Seven Generations
of Iroquois Leadership

The Iroquois and Their Neighbors
Christopher Vecsey, *Series Editor*

OTHER BOOKS IN THE IROQUOIS AND THEIR NEIGHBORS SERIES

Archaeology of the Iroquois: Selected Readings and Research Sources
JORDAN E. KERBER, ed.

Big Medicine from the Six Nations
TED WILLIAMS

The Collected Speeches of Sagoyewatha, or Red Jacket
GRANVILLE GANTER, ed.

The History and Culture of Iroquois Diplomacy: An Interdisciplinary Guide to the Treaties of the Six Nations and Their League
FRANCIS JENNINGS, ed.

In Mohawk Country: Early Narratives of a Native People
DEAN R. SNOW, CHARLES T. GEHRING,
and WILLIAM A. STARNA, eds.

Iroquoia: The Development of a Native World
WILLIAM ENGELBRECHT

Iroquois Medical Botany
JAMES W. HERRICK AND DEAN R. SNOW, eds.

The Mashpee Indians: Tribe on Trial
JACK CAMPISI

Oneida Iroquois Folklore, Myth, and History: New York Oral Narrative from the Notes of H. E. Allen and Others
ANTHONY WONDERLEY

The Reservation
TED WILLIAMS

Seven Generations of Iroquois Leadership

THE SIX NATIONS SINCE 1800

Laurence M. Hauptman

SYRACUSE UNIVERSITY PRESS

Permission to reprint the following material is gratefully acknowledged: chapter 2: "Governor Blacksnake and the Seneca Indian Struggle to Save the Oil Spring Reservation," *Mid-America* 81 (Winter 1999): 51–73; chapter 3: "Samuel George (1795–1873): A Study of Onondaga Indian Conservatism," *New York History* 70 (Jan. 1989): 5–22; chapter 4: "The Two Worlds of Aunt Dinah (1774?–1883), Onondaga Indian," *New York History* 87 (Winter 2006): 5–28; chapter 7: "'War Eagle': Lieutenant Cornelius C. Cusick," in *The Iroquois in the Civil War: From Battlefield to Reservation,* ed. Laurence M. Hauptman (Syracuse, N.Y.: Syracuse Univ. Press, 1993), 39–45; chapter 9: "Designing Woman: Minnie Kellogg, Iroquois Leader," in *Indian Lives: Essays on Nineteenth and Twentieth Century Native American Leaders,* ed. L. G. Moses and Raymond Wilson (Albuquerque: Univ. of New Mexico Press, 1985), 159–88.

The paper used in this publication meets the minimum requirements of American National Standard for Information Sciences—Permanence of Paper for Printed Library Materials, ANSI Z39.48–1984.∞™

For a listing of books published and distributed by Syracuse University Press, visit our Web site at SyracuseUniversityPress.syr.edu.

ISBN 978-0-8156-3165-1 (cloth)   ISBN 978-0-8156-3189-7 (pbk.)

Library of Congress Cataloging-in-Publication Data
Hauptman, Laurence M.
Seven generations of Iroquois leadership : the Six Nations since 1800 / Laurence M. Hauptman. — 1st ed.
p. cm. — (The Iroquois and their neighbors)
Includes bibliographical references and index.
ISBN 978-0-8156-3165-1 (hardcover : alk. paper) — ISBN 978-0-8156-3189-7 (pbk. : alk. paper)
1. Iroquois Indians—Kings and rulers—Biography. 2. Iroquois Indians—Politics and government.
3. Iroquois Indians — History. 4. Leadership—North America. I. Title.
E99.17H35 2008
974.7004'9755—dc22
2008020581

Manufactured in the United States of America

To the memory of
Beth Sara Hauptman

LAURENCE M. HAUPTMAN is SUNY Distinguished Professor at SUNY New Paltz, where he has taught for the past thirty-seven years. He is the author, coauthor, or coeditor of fifteen books on the Iroquois and other Native Americans, including *Conspiracy of Interests: Iroquois Dispossession and the Rise of New York State,* published by Syracuse University Press in 1999. He has served as a historical consultant for the Cayugas, the Mashantucket Pequots, the Senecas, and the Wisconsin Oneidas. Professor Hauptman has been honored for his research and writings by both the Iroquois nations and the New York State Board of Regents.

Contents

Illustrations

Preface

Today, the Iroquois Indians—the Cayugas, Mohawks, Oneidas, Onondagas, Senecas, and Tuscaroras—live on seventeen native settlements/reservations/reserves in New York, Oklahoma, and Wisconsin as well as in Ontario and Quebec. Approximately one hundred thousand Iroquois live in these communities or in major urban centers stretching from Montreal to Milwaukee and beyond. Each of their reservations/reserves has its own leadership, either councils of chiefs raised in the ancient manner or elected systems that became a feature of Indian political systems in the nineteenth and twentieth centuries. Many of these communities, but not all, still have ties to two central fires, with Iroquois Confederacy Councils at the Onondaga Reservation near Syracuse, New York, and at Ohsweken on the Six Nations Reserve near Brantford, Ontario.

Unfortunately, the standard textbooks on the history of the Empire State are either outdated or neglect Native American history; they also omit the presence of the Iroquois over the past two hundred years of the state's history.[1] Consequently, I resolved to correct these omissions by writing a book that could be used as a supplemental reading in courses in New York history as well as one that could be used in classes in Native American studies. I should point out that the Iroquois do not see themselves as "New York Indians" or as "racial minorities," even though they are often designated that way by outside non-Indian observers. They view themselves more in international terms, not in terms of how governmental officials in Albany, New York; Madison, Wisconsin; or Ottawa, Ontario, label them.

Seven Generations of Iroquois Leadership: The Six Nations since 1800 is a work that is not designed to be an all-inclusive history, a nearly impossible task because of the divergent paths of the Iroquois peoples over the past two centuries. The book's focus is thus on what constitutes leadership in Six Nations communities. By collecting five previously published essays and adding six additional ones with introductory materials written specifically for this volume, I attempt to tell the story of the modern Iroquois in the two-hundred-year period after Handsome Lake, the Seneca Prophet, had his visions. Although five of the chapters are reprinted with permission, it should be noted that two-thirds of the material presented here is new to this volume. Of the five previously published chapters, only one—chapter 9 on the life of Laura Minnie Cornelius Kellogg—has been edited and revised to correct and take into account new information acquired since its publication by the University of New Mexico Press in 1985.

After an introductory chapter describes Iroquoia in 1800, the book is then divided into six distinct parts: (1) the prophet's disciples, (2) leadership in the diaspora, (3) war chiefs, (4) the keepers of the kettle/mothers of the nation, (5) the voices of nationhood, and (6) women's leadership, a memoir. The book concludes with a chapter attempting to explain the confusing state of Iroquois leadership at the turn of the twenty-first century. Given that Iroquoian social organization and gender roles are not carbon copies of Western models, four chapters focus on women's leadership. Although there appears to be an imbalance in the number of chapters on men compared to women, I should point out that, unlike other biographies presented, chapter 11 is a composite portrait of leadership and examines the role of not one but thirty-five Iroquois women in rebuilding the Seneca Nation after the Kinzua Dam crisis. Four of the chapters concentrate on Indians outside of their seventeenth-century New York homeland, because more than 70 percent of all Iroquois today reside in Wisconsin, Oklahoma, Ontario, and Quebec. While there are two articles each on the Oneidas and Onondagas, and three on the Senecas, every nation of the Six Nations is represented in this volume. Because my research and fieldwork have largely, but not exclusively, been in New York and Wisconsin, these communities receive much more attention than those in Oklahoma, Ontario, and Quebec.

Unlike *A History of the New York Iroquois*, clergyman-anthropologist William M. Beauchamp's 1905 work,[2] I take the story well beyond the

Empire State and extend the time frame down to the present. Unlike Dean R. Snow's useful survey *The Iroquois,* published in 1994, in which he devoted four of thirteen chapters, a total of eighty pages, to post–Handsome Lake history, the present book focuses on the last two centuries. Differing from Beauchamp or Snow, I employ a biographical approach in an attempt to reveal why the Six Nations have survived as a distinct people in the face of overwhelming pressures.[3] To me, leadership was a major factor in cultural persistence, and therefore this leadership must be examined from inside the communities outwardly, not just from the far-off perspectives of officials in Ottawa or Washington, D.C., or Albany, Madison, or Oklahoma City. My emphasis is not on analyzing the "roll call of chiefs" or on describing chiefly titles and responsibilities, but on how Iroquois leaders use the past to deal with cultural, economic, and political survival.

More than a quarter of a century ago, Benjamin S. Cohn of the University of Chicago pointed out that "history can become more historical in becoming more anthropological." According to Cohn, "The historian needs the direct experience of another culture through systematic fieldwork. It is not just the idea of the exotic, but the sense one gets that other systems work, that there are such things as cultural logics, that there is as much rationality in other societies as in our own even though they flow from other principles." Nevertheless, the employment of fieldwork techniques by historians should not lead them to be overly reliant on oral history, which itself is fraught with inherent dangers and limitations. As Cohn insisted, historians should not neglect archival research. Instead, they should learn "how the particular documents being used were produced" as well as test them for reliability.[4] Thus, as I have found, documents must be read not only for their facts but for the meanings intended. In this respect, fieldwork has helped me uncover the subtleties of the written word found in numerous archives and manuscript collections in the United States and Canada. Consequently, my methods combine archival research with fieldwork on reservations/reserves/urban centers of the Mohawk, Oneida, Onondaga, Cayuga, Seneca, and Tuscarora Indians. Trained in diplomatic history, I have attempted to look at both sides of the divide, not simply focusing on how federal and state policies have shaped the Native American world. I have benefited by studying Iroquoian cosmology, in-group feelings of identity, kinship networks, gender relationships, land-use patterns, politics, and views about the nature of federal-Indian and state-Indian relations.

Past accounts tend to oversimplify Six Nations existence. Too often the Iroquois polity is defined as "factionalized," deemed divided between "traditionalist" or "progressive" (more assimilated), between Longhouse or Christian, between chiefs councils and elected systems. These simplistic categories deny the long-lasting intergenerational dimensions of Iroquois politics and political systems. To me, the diversity of opinions on strategies, as described in these twelve chapters, were and are a strength, not altogether a weakness.

Several caveats to this study need to be stated. First, because most of my research has been on the U.S. side of the international boundary, Iroquois in Canada and Canadian Indian policies receive less attention. Second, since the late 1960s, much of my research has focused on Seneca and Oneida history, and this emphasis continues in this book. Third, I concentrate almost exclusively on reservation/reserve leadership, not on the emergence of the urban Iroquois, a sizable population in both the United States and Canada. Fourth, because the Iroquois are composed of two confederacies as well as numerous individual tribal governments that have been at times in conflict with each other, I have tried to present distinct points of view, an often difficult, if not impossible, balancing act for a non-Indian scholar.

I should like to acknowledge the help of my friend and coauthor/coeditor on several projects, L. Gordon McLester III of Oneida, Wisconsin, who greatly influenced me in understanding his people and Six Nations history. Chapter 6 of this book could not have been written without his assistance. I also want specifically to thank Ramona Charles of the Tonawanda Senecas, Marlene Johnson of the Seneca Nation of Indians, and Salli Benedict of the Mohawk Nation of Akwesasne for their encouragement of my research over the years. Professor Christopher Vecsey of Colgate University and Glenn Wright of Syracuse University Press also encouraged this project right from the beginning. Heriberto Dixon and the late Roy Black have contributed to my understanding in our many discussions about their own Native American experiences. Once again David Jaman of Gardiner, New York, has helped me immensely on a book project. He has been there to discuss every phase of the project and has introduced me, a "Luddite," to the confusing technological world of the modern age. More important, both he and Roy Black, as dear friends, have contributed immeasurably to my well-being during a most difficult time of my life.

Above all, without the love and support of my wife, Ruth, I would not have been able to finish this concluding chapter of my lifelong study of the Iroquois. This is not just an author's obligatory acknowledgment of his spouse. Although I have written these words before in my other writings, they are especially important to say again because unfortunately I now realize that life can be fleeting and that expressions of love if not made and repeated can be lost forever.

Laurence M. Hauptman
New Paltz, New York
February 3, 2007

Introduction

From Alvin M. Josephy Jr.'s *The Patriot Chiefs,* published in 1961, to R. David Edmunds's *The New Warriors,* published in 2000, most historical writings on Native American leadership have been disparate essays that attempt to make sweeping generalizations, however diverse or distinct those societies were and are from each other.[1] Although there have been outstanding biographies of individual Native American leaders published in the past two decades, especially Robert M. Utley's work on Sitting Bull and John Sugden's work on Tecumseh, these books have a limited time frame.[2] By focusing on the Six Nations, communities with greater cultural ties to each other, and by extending the study over two centuries, my attempt is to answer the question of how the Iroquois have survived the onslaught of "civilization."

After more than a half-century of studying the American presidency, the prominent political scientist James McGregor Burns defined leadership as "leaders inducing followers to act for certain goals that represent the values and the motivations—the wants and needs, the aspirations and expectations—of *both leaders and followers.*" Burns isolated two types of leadership: transactional and transforming. Neither is "naked power-wielding." Transactional is less enduring and "occurs when one person takes the initiative in making contact with others for the purpose of an exchange of valued things" that Burns suggested could be of economic, political, or psychological importance. Transformational leadership, one that I see applies to the Iroquois, occurs "when one or more persons *engage* with others in such a way that leaders and followers raise one another to higher levels of motivation and morality."[3] Nevertheless, Burns's model is incomplete and based largely on Western leadership patterns.

The discipline of anthropology offers the best scholarly insights into Iroquois leadership. Two extraordinary scholars of the Iroquois have written award-winning books over the past four decades: Anthony F. C. Wallace's *Death and Rebirth of the Seneca* (1970) and William N. Fenton's *The Great Law and the Longhouse* (1998). Both masterpieces of anthropology described Iroquois ritual and spiritual beliefs and the cultural and political changes wrought over several centuries in the face of European contact. Both anthropologists stressed the adaptability of Iroquois leadership to change within the framework of cultural continuity. Wallace analyzed the origins of Handsome Lake's visions and the establishment of the Longhouse religion, which he insisted was affected by ancient precedents as well as by the Quakers and other Western influences. Wallace concluded his brilliant work with the death of the prophet in 1815.[4]

Fenton's magnum opus was based on his six decades of research and fieldwork among the Iroquois. Focusing on the years before Handsome Lake, Fenton described these Native people's cosmology known as the Great Law and its rituals, a living tradition that dates from the founding of the League in the years before European contact. As Wallace before him, Fenton emphasized that Iroquois leadership was able to adjust to the European presence—trade, wars, land pressures, accculturative forces—by maintaining cultural strengths such as the Condolence Council ceremony. As did Wallace, Fenton emphasized Iroquois cultural continuity even while these Indians adapted to new circumstances and outside interference in their lives and societies. Despite his massive work, Fenton ends his exceptional narrative with the federal treaty with the Six Nations in 1794, the Treaty of Canandaigua, the most important accord made between the Iroquois and Washington officials, which is commemorated by the Indians every November 11 at Canandaigua, New York.[5] It is important to note that these two extraordinary scholars built on the long-time connection between anthropologists and the Iroquois that started in 1851 with the publication of Lewis Henry Morgan's groundbreaking *The League of the Ho-de-no-sau-nee, or Iroquois*.[6] Later, two anthropologists, J. N. B. Hewitt, a Tuscarora, and Arthur C. Parker, a nonenrolled Seneca, added their own scholarship to the body of knowledge about the Iroquois.[7]

The Hotinohsyóni⁷ (Hodenausaunee or Haudenosaunee), meaning in the Seneca language "they [who] are of the extended lodge," are a most remarkable people.⁸ Their leaders' ability to draw strength from the past to survive over 450 years of Euroamerican contact and to maintain a cultural as well as political presence in their homeland sets them apart from many other Native peoples east of the Mississippi. This adaptability is built into the very fabric of their ancient League of the Iroquois and its rituals.

Each of the nations had League chiefs, called sachems. Although each nation was not equally represented in council, the League did not act as a Western-style political unit and thus was not based on majority-rule voting. Instead, all decisions were focused on achieving consensus, which often required long debate over days, months, or years, or was never achieved. Hence, until the crisis caused by the American Revolution, these nations avoided internecine conflict, because agreeing to disagree was a basic axiom accepted by the sachems. If consensus was not achievable, member nations were allowed to follow their own path.

At the core of the League's rituals was the Condolence Ceremony, the *Hai Hai,* where deceased chiefs were replaced by new ones; while attending to grief, the ceremony tied the exploits of great leaders of the past to the present. When a chief died, the eldest matron of his clan chose his successor, and the one chosen would assume the title and identity of the deceased. Thus, through the Condolence Ceremony, the people were reminded of past history and leadership as well as of the glorious achievements of the League.

The Iroquois' Great Law *(Kaianerekown)* defined the duties and rights of chiefs, clans, and nations, but also evidenced flexibility. At times, if there was no suitable replacement, a chief might be borrowed from one clan or one nation to serve. Men of ability, but not "condoled," would be recognized with honorific titles such as Pine Tree or War Chief. The women had the inherent right to choose the new sachem or force an unworthy one out, symbolically removing his badge of honor, his antler horns, from his head.

In the seventeenth and well into the eighteenth century, Iroquois leadership extended outward. Even though they were not the most numerous of woodlands Indians, they learned how to seem more powerful than their numbers. They mastered forest diplomacy and projected power even long after it had waned. The Iroquois excelled at playing off the powerful English and French empires as well as at manipulating other Native communities to serve their interests.[9] At this time in their history, the Iroquois defeated and/or adopted numerous Native peoples. In bringing in diverse peoples and distinct nations, they used the metaphor "extending the rafters." Besides the Tuscarora, who became the sixth nation of the League, the Iroquois brought in Conoy, Delaware, Mesquakie, Nanticoke, Saponi, Susquehannock, Tutelo, and others. Even though they were and are a multicultural reality, the Iroquois then and now have a collective sense of nationalism that affects their leadership right down to the present day. In the late 1950s, the noted writer and social/literary critic Edmund Wilson, who visited the reservations in New York and at Six Nations Reserve in Canada, recognized their diversity. He especially admired the Iroquois tenacity of leadership and their unique worldview, which set them apart and allowed them to survive.[10]

The twelve essays in this book clearly show the interplay of the past with the present and the great adaptability of Iroquois leadership. Part one of *Seven Generations of Iroquois Leadership: The Six Nations since 1800* describes the life of two extraordinary chiefs—Governor Blacksnake (Seneca) and Samuel George (Onondaga)—who understood the need for change and accommodated to change within the overall framework of Iroquois conservatism. Chapter 4 in part two focuses on Dinah John (Onondaga), who realized that cultural survival depended on a level of economic interaction with the non-Indian world of central New York. In chapter 5, the long-held role of women as "mothers of the nation," protectors of the Indian land base, is explored by recounting the life of Alice Lee Jemison, a twentieth-century Seneca Indian activist-journalist. Focusing on the Iroquois diaspora, part three examines the life of Chief Daniel Bread (Oneida), who resurrected elements of the ancient Condolence Council ceremony in order to rebuild his nation's existence in the West. Part four shows that the military career of Chief Cornelius Cusick (Tuscarora), a Civil War hero, replicated the actions and responsibilities of past war chiefs; his actions in some ways resembled modern-day Iroquois leaders in charge of crews in the dangerous work of high-steel construction.

Both Levi General (Cayuga) and Ernest Benedict (Mohawk), treated in part five, attempted to remind the British, Canadian, and U.S. governments of their obligations under treaties (Haldimand, 1784, and Jay, 1794), and emphasized the Iroquois' right to freely speak and travel wherever they desired. In the same section, a chapter treats Laura Minnie Cornelius Kellogg (Oneida), a controversial leader pressing the two-hundred-year-old Iroquois land claims. In part six, a composite portrait of contemporary Iroquois women living on Seneca reservations further ties the present to the past and illustrates that Iroquoian women's roles in some ways have changed far less than previously believed.

Iroquois leadership has not been static, but continues to change within a cultural framework set well back in history. Even in the "age of casinos," leaders must speak in "ancient tongues," namely use the traditional metaphors and make appeals to the past and the greatness of the "League of Peace and Power." The careful employment of metaphors of the past is not just slick politics by modern Iroquois politicians, but an effort (like that expressed in the Condolence Council ceremony) to tie the present to the past and reaffirm the uniqueness of the Iroquois even in the modern world. Iroquois references to ensuring survival for those "seven generations to come" are not mere shibboleths, but once again tie past requirements of leadership to present and future responsibilities.

Timeline

1820–46	Under intense land and transportation pressures, most Oneidas leave New York for Wisconsin (Michigan Territory) and Canada
1822	[Anglo-American] commission establishes U.S.-Canadian boundary line that transects Akwesasne Mohawk territory
1826	Senecas dispossessed of Genesee Valley lands
1831	City of Buffalo is incorporated
1831–32	Ohio Iroquois (Senecas and Cayugas) are removed to Indian Territory under the provisions of two federal treaties
1838	Buffalo Creek Treaty temporarily ends Seneca existence in New York and "encourages" removal of all Iroquois to Kansas
1840–41	New York State Legislature passes first acts taxing Indians
1842	U.S. treaty with the Senecas (Compromise/Compromised Treaty)—two reservations (Allegany and Cattaraugus) "returned" to the Seneca Nation
1848	The Seneca Nation of Indians is established with an elected system of councilors
1856	Thomas Indian Asylum (later the Thomas Indian School) opens
1857	The U.S.-Tonawanda Seneca Treaty provides for the repurchase of part of the Tonawanda Reservation
1861–65	Six hundred Iroquois fight for the Union in the Civil War; Lieutenant Cornelius Cusick cited twice for heroism; Colonel Ely S. Parker drafts surrender terms at Appomattox Courthouse
1868	Ely S. Parker named commissioner of Indian affairs
1868	Hampton Institute is established; hundreds of Iroquois attend between 1878 and 1923
1873	Levi General is born
1879	U.S. Indian Industrial School at Carlisle, Pennsylvania, is established; over one thousand Iroquois attend until its closing in 1918
1887–1933	Allotment era: Wisconsin Oneidas' land loss totals 65,000 acres in this period—the General Allotment Act (Dawes

	Act), 1887; the Burke Act, 1906; the Federal Competency Commission, 1917
1888–89	New York State Assembly Legislative Committee drafts major report (Whipple Report) urging the allotment of Indian reservations in New York and an end to separate Indian status
1901	Alice Lee (Jemison) is born
1911	Society of American Indians is founded
1914–17	World War I: Iroquois Confederacy declares war on Central Powers in 1917, and hundreds serve
1918	Ernest Benedict is born
1921–24	Levi General (Deskaheh) takes the Six Nations case to the League of Nations
1922	New York State Assembly Report (Everett Report) states unequivocally that the Six Nations have legitimate land claims for millions of acres
1923–24	Canadian government invades the Six Nations Confederacy Council House in Ohsweken and establishes an elected council, recognizing it as the band government in place of the chiefs
1924	U.S. Congress passes Indian Citizenship Act; Iroquois Confederacy objects to it
1927	*Deere v. St. Lawrence Power*: federal court dismisses Six Nations land claim
1934	Indian Reorganization Act: Wisconsin Oneidas establish new tribal government (Oneida Business Committee) and begin reacquiring lands lost in the allotment era
1934–42	Two major WPA projects—the Seneca Arts Project in New York and the Oneida Language and Folklore Project in Wisconsin—help preserve Iroquoian traditions
1936	Oklahoma Indian Welfare Act; the consolidated Seneca-Cayuga Tribe of Oklahoma is incorporated under its provisions the following year
1936–37	The Tonawanda Indian Community House is built and dedicated

1939–45	World War II: hundreds of Iroquois in Canada join the war effort in 1939, and Iroquois in the United States join after Pearl Harbor is attacked; U.S. Congress passes the Selective Service Act (1940) and for the first time drafts Iroquois (Canada did this in World War I, but not in World War II); Iroquois draft resistance and three federal cases were initiated but fail
1944	National Congress of American Indians is founded
1946	Indian Claims Commission is established
1948–50	U.S. Congress transfers criminal and civil jurisdiction over the Iroquois to New York State
1950–53	Korean War
1950–75	U.S. involvement in Vietnam leads to full-scale war
1953	U.S. Congress passes House Concurrent Resolution 108 and formalizes "termination" policy; Wisconsin is given jurisdiction over the Indians in criminal and civil matters; urban relocation policies speed up
1954–66	Major Iroquois land loss: Kinzua Dam floods more than nine thousand acres of Seneca lands at Cornplanter Tract; Tuscaroras lose 550 acres to New York State Power Authority Niagara Power Project; the St. Lawrence Seaway project affects Mohawks at Akwesasne and Kahnawake, who lose lands from their reserves; Akwesasne Mohawks face increased environmental degradation caused by new industrial corridor; new presence of Canadian customs officials in their territory
1961	American Indian Chicago Conference brings national attention to Indian concerns
1965	Robert L. Bennett (Oneida) is named commissioner of Indian affairs
1968–77	Red Power Era: Mohawks block flow of traffic across bridge at Cornwall (December 1968 and February 1969); Mohawks and Onondagas lead school boycotts; *Akwesasne Notes* founded; Onondagas lead sitdown on Interstate 81 and protest widening of highway;

participate (Richard Oakes, a leader) in takeover at Alcatraz (1969–71) and in Trail of Broken Treaties (1972); send delegation to Wounded Knee occupation (1973); Kahnawake Mohawks occupy Eagle Bay and claim it as Mohawk territory—later given land in Clinton County (Ganienkeh); birth of new Warriors' Movement, inspired by the writings and teachings of Louis Hall

1969   Louis R. Bruce, Jr. (Mohawk-Sioux) is named commissioner of Indian affairs

1974   Oneida Indian land claims case decided by U.S. Supreme Court; overturns 133 years of federal law by giving the Oneida Nation access to federal courts

1975   Ernest Stevens, Jr. (Wisconsin Oneida) is named to the American Indian Policy Review Commission

1979   Tensions build at Akwesasne; Mohawk occupation at Racquette Point

1985   Oneidas win test case on their land claims in the U.S. Supreme Court

1987–88   Cabazon case allows Indian casino operations; U.S. Congress passes American Indian Gaming Regulatory Act

1990   Seneca Nation Settlement Act provides monetary compensation for federal failure to supervise ninety-nine-year lease agreement on Allegany Reservation

1990–91   Mohawk civil war erupts at Akwesasne

1990–91   Kahnesatake protest and setup of barricades over development of a golf course on lands Mohawks claim as theirs; demonstrations spread to Kahnawake and reverberate throughout Canada

1991   First Gulf War

1992, 1997   Iroquois sales tax "wars" led by the Seneca Nation; Route 17 and the New York State Thruway are temporarily closed

1993–2007   Iroquois nations—Wisconsin Oneida, Oneida Nation of New York, Seneca Nation of Indians, and Mohawk Nation—establish casinos

2000–2005   Cayuga land claims case argued in federal courts; despite favorable decision for the Cayugas at the district court level, the decision is reversed on appeal

2001   World Trade Center terrorism attack; Mohawk ironworkers aid in rescue efforts

2001   Afghanistan War

2001   Iroquois border crossing rights under Jay Treaty denied by Canada's Supreme Court in the Mitchell case

2003– present Iraqi War

2004–7   Seneca claims to Grand Island rejected by federal courts

2005   Sherrill case decided against the Oneida Nation of New York by the U.S. Supreme Court

2006–7   Caledonia, Ontario, occupation by Six Nations Indians claiming land under the Haldimand Treaty (1784)

2007–8   Carl Artman (Wisconsin Oneida) serves as assistant secretary of the interior for Indian affairs

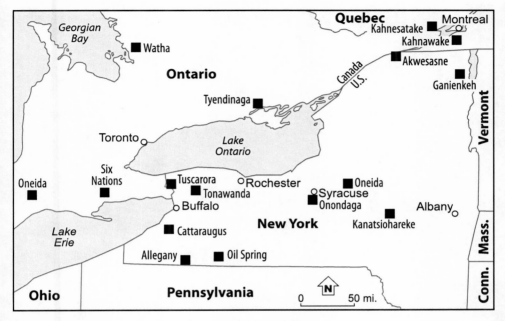

Map 1. Eastern Iroquoia Today. Map by Joe Stoll.

Map 2. Western Iroquoia Today. Map by Joe Stoll.

Seven Generations
of Iroquois Leadership

1

The Iroquois in 1800

The American Revolution and the two decades that followed shattered the Iroquois world forever. Iroquois Indians were on both sides of the conflict, with the Oneidas and Tuscaroras making significant contributions to American military efforts and the Senecas, Cayugas, Mohawks, and Onondagas to the British. The Sullivan-Clinton Campaign of 1779 devastated Iroquois villages in central and western New York and drove many of the Indians to seek refuge with the British at Fort Niagara. With the burning of the Onondaga villages by the American army in 1778 and 1779, the Confederacy council fire was shifted for the next sixty years to Seneca Territory along Buffalo Creek in western New York. After the conflict, numerous Iroquois Loyalists to Great Britain, led by Mohawk war chief Joseph Brant, resettled along the Grand River in Ontario, Canada, founding a second Confederacy Council. Hence the war helped make the Iroquois Confederacy a "two-headed organism," one centered at Onondaga, near Syracuse, returning in the 1840s, and the other at the Six Nations Reserve near Brantford, Ontario.[1]

With the Treaty of Paris of 1783 and later more clearly defined by an Anglo-American Boundary Commission in 1822, outsiders—the British and the Americans—for the first time placed an international boundary that separated Iroquois communities from each other and intruded on nearly every aspect of Indian existence. Despite what the Iroquois believed were assurances of Indian free and unlimited trade across this boundary line set forth in the Treaty of Amity, Commerce and Navigation—the Jay Treaty—of November 19, 1794, this claimed aboriginal right was frequently denied and continues to this day as a source of contention.[2]

In the quarter-century after the American Revolution, the Iroquois were dispossessed of over 95 percent of their land base. From 1784 onward, the Senecas lost most of western New York with the exception of eleven reservations "guaranteed" by the federal Treaty of Big Tree in 1797; the Oneidas, more than five million of their six million acres of tribal land; and the Onondagas, more than one hundred square miles of their territory in 1788 and other lands in and around Onondaga Lake in 1793 and 1795 that contained vast deposits of salt; while the Cayugas lost all of their tribal territory between 1795 and 1807.[3] Most of the three dozen state treaties made with the Iroquois after the U.S. Constitution's ratification did not follow federal law as set out in the Trade and Intercourse Act of 1790 and later acts, which required that a federal commissioner be present and negotiations had to be held at a public treaty council under the auspices of the United States.[4] Few of these state treaties were ratified by the U.S. Senate and proclaimed by the president of the United States. Even when a federal commissioner was present, as in the Mohawk treaty of 1796, known as the Treaty with the Seven Nations of Canada, the Indians lost out as well. The Mohawks at Akwesasne were dispossessed of six million acres, except for a six-mile-square reservation along the St. Lawrence River in an "accord" negotiated and signed by several non-chiefs and by at least two Mohawks from another reserve (Kahnawake).[5] As in the New York State–Cayuga Treaty (Treaty of Cayuga Ferry) of 1795, land "purchased" by state treaty for fifty cents an acre was sold for seven to ten times its original purchase price from the Indians, in clear violation of New York State law.[6]

Often federal officials in Washington or on the ground in New York looked the other way when politicians and Empire State land speculators violated federal laws. In 1784 the federal government itself had imposed harsh terms on the Iroquois in the Treaty of Fort Stanwix, choosing to treat four of the nations—Mohawk, Onondaga, Cayuga, and Seneca—as conquered nations, thereby exacting land concessions.[7] They did nothing to protect the Oneidas, their allies, when New York State officials initiated treaty making at Fort Herkimer in 1785 and Fort Schuyler in 1788 that dispossessed these Indians of millions of acres of land.[8] President Washington's emissary, Timothy Pickering, U.S. commissioner to treat with the Six Nations, returned lands to the Senecas and gave promises of protection to all of the Iroquois in New York at the Treaty of Canandaigua in 1794; however, less than a year later, federal officials looked the other way when state officials violated federal law and dispossessed the Cayugas, Onondagas, and Oneidas in succession.[9] In the Treaty of Big Tree of 1797, federal officials facilitated the nefarious work of Robert and Thomas Morris and the Holland Land Company at getting the Seneca land base. Later, although the Seneca reserved eleven communities under the treaty, the Holland Land Company, succeeded by the Ogden Land Company, acquired the "pre-emptive right" to all of the Seneca lands with the exception of Oil Spring Reservation.[10]

Long before the opening of the Erie Canal in 1825, New York State was undergoing a transportation revolution that had a long-term impact on the Iroquois and spurred future non-Indian development. The establishment of the Western Inland Lock Navigation Company in the early 1790s brought surveyors and canal engineers into central and western New York, the heart of Iroquois Country, as well as entrepreneurs interested in land speculation and the development of the salt and timber resources. Land speculators such as the agents of the Holland Land Company promoted this development as well as the improvement of roads and turnpikes, such as the Seneca Turnpike, also known as the Genesee Turnpike and later the Great Western Turnpike, that traversed the state from Albany to the Genesee Valley. These land speculators fully understood that improved transportation networks clearly made land values rise. Iroquois dispossession soon followed as these agents greased the wheels of powerful legislators such as Philip Schuyler, the major canal developer and founder of the Western Inland Lock Navigation Company, or political mechanics such as Aaron Burr, who served the interests of these entrepreneurs in the corridors of the state legislature.[11]

Although the Iroquois were largely unaware of the machinations of Albany politicians and their direct connections to land and transportation interests, Six Nations communities were affected by their growing powerlessness in the wake of these pressures. The "politics of blame" led to further divisions within tribal communities. Someone had to be held responsible for the failures to stem the tide. Moreover, Anthony F. C. Wallace and other scholars have also noted that this post–Revolutionary War period was marked by increasing evidence of social disintegration among the Iroquois, namely alcohol abuse and with it internecine violence.[12] As in other Native American communities of the time faced with these rapid changes, the Iroquois attempted to find a way to deal with these debilitating circumstances. Unlike the numerous Indians who took to the warpath in response to land loss and outside domination, the Iroquois chose different routes: Christian conversion or Native American religious revitalization.

Christianity was not new to the Iroquois at the end of the eighteenth century. Jesuit missionaries had come to central New York as early as the 1650s. During the Great Awakening from the late 1730s to the American Revolution, Presbyterian missionaries such as Samuel Kirkland won converts within the Oneida Indian communities. With the migration of Loyalist Iroquois, the Anglican church became more influential among the Six Nations in Canada. In the early nineteenth century, Baptist ministers made inroads at Buffalo Creek and at Tuscarora. Indeed, these influences were not short-lived changes in Iroquoia, given that today a vast majority of Six Nations people are Christians—mostly Adventist, Anglican, Baptist, Episcopal, Mormon, Presbyterian, and Roman Catholic.

Perhaps the most significant of these Christian proselytizing efforts occurred among the Seneca. There the Society of Friends established their mission, the Tunessassa School, and other economic and social experiments aimed at transforming the Indians "for their own good." Besides efforts at converting and promoting the road to American citizenship under law, these Quakers, as well as other missionaries, also encouraged temperance, pushed for changes in traditional men's and women's roles, and brought Christian theology—concepts of sin and divine punishment—into Iroquois communities.[13] Apparently Christian missionizing and its call for the Iroquois to change had other consequences not altogether intended by these clergymen. Wallace has made clear that these Christian stirrings also had some effect on the major Native non-Christian religious revitalization of the era, namely Handsome Lake's theology.[14]

Handsome Lake, the Seneca prophet, stirred Iroquoia in 1799 and 1800, changing it forever. He looked back to the ancient past, but at the same time advocated the acceptance of the need for change. Until his series of three visions, Handsome Lake was overshadowed by the political career of his younger half-brother, the Cornplanter. As a notorious drunkard before his visions, Handsome Lake had scarcely played a central political role in the affairs of the Seneca Nation although he had been in attendance and had signed the ignominious agreement, the Treaty of Big Tree, in 1797.

In June 1799 Handsome Lake lay ill, bedridden in his cabin. The Indians living at the old village on the Cornplanter grant had experienced much travail that spring, including drunken brawls, accusations of witchcraft, and even the execution of a witch who was blamed for the death of Cornplanter's and Handsome Lake's niece. Leaving his cabin at Cornplanter on June 15, Handsome Lake collapsed and was aided back to bed by his nephew Governor Blacksnake. Most Senecas believed that he was about to die. After two hours in a near-catatonic state witnessed by other Indians, Handsome Lake opened his eyes and began to recount a religious message that he had just had. His vision included three well-dressed messengers who had come to him with the Creator's commands. The prophet was to choose his sister and her husband as his medicine persons who were to join him and attend the Strawberry Festival. There the prophet was to preach the message of *Gaiwiio (Gaiwi:yoh)* the Good Word, a message that condemned whiskey, witchcraft, love potions, and abortion. All wrongdoers had to confess and repent their wickedness or be punished.[15]

This first vision, later followed by two others, was to have a profound influence on the Iroquois who were faced with disaster in the aftermath of the American Revolution. In part, the origins of the Handsome Lake religion stemmed from the splintering of the Iroquois Confederacy, substantial Indian land loss, constant white land pressures, social disintegration as reflected in increased alcoholism and murder rates, and growing economic dependence on the non-Indian world.[16]

In the following months Handsome Lake had other visions, falling into trances and seeing many wonders, and gaining insights relating to moral and social reform. He saw the punishment of wrongdoers: wife-beaters, drunkards, gamblers, witches, sinners. He traveled to the realm of the blessed, learning in this pleasant world how families among the Iroquois should live in peace in their own communities. Instructed by the sacred messenger who accompanied him on his spiritual journey, he was urged to continue to perform the Iroquois' religious ceremonial cycle.

In his third vision, which took place in 1800, he was commanded to write down the *Gaiwiio* to preserve it for all time and to carry the message to all the peoples of the Six Nations. Although Handsome Lake never preached among the Oneidas, the Good Word spread there. Handsome Lake combined his teaching with an emphasis on family values, condemning gossip, philandering, abortion, and alcohol, all of which were rampant at the time. He claimed to have received the Good Word from messengers of the Creator to advise his people, summarized by the anthropologist Elisabeth Tooker:

> They said that the people should stop drinking, that the witches should confess and cease their activity, that the use of charms [i.e., charms employed in witchcraft] should cease, and that women should cease aborting themselves. These were the first four "words." Other messages included the admonitions that husbands and wives should not desert each other, that they should love each other and their children, and that they should not commit adultery. Children should be treated kindly and listened to; childless couples should adopt children of the wife's sister—if she had them. Old people unable to work should be helped by their grandchildren. Then the messengers said: if a visitor comes when a family is about to eat, the visitor should be invited to eat; children playing near the house should be invited to eat when those in the house are eating; orphans should be helped; the people should not gossip or spread evil reports; and people should not boast. The messengers also said that it was right that men cultivate lands as the white man did, build houses as he did, and keep horses and cattle as he did. At least some children should be sent to school to learn the white man's ways. People should help one another, should not steal, and should not perform dances in honor of the "totem animals" [i.e., should not perform the medicine society dances]. The messengers added, however, that the Creator has given four rituals—Feather Dance, Thanksgiving Dance, Personal Chant, and Bowl Game—which are to be performed. The Creator ordered that Thanksgiving ceremonies should be given at certain times. He also said there should be chiefs and that they should do good for the people.[17]

The Seneca prophet also promoted men's participation in horticulture, which had been the traditional women's domain. Despite this radical departure, the prophet was perceived by his contemporaries as a conservative, "attempting to restore and revitalize an existing system of beliefs and ceremonies that had been falling into disuse." While promoting changes, Handsome Lake was a callback to an ancient faith, one that did not challenge the "old pantheon, the old annual calendar, the old myths, the old dream rites." He endorsed these traditions except for those that had been contaminated by alcohol or witchcraft.[18] In spite of this conservative message, however, he added strong warnings against any further alienation of Indian lands and land sales to whites as well as proscriptions against Iroquois warrior participation in another white man's war—both ignored by many Iroquois Indians, including Governor Blacksnake and Samuel George, long before the prophet's death in 1815.[19]

Handsome Lake's message clearly contained Christian influences.[20] Wallace states, "Recognition of Christian theology is made in the code in his encounter with Jesus Christ, whom the prophet regarded as his counterpart among the whites. The images of heaven and, most particularly, hell seem clearly to have been based on a Christian model."[21] By incorporating select elements of Western theology and thought and preaching a level of accommodation, unlike the militant message of Tenskwatawa, the Shawnee Prophet, Handsome Lake's contemporary, the Seneca prophet won growing acceptance throughout Iroquoia. Even the Presbyterian missionary Samuel Kirkland expressed some praise for Handsome Lake's message of temperance.[22] Importantly, his disciples, who included Jemmy Johnson as well as Governor Blacksnake and Samuel George, described in the next two chapters, helped carry forth the prophet's message and allow Iroquoian beliefs to adapt and survive in the future. Their task was a most difficult one.

Where fewer than two thousand non-Indians lived in twelve counties of central and western New York in 1790, a half-century later, more than a half million non-Indians had flooded the region and had transformed Iroquoia into the "Empire State."[23]

PART ONE The Prophet's Disciples

Introduction

In a recent work on Six Nations history from the time of the French and Indian War through the first decade of the nineteenth century, Pulitzer Prize–winning historian Alan Taylor concentrated much of his work on the creative nature and adaptability of Iroquois leadership in these crisis years. He focused on two male leaders—the Mohawk Joseph Brant and the Oneida Good Peter—and one extraordinary woman—the Oneida Sarah Ainse (Montour). Taylor wrote, "Realistic about the power of settler numbers, these native leaders tried to manage, rather than entirely to block, the presence of settlement." He added, "They did so to ensure a level of Indian autonomy and economic survival as a people. They selectively adapted from the new settler culture that now surrounded them."[1]

The two chapters in part one illustrate Taylor's point but focus on a slight later period. Both Tenh-wen-nyos, "Chainbreaker" (literally "awl breaker"), known to the Americans as "Governor Blacksnake," and Hononwirehdonh ("The Great Wolf"), known to the Americans as "Samuel George," lived through the worst series of crises in Iroquois history: the American Revolution and its immediate aftermath with the loss of most of the Six Nations' homeland; permanent splits of the Six Nations into two confederacies, one based at Onondaga in central New York and the other at Ohsweken in southern Ontario; a second civil war in Iroquoia known in history as the War of 1812; the constant efforts by government officials in Albany, Ottawa, or Washington, D.C., or by missionary societies to inculcate non-Indian ways or to push the Iroquois out of their homeland; and the flood of non-Indian settlement into their territory spurred on by the establishment of turnpikes, canals, and railroads.

The world of the Iroquois was also circumscribed by New York State legislation. The legislature first became involved in Indian statutory law in 1813, with regulations banning the cutting of timber on tribal lands. In 1821, Albany transferred the enforcement of the 1813 law to county district attorneys. By 1835 the legislature, without federal approval, began permitting as well as ratifying leases made by non-Indians on the Allegany Indian Reservation. By 1840 and 1841, New York State attempted to tax Indians for the first time. (New York State efforts to tax Indians has been a continuing source of tensions and conflicts right up to the present time.) In 1846, Albany enacted a law providing for school buildings and annual appropriations for the education of American Indians on four of the reservations: Allegany, Cattaraugus, Onondaga, and St. Regis. Later, state-administered schools were specifically established at Tonawanda and Tuscarora in 1855 and Oneida in 1857. Moreover, New York State underwrote the building of canals, state roads, and/or turnpikes through Indian lands, beginning in the 1790s and continuing to the construction of the New York State Thruway in the 1950s and Route 17 in the 1970s and 1980s.[2] In 1867, the legislature created the Board of State Charities that in 1873, the year of Chief George's death, was renamed the New York State Board of Charities, which administered poorhouses, institutions for the mentally and physically handicapped including "lunatic and idiot asylums," the state school for the blind, the Sailors and Soldiers Home, immigration "clearinghouses," reformatories and orphanages to care for dependent children, and, in 1875, the administration of a formerly private Indian orphanage, the Thomas Asylum, founded in 1856. The Thomas Asylum, later renamed the Thomas Indian School, continued in operation until 1957.[3]

In the wake of these overwhelming changes and beginning in the decades after Handsome Lake's death and burial under the old longhouse floor at Onondaga in 1815, the Seneca prophet's visions were transformed into a religion. Anthropologist Elisabeth Tooker has written that Handsome Lake was "by no means universally accepted as a prophet, his following among the Iroquois was somewhat limited, his views conflicting with those of various Iroquois leaders at the time." His message "continued to be controversial, and it was only through the efforts of a few devoted followers that they came to be transformed into a religion and accepted generally by those Iroquois who did not become converts to Christianity."[4]

Although the religion was initially influenced by Iroquois preachers such as Jemmy Johnson, Sose-há-wä, the only appointed successor to the prophet, others, as Tooker has pointed out, affected the formal establishment of the *Gaiwiio*, the Code of Handsome Lake. Indeed, the religion evolved slowly throughout much of the nineteenth century.[5] As the following chapter describes, Governor Blacksnake was the nephew of the prophet, and his family became the trustees of Handsome Lake's legacy. Later, Owen Blacksnake, Governor Blacksnake's son, was especially instrumental in establishing the religion, making his uncle's message better known and contributing to Handsome Lake's fame as the Seneca prophet.[6]

Both Governor Blacksnake, the Seneca, and Samuel George, the Onondaga, were advocates of selective change. Realizing that power realities had shifted after the American Revolution and that the homeland, however reduced in size, had to be secured, both became flexible conservatives willing to adapt and encourage their tribesmen to change, while steadfastly holding onto their traditional views of Iroquois nationhood. Both allowed missionaries into their communities. They also did not oppose the efforts of Albany officials or missionary societies to establish schools on the reservations.

Although both were followers of Handsome Lake, they modified the prophet's message because they were pragmatists facing a hostile setting. As chiefs of nations whose representatives had signed the much-revered Treaty of Canandaigua of 1794, they understood that they had to reaffirm this agreement by remaining loyal to the Americans.[7] They did so, even at the expense of fighting their pro-British kin from Grand River in the War of 1812. By participating in this war (and in later conflicts such as the Civil War), the Iroquois were rejecting one important belief set forth by Handsome Lake, namely the Seneca prophet's proscription against taking up arms in another white man's war.[8] Governor Blacksnake, a hero to Allegany Senecas to this very day, made compromises that were far more controversial than those of Samuel George. In 1826 and 1842, he put his name to two federal treaties at Buffalo Creek that ceded large chunks of Seneca lands.[9]

Both Governor Blacksnake and Samuel George had to deal with the constant efforts to dispossess the Iroquois and send the Iroquois to the West or to British Canada. Their sophisticated understanding of Euro-American power realities and outside forces, and their own diplomatic skills, were not simply learned in their own lifetime. A century earlier, their ancestors had learned this survival "game."[10] As their power waned in the eighteenth century, the Iroquois developed added diplomatic skills to deal with the non-Indian world.[11] Hence, learning from the past, Governor Blacksnake and Samuel George, in their efforts to protect their shrinking world and guarantee survival for "seven generations to come," an Iroquois metaphor that is used to this day, had not only to be crafty but adaptable at the same time. Thus their conservative but flexible leadership style was—and is—a major reason for Iroquois cultural existence in their homeland right down to the present time.

As the following chapter reveals, Governor Blacksnake was instrumental in saving the Oil Spring Reservation, land personally reserved for Handsome Lake. As the custodian of Handsome Lake's official papers as well as his uncle's religious legacy on the Allegany Reservation, the centenarian Governor Blacksnake was successful in fighting off land speculators in the 1850s.

2

Governor Blacksnake and the Seneca Indian Struggle to Save the Oil Spring Reservation

To the Seneca Indians who reside on the Allegany Reservation in south-western New York, "Tenh-wen-nyos," the Chainbreaker, more commonly known as Governor Blacksnake, is considered among his people's greatest leaders.[1] Although his personal memoir has been published, much of it focuses on Blacksnake's involvement in the American Revolution.[2] Despite his centrality to the history of Gaiwiio, or Code of Handsome Lake—the Iroquois Longhouse religion that still exists in New York, Wisconsin, and Canada—Blacksnake's role in preserving and adapting the Seneca prophet's message and his remarkable efforts at holding onto the prophet's sacred land, the Oil Spring Reservation, have never been completely told before. Indeed, although scholars have written about other disciples of Handsome Lake, such as Jemmy Johnson and Samuel George, and about the development of the Longhouse religion among the Iroquois, they have largely ignored Blacksnake's key involvement in the formulation and institutionalization of this religion.[3]

Anthropologist Elisabeth Tooker has emphasized that the development of the *Gaiwiio* was not a straight, smooth path and that the religion of Handsome Lake "was periodically beset with crises threatening survival." Handsome Lake himself was hardly "universally accepted as a prophet" during his own lifetime and his views conflicted with those of other Iroquois leaders of the time. Tooker insisted, "After his death, they continued to be controversial, and it was only through the efforts of a few devoted followers that they came to be transformed into a religion."[4] One

15

of Handsome Lake's most devoted followers was his nephew, Governor Blacksnake.

Blacksnake did not reject change outright and did permit Western education among his people, but he was also a strong advocate of Indian sovereignty and treaty rights. After his involvement in the American Revolution on the British side, he at times, much like Handsome Lake earlier, urged an accommodationist approach to deal with the problems caused by American encroachment. On other occasions, he became directly involved in efforts to stop Indian land loss. Like Seneca Indian conservatives then and now, he charted a separate independent course and opposed total amalgamation into the American body politic. Yet Blacksnake was no ordinary chief. The famed Allegany Seneca was the nephew of both Cornplanter and Handsome Lake. Blacksnake's mother was the sister of these two prominent Indians. It should be emphasized that the relationship of mother's brother to sister's son is very significant in matrilineal societies such as the Senecas.[5] His monument at the cemetery near Onoville on the Allegany Indian Reservation reads in part: "Devoted his later years to work among his people. *Absolutely honest and truthful* and enjoying the confidence of Indian and Pale-Face."[6]

Governor Blacksnake was born in the hamlet of Kendaia on Seneca Lake around 1753 and lived his early life at Canawaugus, today's Avon, New York. An impressive figure and orator, Blacksnake was a slim man of slightly more than six feet in height. During the American Revolution, he, as most other Senecas, served the British Crown throughout the conflict. After the British defeat and the humiliating treatment of four of the Iroquois nations at Fort Stanwix in 1784, Blacksnake accompanied his uncle the Cornplanter on special missions to see General George Washington as well as to members of the Continental Congress. He also was in attendance at the major Seneca councils and land negotiations with federal officials and land jobbers after the Revolution. When Blacksnake's home village of Canawaugus was included in the Phelps-Gorham Purchase of Seneca lands in 1788, he and his family moved to his uncle's lands, on the Cornplanter Tract, a few miles downriver from the Allegany Reservation.[7]

The Six Nations of the Iroquois Confederacy, whether they supported the colonists' cause or remained loyal to the Crown, were all losers in the

1. Governor Blacksnake, chief of the Allegany Senecas, c. 1850. Thomas Donaldson, comp., *Extra Census Bulletin of the Eleventh Census (1890) of the United States* (Washington, D.C.: U.S. Census Printing Office, 1892).

American Revolution. The loyalist groups were forced to give up their New York lands and move to Canada; the remaining Iroquois, those who stayed in New York, soon began to suffer incursions from the newly independent Americans. They were almost completely at the mercy of white land speculators and politicians, and between 1784 and 1842 they lost 95 percent of their lands. In the subtler areas that made up an Iroquois way of life, they suffered throughout the late eighteenth and nineteenth centuries endless impersonal bombardment of American civilization as it related to language, custom, consumer goods, and communication. It is thus quite remarkable that there was continuity in Iroquois society and that Iroquoian culture persisted in a variety of traditional forms. Many individuals contributed to this cultural tenacity. One of these was Governor Blacksnake, a man whose career contributes to a fuller picture of Indian life in New York during a period when Iroquoian culture faced its greatest challenge.[8]

At Cornplanter, Blacksnake was converted to the new religion espoused by his uncle, Handsome Lake. During the prophet's lifetime, Blacksnake, as a major supporter, contributed to the proselytizing of the new religion. He served as a key adviser, described by Wallace as the prophet's "privy counsellor."[9] After a dispute with Cornplanter in 1803, Handsome Lake, Blacksnake, and their followers moved from the Cornplanter Tract to the Allegany Indian Reservation where they founded the community of Coldspring. For the remainder of his life, the Chainbreaker resided a mile and a half above Coldspring in a small frame house. When Handsome Lake began sanctioning the execution of witches, support for the prophet's message waned. Eventually Handsome Lake left the Coldspring community for Tonawanda. Blacksnake, still a devoted follower of the Seneca prophet, stayed behind at Allegany where he remained until his own death in 1859.[10]

Even before Handsome Lake's death in 1815 on a visit to Onondaga, Blacksnake was modifying the message that the prophet had conveyed. He rejected Handsome Lake's proscription against Indian participation in the "white man's wars." By July 1813, Blacksnake, by then in his mid-sixties, volunteered his services on the side of the Americans.[11] In most other respects, he continued to advocate temperance, morality, and adherence to the overall principles of Handsome Lake.

After the War of 1812, the agents of the Ogden Land Company began to advocate the removal of all Iroquois Indians from New York State. At the time, the Ogden Land Company had the preemptive right to Seneca lands if the Indians could be "convinced" to sell their estate. In response to an 1817 proposal to divide Seneca lands in severalty, Blacksnake rejected this course of action. He insisted that this would lead to the Ogdens' gaining title to Seneca lands because fee simple title would make the lands subject to taxation and debt foreclosure. Blacksnake, wisely predicting later arguments against the General Allotment Act (Dawes Act) of 1887, maintained that this division would lead to the loss of the Senecas' estate and worse.

Besides, the Chainbreaker insisted, too many whites on the frontier who owned individual parcels of land were poor examples for the Indians.[12]

In response to the pressures for the Senecas to cede land, some Indian leaders such as Cornplanter became increasingly hostile to all whites, including the missionaries. Blacksnake rejected this course of action. He, Jemmy Johnson at Tonawanda, and other Senecas at Buffalo Creek countered the increasing antiwhite feelings. They observed that a "policy of uncompromising refusal to accept *any* whites customs would be destructive for its adherents, would deepen the schism within the tribes, and would drive many reasonable people into the hands of the Christian faction."[13] Thus Blacksnake permitted missionaries and Western schooling to operate at Allegany.[14] One contemporary white observer wrote of Blacksnake: "Although a pagan, he is yet tolerant, and makes no serious opposition to missionary efforts."[15] Blacksnake urged all followers of the *Gaiwiio* to secure more of the white man's education, not less, to cultivate their fields and build comfortable homes, and to aim to achieve social harmony, not divisive religious factionalism. Consequently, in the three decades that followed, these efforts, which appealed to the memory and teachings of the prophet, led to the institutionalization of a new religion, the Longhouse.[16] Even past his ninetieth year, Blacksnake was an essential participant in the Iroquois Condolence Council.[17] Importantly, by the 1840s, Blacksnake himself had formulated his specific version of the *Gaiwiio* "beginning with the account of the first vision" and mandating "twelve commandments prohibiting whiskey, witchcraft, love magic, divorce, adultery, premarital sex, refusal of the wife to live with her husband's parents, failure of parents to discipline unruly children, unwillingness to love all men, enmity, and gossip."[18]

The adaptive religious leadership of this aged warrior and major disciple of Handsome Lake at Allegany was essential at this time. A hardened antiwhite stance would have led nowhere because Senecas were powerless and they needed white cooperation to save what they could of the Seneca estate. The weakened position of the Senecas was clearly evident throughout this period. Blacksnake bore witness to the rapid dispossession of his people. From 1797 to 1826, he attended treaty councils in which land cessions were made; however, later in 1838, Blacksnake refused to place his name on a federal treaty ceding Buffalo Creek, much of the present city of Buffalo, and all the remaining Seneca lands except for the Oil Spring Reservation. He remained a holdout to the end. After being convinced by the Hicksite Quakers that his Allegany Indian Reservation, as well as the Cattaraugus Indian Reservation, could be returned only if he agreed to sign the Seneca Treaty of 1842, the elderly man signed this so-called "compromise treaty" that recognized the permanent loss of the Buffalo Creek and Tonawanda Indian Reservations.[19]

One of Blacksnake's greatest moments was to occur in the 1850s, even though he was well beyond one hundred years of age at the time. Continuing to see himself as the faithful disciple of Handsome Lake, Blacksnake protected the prophet's domain, namely the Oil Spring Reservation, saving it for Seneca posterity.

The Oil Spring Reservation is a parcel of Seneca land one mile square, near Cuba, New York. Nearly two-thirds of the reservation is in Allegany County and the rest is in Cattaraugus County, New York. Even though the Oil Spring was not one of the Seneca lands reserved specifically in the Treaty of Big Tree of 1797, Seneca title to the land was later recognized by Robert Morris, Thomas Morris, and agents of the Holland Land Company, who reserved the one-mile tract for Handsome Lake, the Seneca prophet, as confirmed in a Joseph Ellicott–Holland Land Company map of 1801 and later, as a result of Blacksnake's efforts, in a New York State Court of Appeals case in 1860–61.[20]

The "spring" is "a natural flow of petroleum, which the Senecas used to gather and use for a liniment to treat rheumatic pains and old ulcers."[21] The earliest unequivocal citation in the historical record to the oil spring is in the *Jesuit Relations* in 1656, which made reference to a petroleum spring: "As one approaches nearer to the country of the cats [Erie Indians] one finds heavy and thick water, which ignites like brandy and boils up in bubbles of flame when fire is applied to it."[22] Until his death in 1815, Handsome Lake, according to anthropologist Anthony F. C. Wallace, viewed this land with special interest and as his personal domain, perhaps because of his practice as a shaman.[23]

The fame of the Oil Spring was increasingly publicized in the early years of the nineteenth century. Writing in 1804 describing the Genesee

Country, Robert Munro observed, "Near the head of the Genesee River there is a remarkable spring, the water issuing from it being covered with a sort of oil, called by the Indian Seneca Oil, which is excellent for wounds and other medicinal uses."[24] More importantly, De Witt Clinton, while touring New York for the Board of Canal Commissioners in 1810, visited the Oil Spring, commenting, "Seneca Oil is procured from a spring in Olean, on the Allegany River, by dipping a blanket on the surface, which attracts the oil and then brushing it into a receiver."[25] Despite his mistakes in geography, Clinton's 1810 memoir provided the boosterism not only for canal development, but also for Genesee Fever, a land rush of immense proportions. In his journal, he stated unequivocally, "It is not perhaps too exaggerated to say that the worst lands in the western country [of New York State] are nearly equal to the best in the Atlantic parts of the state."[26]

Much of what happened to the Oil Spring Reservation and environs after Handsome Lake's death in 1815 was the result of the City of Rochester's emergence as a major metropolis. Virtually nonexistent in 1814, Rochester grew to over 36,000 people by 1850. Monroe County, which was not organized as a separate entity before the War of 1812, had over 60,000 residents by 1840. Most of this growth was attributable to the completion of the Erie Canal just south of the city at Pittsford and its elaborate connections to the Irondequoit Creek and the Genesee River in 1822. By that date, the Erie Canal ran from Little Falls to Rochester, 180 miles of inland navigation, resulting in a land and commercial rush in the Genesee. The area became a breadbasket overnight, producing substantial wheat. By 1840, Monroe County alone harvested a million bushels of wheat, while Genesee, Livingston, Ontario, and Orleans produced a comparable harvest. Each of these counties as well as nearby Wayne County produced a substantial corn crop as well, with Monroe leading the way with more than 400,000 bushels by 1840.[27]

Pressures to further open up the Genesee country intensified. By the mid-1830s, Rochester had become the leading granary of the Genesee situated in the greatest wheat-growing region of the state. Outside of Buffalo, it had more natural advantages than any other canal town because of its great access to both agricultural products and the extensive water power of the Genesee River. Thus it was no coincidence that Rochester became the flour capital of the United States. As early as 1835, twenty-one mills were operating in the city. These water-powered mills ground the grain into flour. The end-product was then packed into barrels and trans-shipped eastward by canal boats.[28]

Rochester, which also became the flower capital of the United States in the same period, thrived based on its water power and on its lucrative lumber industry, because rafts and logs could easily be floated down the Genesee River to the city's numerous sawmills. "The Water Power City," as it became known, became a boom town much like mining towns such as Denver, Helena, Sacramento, San Francisco, Seattle, and Tucson later did in the trans-Mississippi West. Hence it was no accident that the city fathers pushed for the expansion of transportation networks southward, hoping to secure trade as far as Pittsburgh and the Ohio River. They urged the creation of a Genesee Valley Canal to connect Rochester with the Allegany River and beyond.[29]

During his extraordinary long life, Blacksnake had witnessed the substantial shrinking of Seneca Country as a result of pressures from land speculators, transportation interests, and governmental officials. In the first four decades of the nineteenth century, the Senecas were permanently dispossessed of six major reservations—Buffalo, Caneadea, Canawaugus, Gardeau, Little Beard's Town, and Squawky Hill—an incredible estate of well over two hundred square miles of western New York State! These lands included some of the choicest agricultural parcels and the bottom lands of the Genesee Valley, as well as the great transshipment center of the nation's grain at Buffalo. Indeed, all of the Seneca reservations, including Allegany, Cattaraugus, and Tonawanda, with the exception of the Oil Spring Reservation, had been taken from the Senecas in the Treaty of Buffalo Creek in 1838; however, as a result of a nationwide protest organized by the Hicksite Friends, the Allegany and Cattaraugus Reservations were returned in 1842. The Tonawanda Senecas had to fight until 1856 to gain the "right" to repurchase some of their reservation lands back, confirmed by federal treaty the next year. It is important to note that the ambiguity about the legal status of the Oil Spring Reservation and the conscious efforts by Blacksnake to save this one-mile-square parcel were two of the major reasons for the Senecas' retaining this holy place in their history.

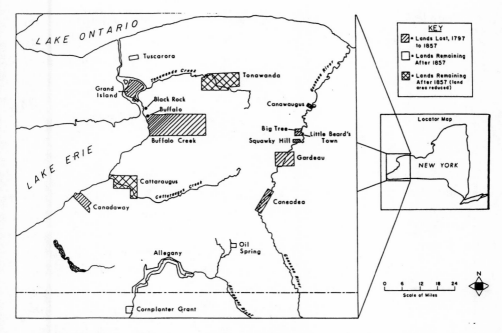

Map 3. Seneca Lands and Dispossession, 1797–1857. Map by Ben Simpson.

In 1836, the New York State Board of Canal Commissioners finally chose the Rochester-to-Olean route for construction of the Genesee Valley Canal. An immediate sense of urgency gripped Rochester merchants about the need for rapid construction because they feared that the recently opened canal-rail connection between Philadelphia and Pittsburgh would threaten their ambitious plans to corner north-south commercial routes to the Ohio River. Greed and pork-barrel politics supplanted reality given that the route chosen in 1836 was hilly terrain, had scant water supply for canal purposes in the highlands near Mount Morris, and construction costs of the venture—ultimately $6 million, the second most expensive canal project in the history of New York State—proved much more than originally calculated.[30]

The construction on the southern section of the Genesee Valley Canal began in 1839. Because of a major New York State budget crisis, the canal construction came to a halt in 1842. Construction resumed in 1846. As a result of the difficult hilly terrain and excessive cost of the project, final completion of the canal was delayed until 1858 (except for work on an eleven-mile extension spur near Dansville). The resulting Genesee Valley Canal, 128 miles long with 112 locks, connected the Erie Canal near Rochester to the New York and Erie Railroad at Olean, New York, a major railway that had opened in 1851.[31]

The building of the Genesee Valley Canal, the second most expensive canal in New York State to build, required the acquisition of land as a feeder for the canal. The Oil Spring Reservoir (Cuba Lake) was created in 1855 by construction of a dam on Oil Creek, 56 feet in height. In 1863 and then again in 1868, the New York State Legislature authorized the expansion of the spillway and the raising of the water level of Oil Creek Reservoir. Before this 1868 take and without federal or Indian approval, the New York State Board of Canal Commissioners expropriated 45 acres of the Oil Spring Indian Reservation in the creation of the Genesee Valley Canal project. Charles Congdon indicated that "47 acres of reservation lands were affected, of which only 13.19 acres were appropriated for the reservoir, but certain other quantities were liable to be damaged and flooded, used for roads, spoilbanks, etc."[32] Although New York State later claimed that it subsequently, in 1927, received retroactive federal approval of the original "take" of 45–47 acres of land *before* 1865, it never before or since received federal consent to later "takes."[33] Indeed, the secretary to the New York State Conservation Commission readily admitted in 1914, "About the year 1872 there was also acquired [by the state] 1.48 acres in the same reservation."[34]

As early as December 1835, Blacksnake and other Seneca chiefs and warriors of the Seneca Nation of Indians had made a thirty-year lease with "Irvine, Lowry, and Macomber one mile square on the Oil Spring Reservation in the county of Allegany, 'with full power to search for any and all kinds of minerals or ore.'" This agreement went beyond Oil Spring Reservation; it also allowed for the company's construction of three mills, hydraulic works, and dams along the Allegany River in Seneca Country. In return, Irvine, Lowry, and Macomber agreed to pay the Seneca $400 annually, promised to instruct the Indians in agriculture, and insisted the firm would prevent "any trespass committed by other individuals, such as cutting and carrying away timber." Seeing the potential of the proposed

Genesee Valley Canal, which might be compromised by this private agreement, the New York State Legislature rejected the Seneca petition to confirm this individual lease.[35]

Why the Senecas went to the New York State Legislature for confirmation of this lease is unclear. Perhaps in the Age of Jackson, Indians were reluctant to go to Washington to seek protection. Another possibility, a more likely one, is that the Indians were trying to delay or even stymie the building of the Genesee Valley Canal and were playing off private interests (Irvine, Lowry, and Macomber) against those of the New York State Board of Canal Commissioners. After all, the New York State Legislative Report maintained,

> By the terms of the contract, the leasees would have the entire control of the Allegany river, for a distance of about forty miles for the term of thirty years, which, in the opinion of your committee, is a power that should never be surrendered by the State, to any individual, or number of individuals, however respectable they may be, over a navigable river of so much importance as the Allegany, particularly when it is in contemplation to connect that river with our great commercial metropolis by splendid projects of internal improvement.
>
> Should the projected improvements of this State be constructed, the Allegany river is destined to become the great thoroughfare from the city of New York to the valley of the Ohio and the Mississippi, and should the Legislature confirm the contract made by the Indians, they might thereby legalize a destruction of the navigation of that noble river, and have the sad consolation of knowing they had tied up their own hands for the space of thirty years, and given to a company of individuals what they would consider a *"vested right,"* and thereby prevent any further legislation on the subject.[36]

Pressures had actually mounted in and around the Oil Spring Reservation long before the construction of the Genesee Valley Canal. Because the region contained a significant growth of pine, oak, chestnut, beech, and maple, General Calvin T. Chamberlain, after the War of 1812, had established the first sawmill in the environs of the reservation. Indeed,

Chamberlain's family, as well as the Clarks, were the founding fathers of the region. They had purchased sizable holdings from the Holland Land Company adjacent to the Oil Spring Reservation. In 1822, the New York State Legislature incorporated the village of Oil Creek, which also included Clarksville and Genesee. In the same year, a turnpike opened from Oil Creek to Olean. By the mid-1830s, this village became a separate entity from Clarksville, taking the name of Cuba. At precisely that time, General Chamberlain and Stephen Smith, the two founders of the village, along with other leading citizens of the region, met to organize the lobbying effort for a grand canal between the upper Genesee and the upper Allegany Rivers. The coming of construction in the southern section of the Genesee Valley Canal served as a catalyst and accelerated later developments along the canal. Cuba, now a town, reached 2,243 in population. With it also came land speculators, land squatters, and timber strippers onto Seneca lands in the region.[37] In the Age of Jackson, it seemed inevitable that the Senecas would lose their claim to Oil Spring, just as they had to the rest of their Genesee lands.

A decade later, Stanley Clark, a descendant of one of the leading pioneer families of southwestern New York, was elected to Congress from the area. A dabbler in Allegany and Cattaraugus Counties real estate, he and his partners, Benjamin Chamberlain and William Gallagher, soon became aware that the Oil Spring Reservation had never been reserved under any federal-Seneca treaty. At that time, the three men's lands, obtained earlier from the Holland Land Company, were adjacent to the reservation. Clark, without Indian authorization, then went onto the Oil Spring Reservation, surveyed it, and claimed it for the three men. They then conveyed one-quarter of the reservation to Horatio Seymour, later governor of New York, Democratic candidate for the presidency in 1868, and major promoter of New York State's canal system. Another quarter, which included the Oil Spring itself, was conveyed in the mid-1850s to Philonus Pattison, who immediately cleared and fenced eighty acres, planted an orchard, and built a house.[38] Hence, by the mid-1850s, the dispossession of the Senecas from Oil Spring seemed a fait accompli.

From 1855 to 1861, the Seneca Nation fought to save the entire reservation from squatters. It began a major ejectment case, *Seneca Nation of*

Indians v. Philonus Pattison, which ended up in the New York State Court of Appeals. A second action was directed by the Seneca against Seymour, Gallagher, Chamberlain, and Clark for the northeast quarter of the Oil Spring tract. The reason why it ended up in a state court is not altogether clear; however, it may be suggested that because of the political turmoil following the Seneca revolution of 1848, and the establishment of a new Indian republican elected government incorporated under New York State laws, the Seneca's attorney Daniel Sherman (later federal Indian agent) was hardly concerned with Indian sovereignty issues. The case turned on evidence produced by Blacksnake.[39]

The counsel for the defendants repeatedly attempted to challenge the Senecas' right to ownership of the Oil Spring Reservation because the lands had never been specifically reserved in any federal treaty. Yet, in April 1857, Daniel Sherman, now attorney for the Senecas, produced a deposition by Governor Blacksnake about the negotiations, which he had attended, relating to the Treaty of Big Tree of 1797. In it, Blacksnake made clear that it was the intent of both the Senecas and the Holland Land Company to include these lands in the treaty, but they had been inadvertently omitted. Joseph Ellicott himself had surveyed the lands, along with other Seneca parcels, in 1798, and had produced a map indicating Seneca ownership of the property.[40]

On August 27 and 28, 1858, Blacksnake appeared before Judge Cobb in Cattaraugus County Court in the sleepy hamlet of Little Valley, New York, and testified about his earlier deposition. Indicating he was 108 years of age, he recounted his long and extraordinary life—his childhood on the Genesee, his involvement in the American Revolution, his appointment as chief, his five meetings with General Washington. He stated that he was well "acquainted with the Oil Spring Reservation" and that he had been frequently there long before the Treaty of Big Tree because the "Indians used the oil of the spring a good deal for medicine." He then described the treaty negotiations at Big Tree that he and other chiefs had signed. After failing to recollect any talk there about the Oil Spring, he noted, however, that two or three years later, he noticed that the reservation boundaries had been marked: "The marks on the trees looked fresh and were the same as around the other reservations." Moreover, about a year or two after the

Treaty of Big Tree, Blacksnake saw a map in which the Oil Spring Reservation was marked red like the others reserved under the treaty. He took the map from Ellicott, copies of which the Holland Land Company agent had made for all the Seneca parties to the agreement, and then filed it with the chief's other important papers in a chest underneath his bed. The court found for the Senecas, and Pattison, Chamberlain, Clark, Gallagher, and Seymour were eventually ejected from the reservation after their appeals to the New York State Court of Appeals failed by 1861.[41]

Blacksnake, who died in 1859, never lived to see the Senecas' legal victory before the New York State Court of Appeals. His testimony had assured formal state recognition of Oil Spring as Seneca Country against the greedy efforts of individual land speculators; nevertheless, formal recognition did not mean that Albany officials, most notably the New York State Board of Canal Commissioners, would cease and desist from increasing the size of the spillway needed for the Genesee Valley Canal, which they continued to expand for more than a decade after Blacksnake's death.

The Oil Spring Reservoir, now known as Cuba Lake, an area of nearly 1,600 acres and the largest artificial body of water in the state when it was created, eventually became a leading pleasure resort. The nearby town of Cuba encouraged tourism and the lake became famous for anglers from around New York State as well as from Pennsylvania. Thus, in effect, part of Oil Spring, Seneca holy ground, became a dammed playground for non-Indians. Indeed, tourism became a mainstay of the entire region that Handsome Lake and his disciple Blacksnake traversed and saw as their holy land. Even the old Caneadea Council House was eventually disassembled and sent up the Genesee Valley Canal. Later it was reassembled by William Pryor Letchworth and placed near Mary Jemison's cabin at Letchworth State Park, the site of the old Gardeau Indian Reservation. Thus some of the holiest spots in Iroquoia were now simply seen by non-Indians as fishermen's paradises, or relics, "curiosities" to generate tourist dollars.[42]

In October 1872, before the council house was removed, many prominent Iroquois Indians gathered for the last time at Caneadea. One of the Senecas in attendance was William Blacksnake, "Sho-noh-go-wah," the grandson of the famous Chainbreaker. The Indians solemnly recalled earlier councils at the site, at a time when Seneca villages stretched in a line from the Upper Genesee to the Upper Allegany.[43] While the last boats were moving down the Genesee Valley Canal, soon to be replaced by a new mode of transportation—the railroad—the Indians nostalgically looked back to the time of the disciple, Handsome Lake's nephew, who kept a watchful eye on the Seneca holy lands as a custodian of the prophet's domain. Although he did not achieve total success, Blacksnake's actions did help to define Oil Spring as Seneca Indian land, which it remains, except for some acreage under water today at Cuba Lake.

3

Samuel George (1795–1873)

A *Study of Onondaga Indian Conservatism*

The Six Nations of the Iroquois Confederacy, whether they supported the colonists' cause or remained loyal to the Crown, were all losers in the American Revolution. The loyalist groups were forced to give up their New York lands and remove to Canada; the remaining Iroquois, those who stayed in New York, very soon began to suffer incursions from the newly independent Americans. They were almost completely at the mercy of white capitalists and politicians, and between 1784 and 1842, they lost 95 percent of their lands. In the subtler areas that made up an Iroquois way of life, they suffered the assaults of white missionaries and, inevitably, the endless impersonal bombardment of American civilization as it related to language, custom, consumer goods, communication. It is thus quite remarkable that throughout the nineteenth century there was a continuity in Iroquois society and that Iroquoian culture persisted in a variety of traditional forms. Many individuals contributed to this cultural tenacity, a number of whom have all but disappeared from the historical record. One of these was Samuel George of the Onondaga, a man whose career contributes to a fuller picture of Indian life in New York during a period when Iroquoian culture faced its greatest challenge.

It should be noted immediately that historical sources relating to George are not plentiful. His life spanned a period, 1795 to 1873, when the historical record was erratically maintained. Unlike later Iroquois leaders—Ely Parker and Clinton Rickard come immediately to mind—he did not live in a place or time that gave emphasis to the keeping of personal records, nor did he have a historical mentor to encourage him to do so.

2. Samuel George, chief of the
Onondagas, c. 1859. Painting by
Sanford Thayer. Courtesy of the
Onondaga Historical Association.

Samuel George was an Onondaga. Scholars writing on the history of the
Iroquois in nineteenth-century New York have focused most exclusively
on the Senecas.[1] All these factors have combined to exclude George from
his appropriate place in recorded history. F. D. Huntington, the Episcopal
bishop of central New York, speaking in 1889, labeled him "the ablest
pagan chief of this generation."[2] Despite a certain cultural myopia, Huntington's appraisal was accurate. George was among the most influential
Onondaga of the century. He was also the consummate Onondaga conservative. Unlike other Onondaga leaders of the same period, such as Chief
Albert Cusick, who converted to Christianity, George held steadfast to his
native beliefs.[3] He did not reject change outright and did permit western
education among his people, but he was also a strong advocate of Indian
sovereignty and treaty rights. Like Onondaga conservatives then and now,
he urged a separate course for the Iroquois and opposed amalgamation
into the American body politic.

Samuel George was born into the Wolf Clan of the Onondaga on the
Buffalo Creek Reservation in 1795. This level and well-wooded tract of
83,555 fertile acres along Cayuga, Cazenovia, and Buffalo creeks, which
included much of the present-day city of Buffalo, was the central fire of

Indian life in New York in the sixty years that followed the American Revolution. It attracted a substantial number of Iroquois refugees from all member nations of the Six Nations. Although the Seneca were the most numerous and politically influential on the reservation, the Onondagas were well represented. In 1816, out of a total of 450 Onondaga in New York, 210 were residing at the Buffalo Creek Reservation. As late as 1837, there were 197 Onondaga on the reservation—approximately 40 percent of all Onondaga in New York State. They occupied a square-mile tract on the southerly side of the reservation along Cazenovia Creek.[4]

The Seneca prophet Handsome Lake, at times a resident of the Buffalo Creek Reservation, received his first vision in 1799, when George was still a small boy. The word of the prophet spread quickly. He spoke against the use of alcohol and against witchcraft and urged the Iroquois to return to traditional ceremonies. At the same time, he urged the Indians to learn to farm in the white manner, and he gave religious sanction to a male role in agriculture. He also preached the transformation of the Indian family structure—from the traditional extended family or clan to the parent-centered family structure of Europeans. And he urged his people not to give any more land to the white man and to take no part in the wars of the whites.[5] While clearly innovative in some respects, Handsome Lake's movement was basically conservative in that it called for the restoration of Iroquois beliefs and ceremonies that had fallen into disuse. He accepted the myths, the ancient dream rites, the old annual calendar.[6]

It is not surprising that Samuel George's nation, the Onondaga, was receptive to the prophet's conservative preaching. The Onondaga had clearly not prospered under white domination. The millions of acres that they had held in 1776 were gone. By the 1820s they were reduced to a reservation of 6,100 acres at Onondaga and to living with other members of the Six Nations at Buffalo Creek and along the Grand River near Brantford, Ontario. Divided by the events of the American Revolution, by the proselytizing of white missionaries, and by the power plays of their own leaders, they were impressed by Handsome Lake's call for solidarity and temperance. Many Onondagas converted to his ancient beliefs. The prophet died, in fact, while visiting the Onondaga Reservation in 1815 and was buried beneath the floor of the old Onondaga council house, a site marked today by a monument in the center of the reservation.[7]

Samuel George was twenty when the prophet died. The historical record, not surprisingly, gives no hint of contact between the two, and in one respect, George, like many Iroquois, ignored Handsome Lake's message-proscription against Indian participation in the white man's wars. The Iroquois, including a sizable detachment of Onondagas, served on the American side in the War of 1812. They viewed themselves as citizens of their separate nations and as allies of the United States under the direct command of their own chiefs, especially the Seneca leader Farmer's Brother. Onondagas, including Samuel George, followed the leadership of their chiefs, Captains Cold (Cole) and LaFort.[8] Ironically, the Onondaga came face-to-face with British-allied Iroquois, including Onondaga, from the Six Nations Reserve in Ontario. Once again, the Onondagas were split, participating as auxiliaries in the white man's "war of brothers," as they had done in the American Revolution.[9]

The Iroquois, including the Onondagas, derived little benefit from the war. They suffered casualties in battle and endured smallpox epidemics, while several of the fiercest engagements of the war took place on their lands along the Niagara River.[10] But for Samuel George, the war was a theater in which he displayed courage, endurance, and physical prowess, all of which play a role in the making of a leader among the Iroquois. Serving along the Buffalo-to-Albany corridor during the conflict, George was to excel as a runner. A thin, sinewy man with strongly marked features, his physical appearance was frequently mentioned in the records. He was viewed by one of these observers as "a noble specimen of a man" for his athletic prowess and presence. George's greatest achievement during the War of 1812 was to run from American headquarters at Buffalo to the arsenal at Canandaigua and back, a distance of 150 miles, in two days![11]

George's running abilities were legendary. Orlando Allen, a man later involved in cheating Iroquois Indians out of their lands, wrote that George was virtually unbeatable in foot races. The only challenge to his string of victories came from John Titus, a Seneca Indian from the Allegany Reservation. According to Allen, Titus was able to defeat George only once:

On one occasion Titus achieved by strategy, what he could not by speed, and that was by keeping close up to George until within a few steps of the goal, and then just before crossing the line, putting forth all of his powers, slipped by leaving George no time to recover the lost race, as he probably could have done in ten strides. George was exceedingly mortified at the result and was careful not to be thus outwitted again. I think he was on no other occasion beaten in these races.[12]

The importance of "runners" in Iroquois history should not be under-estimated. They were not merely gifted athletes intent on "going for the gold." Iroquois runners summoned councils, conveyed intelligence from nation to nation, and warned of impending danger. George's contemporary, Lewis Henry Morgan, in his classic *League of the Ho-de-no-sau-nee, or Iroquois* (1851), observed, "Swiftness of foot was an acquirement, among the Iroquois, which brought the individual into high repute."[13] Consequently, George's rise to power and influence in the Iroquois councils was a direct result of his physical prowess. It is also important to note that the contemporary Onondaga still designate "runners," using the term to describe people who serve the council as a conduit for the conduct of essential business, and who are accorded respect as community leaders worthy of other higher positions of authority and prestige in the nation. Significantly, runners still convey official messages and carry stringed wampum to symbolize their official role, diplomatic protocol, and/or truth.[14]

George later received a pension of $120 for his participation in the War of 1812. His pension request for three years of service in the defense of the Niagara Frontier is quite revealing. He asked to be compensated for the following: 1 hat ($5.00), ordinary (non-uniform) coat ($25.00), 1 vest ($3.50), 1 pair of "leggins" ($3.50), 2 blankets ($10.00), 1 knapsack ($3.00), 1 canteen ($.25), "use" of 1 rifle ($10.00), 1 canoe ($6.00), 2 belts ($7.00), 2 pair of stockings ($1.00), 2 shirts ($4.00), 2 pair of moccasins ($2.00), 1 neckerchief ($1.50), and 1 "scalping knife" ($.50).[15] He also requested $2.00 compensation for his transportation expenses between Buffalo Creek and Fort Niagara (eighty miles round trip).

From the end of the War of 1812 until the mid-1840s, George virtually disappears from the historical record; it is nevertheless possible to reconstruct a part of this period of his life. George and his people came face-to-face with tribal destruction in the three decades after the War of 1812. Following the opening of the Erie Canal in 1825, population rapidly increased in central and western New York. The City of Buffalo was formally incorporated in 1831 and soon became a major Great Lakes port, creating further pressures for expansion; however, Buffalo Creek Reservation blocked the city's expansion to the southeast. Land speculators soon took advantage of the Iroquois, who were bitterly divided by a number of matters—land sales, methods of selecting chiefs, education, religion—that separated the Indians into different camps and made them susceptible to manipulation.

Land speculators and corrupt federal officials took advantage of the situation, employed bribery and coercion, and induced some of the chiefs to sign the Treaty of Buffalo Creek in 1838, by which the Indians lost the Buffalo Creek Reservation. Among the Iroquois signatories to the treaty were two Onondaga warriors, William John and Noah Silversmith, who acted without authority from the chiefs and received $2,000 for their "cooperation." The Onondaga were in fact the most resistant to change of all the New York Iroquois. One article of the treaty offered them cash compensation totaling $4,500 to move to the American West. Few of them did so, in sharp contrast to the substantial number of Cayuga and Oneida who left New York after the signing.[16]

The Onondaga and Tonawanda chiefs vociferously opposed the Seneca political revolution of 1848 that had overturned the old chieftain system of government and had established a republic, the Seneca Nation of Indians, an elected political system set apart from the Iroquois Confederacy. For more than two decades, they tried to restore the old chieftain system of government on the Allegany and Cattaraugus Reservations. Samuel George was one of the Onondaga leaders who gave support to Senecas attempting to restore the traditional government. Writing in 1850, he praised the Old Chiefs party at Cattaraugus and urged them "to defend the rights of the system of our old Indian government . . . so highly important to us all to maintain."[17]

Onondaga conservatism was also reflected in their resistance to missionaries. Jabez Backus Hyde, a missionary at Buffalo Creek from 1811 to 1820, commented in his journal that the Onondagas were strongly opposed to conversion. Despite the frequent visits of Episcopal, Methodist, Presbyterian, and Quaker missionaries and the building of a Methodist and Episcopal church as well as an Episcopal school at Onondaga in the nineteenth century, a minority of Onondaga were converted. Although the Onondaga chiefs permitted these sects on the reservation, the missionaries' Christian message was not universally accepted. As late as 1890, there were only 68 Christians at Onondaga out of a population of 494 residents (including 86 Oneidas).[18]

As a consequence of the loss of the Buffalo Creek Reservation in 1842 and after the death of Captain Cold (Ut-ha-wah), the Onondaga returned to their homeland in central New York. The Confederacy's council fire that had burned at Buffalo Creek was rekindled at the Onondaga Reservation and the sacred wampum was returned to the Onondaga longhouse in 1847. After a brief residence at the Cattaraugus Reservation in the mid-1840s, Samuel George moved his wife and five children to Onondaga. It was there in 1850 that he became a chief, taking the name *Hononwirehdonh,* the "Great Wolf," the hereditary keeper of the wampum held by a member of the Wolf Clan of the Onondaga Nation.[19]

The attainment of this League title, which he held until his death in 1873, was the culmination of four decades of apprenticeship for leadership. Hononwirehdonh was no ordinary title. As Annemarie Shimony stated, "He is arbiter of disputes and the tie-breaker in voting. To him are left decisions of referral back to the individual phratries, and to him accrues the task of 'cooling down the fire' when arguments break out." He is also, she noted, "the wampum keeper of the League, and the only chief to constitute a phratry [a tribal social subdivision] all by himself."[20] Thus, at a time of bitter dissension caused by the Buffalo Creek Treaty of 1838 and its aftermath and continued talk by federal and state officials of Iroquois removal from New York, the Hononwirehdonh, with his responsibilities to help create consensus and pacify diverse elements, held a strategic position in the struggle for Iroquois survival.

George and the Onondaga Council of Chiefs were soon faced with repeated state policies of forced assimilation. This so-called Americanization process comprised a four-pronged formula: The christianizing activities of missionaries on reservations in order to stamp out "paganism"; the exposure of the Indian to white Americans' ways through New York State–supported schools established from the mid-1840s onward; the division of tribal lands among individual Indians to instill personal initiative, allegedly required by the free enterprise system; and finally, in return for accepting land-in-severalty, the "rewarding" of Indians with U.S. citizenship.

The New York State superintendent of common schools wrote in 1849, "Is it not obvious that the practical *communism* imposed by our laws upon the Indians, obstructs their advance in knowledge and civilization, and deprives them of the chief stimulus to industry and frugality[?]" The superintendent added, "If the Indian is to be civilized and educated, he must cease to be a savage. We must allow him to partition and cultivate his land, if we would not have all our efforts to educate and enlighten him prove illusive and futile."[21] Sixteen years later, this assimilationist message was even more elaborately presented by the superintendent of the Onondaga Indian Schools. In his report in 1865, he advocated the state's abandonment of "the letter of old treaties" in order to save the Indians "from extinction." He urged that the course of citizenship and state jurisdiction work upon Indian lives in the same manner that it worked to fuse "the lower type of emigrants from foreign lands" into American society.[22]

Most Onondagas rejected this "Americanization" program; to preserve tribal identity they retained their separate existence, spoke their own languages, performed their ceremonies, and continued to observe their native religion, not pushing for state or federal suffrage and viewing themselves as citizens of sovereign nation-states. Most importantly, they protested against every effort to undermine their tribal land base. In the early 1850s, a bill to survey the Onondaga Reservation was introduced and passed in the New York State Assembly without the prior approval or knowledge of the Onondaga Council of Chiefs. When the chiefs learned of this bill, they protested, insisting that surveying was the first step in the division of the reservation into individual allotments and ultimate Indian land loss, "thereby destroying that bond of common interest which unites and holds Indian communities together."[23] The bill failed to pass the New York State Senate, but these efforts continued well into the late nineteenth and early twentieth centuries. It should be noted that the movement to survey and allot the reservation was supported by disgruntled Onondagas, some of whom were Christian converts, who objected to the power of the traditional Council of Chiefs. They accused the chiefs of personally profiting from their position by allowing whites to strip timber on the reservation. There is also evidence that some Onondagas did not welcome Indian refugees from the Buffalo Creek Reservation with open arms.[24]

During the Civil War, Samuel George was the leading spokesman of the Iroquois Confederacy in dealing with Washington. By 1863, federal officials had awarded him the honorary rank of brevet general and acknowledged him to be the "Principal Chief of the Six Nations." Considerably more than three hundred Iroquois Indians joined the Union side during the American Civil War.[25] Although there appears to have been Indian willingness to enlist in the conflict, the Iroquois reacted strongly to certain abuses in the recruitment process.

Much of the Iroquois criticism centered on the military conscription system. The Enrollment Act of 1863, which set categories of priority for conscription of all able-bodied male citizens, allowed a significant number of reasons for exemptions. The Act exempted anyone who could pay a $300 exemption fee or provide a substitute.[26] Though there seems to be little evidence that New York Indians were drafted during the Civil War, which is in sharp contrast to World War II and Vietnam, they were nevertheless affected by the Enrollment Act.[27] Because most of the Indians were poor, they found themselves subject to bounty inducements and many became substitutes. Non-Indian "bounty-brokers" actively recruited Indians as substitutes because of the attractiveness of the substitute fees to poor reservation residents. But the Indians were often the victims of unscrupulous brokers. By 1864, forty-three Iroquois, mostly Senecas, serving in the 24th New York Cavalry; the 86th, 97th, and 100th New York Volunteers; and the 13th and 14th New York Heavy Artillery, asked to be released from service. They claimed they had never received their promised bounties or that they were underage recruits, some being only fifteen or sixteen years of age.

Iroquois leaders soon objected to the operation of the Act, and Samuel George led the protest. In November 1863, he met with President Lincoln to discuss this matter. As a designated official of the Six Nations, George followed the traditional course established by earlier chiefs, who held that negotiations affecting the Iroquois must be made directly with the president of the United States on a nation-to-nation basis between equals.[28] In his talk with Lincoln, George undoubtedly reaffirmed the federal-Indian treaty relationship and questioned the right of Congress to pass legislation such as the Enrollment Act without the prior deliberation and approval of the Confederacy Council.

George convinced Lincoln to intervene on behalf of the Indian recruits. On November 20, 1863, Lincoln wrote Secretary of War Edwin Stanton, "Please see and hear the Sec. of Interior and Comm. of Indian Affairs with Genl. George, Indian Chief and discharge such of the men as the chief applies for and who have not received bounties." Seventeen days later, the assistant adjutant general's office issued Special Order No. 542, which allowed for the discharge of thirteen Iroquois Indians serving in the 13th New York Heavy Artillery and one in the 86th New York Volunteers.[29] On December 23, thirteen of the fourteen Indians were released from their military service. Importantly, the order read: "Discharged by direction of the President at the request of the Chief of the Six Nations Indians."[30]

George was less successful in securing the discharge of the other Indians, though he and the Seneca frequently petitioned for their release. In June 1864, Seneca leaders insisted that they had "authorized Samuel George head chief among the Onondagas and representative of the Six Nations to present our supplication." The Seneca reiterated George's arguments to Lincoln, maintaining that there was no law allowing for the drafting or enlistment of Indian minor children and objecting to conscription of Indians into military service without prior tribal consent, which went against historic precedents and treaties.[31] A month later, George wrote the commissioner of Indian Affairs. Recalling his official visit to Washington and interviews with politicians nine months earlier, George repeated his stand about discharging the Indians: "We agreed [that] those who have not received Bounty [sic] from the Government shall be discharged from the service, notwithstanding many of our young men taken away . . . I hope that you will discharge them without further delay."[32]

After substantial negotiations, the remaining Indians won the right to be discharged but only after they were required to pay back whatever bounty they had received. Unfortunately, most of these Indians had already spent the money, and though at least three repaid the bounty and were discharged, the majority stayed in military service to the end of the Civil War. At least two of these Indians, Privates Ira Pierce and John B. Williams, died in the conflict—Pierce at Petersburg and Williams as a prisoner of war at Andersonville Prison.[33]

Despite his limited victory, George's efforts helped reinforce the Iroquois traditional belief in their own separate sovereignty. Reaffirming treaty rights, meeting with the Great Father in Washington City, and rejecting conscription without tribal consent are as strongly established in the conservative agenda of the Onondaga today as they were more than 140 years ago during the Civil War. Although success is important, symbolism, form, and style are equally important in the Iroquois traditional mind.[34]

Following the war, George continued to serve as Iroquois spokesman. In March 1870, as "Head Chief," he wrote to Governor John Hoffman of New York State to complain about timber stripping by whites on the Onondaga Reservation, to inquire about the status of an Indian agent, and to raise questions about leasing. In June 1870, he asked Hoffman for information about moneys owed to the Indians by New York State.[35]

From 1869 to 1873, George was formally licensed to practice medicine and was appointed "government physician" to the Onondaga after a petition was signed by thirty-three leading Indians and non-Indians in the environs of Syracuse. His long involvement as a "traditional medicine man" is clear from the historic record. R. H. Gardner, the Indian agent at that time, formally endorsed George's appointment: "I believe Captain George can doctor the Indians as well as a white man. After considerable experience on the subject, I believe that the Indians live under his treatment and are as healthful as when treated by any other physician."[36]

During the last two decades of his life, George's gift of oratory was noted by observers of the Indian world. According to William Beauchamp, the Episcopal minister and keenest observer of the Onondaga world of the nineteenth and early twentieth centuries, George "was both shrewd and eloquent" and "full of official dignity and seldom condescending to speak English." Although "thin and rather fun-looking," George was frequently a featured speaker at public events where his speeches were translated from Onondaga into English. His fame as a storyteller was widespread and undoubtedly added to his prestige and power among his own people and outsiders in the non-Indian environs of Syracuse. Beauchamp added, "I have heard him speak, and he was fond of story-telling, having a good stock to draw upon. He remembered when the Onondagas moved up the valley to their present reservation village, many building bark houses at that time."[37]

Oratory was a path to leadership among the Iroquois. Lewis Henry Morgan observed in 1851, "By the cultivation and exercise of this capacity [of oratory], was opened the pathway to distinction; and the chief or warrior gifted with its magical power could elevate himself as rapidly, as he who gained renown upon the warpath."[38] George's speaking abilities, in combination with his diplomatic and medical skills and his physical prowess, gave him a position of particular influence at the council fires of the Iroquois Confederacy. It is worth noting that oratorical skill is still valued in the Iroquois polity. One of the factors in the reemergence of Onondaga power within the Confederacy over the past few decades, apparently, is the substantial oratorical skills of two of its present Onondaga chiefs.[39]

Until his death on September 24, 1873, George lived in a small frame single-story house just northeast of the Onondaga Council House, about a quarter of a mile from the center of the reservation. He remained a "traditional" to the end, never converting to Christianity. Although a Christian sermon was presented by Bishop Huntington and other Episcopal leaders at his funeral, George was buried with Indian rites as prescribed by the Great Binding Law of his Iroquois people.[40]

Samuel George had witnessed striking changes in the status of the Iroquois during his lifetime. He was directly involved in two wars—in the War of 1812 as a combatant and in the Civil War as an Iroquois spokesman. He undoubtedly observed, as he was affected by, the Iroquois revitalization movement inspired by Handsome Lake's visions, which stimulated changes in the agriculture, the basic family patterns, and the religion of the Iroquois. He lived through a period of explosive growth in the white population of central and western New York—decades in which his people lost substantial amounts of land and suffered environmental deterioration and social circumscription. He endured a failed Indian leadership that was incapable of stemming the tide of land speculators and missionaries, as he endured the increased dependence of the Indian on the white man, caused by the economic and political changes brought about by American industrialization in combination with a shrinking Indian land base.

Despite these revolutionary changes, George remained an Iroquois conservative to the end. His rise to influence among his people had been along the traditional paths to authority. His brand of conservatism allowed him to accept but modify the teachings of Handsome Lake. Although he faithfully ascribed to the ceremonials, kept his Iroquoian language alive, and rejected alienation of Indian lands, he served the American cause in two major wars. He also permitted missionaries and schools to be maintained on the Onondaga Reservation and was a well-known and admired "personality" off the reservation. While dealing with the likes of Bishop Huntington, Governor Hoffman, or President Lincoln, George attempted in a practical but mostly traditional way to serve his people and to express Indian concerns despite the often debilitating internal discord that was reflected in the Iroquois polity and the incredible pressures from the non-Indian world. Although today his reputation as "the runner" remains in Indian oral tradition and overshadows his other accomplishments, George's steadfastness in maintaining tradition, however flexible in approach, makes him worthy of study and explains much about Iroquois survival well over a century after his death.[41]

PART TWO The Keepers
of the Kettle/Mothers
of the Nation

Introduction

Before my attendance in July 2005 at a symposium devoted to teaching teachers Native American history, Dr. Lloyd Elm, the prominent educator of Onondaga-Oneida ancestry, suggested that I present an aspect of Hotinohsyóni? women's history to the gathering, rather than simply lecturing on Iroquois warriors in the Civil War as I had been scheduled to do. In an instructive manner, he pointed out, "To understand us [Hotinohsyóni?], you have to understand our women and their roles in our world."[1] His words made perfect sense to me from the time my research on the Six Nations began in 1971.

Although often mistakenly presented as a "matriarchy," traditional gender roles among the Iroquois were balanced ones. Men did not dominate, and women were not subservient. Theirs were two distinct provinces: the clearing in which women played key economic roles and raised the chiefs to leadership; and the forest world where the men's domain was largely in hunting, war, and diplomacy.[2] Thus women had their own separate arenas of influence and power that included adopting of captives, assigning of the fields, arranging marriages, naming, and so forth. Their roles were reinforced by the Iroquois cosmology: their creation belief with the key role of Sky Women and women's significance in the development of horticulture and ritual, and in the recounting of the founding of the League of the Iroquois where Jigonsasee, a Neutral Indian and known as the "Mother of Nations," became the first person to accept the message brought by the Peacemaker (Deganawidah).[3]

Most studies of Iroquoian women have been fraught with generalizations and focused on "declension" studies, emphasizing the reduction of women's power since the late eighteenth century. Most of these studies point out that the Seneca Nation of Indians did not allow women to vote or hold office until the mid-1960s.[4] Iroquois women's roles did rapidly change before and after the American Revolution, and their control of the clearing became shared with men. No longer, as in the past, did clan mothers "raise" chiefs to a position of authority in all of the Iroquois communities, although this role still continues on some of their reserves/reservations today. While the major role of clan mothers has definitely declined and the economic control of horticulture by women has disappeared, Iroquois women continued to play essential roles—economically, culturally, and politically—in each of their communities. In some cases, as the two chapters in part two illustrate, their roles had characteristics similar to ones in their earlier history.

The life of Dinah John, the best known Onondaga woman of the nineteenth century, is a case in point. The noted historian Theda Perdue has observed that "another possibility of gendering the past is economic history."[5] The reality of separate economic roles for men and women continued well into the twentieth century. John, an aged Onondaga potter and basket maker, brought her wares three and one-half miles to downtown Syracuse and back along Salina Street, just as Iroquois women selling sassafras and baskets did until the years immediately after World War II.[6]

In a revisionist study, Kees-Jan Waterman, in his edited work on the Wendells, an Albany trading family, has pointed out that women played a much greater role in Indian-white economic exchange in the late seventeenth and early decades of the eighteenth century than previously acknowledged by scholars.[7] John, much as was true of these earlier women, used her gender, seen by the white citizens of Syracuse as less threatening than the presence of Onondaga males in the city's commercial district. This perception allowed her to sell her wares. In a sophisticated and calculating way, she played the role of the self-effacing Onondaga outwardly friendly to all, while at the same time maintaining her Hotinohsyóni? identity. Although not a political-religious leader of her community as was Samuel George, she, nevertheless, showed all Onondaga women that they could be as self-reliant as their menfolk and that they could be as active in efforts at economic and cultural survival as their mothers, grandmothers, and great-grandmothers had been in the past.

The life of a twentieth-century Seneca woman offers the reader another perspective of how traditional roles of women are modified and used in more contemporary times. To outsiders, it may seem strange that the Seneca Nation did not allow women suffrage or permit women to hold office until the 1960s. Yet, the second chapter in part two on Alice Lee Jemison shows that these restrictions did not mean that all Seneca women were powerless. They and other Iroquois women have periodically asserted their roles as "Mothers of the Nation."

In the early 1970s, while beginning my research for the book *The Iroquois and the New Deal* (1981), I came across two documents. The first one, housed at the Buffalo and Erie County Historical Society, was written in 1933 by Ray Jimerson, president of the Seneca Nation of Indians; attached to it was the résumé of Alice Lee Jemison. Jimerson's letter enthusiastically recommended Jemison, then his "girl Friday," for a position in Washington, D.C., in the newly elected administration of President Franklin D. Roosevelt.[8] A second letter, found in the Franklin D. Roosevelt Presidential Library, was Jemison's four-page letter to the president, written in 1935, condemning New York State officials for their lack of concern for the health of the Indians of Cattaraugus Indian Reservation, caused by failures to prevent the continued environmental contamination of the community. She also accused Albany of violating Seneca treaties, and criticized President Roosevelt's actions in stymieing a bill protecting Indian hunting and fishing rights.[9]

Increasingly through the 1930s, Jemison, a journalist influenced by the Yavapai physician and intellectual Carlos Montezuma, who had earlier called for the abolition of the Bureau of Indian Affairs, became a major activist in national circles. Because of her willingness to work with any and all Roosevelt administration-bashers, however unsavory, her reputation was soon dragged through the mud by Harold Ickes, the secretary of the interior, and John Collier, the commissioner of Indian affairs. Because of her vitriolic attacks on the New Deal, her efforts in organizing the American Indian Federation—an umbrella organization committed to the abolition of the BIA and numerous other concerns—and her strong objection to the Selective Service Act of 1940 and the forced conscription of American Indians into military service, she was condemned by the Roosevelt administration, especially Ickes and Collier, as a "mixed blood," a "fascist," and a Nazi tool of Adolph Hitler.[10] She was placed under political surveillance by the FBI from 1938 to 1948, yet even J. Edgar Hoover conceded she was not a subversive.[11]

Only by doing fieldwork in the 1970s at her home on the Cattaraugus Indian Reservation was I able to uncover the real life of Alice Lee Jemison. Despite the negative assessments, she was a sovereignty-minded Seneca (her mother was a Seneca and her father a Cherokee) who served as a lobbyist for the Seneca Nation of Indians. Her uncle Cornelius Seneca is considered to have been the finest president of the Seneca Nation of the twentieth century. Her daughter Jeanne Marie Jemison was the surrogate judge of the Seneca Nation.[12] Alice Lee Jemison's motivation was not mimicking words coming out of Berlin or Rome; it was the actions of her powerful women of the past, "Keepers of the Kettle," whose main responsibility was preserving the clearing from apparent dangers. To her and to many Iroquois Indians in New York, the Roosevelt administration's plans had to be resisted at all costs.[13] Although rooted in the past, Jemison's political activism was also the harbinger of Iroquois activism that emerged in the last half-century.[14]

4

The Two Worlds of Aunt Dinah John (1774?–1883), Onondaga Indian

Today, the Onondaga Indians teach their children about the *Kaswentha,* the Two Row Wampum. The belt contains two parallel purple rows of shell with three white rows of shell interspersed. Indeed, the belt's design is included in the recently constructed Tsha' Hon'nonyeadakhwa', the impressive Onondaga Nation Arena, the ice hockey and indoor lacrosse facility on the reservation just south of Syracuse. To the Onondagas as well as to other members of the Six Nations in the United States as well as in Canada, the two purple strands represent two vessels, an Iroquois canoe and a Euro-American ship, symbolic of two distinct peoples going down the river. One vessel, the canoe, represents the Iroquois world; the other, the ship, represents the Euro-Americans and their laws, mores, and values. In order to successfully navigate the river, the vessels must not interfere with each other, meaning that Indians and non-Indians respect each other's way of life.[1]

Modern-day Iroquois often add a further meaning to the Two Row Wampum, warning their people that it is nearly impossible to go down the river with one foot in the Indian canoe and the other in the Euro-American ship; however, as this chapter shows, one Onondaga woman, Dinah A. John (c. 1774–1883), did accomplish that very feat. In part, she did so under enormous pressures in the century after the whirlwind of the American Revolution by becoming "Aunt Dinah" to the outside white world. Although at a cost, she succeeded in navigating the white-water rapids that at times threatened to submerge her and her Indian people. Yet hers was not a story of failure but one of cultural adaptation, persistence, and survival in the face of overwhelming odds.

49

John was among the most prominent Iroquois women of the nineteenth century in New York. Only the Seneca Caroline Parker Mountpleasant and Mary Jemison, the famous white captive adopted by the Senecas, are more renowned in this period.[2] John, a leading Onondaga basket maker and potter, was one of the first Iroquois women depicted in portraiture. In 1876, Philip S. Ryder photographed her, a painted copy of which now hangs in the Onondaga Historical Association in Syracuse. Ryder's popular photograph of this Onondaga centenarian was widely distributed throughout central New York and later partially reproduced in Thomas Donaldson's *Six Nations of New York,* a federal census publication of 1892. Both the Ryder original and the Donaldson copy showed "Aunt Dinah" as a shriveled old woman, seated in her rocking chair with a cane in her left hand.[3]

Although John had no official birth certificate, Donaldson, in the same publication, estimated the age of the Onondaga elder and described her extraordinary vitality: "Old Aunt Dinah, who died at the age of 107, on the Onondaga reservation, is kindly remembered by the citizens of Syracuse, as well as by her own people. After the age of 90, she walked 7 miles to the city and back." Despite her Longhouse funeral, Donaldson notes, "When asked as to her church relations, she placed her hand upon her head, saying 'I'm Piscopal here'; then, placing her hand upon her heart, she added: 'I'm Methodist here.'"[4]

William M. Beauchamp, the prominent Episcopal minister and anthropologist, included "Ta-wah-ta-whe-jah-quan or Aunt Dinah John" in his thumbnail sketches/field notes found in the New York State Library's Manuscript Division. He suggested that she could have been born as early as 1774 and that her Onondaga name meant "the earth that upholds itself." Beauchamp added that she "was for many years, one of the best known women in the county [Onondaga County]" and continued to visit Syracuse often, even after she was said to be a hundred years old. The Episcopal minister indicated that John had seen George Washington when she was a child and that New York Governor Horatio Seymour, the Democrats' presidential candidate in 1868, had been cradled in her arms as an infant when he had lived in nearby Pompey, New York. Beauchamp, who knew her and visited her home on the reservation on numerous occasions, insisted that the Onondaga elder "was very jolly, a general favorite everywhere and

3. Dinah John, Onondaga elder, c. 1876. Photograph by Philip S. Ryder. Thomas Donaldson, comp., *Extra Census Bulletin of the Eleventh Census (1890) of the United States* (Washington, D.C.: U.S. Census Printing Office, 1892).

welcomed at every home." Although most evidence is to the contrary, Beauchamp later noted that Dinah John "may have been ten years younger [than 109 years of age at the time of her death as he had previously claimed]. She was well known throughout the county, especially in Syracuse, and was an estimable woman."[5]

During the long life of Dinah John, Iroquois Indian life underwent tumultuous change. At the time of her birth, the Onondagas had ten villages in the upper Susquehanna Valley. Soon the child's world was disrupted by the American Revolution. On April 19, 1779, Colonel Goose Van Schaick with soldiers of the American Continental Army invaded the Onondaga country by way of Oneida Lake. Some sources claim that Dinah was old enough to remember Van Schaick's military expedition. The American colonel marched his soldiers out of Fort Stanwix and onto the major Onondaga village along the bottomlands of Onondaga Creek below the present town of Nedrow, just south of today's Syracuse, where he laid waste to the entire settlement. The American army killed at least twelve and took thirty-three Onondagas, mostly women who had been trapped in a cornfield, as prisoners of war. The Indians later alleged that the women were sexually abused while they were incarcerated by Van Schaick's soldiers, a charge that was later denied by American officers. Later that year, a hundred-man detachment from the Sullivan-Clinton campaign finished Van Schaick's work of destruction by burning the other Onondaga villages.[6] The result was that a majority of Onondagas fled to the Niagara frontier and resettled at what became the Seneca's Buffalo Creek Reservation or fled to British Canada and established a new Iroquois Confederacy at Ohsweken, Ontario, what became the Six Nations Reserve. Yet John remained behind in central New York at a time when white land pressures grew exponentially.

John's long life provides insights into how Iroquoian women dealt with the rapidly changing and increasingly urbanized world around them. By 1806, only 143 Indians, including Dinah Anthony (John), were residing at the Onondaga Reservation.[7] The population of what became Onondaga County increased from a few whites in 1790 to over 117,000 non-Indians by 1880. At the same time, Syracuse, which borders the 6,100-acre Onondaga Indian Reservation, became an instant city, with a population of over 51,000 people by the time of John's death in 1883.[8] In sharp contrast, the total population on the Onondaga Reservation numbered fewer than five hundred Indians by 1890.[9]

On September 12, 1788, in a state treaty, the Onondaga "ceded" (the Indians to this day insist it was a lease) a one-hundred-square-mile tract running from Lake Ontario southward to the Pennsylvania line for "one thousand French Crowns in Money and two hundred Pounds in Cloathing," and an annuity of "five hundred Dollars in Silver" forever, with the option of converting the annual annuity to a payment in clothes. In the "treaty," the Onondagas were dispossessed of all their lands in Cayuga, Cortland, Oswego, Tompkins, and Wayne Counties and some in Onondaga County.[10] Much of the remaining Onondaga land, including the city of Syracuse, was lost in a second state "treaty," consummated on July 28, 1795.[11] By 1797, Albany officials had established the New York State's Salt Spring Reserve around today's Salina, Geddes, and Syracuse, which along with canal development over the next several decades led to the rapid white settlement of the Military Tract lands that surrounded the Onondaga Reservation.[12]

Around 1811, Dinah Anthony began cohabiting with Thomas John. Their relationship began when she was well into her thirties, suggesting that she may have been married previously and possibly to an Oneida since Anthony (Antone) is an Oneida surname. Dinah later claimed that she was "formally" married after the end of the War of 1812. Although no official record of their marriage exists today, Iroquois men and women of the time exchanged gifts in the longhouse as part of a traditional ceremony, in lieu of marriage certificates issued by a church or state to verify the occasion.[13] The traditional manner of Dinah's and Thomas's marriage, as will be subsequently shown, was to lead the Onondaga woman into a Herculean struggle with the federal government over a military pension.

In the summer of 1812, the Onondagas in central New York, allied with the United States since the Treaty of Canandaigua of 1794, joined in with the Americans against the British.[14] Thomas John served for over two years in two different units, with Tall John's company of New York Indians and with Captain Cold's (Ut-ha-wah's) company of New York Militia. He fought at the Battles of Chippawa and Fort Erie and was wounded at Lundy's Lane.[15] Dinah went to war with her husband for a brief time, serving as a cook in these all-Indian regiments. It should be pointed out that at least fourteen other Indian women served in the American army during this war, and four received pensions as military cooks long before Dinah: Julia John (Seneca), Susan Jacob (Onondaga), Polly Cooper (Oneida), and Dolly Schenandoah or Skanandoah (Oneida).[16]

When her husband returned from war, the Johns settled in their home, a one-and-a-half story house that was just south of the council house on the reservation.[17] There she raised two children, a son named Abram and a daughter, Elizabeth Tallchief George. Along with her famous Onondaga contemporary and friend Captain Samuel George, she was rooted in Onondaga traditions, but she understood that the world around her was rapidly changing.[18] After the War of 1812, while the Iroquois land base was reduced substantially, the Onondagas clung to their small reservation adjacent to the rapidly growing city of Syracuse. Although two Onondagas signed the Buffalo Creek Treaty of 1838 that was designed to force the Iroquois out of New York to lands in Kansas, neither Thomas nor Dinah John agreed with Indian removal and leaving Onondaga Territory.[19] She and her family were among the 187 out of 296 Onondagas who resisted relocating to Kansas lands.[20]

The Schoolcraft Census of the Six Nations in 1845 throws further light on the Onondaga woman's life. In the census, Thomas John appears as head of a household of nine, including himself and three other males and Dinah and four other females. At least one married daughter, in traditional matrilocal fashion, was living in the household. Two other members of the household, a male and a female, had died in the previous year. Thomas and Dinah John apparently had two surviving children, Abram and Elizabeth. Their grandchildren were undoubtedly in the household given that three unmarried females under sixteen years of age and one unmarried female between sixteen and forty-five years of age were enumerated. The state school was founded at Onondaga in 1845, and several members of the household are listed as attending school.[21]

As revealed, Thomas and Dinah lived on a fifteen-acre plot on tribal lands at Onondaga. On three acres, they raised and harvested corn—fifty bushels a year—and had three cows total, two of which were milk cows, and six pigs. The Johns produced twenty-six pounds of butter, and two acres of meadow were cut for hay. The value of their garden and horticultural products was $25, the third highest on the reservation. Most of their income, however, came from leasing. They leased twelve out of fifteen acres at $2.50 per acre. The Johns' land values were the fifth largest on the Onondaga Reservation, in a community that was barely surviving economically.[22]

Onondagas, including their women, accommodated to change to deal with numerous crises—devastation of their villages in the American Revolution, pressures to cede more and more land and remove west, the presence of mission- and state-operated schools designed to transform their society, and state and federal efforts at tribal dissolution that pushed for the allotment of their reservation, fee simple title, taxation, and U.S. citizenship.[23] "Aunt Dinah" and other Onondaga women in the nineteenth century worked as domestics in white homes and/or supplemented their income by selling sassafras or Iroquoian sewing baskets and pots at Indian fairs or in a variety of public spaces allowed by whites. Women's roles were not static, and, in some cases, were in direct conflict with Iroquoian religious proscriptions laid out in the *Gaiwiio,* the Code of Handsome Lake. John served in the War of 1812, directly against Handsome Lake's warnings about Iroquois joining a conflict between white men.[24] Unlike the Seneca orator Red Jacket, John was respectful of missionaries who did not object openly to their presence at Onondaga. Nor did she object to the presence of a state-run school at the reservation.[25]

In her recent first-rate analysis of the urbanization process in nineteenth-century Syracuse and Rochester, architectural historian Diane Shaw observed that "Native Americans were at the bottom of the social and spatial hierarchies in the public space of these new citizens." Shaw specifically pointed out that the Onondagas "were isolated to their own section on the contemporary Onondaga Reservation." To Shaw, the Indians were fleeting figures on the streets of Syracuse, accepted in urban space only when they received their treaty annuities and had money to spend or when they were needed to serve as magnets to attract customers to Phinney's Museum at Clinton Square. At most times, Shaw indicated, Indian men were too frequently seen as impoverished intruders, prostrate drunks, or a "gang of vagabond natives." Indian women were likewise unwelcome in this hostile environment and reacted to leering whites, showing their displeasure by making head and hand gestures and turning their backs on annoying males.[26]

Dinah John was an exception to what Shaw suggested. The Onondaga elder was able to navigate herself through both the Iroquois world and the white man's space of Syracuse and beyond. Even though she remained an Onondaga conservative to the end of her life, she became "Aunt Dinah" to whites in central New York. She used her gentle demeanor, advanced age, gender, and merchandising skills to win favor and sell her handicrafts in Syracuse's central commercial district.

John lived in one world, the Onondaga Indian Reservation, but needed the other, Syracuse, to survive. Using an accommodationist strategy, she consciously ingratiated herself to local whites to sell her wares in the restricted spaces of the city. She also hired several different white attorneys in her lengthy pursuit of a military service pension from the War of 1812. Thus, to the white people of central New York who frequently read about her in local newspapers or saw her on the streets, "Aunt Dinah" was a non-threatening loyal American, a kind, dignified old Indian lady who bridged the "uncivilized" and "antiquated" world of the local reservation down the road with that of modern industrial Syracuse. At a time when white civic leaders in central New York and Albany politicians were still labeling the Onondagas as "savages," describing reservation life as "depraved," and urging the replacement of the traditional council of chiefs with an elected system,[27] John became the noble exception, the vanishing "full blood," the friendly native woman with artistic, entrepreneurial, and social skills who was allowed to freely enter the white space of Syracuse's downtown commercial center.

Reporters frequently commented about her deference toward and respect for local Episcopal and Methodist clergymen, suggesting to local whites that she was no immoral "pagan" incapable of salvation, unlike most of her Onondaga counterparts, especially males, who were portrayed in a negative way in the same period. After all, throughout much of her exceptionally long life, she was to be seen as a hard-working entrepreneur off the reservation. Until well past the age of ninety, she walked the three-and-a-half miles nearly every morning from the Onondaga Reservation to the downtown business area of Syracuse to sell her Indian baskets and pots. When she completed her task, she would walk back the three-and-a-half miles to her home. When she was not on her regular street corner politely selling her wares, newspapers reported on her infirmities much as they did the local weather forecast. The real "Aunt" Dinah—Dinah John, Onondaga elder—was less important to central New Yorkers than the symbol that she became, namely "Aunt Dinah," the friend of the white populace of Syracuse.[28]

Her age was also a factor in how she was perceived and in her designation as "Aunt" by whites in central New York. She was not the only centenarian among the Iroquois in the nineteenth century, including the Seneca Governor Blacksnake and the Oneida Skenando, both of whom were lauded for surviving so long.[29] At a time when the median age in the United States was twenty-one and only one-third of America's population lived to age seventy, the very elderly, especially centenarians, intrigued the readers of local newspapers. As one of the oldest New Yorkers, she was always newsworthy, and stories about her longevity and health were especially popular. As a result, politicians frequently wanted to be seen with her to get favorable publicity.[30] To Onondaga County residents, she was a woman who had lived through the stirring events of the Revolutionary era, albeit as a child-refugee fleeing the invading patriot army. To Americans, anyone, including Native Americans, connected directly to the era of America's founding was worthy of honor.[31]

In ways less visible to whites, Dinah John was a determined fighter. As a woman immersed in Iroquoian culture, she was married in the ways of her ancestors; spoke Onondaga, rarely communicating in English except to sell her Indian sweetgrass baskets and pots or to make small talk, in broken English, to local whites; and refused to take oaths of allegiance to the U.S. Constitution, seeing herself, as modern Onondagas do, as Hotinonshiónni citizens and allies of Washington. Women's subsistence efforts as horticulturalists had largely disappeared, and now many had to survive economically by adapting to day labor in the white world. Women such as Dinah John struggled in an increasingly threatening world but developed ways to survive for themselves, their families, their Indian nations. Although she appeared to be a compliant "good Indian," Dinah John remained a Hotinonshiónni.

Despite the outward appearance of accommodation with the non-Indian world, Dinah John's long struggle with the U.S. Bureau of Pensions in Washington reveals a more forceful side of her personality. She was resolute, pursuing a military service pension for a quarter of a century. Her determination was based on her refusal to abandon her Onondaga values. To her, adaptation did not mean abandoning her identity as a strong-willed Iroquoian woman. Besides hiring three outside white legal attorneys from Syracuse and Buffalo, she sought out support from clan matrons as well as from the Onondaga chiefs.

In the late summer of 1857, Thomas John applied for a military pension of $96 from the State of New York for his military service in the War of 1812. A portion of this award—$42—was for equipment, boots, and clothes "worn out, lost and destroyed in said service." The rest was for his "services and contingent expenses as Volunteer or draft in the Militia of said State, for its defence during said war." Subsequently, he was awarded only $37.50 of the total amount.[32]

Thomas John was also eligible for a monthly stipend for his military service; however, before he could secure this pension, he died, leaving it up to his widow to secure payment. Under the Acts of April 24, 1816, and March 3, 1817, soldiers and officers of militia units as well as those in the regular army in the War of 1812 were entitled to $8 per month, while half-pay pensions for a five-year period, although later renewable, were allocated to widows and orphans of military personnel. Before the Civil War, pensions were extended to all surviving War of 1812 widows whose husbands had died as a result of wounds or disabilities incurred in service.[33]

Dinah John repeatedly made efforts to get a "widow's pension," because she could not prove her own service. On August 1, 1857, four months after the death of her husband, she filed an affidavit seeking money. She swore that she had been married to Thomas according to the laws and usages and customs of the Onondaga Indians. Since she could not write English, she hired Henry Oras of Syracuse to help her secure the pension. Her pension application had conflicting information about her exact age and the exact date of her marriage, perhaps because of problems caused by her inability to make her Onondaga explainable in English for her lawyer's filing of the required forms; nevertheless, on the application and in subsequent filings, she insisted that her husband had enlisted at Onondaga on July 15, 1812; that he had served for over two years, including in Captain Cold's (Ut-ha-wah's) New York State Militia; and that he had participated in major military engagements such as the battles of Chippawa, Fort Erie, and Lundy's Lane. In 1858, Dinah's application was denied.[34]

The Onondaga woman did not give up in her efforts to secure a pension. In 1871, Congress passed a new pension act for veterans of the War of 1812. The legislation granted pensions to all surviving soldiers and sailors who had served for at least sixty days, were honorably discharged, or who had received special recognition from Congress during the war. The act required these veterans to have been loyal to the Union during the Civil War and to have taken an oath to support the Constitution of the United States. Surviving widows of veterans were eligible as long as they had been married prior to the end of the war and had not remarried. Qualifying veterans and widows were to receive $8 a month for life.[35]

Almost immediately after the congressional passage of the act, Dinah refiled her application, this time hiring John C. Bennett, a non-Indian attorney from Syracuse, to help her, as well as Chief Samuel George of the Onondagas. The well-respected George, who had known Thomas and Dinah John for over seventy years, had been a hero of the War of 1812, serving as a famous runner carrying messages between the federal arsenal at Canandaigua and the Niagara Frontier (see chapter 3). As an Onondaga of note and an Iroquois Confederacy spokesman, he had met with President Lincoln during the Civil War. Despite the support of George as well as of other surviving veterans and prominent Onondagas, Aunt Dinah's application was rejected once again; however, the applications and the correspondence relating to this rejection throw more light on Dinah, her marriage, her role in the War of 1812, and the almost insurmountable problems Indian women faced in fighting the federal bureaucracy.[36]

In her personal affidavit sworn in front of missionary George B. Wathan, she indicated that her husband, Thomas, had left for war four times between 1812 and 1814. She then revealed her own role during the conflict. She indicated that on his second mission from Onondaga, she went with her husband to war "until the snow was about 18 inches deep," but returned to the reservation later. Unwilling to lie or fabricate the date of her marriage, she admitted that she was formally "married after they came back," which occurred about a year after the war had ended. Seeing no immorality about her long relationship with her husband, she honestly admitted that she "lived and cohabited together as such as man and wife" according to tribal custom since June 1811. Significantly, Dinah once again refused to swear allegiance to the U.S Constitution.[37]

Under the Act of 1871, the applicant had to show proof of a church or public record of marriage or an affidavit of a clergyman, impossible for Onondaga men and women who had traditionally exchanged gifts, not written certificates, in the longhouse or council house ceremonies of the early nineteenth century. The act did allow affidavits of two or more eyewitnesses to the ceremony and two or more witnesses swearing to the couple's date of marriage, period of cohabitation, and length of marriage. Yet, by the time Dinah refiled her application under the Act of 1871, there was no living witness to her marriage.[38] As a result of her remarkable longevity, then over ninety years of age, Dinah had outlived her contemporaries. Except for assistance from her attorney John Bennett, Onondaga chief Samuel George and his wife, Hannah, and Harry Webster, an aged veteran of the War of 1812, she was left to challenge the federal bureaucracy alone; however, she persisted and never gave up the fight.

The Onondaga woman's constant prodding created a backlash. J. H. Baker, the U.S. commissioner of pensions, sent John S. Parker, a special agent, to investigate the matter. Ignoring Dinah's claim that her cohabitation as early as 1811 was "after the usages of her people," Parker insisted that Thomas and Dinah had been married sometime between 1818 and 1822. Agent Parker then interviewed Susannah Peters, a seventy-eight-year-old Onondaga, who stated that Thomas and Dinah John had been formally married after the war. She indicated that Thomas had served in the War of 1812, but not as a warrior with Ut-ha-wah. Peters, who was only a teenager during the War of 1812, never referred to the couple's cohabitation before the war and was mistaken about Thomas's military service given that Dinah's husband had served in not one but two separate regiments, including with Ut-ha-wah. Agent Parker then interviewed Samuel George, quickly dismissing the chief as a liar. He discounted the chief's affidavit, suggesting that George would swear to anything and that he was in cahoots with attorney Bennett to swindle the federal government out of pension funds.[39] Despite Parker's disparagement of this Onondaga chief, George, a respected elder in both the Indian and non-Indian worlds of New York and a hero of the War of 1812, had obviously told the truth. He had sworn that Dinah had cohabited with Thomas John from 1811 onward but had married him in and around 1816 and that Dinah remained a faithful wife until her husband's death. Chief George also swore that he had known Dinah and Thomas for over seventy years and that Thomas's military record was unblemished, his having served from August 10, 1812, to October 15, 1814.[40] In the end, for whatever reasons, Agent Parker recommended that the pension application be denied.[41]

By the mid-1870s, Dinah John was approaching one hundred years of age and her financial situation was becoming desperate. Throughout the nineteenth century, the Onondagas had received about $2,400 a year in state Indian treaty annuities. The state Indian agent distributed between $15 and $20 a year per family. On one occasion, the state Indian agent, R. H. Gardner, commented about Dinah's surprising appearance at the annuity distribution, given that she was well over one hundred years of age at the time. On June 13, 1878, Gardner wrote that John had sprightly come to receive her payment of $19.28: "This squaw is 104 years old. She came to the table and took her money as if but 50 years old."[42] What Gardner never indicated was that "Aunt" Dinah, an aged widow, was now in desperate financial straits. Despite being included in the American centennial celebration in Syracuse on July 4, 1876, she had not yet received her federal pension for her husband's service in the War of 1812. No longer was she seen as a fixture on the streets of Syracuse selling her pots and baskets. Infirm and nearly blind, she depended on the sale of the Ryder photograph and the generosity of prominent visitors to her home at Onondaga.[43]

The Beauchamp manuscripts in the New York State Library describe John's declining health by the early 1880s: "She goes no more to the city, but sat in her chair with her shawl over her head, and said she was 'very sick, very sick.'"[44] On another visit by the Beauchamps, John told them that she was 107 years of age and that she was blind and somewhat deaf. Despite these infirmities, a Beauchamp family member called her a "chatty" and "cordial" woman who liked "to have visitors, if they bring her a present. She particularly likes to have a paper of sugar put into her hands."[45]

In 1878, Congress passed its most liberal pension act relative to the War of 1812. Veterans had to have served only fourteen days and had to have received an honorable discharge. No loyalty oath was required, except for a provision indicating that the soldier had not fought on the British side against the United States. Eight dollars a month were provided all widows of veterans whether they were married before or after the peace treaty that ended the war. Consequently, the number of widows of veterans of the War of 1812 who received pensions rapidly expanded. Under this third act of Congress, 24,661 widows received pensions totaling approximately $2 million.[46] Employing Samuel Lake, an attorney from Buffalo, Dinah John this time was finally successful. In June 1882, less than one year before her death, the Bureau of Pensions awarded her $8 a month and a one-time back payment of $400 under the Act of 1878.[47]

At her death in May 1883, Dinah remained true to her Onondaga ways. Her funeral procession went from a Syracuse funeral parlor directly to the Council House, and only after this to the Methodist chapel and cemetery. According to the reports of her funeral, Dinah "desired some of the customary pagan rites at the council house," which she had left in her instructions to her daughter Elizabeth John Tallchief George.[48] Indeed, according to one newspaper account, "forty or fifty pagan Indians" protested giving Dinah John a Methodist funeral service until the Onondaga centenarian had been properly memorialized in a traditional longhouse service.[49] A Syracuse newspaper recorded her commitment to the ancient ways of the past:

> Dinah retained many Indian superstitions. There used to be a tradition that *To-oun-ya-wat-ha,* the deity who presided over fisheries and hunting grounds, saw many strange things and performed many wonderful acts in the vicinity. She was always a believer in this god, as also in many queer Indian notions. In the house from which her body was taken yesterday, the face of the clock and a small mirror were covered with cloth, in obedience to some superstitious belief.[50]

In this story, the reporter revealed his or her cultural myopia. But Indian identity cannot be defined solely as outsiders see it, and the "queer notions" and "superstitious belief" of this very significant woman were in fact her religion, a key to why the Onondaga have survived as a separate and distinct people. In July, less than two months after Dinah John's death, the people of Syracuse dedicated a monument to the Onondaga's memory, a five-foot-high headstone fashioned out of Oneida sandstone that cost one hundred dollars. Not in the white man's space of downtown Syracuse, the "Aunt Dinah" monument is on the Onondaga Reservation, symbolic of how this elder saw herself throughout her life.[51]

The "Aunt Dinah" story did not end with her death in 1883. Despite her own heroic struggles to survive in a world not of her making, Dinah John's name became appropriated by politicians intent on transforming the Onondagas in ways she would never have approved. In 1888, the New York State Assembly appointed a special committee to investigate the "Indian problem." Their report, named after the committee's chairman, J. S. Whipple of Salamanca, New York, was issued on February 1, 1889. This Whipple Report, followed by similar ones in 1900 and 1905 by other state investigations, concluded that the "Indian problem" could be solved only by ending the Indians' separate status, giving them full citizenship, and absorbing them "into the great mass of the American people."[52] The Whipple Report cited the testimony of disgruntled Onondaga political leaders as well as testimony and earlier Albany-sponsored "studies" pushing for the overthrow of the traditional Indian government and the allotment of the Onondaga Reservation.[53]

The Whipple Report had its harshest words for the Onondagas because both missionaries and state officials apparently were most frustrated in dealing with their conservatism and resistance to change. With no conception of cultural relativism as we understand it today, the report condemned the traditional governmental leadership on the reservation as "corrupt and vicious," characterized the religious practices as depraved, immoral, and superstitious, and described the social and industrial state as "chronic barbarism." It insisted, "Their present condition is infamously vile and detestable, and just so long as they are permitted to remain in this condition, just so long will there remain upon the fair name of the Empire State a stain of no small magnitude." The Whipple Report maintained that reservation lands be allotted in severalty among tribal members with suitable restrictions as to alienation of whites and protection from judgments and debts. It urged the extension of state laws and jurisdiction over the Indians and "their absorption into citizenship."[54] Whipple committee members nostalgically made reference to the departed "full blood" Dinah John, appropriating her legacy for their push for "regime change" at Onondaga.[55] Although her daughter Elizabeth broke with the chiefs and supported governmental change at Onondaga, Dinah John would never have espoused that cause.[56]

In sum, Dinah John was forced to live and survive in two worlds, a decision not of her own choosing. As a sovereignty-minded Onondaga, she did not see herself as a New Yorker. Her constitution was not drafted in

1787 but much earlier. She never compromised her principles, as indicated by her tenacity in fighting the Washington bureaucracy over her War of 1812 pension. Her primary world was not downtown Syracuse, where by day she earned a living selling baskets and pots, but Onondaga Territory, just a few miles to the south, where she returned every night and where she is buried. In effect, she was able to balance herself with a foot in two vessels while navigating the rapids.

5

Alice Lee Jemison, Seneca Journalist as Activist

Alice Mae Lee Jemison was the most prominent American Indian journalist in the United States from the early 1930s until her death in 1964. She was pictured by federal officials as a dangerous subversive and put under FBI surveillance because of her unyielding criticism of U.S. government Indian policies.[1] Jemison's political activism was well rooted in Seneca culture and history; she was courageous, strident, bold, and fanatical in her defense of the Seneca Nation. Despite being falsely labeled as a troublemaker, as an unrepresentative "mixed blood," and as a Nazi, a fascist, and a communist by Interior Department personnel and by FBI informants, Jemison was much more a representative voice of Seneca women than her enemies ever acknowledged.[2]

Scholars have long been intrigued by the role of women in Iroquoia, especially Seneca Indian society. Much of the recent literature has focused on three areas: (1) the traditional roles of Seneca women in the early European contact period;[3] (2) the persistence of certain women's roles into the contemporary period;[4] and (3) the declension of women's economic and political roles during the past two hundred years.[5] It should be pointed out that there are two Seneca governments in New York State: the Seneca Nation of Indians, an elected system of government created in a political upheaval in 1848 that administers the Allegany, Cattaraugus, and Oil Spring Reservations in southwestern New York; and the Tonawanda Band of Senecas, a traditional government on the Tonawanda Reservation, which is the "Western Door" of the Iroquois Confederacy and where clan mothers ideally still raise the chiefs of the nation. Much of the literature dealing with cultural persistence or declension of women's roles has focused on women of the much larger Seneca Nation of Indians, not on the Tonawanda Band of Senecas.

Seneca society in the precontact and the immediate postcontact periods was organized around complementary gender roles. Anthropologist Elisabeth Tooker refers to the division of male/female roles as the dichotomy between the forest world and the clearing. The Iroquois village with its horticultural focus was the world of the women, matrilineal descent, and matrilocal residence. The world beyond the village was the arena where men absented themselves to conduct diplomacy, go on the hunt, or take the warpath.[6] With the process of Euro-American colonization came vast disruptions in Seneca existence. Senecas changed from extended longhouse residence to nuclear households and to a patrilineal naming system. From 1784 to 1842, they were victims in fraudulent treaty negotiations and came face-to-face with scheming land speculators such as the Phelps-Gorham, Holland, and Ogden Land companies. As a result of these forces and the corruption of some of their own chiefs, they were dispossessed of the Buffalo Creek Reservation in 1838, which led the Cattaraugus and Allegany Senecas to depose their chiefs in 1848 and establish the Seneca Nation of Indians. They adopted a written constitution with elected officials, creating a republican form of government, thus breaking with the traditional Iroquois Confederacy structure.[7] Under the 1848 constitution, only men over the age of twenty-one could vote, although Seneca clan mothers continued to have voting rights on land issues.[8]

Throughout the nineteenth and well into the twentieth centuries, the Seneca Nation accommodated Euro-American culture, religious traditions, and values, and with them certain restrictions on the role of women in its society. Despite not having the right to vote or seek public office until 1964, women continued to be "politically visible when major issues divided the nation."[9] Indeed, women as a separate group petitioned the federal government to accept the results of the Seneca revolution of 1848 and to allow it to stand. Speaking as mothers or potential mothers of the nation, they insisted they had the right to speak for the seven generations to come. At this time and in subsequent crises, women, in order to ensure stability, came to the fore. Significantly, despite electoral restrictions, Seneca laws nevertheless continued to respect women's roles, recognizing that husband and wife would each keep control of their own property. While women's roles in horticulture declined throughout the nineteenth century, men's roles did also, although men had more alternative economic avenues to pursue.[10] Anthropologist Joy Bilharz describes the roles of women at the time of Alice Mae Lee Jemison's birth in 1901:

> By the beginning of the twentieth century, their economic roles consisted of homemaking, with few, if any, holding outside employment. Wage labor was within the domain of men, many of whom now worked for the railroads that ran through the Allegany Reservation. In a way, the old forest/clearing dichotomy continued, albeit in modern guise, with women's roles devalued, at least by white society, because they were not income producing. Seneca women probably did not feel the status loss that appears great to non-Indian women of the late twentieth century. At Allegany, women still collected fruits and berries, made medicines, wove baskets, and planted their gardens. Some worked as domestics for white men in nearby villages and by midcentury a few held clerical jobs.[11]

A new generation of outstanding women, beginning with Jemison in the late 1920s, slowly began to transform women's roles from behind-the-scenes to a more visible role in Seneca Nation politics. By the 1960s, in a conscious attempt to rebuild the Seneca Nation of Indians after the flooding of over nine thousand acres of their lands at the Cornplanter Tract and along the upper Allegany River by the construction of the Kinzua Dam, women and women's societies emerged once more. Bilharz clearly shows that during the Kinzua crisis Seneca women resurrected their image as "mothers of the nation," namely protectors of Indian cultural identity. She adds that during this crisis, Seneca children "saw their mothers (and fathers) as active, often angry, participants rather than as passive, withdrawn victims. . . . By maintaining and building upon traditional Iroquois gender roles, they provided good models for their children, both male and female, so that a pattern of dysfunctional families was not established."[12] As a result of the Kinzua crisis and the lobbying efforts of Genevieve Plummer, Reva Barss, and George Heron, Seneca women finally achieved the right to vote and to hold political office. Since the election of Martha Buck-tooth to the council in the mid-1960s, women have been frequently elected or appointed to key positions within the tribal government, although not one woman has yet been elected president of the nation.[13]

These more visible roles were increasingly apparent by the mid-1970s. Faced with a major health crisis, land loss in the final completion of New York State Route 17, the ending of the ninety-nine-year lease to the City of Salamanca, and a bitter tax struggle with New York State, Seneca women were no longer detached from politics nor played politics from behind the scenes in the traditional way, but were active participants in the events that transpired. As a result of a highly organized group of women, the Seneca Nation Health Action Group, led by Hazel Dean John, Norma Kennedy, Wini Kettle, and others, the Senecas established two modern Indian Health Service facilities at the Allegany and Cattaraugus Reservations and designated Lionel John, later president of the Seneca Nation, as their spokesman.[14] After raising support for a tribal commemoration of the twenty-year anniversary of the Kinzua Dam tragedy in 1984, numerous young Seneca women, a year later, actively participated in protesting the completion of New York State Route 17.[15] Between 1985 and 1991, Seneca women such as Loretta Crane, Cheryl Ray, and others played key roles in the final settlement of the Seneca Nation–Salamanca lease controversy, one that had lingered for a century.[16] In 1992 and especially in 1997, Indian women were among the key organizers of the resistance to New York State's efforts at collecting sales taxes on Indian reservations. During the "Tax Wars" of both 1992 and 1997, the New York State Thruway and Route 17 were closed.[17]

Despite the nontraditional, namely outward and activist, aspects of Seneca women's roles over the past six decades, these women have helped resurrect the image of women as "mothers of the nation," guardians of tradition in the face of overwhelming odds and crises, some of which involved face-to-face confrontations with heavily armed state troopers.

Alice Mae Lee Jemison set the tone for the increasing activism of Seneca women in the twentieth century. Her relentless commitment to Iroquois sovereignty-minded views and her willingness to take extreme measures, even at all costs to her reputation, made her a formidable opponent of

4. Alice Lee Jemison, Seneca
journalist-activist, c. early 1930s.
Courtesy of Jeanne Marie
Jemison.

Washington- and Albany-directed Indian policies from 1930 to her death
in 1964.

Jemison was born at Silver Creek, New York, near the Cattaraugus
Reservation of the Senecas, on October 9, 1901. She was the daughter of
Daniel A. Lee, a cabinetmaker of Cherokee descent, and Elnora E. Seneca,
a member of a prominent Seneca family. Her parents met while attending
Hampton Institute. Jemison's youthful ambition to become an attorney was
frustrated by her family's poverty. Her formal education ended with her
graduation in 1919 from Silver Creek High School, where she had studied
debating and journalism. That same year she married Le Verne Leonard
Jemison, a local Seneca steelworker. They were separated nine years later as
a result of her husband's chronic alcoholism, and, as a single parent, Jemison thereafter had to support her mother and her two children. Living on
the Cattaraugus Reservation through the 1920s, she struggled to provide for
her family, working in a factory and as a clerk, peddler, dressmaker, practical nurse, stone and gravel hauler, and legal researcher for a Buffalo attorney. In 1929 she became the secretary to, and researcher for, Ray Jimerson,
then president of the Seneca Nation. The next year Jemison worked for the
U.S. Bureau of the Census, gathering information on the reservation.[18]

By 1930, Jemison's worldview had already been firmly shaped. As a woman growing up in Seneca society, with the ever-present role of powerful women who still served as clan mothers and faithkeepers, she was constantly reminded that women were traditionally protectors of the Seneca lands and, with them, identity. After all, to this day, only children of Seneca women can achieve tribal enrollment. Moreover, as the head of a single-parent household with two young children and an aging mother to care for after the collapse of her marriage, Jemison was forced to be even more self-reliant.[19] As a hardworking woman from a proud and distinguished Seneca family lineage, she looked on both Washington and Albany as enemies fostering Indian dependence and welfare. As an Iroquois traditionalist, she insisted that what was needed was the carrying out of federal-Iroquois treaties, most specifically the Canandaigua Treaty of 1794. Any other course of action was wrong, and she repeatedly pointed out that the Indians did not need any more reforms such as the Indian Reorganization Act, because they only added new levels of bureaucracy that, to her, benefited only government workers. To her, a bloated and corrupt Bureau of Indian Affairs in Washington or New York State programs that delayed Indian land claims settlements or did not recognize Indian hunting and fishing rights were hardly beneficial to the Indians.

As a disciple of the famous Yavapai journalist and physician Carlos Montezuma, she could easily find fault with both federal and state Indian policies. As was true of Montezuma, she became an ardent abolitionist, calling for an end of the role of the Bureau of Indian Affairs.[20] After all, both Montezuma and Jemison could condemn an agency that had done little to prevent the alienation of over ninety million acres of the Indian land base since the passage of the Dawes General Allotment Act of 1887. By 1933, Indians retained approximately forty-eight million acres, much of it arid, unusable land. Moreover, 49 percent of the Indians on allotted reservations were landless. Even before the onset of the Great Depression, 96 percent of all Indians earned less than $200 per year, and only 2 percent had a per capita income greater than $500 per year.[21]

Jemison's worldview had been shaped by other factors. In the 1920s, she was witness to a growing resurgence of Iroquois nationalism. During and after World War I, a renewed Iroquois land claims movement arose.

In 1922, a New York State legislative committee, the Everett Commission, insisted that New York State held clouded title to millions of acres taken from the Iroquois in the six decades after the American Revolution.[22] At approximately the same time, in response to an earlier favorable ejectment case, *U.S. v. Boylan,* involving Oneida lands in New York, a Six Nations land claim arose, fostered by Laura Minnie Cornelius Kellogg, a charismatic, spellbinding Oneida orator; although the court case *Deere et al. v. State of New York et al.* was eventually dismissed in 1927, the so-called "Kellogg movement" stirred Iroquois nationalism to a resounding pitch.[23] Other claims assertions followed. Cayuga efforts at securing justice led to a United States–Great Britain arbitration commission in 1926. Iroquois vocal assertions of their sovereignty included sending delegations to the League of Nations in Geneva, Switzerland, and to Great Britain's Board of Trade in the 1920s under the leadership of that great Iroquois nationalist Chief Deskaheh.[24]

Alice Lee Jemison's Senecas were also not idle in this regard. During World War I, their attorney George Decker, later the attorney for Chief Deskaheh, was hired to assert the Seneca claims to the Niagara River.[25] More important to Jemison, instead of responding to Seneca insistence that these Indians had the right to fish on their own tribal lands without a New York State license, Congress in 1927 "awarded" both the Senecas and New York State joint jurisdiction on Indian reservation lands. Moreover, in the same act, as a result of lobbying by New York's attorney general, Congress retroactively confirmed the state's "take" of some of the Seneca lands at the Oil Spring Reservation, an illegal state move that had been made in clear violation of the federal trade and intercourse acts and one that had never been approved by the U.S. Senate.[26] This act, known as the Seneca Conservation Act, was a major turning point in Jemison's political awakening.

Another turning point in Jemison's life came with the Marchand murder case of 1930, the most notorious event in Buffalo's history since the 1901 assassination of President William McKinley. Two American Indian women were accused of killing a white woman, Clothilde Marchand, the wife of noted artist and museum designer Jules Henri Marchand. Jemison moved to Buffalo to work with Iroquois leaders who were seeking federal intervention in the case and challenging disparaging portrayals of Indians.

Jemison wrote letters to public figures and began writing for the *Buffalo Evening News*. The two women were convicted, but after serving time in prison they were freed because of legal questions involving the fairness of the trial. The experience Jemison gained in lobbying and publicity and the contacts she made in the journalistic world became her springboard for a new career. By 1932 her articles were being syndicated by the North American Newspaper Alliance and were reaching a wide audience.[27] As a result of her work for the Senecas, she was nominated by the Seneca Nation Tribal Council for positions in the Indian Service on at least two occasions.[28]

In 1934 Jemison moved to Washington, D.C., and began writing for the *Washington Star*. She also served as a lobbyist for the Seneca Nation and monitored congressional activities on Indian affairs. As both a staunch defender of Iroquois treaty rights and a political conservative, she was suspicious of Indian policies emanating from the federal government. Influenced by the thinking of Montezuma, Jemison argued for the abolition of the BIA. She soon became the major publicist-lobbyist for a new nationwide Indian organization, the American Indian Federation (AIF).

Cutting through its extremist right-wing language of protest that was as much rhetoric and tactic as ideology, the AIF was a loose umbrella-like organization that was composed of many strands of Indian thinking: the Indian National Confederacy of Oklahoma, which included members of the Five Civilized Tribes; the Mission Indian Federation of California; the Intertribal Committee for the Fundamental Advancement of the American Indian, based in Buffalo and Detroit and largely dominated by Iroquois Indians; and the Black Hills Treaty Council, composed of a substantial number of Sioux Indians opposed to the Indian Reorganization Act (IRA). Moreover, the organization was substantially different in 1939 from the AIF at its inception five years earlier, and this fact must be taken into account in any analysis that attempts to explain how it operated. Hence, the organization was as diverse as Native America itself, with Indians coalescing in a national lobbying effort largely because of local reservation grievances, some of which preceded the New Deal.[29]

Throughout the debate over the "Indian New Deal," Jemison served as spokeswoman for the AIF. She edited the federation's newspaper, *First American*, and served as the organization's major lobbyist on Capitol Hill.

From 1934 until her resignation from the federation in 1939, Jemison appeared at more congressional hearings on Indian affairs than any other Native American. In addition to her objection on principle to the BIA, Jemison criticized the reformist policies, the IRA, proposed by Franklin Roosevelt's commissioner of Indian Affairs, John Collier, and supported by Secretary of Indian Affairs Harold Ickes, both of whom she believed did not understand the diverse world of American Indians. The IRA, passed by Congress in June 1934, provided for the establishment of tribal elections, constitutions, and corporations; a revolving loan fund to assist organized tribes in community development; and the encouragement of Indian employment in the Indian Service by giving preference in hiring through the waiving of civil service requirements. The act also created an educational loan program for Indian students seeking a vocational, high school, or college education. Moreover, the act directly related to Indian lands, ending the land allotment policies of the Dawes Act and providing for the purchase of new lands for the Indians. Unallotted lands were to be returned to tribal councils. Conservation efforts were also encouraged on existing Indian lands by the establishment of Indian forestry units and by herd reduction on arid land to prevent range deterioration.[30]

Jemison viewed this far-reaching IRA as simply adding new levels of bureaucracy to Indian life and as intruding on tribal sovereignty by requiring Secretary of the Interior approval on nearly every provision of the act. She challenged Commissioner Collier by insisting that no act or uniform program dictated by Washington could do justice to the diverse needs of Native Americans across the United States. Many Indians, too, objected to the provisions for tribal plebiscites, required with the acceptance of the terms of the IRA. Jemison furthermore accused the BIA of manipulating congressional hearings on the legislation by looking more favorably on requests for travel funds from the act's supporters than from its opponents.[31]

To Jemison's own Senecas, who operated already under an elected system, IRA provisions calling for a new constitution and a new elected system were superfluous. With over 50,000 acres of tribal lands remaining in their hands, many Senecas feared that the whole reform was a new scheme to get at their land base. One contemporary of Jemison wrote Commissioner Collier, "We have been fooled time after time that most of the Indians have lost faith in the Saxon race we certainly have had some raw deal in back history we have never had a square deal."[32] Much like Alice Lee Jemison, President Ray Jimerson viewed the forty-eight-page IRA as "too long and complicated . . . full of new rules and regulations . . . and subject to Bureau interpretation."[33] Hence Jemison, as a "mother of the nation," saw that her role was to save her people and her people's homeland at all costs.

Jemison's activism was also prompted by the terrible conditions found on her reservation. Because most Senecas worked off the Cattaraugus Reservation in factories in or near Buffalo or were employed as structural iron-workers, they were not insulated from the devastating effects of the Great Depression. Unemployment was high, and many Indians depended on work relief to survive. Throughout the period after 1929, these Indians frequently complained that state and later federal programs designed for their needs—including road work and school construction projects—discriminated against the Indians by hiring only non-Indians or required American citizenship, voter's registration cards, and loyalty oaths that ran counter to Iroquois beliefs in sovereignty.[34] The worst conditions at Cattaraugus were in the area of public health. In 1934, the death rate caused by tuberculosis on the reservation was six times higher than in the non-Indian world.[35] The continued pollution of Cattaraugus Creek, which traverses the reservation, was a major source of the spread of disease.

As a result of these and other Indian complaints against the New York State Department of Conservation, the Seneca Nation Tribal Council appointed Jemison as their lobbyist in Washington to attempt to overturn the Seneca Conservation Act of 1927. From January 1933 to June 1935, she actively campaigned to overturn the act. Working with President Ray Jimerson and Robert Galloway, the attorney for the Seneca Nation, she convinced New York Congressman Alfred Beiter to introduce legislation to overturn New York State Department of Conservation jurisdiction on hunting and fishing on Indian reservations. She used the two arguments that the law violated Iroquois rights as guaranteed under the Treaty of Canandaigua and that state officials were harassing the Indians.[36] In June 1935, just after Iroquois rejection of the Indian Reorganization Act, President Roosevelt, a former two-term governor of New York State, vetoed the Beiter Bill, much to the anger of the Senecas. In reaction, Jemison wrote a four-page letter of protest in which she criticized Roosevelt's action, claiming his veto was motivated by Iroquois opposition to John Collier and their voting down the IRA. She insisted that he reread the treaty of 1794 and fire the commissioner of Indian affairs:[37]

> I know that my people will be deeply grieved at your attitude. Having been Governor of New York State you are in a position to know that the New York State Indians are now and always have been in the status of "quasi dependent nations"; that their lands have been held by the Highest Courts to be "extra territoria"; and that they have always enjoyed the rights of self-government free from any outside direction, under the provisions of the Treaty of Canandaigua made in 1794 with George Washington. Up until you became President of the United States this popularly termed Conservation Act constituted the only existing legislative violation of that treaty.[38]

The failure of this campaign to overturn the Seneca Conservation Act contributed to Jemison's increasing activism in the mid- and late 1930s and to her overwhelmingly negative reaction to Commissioner Collier, the IRA, and the Roosevelt administration as a whole.

Indeed, despite her national focus in her work for the AIF, Jemison was primarily an Iroquois woman, a political disciple of Montezuma as well as an evangelical abolitionist. She feared an omnipotent federal government and was suspicious of all non-Indian governmental authority, be it Washington- or Albany-based. Although her remarks before Senate and House committee hearings echoed much of her organization's right-wing rhetoric of protest and represented much of the sentiment of the Oklahoma faction within the AIF, Jemison's protests also reflected much of the Iroquois thinking of the period. Her belief in Iroquois treaty rights, coupled with an Iroquois vision of sovereignty that never wavered, came into conflict with Commissioner Collier and his views throughout the New Deal years.

At a congressional hearing on February 11, 1935, Jemison affirmed her belief in the sanctity of the Treaty of Canandaigua, insisted that the "situation in New York State is entirely different from any other Indians in the United States," and concluded that, under the terms of this and other treaties with the federal government, "we have always had self-government among the New York Indians."[39] At the same hearing, Collier totally dismissed this interpretation that the Iroquois were independent sovereignties who "never came under the jurisdiction of the United States and only by courtesy and consent under the jurisdiction of the State of New York [and] that they are independent sovereignties, dependent, but not subject to nothing but a ghostly guardianship." After all, Collier argued, the Supreme Court has repeatedly held that the "sovereignty in an Indian group is dependent on the will of Congress, and that Congress may invade, modify, regulate, or abolish it."[40] Hence two divergent belief systems, one ascribed to by Jemison and a significant number of Iroquois and the other held to by the non-Indian world and its legal institutions, clashed throughout the New Deal.

It should also be noted that by 1937 the Indian New Deal as well as the New Deal as a whole was in serious political trouble. The conservative coalition in Congress began to assert the power that it had relinquished during the economic emergency of President Roosevelt's first term. The "court-packing" fight of 1937 also undermined the administration's influence on Capitol Hill. Commissioner Collier and Secretary Ickes, never liked by many congressional leaders, had also begun to face the wrath of a newly assertive Congress. Most of the major pieces of legislation of the Indian New Deal had been introduced and passed during Roosevelt's first administration. Equally significant, Senator Wheeler, by 1937 the leader against Roosevelt's attempt to pack the Supreme Court, introduced a bill to repeal the IRA, the very piece of legislation he had sponsored into law. Just as the president had purged his foes in the congressional primaries of 1938 and 1940, Collier and Ickes, now under attack by Congressman Dies's House on Un-American Activities Committee, began to retaliate against their enemies. It appears as no coincidence, then, that the day after Jemison testified about communism in the Interior Department before Dies's committee, Ickes first alleged that Jemison, code-named "Pocahontas," was a Nazi go-between. The FBI file on Jemison also reveals that her two major accusers of alleged Nazi activity were the secretary of the Interior and the commissioner of Indian Affairs, precisely the same two administrators subjected most to Jemison's attacks.[41]

Jemison's attacks were frequently overblown and extremist in tone. Sometimes branding her opponents as communists or atheists, Jemison herself was accepted by right-wing critics of the Roosevelt administration, ranging from the Daughters of the American Revolution to William Dudley Pelley, the extremist leader of the Silver Shirts of America. In her relentless war against the BIA, she was willing to appear at the same hearing with self-styled fascists, as she did in 1938 and 1940 before the House Committee on Un-American Activities. Such tactics allowed the Interior Department to portray her as an Indian Nazi, a charge belied by the fact that she passed every loyalty check made by the FBI and was able to secure government employment in the Bureau of the Census during World War II. Moreover, Jemison, throughout her life, was closely tied to the political leadership of the Seneca Nation. Importantly, her highly respected uncle, Cornelius Seneca, was elected to the presidency of the Seneca Nation on several different occasions in the 1940s and 1950s.

The Interior Department's portrayal of Jemison as a subversive was furthered by her own actions in defense of Iroquois sovereignty. An equally thorny and volatile issue during this era involved the issue of whether the federal government could draft Iroquois into the armed forces. Once again, despite being labeled as unpatriotic, it was Jemison who led the opposition to the Selective Service Act of 1940, based on her insistence that only the Iroquois Confederacy and/or each nation's tribal council had the ultimate authority to make decisions for war.[42] Furthermore, talk of a new flood control project from 1936 onward that would entail the loss of the Senecas' Cornplanter Tract in Pennsylvania added weight to Iroquois fears throughout the period. This Kinzua Dam project was to materialize two decades later.[43]

Because of family economic necessity, federal limitations on government employees' political lobbying, and the climate of the country after Pearl Harbor, Jemison muted her outspoken stance through the Second World War when she worked for the Bureau of the Census. After the war, Jemison remained in Washington and continued to call for the BIA's abolition while opposing the transfer of criminal jurisdiction over Indians in New York from federal to state government that occurred in 1948. In 1948, when Senator Arthur Watkins of Utah suggested that a lump-sum monetary payment replace the symbolic treaty cloth that the Iroquois annually receive under the Treaty of Canandaigua, which the senator considered to be anachronistic, Jemison angrily responded, "We have kept our shares of the treaties, and we are here to ask that you keep yours. The little amount of calico [treaty cloth] for which the money is appropriated each year by this Congress doesn't amount to very much per person, but it is the significance of that calico which means something to all of us."[44]

The ultimate irony of Jemison's career as a political activist was that her work over three decades was distorted by the congressional establishment of the 1950s through the policy of termination and had the opposite effects on Native Americans than what she had intended. She wanted to help American Indians by abolishing the BIA; however, her arguments for its abolition added fuel to a policy that proved more of a detriment than a cure. Termination, the policy of removing the BIA's role in administering Indian programs by ending the separate legal status of American Indians guaranteed by treaties, was applied in the 1950s and 1960s. Congress "turned certain Indian tribes loose" from federal authority, for reasons not simply related to BIA mismanagement or because of its faith in the ability of Native Americans to rule themselves, as Montezuma and Jemison had maintained. Masking their motives in self-determination rhetoric, conservatives in Congress such as Senators Arthur Watkins and Karl Mundt urged termination for cost-saving reasons, anti–big government sentiment, anti–welfare statism, and basic laissez-faire attitudes. Liberals such as Senator Hubert Humphrey, under the backdrop of the milestone *Brown v. The Board of Education of Topeka, Kansas,* viewed the Indian world in a civil rights context, largely unaware of the cultural separatist nature in much of Native American thinking. Consequently, they urged termination as a means of freeing the Indians from oppression.

Although one is tempted to label Jemison a "terminationist," this overgeneralization is as misleading as the labels given her by Collier. She was an Iroquois woman, a political disciple of Montezuma, an evangelical abolitionist, an individual who, until her death in 1964, had complete faith in Native American peoples to rule themselves. Her agitation of the 1950s was consistent with her early position of the 1930s in her call for the abolition of the BIA. Although Jemison's arguments were used by congressional critics of the Bureau and proponents of termination in the early 1950s, she and other activists among the Iroquois saw the dangers of the proposed legislation of the Truman-Eisenhower administrations. In her newsletter published in February 1954, Jemison predicted with startling accuracy the dangers facing the Indians. She insisted that the "present proposals will accomplish only one thing with any certainty—the termination of Federal expenditures for the benefit of the Indians, and will leave the Indians suspended in a twilight zone of political nonentity, partly tribal, partly State. And twenty years from now another Congress will be considering measures to correct the mistakes of this experiment."[45] It is noteworthy that Congress in 1973, nearly twenty years after the passage of the first termination bill, restored the federal status of the Menominee Nation of Wisconsin.

ALICE LEE JEMISON was a modern woman of the Seneca Nation of Indians, but reflected the ancient values of her people. Instead of swaying her people in behind-the-scenes negotiations as in the past, she was an especially outwardly combative person espousing a most traditional message, namely respect for Iroquois sovereignty and treaty rights. Although she used a twentieth-century weapon—the mass media—to fight back, she saw her role as a "mother of the nation," protecting Seneca land and, at the same time, cultural identity. No longer relegated to the world of the clearing as in olden times, Jemison realized that the Senecas were in a state of crisis. Being powerless people, she attempted to bring her appeal beyond the reservation, use the power of her journalism, grab headlines, and often scurrilously attack her enemies. Her willingness to sacrifice everything for her cause, what she interpreted as her people's survival, was often viewed by outsiders as extreme and even fanatical, and in many ways she might be considered the harbinger of Red Power politics among the Iroquois; however, more accurately, she saw herself as a "mother of the nation," protecting and ensuring Seneca survival into the future.

PART THREE Leadership in
the Diaspora

Introduction

Today the largest populations of Iroquois Indians live outside of their New York homeland. Their communities stretch from Quebec to Oklahoma. The problems caused by refugee status, relocation, and removal required leadership. Although new skills were required to meet these pressures and problems that resulted, both the style and substance of leadership were not entirely new. Traditions of leadership were not totally forsaken whether in Canada or in the two new Iroquois communities in the United States: Oklahoma and Wisconsin.

In the sixty years after the American Revolution, the Iroquois were nearly dispossessed of their entire New York homeland. Many Iroquois, faced with these overwhelming pressures, chose not to remain in New York. After the American Revolution, some of these Indians became Loyalist refugees in the Canadian wilderness. Still others, at the urging of missionaries, government agents, and land speculators, chose Wisconsin and Indian Territory as their "Red Zion." Those Iroquois that made the trek westward were the ancestors of the present Oneidas of Wisconsin and Seneca-Cayugas of Oklahoma.

The Seneca-Cayugas of Oklahoma are Iroquoian peoples relocated from eastern Ohio in federal treaties of removal during Andrew Jackson's presidency. These Indians were joined in the period 1846–52 by Iroquois, mostly Cayugas from western New York, who had agreed to exchange their claims in the East for Kansas lands in the nefarious Treaty of Buffalo Creek of 1838. Although most of these Indians died during the removal process or returned to New York, a small number remained in Indian Territory. After the Civil War, new emigrants, mostly Cayugas, from both the Six Nations Reserve and Cattaraugus Reservation arrived in Indian

Territory. As late as December 1881, thirty-two more Iroquois, twenty-six from Brantford and six from Cattaraugus, arrived. Eleven of these Indians were to return to the East only after much administrative confusion about jurisdiction on the part of Indian agents and their supervisors in Canada and the United States.[1]

Although separated by fifteen hundred miles from New York, these Oklahoma Iroquois Indians were not completely separated from their eastern kin. The Cayuga language was spoken well into contemporary times. Today their ties to the East include receiving annuities under treaty from New York State. The Seneca-Cayugas celebrate the annual Iroquois Green Corn Festival each August. A version of the peach stone game, typically found among Iroquois Indians in New York, is also played by these Oklahoma tribesmen.[2]

The Seneca-Cayugas refer to themselves as "Iroquois at the end of the log." Their connections are largely with the Six Nations at Ohsweken, Ontario, but Longhouse preachers from the Allegany Reservation (and previously Cornplanter Tract) have attended their Green Corn Ceremony for years, educating newer generations about Iroquoian songs and rituals.[3] Currently they reside on a small land base in Miami and Grove, Oklahoma, with a population now numbering five thousand members. Recently they have purchased land in New York and have been active participants in federal courts, suing New York State for lands lost in 1795 and 1807.[4]

The migrations of Oneidas west to Green Bay, Wisconsin, then part of Michigan Territory, and its environs began in 1820; however, the pressures that led to their removal from their central New York State homeland started immediately after the American Revolution. Their homeland, whose center was the short portage between the Mohawk River and Wood Creek, the so-called Oneida Carrying Place, was strategic to the Indians and later to Euro-Americans. To the southeast are the headwaters of the Mohawk, which flows eastward until it joins the Hudson, which connects to the Atlantic Ocean at New York City. On the north is Wood Creek, which, along with Fish Creek, Oneida Lake, and the Oswego River, was a major passageway to Lake Ontario and the rest of the Great Lakes. As a result, Albany policymakers and land speculators saw the region as essential to building a massive transportation network—improved river navigation, canals, and later railroads—that would be attractive to white settlement and economic development.[5]

New York officials built the rising Empire State on profits from Indian land cessions. The Oneidas are a case in point. Between 1785 and 1846, these Indians lost their lands in New York State through a series of "treaties," despite being largely on the patriot side during the American Revolution and despite provisions of protection in the New York State and U.S. constitutions, congressional acts, and federal treaties. Taking advantage of the existence of Oneida divisions, New York State officials began the process of dispossession, defrauding these Indians of over five million acres. Land "purchased" by state "treaty" from the Oneidas for fifty cents an acre was sold for seven to ten times its original purchase price. Meanwhile, the state was pushing settlement. Madison County, with fewer than one thousand settlers in 1800, had thirty-nine thousand by 1840. The Oneidas, already severely divided in their polity and religion, largely found it impossible to resist these pressures, leading a majority of the community, for its protection and survival, to migrate west to Wisconsin in the period 1820–38 or to Ontario between 1839 and 1845.[6]

From the time of their arrival in Wisconsin, Oneidas attempted to rebuild their community. Oneida life in Wisconsin revolved around eight clearly defined neighborhoods. The Episcopal church members settled at Oneida along Duck Creek on the west side of the reservation, and the Methodist followers, the old Orchard Party, settled along the east side near De Pere. The nuclear family was the primary unit, and reciprocal gift giving and assistance in the form of building bees were expected among kin. Marriages were arranged, and rules of clan exogamy were followed in the first decades. The Longhouse religion was not practiced, and certain Iroquois practices—such as the Little Water Society, Iroquoian funerary customs, and employment of herbal medicines—were fitted into the Christian religion. In addition, the Oneidas brought little of their traditional political structure to Wisconsin, although they had a system of chiefs who claimed hereditary rights. The council was comprised of a head chief and twelve "big men," or chiefs, appointed by the senior women of the lineages. This hereditary council could allocate lands, outlaw liquor sales, make contracts for sale of timber, enforce sentences of banishment and execution, and represent the nation in dealings with the federal government, such as in securing annuity payments.[7]

Thus, despite the great crisis caused by dispossession and removal, Oneida society had resilience enough to adapt to its new surroundings. The Oneidas also had an extraordinary leader, Chief Daniel Bread, who dominated Wisconsin Oneida politics for nearly a half-century.[8] Although separated by a thousand miles from their central New York homeland, the Wisconsin Oneidas also maintained connections to it. They retained kinship and cultural connections to other Oneida communities at Southwold, Ontario, and Oneida, New York.

Today the Wisconsin Oneidas reaffirm their past in a variety of ways. They sponsor annual history conferences. Participants include numerous community peoples and a few trusted scholars. Working under contract from the nation, L. Gordon McLester III, an Oneida public historian, who also runs the Oneida History Conferences and who is the founder of the Oneida Historical Society, has conducted more than four hundred videotaped interviews with elders about events, festivities, peoples, places, and traditions.[9]

The Wisconsin Oneidas also maintain an elaborate Cultural Heritage Department and publish a newsletter with its version of these Indians' past, articles that have included aspects of Oneida and Iroquoian cultural and religious traditions from their New York homeland, the impact of the Dawes General Allotment Act, and famous Oneida leaders in history. The Oneida Cultural Heritage Department also houses the voluminous stories collected by Oneida elders from 1938 to 1942 under the auspices of the Works Progress Administration. This Oneida Language and Folklore Project, administered by anthropologists Morris Swadesh, Floyd Lounsbury, and Harry Basehart, is a remarkable oral history collection on every aspect of Oneida life from the time these "New York Indians" arrived in Wisconsin. While there are now fewer and fewer speakers of the native language throughout Iroquoia, the Wisconsin Oneidas have made herculean efforts to preserve and teach Oneida since the late 1930s.[10] They have been the leaders of land-claims litigation against New York State for the loss of millions of acres that they possessed at the end of the American Revolution.[11] Moreover, in 1970, the Wisconsin Oneidas established a Longhouse and they now teach the *Gaiwiio* and hold Iroquois traditional ceremonies there.[12]

The following chapter focuses on the life of Chief Daniel Bread and his political leadership of the Oneida Indians. His is a story of pragmatic tribal leadership in the face of overwhelming odds: transportation and land speculation pressures, state and federal policies pushing the agenda of Indian removal, tense diplomacy with other quite distinct Native American nations to allow for resettlement in the West, and the pressures of nation building. In the process, he modified Iroquoian traditions to fit the new circumstances that the Oneidas faced in Wisconsin. Today's seventeen thousand Oneidas in Wisconsin owe much to his skills.

Bread knew well that it was tough to be Indian, especially in nineteenth-century frontier America. His extraordinary coalition-building efforts to achieve internal cohesion lasted a generation at a critical time in Oneida history. Bread was truly the founding father of his Iroquois nation, ranking in importance with the Oneida chiefs of the past, most notably Good Peter, who had fought so courageously in attempting to lead the nation in New York after the American Revolution. Bread was not a devout preacher in the manner of Good Peter, and Bread used religion in a calculating fashion to further his political ambitions; nevertheless, Bread deserves immense credit for his careful stewardship of the Oneidas in the great transition from Oneida Castle in central New York to Duck Creek, Wisconsin—no simple achievement.

The Gardener

Chief Daniel Bread and the Planting
of the Oneida Nation in Wisconsin

> He [Chief Daniel Bread] is a shrewd and talented man, well educated—
> speaking good English—is handsome and a polite and gentlemanly
> man in his deportment.
> —George Catlin, *Letters and Notes on the Manners,*
> *Customs, and Condition of the North American Indians*

Chief Daniel Bread (1800–1873), "Tekayá-tilu," was the central figure in
the early history of the Oneida Indians in Wisconsin. Bread, a great orator
in the Oneida language and well-trained in English, was the most articulate voice defending tribal interests at a critical time for these American
Indians because of their removal from New York State and adjustment to
new surroundings.[1] As a masterful politician, Bread saw no contradiction
in promoting tribal sovereignty and treaty rights of his Indian people while
at the same time cooperating with Indian agents or accepting the white
man's religion, holidays, and schools, as well as the role of "Great Father"
in Washington. For Bread was a political pragmatist, not necessarily committed to spiritual concerns or idealistic principles.

No Iroquois prophet or war chief, Bread was a savvy tribal politician
who was most responsible for transplanting Oneida existence to Wisconsin,
then known as Michigan Territory, where these Native peoples remain to
the present day. In the three decades before the American Civil War, he
accomplished this herculean task by ameliorating internal political divisions
stemming from earlier divisive battles in central New York and by creating tribal consensus that lasted until the 1850s; by his forceful leadership

5. Daniel Bread, Oneida chief, 1831. Painting by George Catlin. [Smithsonian] National Museum of American Art.

opposing any efforts by federal and state officials to limit the tribal land base or to remove the Oneidas to the Indian Territory; and, finally, and quite importantly, by adapting Iroquoian traditions to the Wisconsin setting.

The chief drew inspiration from the Oneida past and tried to avoid pitfalls—disunity and resulting intertribal party conflict—factors that contributed to his people's removal from central New York.[2] He was a quick learner who operated in the hard-boiled, real world of nineteenth-century America with its harsh racial attitudes about Indians and their future. Bread realized that the Oneidas had lost much: their traditional social organization was fading and their traditional political organization, based on the leadership of condoled chiefs, was a thing of the past by the time these Indians entered Michigan Territory in the 1820s. Despite rapid cultural changes, the Oneidas rebuilt their nation under Chief Bread's aegis by taking cultural elements of the past and modifying them to serve the Indians' needs.

By 1821, seven years before he arrived in Michigan Territory, Bread is listed as a chief of the Oneidas' First Christian Party.[3] Indeed, this was precisely the most desperate time of Oneida existence. The building of major turnpikes and the opening of the central section of the Erie Canal in 1817

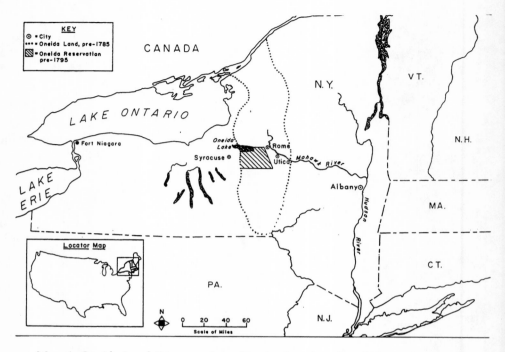

Map 4. Oneida Land Dispossession after the American Revolution. Map by Ben Simpson.

brought thousands of non-Indians into Madison and Oneida Counties. As land pressures mounted, Albany politicians and land speculators lusted after the Oneida estate and "encouraged" Indian outmigration from the Empire State. The Oneidas faced severe internal divisions, splitting into three separate tribal political entities. Moreover, the Oneidas' cohesion was weakened by the rampant alcohol abuse, poverty, and social disintegration that were frequently noted by outside observers.[4]

Shortly after the end of the War of 1812, Bishop John Henry Hobart of the Episcopal church had appointed Eleazer Williams as a lay reader and catechist and, in 1817, as a missionary to the Oneida Indians. An eccentric Mohawk with elaborate goals, unrealistic fantasies, and questionable scruples, Williams expanded a plan first proposed by Jedidiah Morse, the famous minister, geographer, and congressman, to resettle the Six Nations from New York State in the West. Williams led delegations of the Iroquois and other Indians from New York State to Green Bay in 1820–22, where treaties were negotiated with the Menominees and Ho-Chunks (Winnebagos), securing millions of acres of land and settlements in the Fox River Valley at Little Chute and along Duck Creek near Green Bay. Yet Williams's significance in this migration and later events has been exaggerated by historians, and the Oneidas' roles, especially that of Daniel Bread, have been underestimated and misinterpreted.[5]

In several subsequent federal treaties, specifically the Treaty of Butte des Morts in 1827 and the federal Menominee treaty of 1831 (Stambaugh Treaty), Oneida lands in Michigan Territory were reduced by more than 90 percent.[6] Despite arriving in Michigan Territory in 1828, Bread soon became the leader trying to challenge the 1827 and 1831 treaties, because the Oneidas were bypassed during each of these federal negotiations.[7]

In the winter of 1831, Bread, along with representatives of the Brothertown and Stockbridge Indians, took his case to Washington. After holding a religious service in one of the churches of the nation's capital conducted by the Indian clergy of the Stockbridge Indians, the representatives of the "New York Indians" went to the War Department to meet with Secretary Lewis Cass, the former governor of Michigan Territory.[8] Subsequently they went to the White House, accompanied by George B. Porter, the governor of Michigan Territory. There the chief met with Old Hickory and vigorously defended his people's interests, clearly explaining that the Oneida land remaining after the 1831 treaty was not "sufficient in quality or quantity" for his tribe's needs, and suggested an alternative, one that Jackson accepted.[9] Although the Oneidas did not win an overall victory, they did achieve agreement by the president that their lands would be exchanged for better, more fertile lands in the southern part of Menominee Territory, no small achievement in the Age of Jackson.[10]

Afterward, to win political acceptance among the Oneidas, Bread played a careful game, presenting himself as the great defender of Oneida interests, distancing himself from the other "New York Indians," and bad-mouthing the French traders and Métis at Green Bay as well as the Menominee leadership who had promoted the 1827 and 1831 treaties. Throughout the next decade, Bread cooperated with George Boyd, the Indian agent at Green Bay, who had a pro-Oneida, anti-Catholic, anti-French, anti-Menominee bias.

Cooperating with Boyd at every turn, Bread supported schools and Western education and Western public health efforts such as vaccination for his people. Both the chief and the Indian agent also successfully conspired to ostracize Eleazer Williams from all dealings affecting the Oneidas.[11]

In 1836, when the federal government under the nefarious Indian treaty negotiator John Schermerhorn renewed efforts to cut the Oneida land base in Wisconsin, Bread made clear to the territorial governor that his people now refused to "mingle in council with the Menominee" and other Indians. "We have nothing to do in conjunction with them. The Oneida Nation must therefore be regarded as standing alone."[12] Eventually, on February 3, 1838, the Oneidas and federal officials signed the Amended Treaty of Buffalo Creek, also known as the Oneida Treaty of Washington, whereby the United States recognized a separate 65,420-acre reservation for those Indians in the area of today's Green Bay, Wisconsin.[13]

During the 1830s, Chief Bread, fearing that divisions within his nation would once again lead to removal and because of growing territorial and federal pressures, made an alliance with his most prominent Oneida political rival, Chief Jacob Cornelius of the Orchard Party. Cornelius and his followers had arrived in the West in 1834. Oneida weakness forced the two chiefs and their followers to cooperate.[14] Each worked to head off tribal fissures that both chiefs knew might contribute to disaster and removal to Indian Territory. Both men had to face a myriad of problems of resettlement in the early 1830s caused by waves of impoverished Oneidas arriving in the environs of Green Bay from New York State. Even though each man operated as the singular voice of his party and sought separate compensation from Albany officials under New York State treaties, the two joined together on many other issues. These included petitions for the payment of federal annuities under the Treaty of Canandaigua, claims for compensation under the Treaty of Buffalo Creek, and relief for struggling members of each party newly arrived from New York State. They took joint stands against removal from Wisconsin, supported several federal subagents at Green Bay favorable to the Oneidas' interests, and opposed the appointment of others who were seen as enemies of their people. Importantly, both men signed the Oneidas' Amended Treaty of Buffalo Creek of February 3, 1838.[15]

By 1836 Bread's alliance with Chief Cornelius was set down on paper when both men were designated to speak for the entire Oneida Nation in negotiations. On August 31, 1836, long-time First Christian Party chiefs Neddy Archiquette and Elijah Skenandore gave Bread an unqualified vote of confidence for his policies and actions, insisting that the thirty-six-year-old chief was "a fine expression of our views."[16] Two days later, he and Cornelius formally made a pact, one that proved invaluable in the decade and a half that followed and that cemented Bread's role as the single most important voice in council.[17]

Bread prepared the groundwork for the accord with the Orchard Party by carefully leading two waves of these and other Oneida emigrants from New York to Michigan Territory in 1833 and 1834. On his second trip to New York, Bread appealed for relief funds from the New York State legislature. Bread's work on behalf of the Indian refugees of both parties was acknowledged in a report made by the New York State legislature in 1835. The report categorized his relief efforts as "meritorious," stating that he was "prudent, wise and energetic" in facilitating the administration of removal for both First Christian and Orchard Party Oneidas.[18] The accommodation of Bread and Cornelius is even more remarkable because their two neighborhoods on the reservation operated separately, almost as autonomous units, each with its own set of pinetree chiefs, its own church, its own singing and mutual aid societies, its own mission school, even its own lacrosse team.

Bread's role went beyond political and economic concerns. He helped tie the Oneida present of the nineteenth century with the ancient Iroquoian traditions of the past. As the proud descendants of a once-powerful Iroquois Confederacy that had negotiated with representatives of kings, the Oneidas adapted the Condolence Council ritual, at the core of their culture, into the Wisconsin setting. They did this through the annual commemoration of Independence Day promoted by Chief Bread. Every July 4th, Oneida chiefs made their formal addresses to their people and to invited guests in a conscious diplomatic attempt to win friends in a hostile world, to soothe Oneida-white relations, and to build bridges with key members of the surrounding white community. These Indians recalled their glory days and reminded their own people and outsiders of the need for ties to bind them.[19]

The Oneidas' commemoration of Independence Day was not simply the fruit of acculturative white forces working to absorb them. Their Revolutionary War alliance with the American colonists had cost them dearly in lives, and their communities had been devastated. The war had also strained their relations with pro-British elements within the Six Nations; however, the Oneidas were proud of their role as loyal warriors of General Washington.[20] Right up to the present time, July 4th is the date of the Wisconsin Oneida Nation pow-wow at which time Indian veterans are always honored.

Three of the Oneidas' past July 4th celebrations—1849, 1854, and 1857—reveal much about this adaptation. The festivities contained a chief's addresses (although the 1849 one was not fully recorded nor reported on), replies by invited guests, a feast, a lacrosse match, and, at least in one instance, social dancing. The reporting of these festivities, all made by outside non-Indian observers, focused on the good times had by all, the foods, and the lacrosse match.

In the summer of 1849, Alfred Cope, a wealthy Quaker businessman and philanthropist from Philadelphia, visited the Oneidas in Wisconsin. Cope described the July 4th celebration at Oneida, at which time he found that it was customary for Chief Bread to invite his tribesmen and their guests to his house. Over one hundred attended the feast, which included a meal of venison, fresh pork, beef, rice pudding, and coffee. Much like in other American communities, fireworks were set off. The meal was followed by a lacrosse match between teams selected from members of the Episcopal and Methodist churches.[21]

A second account of a July 4th, 1854, celebration at Oneida, published in the *Green Bay Advocate,* adds to our understanding. The chief's address, the reply by any assembled guest, the feast, and lacrosse were once again part of the day's festivities. At the opening of his speech, Chief Bread deferentially stated, much in the manner of Indian council protocol, "If you observe anything on our [Oneidas'] part (as you undoubtedly will), which may appear to you unseemly, you will please . . . excuse us; and . . . [we] shall endeavor to entertain you to the best of our ability, and of the best which we have we offer to you." He then continued by mentioning that the Oneidas had "forsaken many of the customs of our fathers"; however, Bread carefully indicated that despite significant changes, there was still "a wide difference between us." This observation was a conscious effort to teach the outsiders that Oneidas were not willing to be made into carbon-copy whites, but, in the traditional Iroquoian metaphor, paddled a separate canoe down the river. They could not completely enter the white man's ship nor could they straddle with one foot in two vessels.[22]

Bread then told the gathering about the history of the Iroquois and the major role the Oneidas played in the American Revolution: "But the Oneidas, ever friendly towards your fathers, could not be alienated from them either by the threats or persuasions of their foes." In their commitment to General Washington, they "painted their tomahawks red in blood of the enemies of your people." The chief pointed out his people's sacrifice: "Many of their bravest warriors were slain, but their own children known [*sic*] not the resting place of their bodies. There are no monuments erected to show where they fell." Renewing the chain of friendship, he reaffirmed his people's loyalty to the Americans and looked to the president of the United States, "our Great Father in Washington, who will act as the eagle watching over the Oneidas" to protect them "whenever we are in danger of trouble."[23]

On July 4, 1857, Bread once again held forth. In a speech cited by Lyman C. Draper in his annual report for the State Historical Society of Wisconsin, Bread recounted the history of the Oneida people, while lauding American progress. Draper pointed out the observations made by a local reporter: "Our neighbors, the Oneida Indians have an old, time-honored usage of celebrating our national holiday every year, by a sort of festival, in which they are joined, not only as spectators but participants by their pale-faced brethren." Viewing it as an excellent way "to promote unity and harmony between the two races," the reporter praised Bread's and his Oneida people's hospitality given that the assembled were "entertained, and invited to partake of viands cooked in the most tempting style" that the newsman described as a "sumptuous feast." After the address by Bread in the Oneida language, which was translated "through an interpreter, and a reply made by any person present," the day closed "with athletic games by the Indians."[24]

These annual speeches served to remind Indian and non-Indian alike of those who had come before and the responsibilities of the living to the dead.

Fenton has noted, "The ritual paradigm that governed the proceedings [of forest diplomacy] guided the behavior of Iroquoian and Algonquian speakers alike throughout the lower Great Lakes; it survives today in the program of the Iroquois Condolence Council." This council was for mourning dead chiefs, lifting up the minds of bereaved relatives, and installing their successors. The ceremony is essential for understanding the Iroquois and their diplomacy with other Indian and Euro-American nations. It consists of rites known as the Roll Call of the Founders, the Welcome at the Woods' Edge, the Recitation of Laws, the Requickening Address, the Six Songs of Requiem, and the Charge to the New Chief. Invited guests gathered at the "Woods' Edge" and were welcomed into the village, where the chiefs read the "Roll Call of the Founders," recounting the sacrifices of past leaders. Dead chiefs were recognized for their service to the nation, mourned, and their successors raised and validated, in Fenton's words "requickened in the titles of the founders so that the league may endure." Then the face of the new chief was revealed and he was charged in his new duties to carry out the people's will.[25]

Fenton has written that this ritual of mourning and installation of chiefs was filled with numerous metaphors that attempted to "strengthen the house [nation]."[26] Dispelling the clouds and restoring the sun were metaphors used to emphasize the importance of this bereavement and installation ritual. To create alliances of the gathered participants, there were references to keeping the path open by clearing rivers, rapids, and roads; polishing a chain; and maintaining a perpetual fire to bind.[27]

The Iroquois' expectation was that all the guests/outsiders observe and respect these Indians' traditions and learn the proper forms of the ritual. Fenton has observed that, through the seriousness and religiosity of the Condolence Council, the Iroquois attempted to manipulate the forbidding white world to their own advantage. Knowing their great power had waned by the eighteenth century, the Iroquois Confederacy saw alliances as indispensable for survival. Whether weaker Indian nations or more powerful Europeans, one thing was clear, as Fenton has importantly noted: "Whoever came to the Iroquois came on their terms."[28]

The Six Nations' hospitality and generosity during this Condolence Council ceremony were exceptional. The ceremony included the "passing of wampum belts, the distribution of presents and the enormous expense of the expected feast." Besides social dancing that always followed the end of the ten-day period of the Condolence Council, a lacrosse match was held, which was intentionally planned as part of the rite. (A lacrosse match has recently been added to the events of the Oneida Wisconsin July 4th pow-wow.) For lacrosse was more than merely a game. Fenton has written that lacrosse was a "game that anciently discharged social tensions," by discouraging intervillage warfare, keeping the warriors fit, and cheering the depressed relatives of the deceased. Thus the ceremony, in effect, reinvigorated Iroquois existence, renewed political forms, restored society, and built or strengthened alliances.[29]

Chief Bread was the central figure in transforming the Iroquois Condolence ritual into an annual Independence Day ceremony in Wisconsin. Through his brilliant oratory, Bread used the traditional elements of Iroquoian ritualism, modifying them to meet the outside threats of another removal as well as the other political circumstances of the day. In typical Iroquoian diplomatic fashion and with skill to win favor and support for his people, he attempted to educate both his people and friendly whites to the great Oneida leaders and accomplishments of the past and their contributions to the American nation.

Chief Bread's influence was to wane with the challenges to his leadership over controls of reservation timber resources starting just before the Civil War. His alliance with Chief Cornelius collapsed and new leaders—those Oneidas born in Wisconsin—emerged. By the early 1870s, his power had faded away. He died of bilious fever on July 23, 1873.[30] By that time, the Oneidas' roots were strong enough to take hold in Wisconsin, having survived the era of removal. In effect, master politician Chief Daniel Bread had prepared the ground, planted the seed, and ensured the sprouting of his people's future twelve hundred miles from the Oneida homeland in central New York.

PART FOUR

War Chiefs

Introduction

In 1983 the historian Daniel Richter observed that the "plaudits offered to successful warriors suggest a deep cultural significance; societies usually reward warlike behavior not for its own sake but for the useful functions it performs." The primary aim of an Iroquois war chief in the forest conflicts of the seventeenth and eighteenth centuries was to lead his warriors into battle to capture "prisoners and bring them home alive." Richter labels this "mourning-wars," namely to replenish the ranks of depleted Iroquois villages decimated by epidemics and/or earlier conflicts. Importantly, the war chief was to minimize fatalities in his own warrior ranks by quick raids, by avoiding frontal assaults, by employing other defensive tactics that precluded loss of life, or by quickly withdrawing his men from disastrous situations, thus avoiding the "costly last stands that earned glory for European warriors."[1] In the eighteenth century, Iroquois war chiefs led raids well into the Southeast, taking on the likes of the Cherokees and Catawbas. Although mourning-war ended in the late eighteenth century, the war chief ideal became ingrained in the Iroquois psyche and continues to influence Six Nations life today. This ideal is reflected in extraordinarily high enlistment rates among the Iroquois from the Civil War to the Iraqi War, but also in other ways. Indeed, the responsibilities of ironworker crew chiefs in building skyscrapers and bridges are parallel to the ancient role of war chiefs in the distant past.

Although not motivated by traditional "mourning-war," Cornelius C. Cusick, a Tuscarora, personally recruited and was the leader of twenty-five Indians in Company D of the 132nd New York Volunteer Infantry during the American Civil War. In the past, before military conscription, the raising of a war party was "left entirely to private enterprise and to the system of voluntary service." Any individual had the right to "organize a band, and make an invasion."[2] Cusick fit perfectly into this traditional role of leadership.

Other Iroquois have served honorably in combat in American wars, for example Ely S. Parker, the distinguished Seneca sachem who served on General Grant's staff as his military secretary and drew up the articles of surrender at Appomattox Courthouse.[3] Later, A.G.E. Smith, the father of Jay Silverheels, a Mohawk from the Six Nations Reserve, was the most decorated Indian in the Canadian (British) military during World War I.[4] Despite their overall achievements, neither Parker nor Smith led American Indian troops. Indeed, Cusick was the last who led Iroquois troops in combat, a leadership role that has disappeared during the past 150 years.

The twenty-five Indians who served in Cusick's Company D were recruited from May 12 to August 26, 1862. From their dates of enlistment, it is clear that they joined in clusters, on or just off their reservation communities at Lewiston and Suspension Bridge (Niagara Falls), or in Buffalo. Seven men from the Cattaraugus Indian Reservation volunteered on the same day, May 24, 1862. Isaac Newton Parker and two other Senecas—Benjamin Jonas of Cattaraugus and Henry Sundown of Tonawanda—volunteered on June 18, 1862, at Buffalo.

The D Company of the 132nd New York State Volunteer Infantry, known because of Cusick's leadership as the "Tuscarora Company," came into existence when the 53rd New York State Volunteer Infantry was disbanded in the late spring of 1862. Although referred to as the Tuscarora Company, it contained more Germans than Iroquois and had four times as many Senecas as Tuscaroras. Despite its polyglot nature, the men of the company banded together as a fighting unit and there was little, if any, racial discrimination directed toward the Indians.[5]

After receiving assurances that they would receive a $25 bounty, a $2 premium, and a month's pay of $13 for enlisting, the twenty-five Indians were sent to Camp Scrogg in New York City. There they trained on the parade grounds and received regimental inspection. On September 28, 1862, the 132nd New York State Volunteer Infantry was sent to Washington. On October 4, the Indians were mustered into service for three years and sent to Suffolk, Virginia, for duty at Camp Hoffman at Fortress Monroe under General John Peck of Syracuse, New York.

At Christmas in 1862, the 132nd New York State Volunteers and the entire brigade were ordered to prepare to leave Fortress Monroe for North Carolina. Under a cloak of secrecy, the regiment was ordered to New Bern, North Carolina, a major railroad terminus that had been captured by General Ambrose Burnside and his Union forces in an amphibious landing nine months earlier.[6] From the winter of 1862 to the end of the war, the Tuscarora Company was stationed in North Carolina and assigned to guarding the rails. Their first major engagement in combat was the Battle of Batchelder's Creek on February 1–4, 1864. In the battle, Cusick faced a three-pronged onslaught of thousands of Confederates. Eleven of the Indians held the Neuse Bridge for over an hour against the massive enemy force and were later cited for heroism. Only when the Confederates were finally able to bring up artillery pieces did the Indian survivors fall back.[7] One of the Indians was killed in action, and another was captured and later died at Andersonville Prison. Later that year, Cusick and his Iroquois warriors were cited for bravery at the Battle of Jackson Mills. Their last major engagement with Confederate forces occurred on March 7–10, 1865, at the Battle of Wyse (Wise) Forks, near Kinston, North Carolina.[8]

After the war, Cusick secured a commission as an officer, serving for the next quarter-century on the trans-Mississippi frontier. This appointment and his promotion to the rank of captain as well as his long-time service in the regular army are evidence that his leadership abilities were recognized by non-Indians. Importantly, he was able to bring home safely all but two of his Iroquois warriors. Thus, much like war chiefs of the past, Cusick understood that foolish risks endangered the future survival of the Iroquois.

Over the past 125 years, the Iroquois Indians have replicated this ideal in high-steel construction. Just as war chiefs led warriors into battle and carefully watched over and helped modify reckless behavior that threatened the group, the crew chiefs of iron work, who earn their stripes as virtuosos of high steel, warn young laborers to use their safety belts while walking on beams seventy or more stories up. One of these Mohawks, Kyle Karonhiaktatie Beauvais, observed, "A lot of people think Mohawks aren't afraid of heights; that's not true. We have as much fear as the next guy." He added, "*We also have the experience of old timers to follow and the responsibility to lead the younger guys.* There's pride in walking iron" (emphasis mine).[9] Just as past Iroquois young men went off to far-off wars, in more modern times ironworkers "boom out" (their own words), leaving their own communities to join up in massive projects including the Empire State Building, the Chrysler Building, the George Washington Bridge, the Verrazano Narrows Bridge, the San Francisco–Oakland Bay Bridge, and the World Trade Center.[10] These same Iroquois crews were called into service when terrorists hijacked two planes and crashed them into the World Trade Center on September 11, 2001. They heroically aided the recovery efforts, once again risking their health and lives in the tumultuous days that followed.[11]

7

"War Eagle"

Lieutenant Cornelius C. Cusick

Lieutenant Cornelius C. Cusick was the most important Iroquois commander of Indian troops during the American Civil War. Ely S. Parker held a higher rank, that of brigadier general, by war's end; however, Parker, unlike Cusick, never led Iroquois soldiers into combat. Because of Cusick's demonstrated leadership abilities, he received a commission in the regular army at the end of the Civil War and served for more than a quarter of a century as an officer on the trans-Mississippi frontier.

Despite being a "peace chief," having been appointed Turtle Clan sachem after the death of his uncle Chief William Chew around 1857, Cusick was the archetype of the classic ambitious war chief who raised war parties in seventeenth- and eighteenth-century forest combat. His leadership was based on his abilities as well as his prestigious lineage, which for decades had been associated with success on the warpath. Known as "War Eagle," he was the recognized leader of the Tuscarora Company. It was no coincidence that the commanding officers of the 132nd New York State Volunteer Infantry frequently alluded to "Cusick's Indians" and their military prowess during the latter stages of the Civil War and that the Tuscarora oral tradition is filled with references to Cusick's military exploits.[1]

Cusick was born on the Tuscarora Indian Reservation in western New York on August 2, 1835, the son of James and Mary Cusick. His was the most prominent lineage in Tuscarora history. Like the Parker family among the Seneca, the Cusicks were part of a leadership elite who shaped community existence. Cusick's grandfather was Nicholas Kaghnatsho (Cusick), the interpreter for General Marquis de Lafayette, who faithfully served the patriot cause during the American Revolution. Cornelius's father, James Cusick, was the Baptist minister on the Tuscarora Indian Reservation, but because of his leadership of the pro-emigration party and family support for the Treaty of Buffalo Creek, James and his religious efforts fell into disfavor on the reservation during the 1840s. Cornelius C. Cusick's uncle David was a noted scholar, author of *Sketches of Ancient History of the Six Nations,* the "first major work written by an Iroquoian," which was published in 1828.[2] Cusick's grandnephew Clinton Rickard was the founder of the Indian Defense League of North America and a passionate spokesman for Indian treaty and civil rights who fought, until his death in 1971, for the Indians' right of free and unlimited passage across the international boundary between Canada and the United States. His great-grandnephew William Rickard led the unsuccessful fight against Robert Moses's and the New York State Power Authority's condemnation of Tuscarora lands in the 1950s.[3]

Cornelius Cusick belonged to a family tradition directly related to American military service. Clinton Rickard was one of ten soldiers detailed to protect Vice President Theodore Roosevelt on a visit to Buffalo in 1901. Later, Rickard served with distinction in the U.S. cavalry during the Philippine insurrection after the Spanish American War. In his autobiography, Rickard described his family's military tradition:

> Many of my ancestors were soldiers and warriors. I was following in this tradition. My great great grandfather was Lieutenant Nicholas Cusick of the Revolutionary War. He took part in the Battle of Saratoga and also served as an interpreter and as bodyguard to General Lafayette. He was one among many of our Indian people who helped these United States achieve their independence. My grandfather's half-brother, Captain Cornelius Cusick, was a professional army man and fought in the Civil War. Also, my father's eldest brother was on guard at the White House the night Lincoln was shot.[4]

Cornelius Cusick was a mediator between cultures. He was a member of the educated leadership elite that has been part of Iroquoian society since the seventeenth century and that has served as liaison and broker between

6. Cornelius C. Cusick, Tuscarora officer and hero of the American Civil War. National Archives.

the Indian and non-Indian worlds. He spoke eight Indian languages and was recognized in the non-Indian world as an authority on Iroquoian culture, as evidenced by his appointment as assistant director of archaeology and ethnology for the Columbian Exposition in Chicago in 1892.[5] Despite his family's support of the Buffalo Creek Treaty, Cusick apparently was back in favor on the reservation by the Civil War. One source indicates that at the age of twenty-five, Cusick was "installed as a sachem of the Confederacy." Throughout the war and after, his superior officers referred to him as a Tuscarora chief.[6]

In his appeals to federal officials to allow recruitment of "Iroquois warriors" (Cusick's words), he was imitating earlier war chiefs' routes to prestige among his people. The "war path" (Cusick's words) was his route to fame just as earlier Tuscarora warriors served the American government in 1776 and 1812.[7] Because of their strategic location along the Niagara River, which connects Lake Erie and Lake Ontario, the Tuscaroras served the United States as allies during the War of 1812. Three of the thirty-five warriors listed in the records were named Cusick: Joseph, John, and David.[8]

Cornelius Cusick was one of twenty-three Tuscaroras to volunteer for Union service in the American Civil War. In part as a result of Cusick's and Fisk's petitions in the early spring of 1862, Congressman Burt Van Horn of western New York interceded on behalf of the Indians' "right" to serve in the Union army. Seventeen of the twenty-five Iroquois in the Tuscarora Company were credited to Cusick's enlistment efforts.[9]

The records of the 132nd New York State Volunteer Infantry reveal very little about Lieutenant Cusick's Union military service before February 1864. A man of dark complexion and five feet seven inches tall, he volunteered on May 12, 1862, and was promoted to first lieutenant on July 1, 1863. It was ironic that Cusick was sent with his warriors in December 1862 to the New Bern area of North Carolina, where they guarded a rail terminus depot at Tuscarora, the precise spot from which his tribesmen had been forced to flee 150 years earlier during the so-called "Tuscarora Wars." Despite the paucity of records concerning Cusick in the first half of the war, the Tuscarora lieutenant was to make his mark dramatically from February 1 to June 24, 1864, when the general calm of the New Bern theater of the war was shattered.[10]

In early January 1864, General Robert E. Lee recommended that the Confederate armies march on the Union forces at New Bern. Seeking to capture the "large amounts of provisions and other supplies," Lee informed Confederate President Jefferson Davis about his estimate of Union forces there:

New Berne [sic] is defended on the land side by a line of entrenchments from the Neuse to the Trent. A redoubt near the Trent protects that flank, while three or four gun-boats are relied upon to defend the flank on the Neuse. The garrison has been so long unmolested, and experiences such a feeling of security, that it is represented as careless. The gun-boats are small and indifferent and do not keep up a head of steam. A bold party could descend the Neuse in boats at night, capture the gun-boats, and drive the enemy by their aid from the works on that side of the river, while a force should attack them in front.[11]

Lee was also intent on recapturing the railroad at New Bern, which had been guarded by the Tuscarora Company and other Union forces since General Ambrose Burnside's seizure of the area in 1862; however, Lee badly underestimated his enemy's abilities and chose the wrong commander, General George E. Pickett, to lead the strike.

With thirteen thousand men and fourteen navy cutters, General Pickett moved on New Bern on January 30, 1864, dividing his troops into three columns. Confederate General Seth M. Barton and his men were to cross the Trent River near Trenton and proceed on the south side of the river to Brice's Creek below New Bern. He was to take the forts along the Neuse and Trent rivers and then enter New Bern via the railroad bridge, thus preventing Union reinforcement by land or water. Colonels James Dearing and John N. Whitford and their men were to move down the Neuse River and capture Fort Anderson. Generals Robert F. Hoke and Pickett and the remainder of the expeditionary force were to "move down between the Trent and the Neuse, endeavor to surprise the troops on Batchelder's Creek, silence the guns in the star fort and batteries near the Neuse, and penetrate the town in that direction." The Confederate navy was to descend the Neuse, capture Union gunboats, and cooperate with the three Confederate columns.[12]

General Pickett "bungled the New Bern operations," although he shifted blame to Generals Barton and Hoke. Pickett had failed in planning beforehand, underestimating, as Lee did, the task at hand. General Hoke moved quickly to reach Batchelder's Creek before the bridge was taken out by Union forces, but the firing of pickets had warned the Union forces of the enemy's approach. The Union troops then destroyed the bridge to prevent the Confederates' advance. Hoke also failed to capture the Union train and enter the city by rail. Nevertheless, Hoke's men adapted to the circumstances and cut down some trees to make a bridge so that two of

Hoke's regiments could then cross over the creek. Despite Union rein-
forcements, Hoke routed them once his troops crossed Batchelder's Creek.
His men then marched to within a mile of New Bern and waited to join
Barton's forces.[13]

General Barton's men never reached Hoke. After passing through low
swamp country with vast mud holes caused by winter showers, Barton
came in view of the enemy's breastworks close to Brice's Creek at eight
A.M. on February 1. Instead of attacking immediately, which might have
caught the Union forces by surprise, he ordered a reconnaissance while
bringing up his artillery. The reconnaissance found that Union forces were
more entrenched than previously thought. Barton concluded, and then
reported to General Pickett, that his troops were "unprepared to encounter so serious" and "insurmountable" a defense. In the meantime, Union
forces were alerted and their artillery began to hit Barton's position, Pickett
then ordered Barton to join the troops before New Bern for an assault on
that front. Yet to do so, Barton had to cross the Trent River and retrace
his steps, which would have taken more than two days. When Pickett was
informed that Barton and his men could not reach him until February 4,
Pickett withdrew on February 3 and admitted failure. Although the Union
forces suffered more than twice as many casualties—one hundred compared to the Confederate forty-five—the Confederates failed to capture the
supplies they so desperately needed and sought.[14]

Cusick's Indians excelled in this battle at Batchelder's Creek and in
subsequent military engagements in North Carolina in 1864. Captain
Charles G. Smith, the general officer of the day on February 10, 1864, of
the 132nd New York State Volunteer Infantry, commended Cusick and several other commanders at Batchelder's Creek for their "individual instances
of coolness and heroism." After lauding one "Lieutenant Haring" for his
bravery in defending the Neuse bridge, Smith added, "In this he [Haring]
was nobly seconded by Capt. Thomas B. Green, Lieutenant Cusick, and
Companies D and G, with Lieutenants Gearing & Ryan, who were both
badly wounded, the respective companies losing heavily."[15] Later, Captain
R. Emmett Fiske, also of the 132nd New York State Volunteer Infantry,
wrote of the fight at Batchelder's Creek: "Lieutenant Cusick with some thirty
of his warrior soldiers of his tribe, engaged the rebel advance in a sharp

skirmish for several hours and by desperate fighting prevented the dislodge-ment of the picket reserves and the capture of the outpost camp."[16]

Iroquois veterans of the Battle of Batchelder's Creek had to contend with vicious rumors disparaging their military service for the next thirty-five years. Colonel John N. Whitford and his brother Major Edward Whit-ford, who were in the command of the 67th North Carolina Volunteer Infantry in the vicinity of New Bern at Beech Grove, North Carolina, later accused the Indians of the 132nd New York of "scalping" the Confeder-ate wounded at the Battle of Batchelder's Creek. These efforts to discredit Cusick's troops were finally laid to rest when Hugh Hastings, the New York State historian, published an exposé of the alleged affair in 1897, dis-counting the accounts as war propaganda because none of the Confederate wounded was left behind on the battlefield. Colonel Claassen once again praised Cusick's Indians for their valor at Batchelder's Creek and other military engagements.[17]

In June 1864, Colonel Claassen's men were sent on an expedition from Batchelder's Creek to the vicinity of Kinston, North Carolina. While on reconnaissance "into the enemy country," Lieutenant Cusick, "leading his Indians in a flank movement, distinguished himself by materially assisting in the capture of the commandant of Kinston, N.C., Col. Foulke [Folk], (6th N.C. Cav.), together with five of his officers and upwards of fifty of his rank & file." The regiment's captain, Thomas B. Green, and his officers and men were cited in the official record for the success of the operation, which was attributed to their "endurance and determination."[18] Claassen later wrote that at Jackson's Mills, North Carolina, Cusick and his "dusky warriors," lying in wait in a "roadside thicket, with instructions to closely guard the rear," trapped the rebels.[19]

The ambitious Tuscarora chief soon began to promote his exploits. Even before the end of the war, his goal was to receive a commission in the regular army. In January 1865, he wrote President Lincoln asking for an appointment as second lieutenant in the regular army. In seeking the pro-motion, Cusick mentioned that "with the assistance of Colonel John Fisk, late Colonel 2nd NYM Rifles, I sent a petition to the Secretary of War" requesting that Indians be allowed to volunteer. As a result of their efforts, "300 sturdy warriors" took the "war path."[20] The same month, Cusick's colonel, Peter J. Claassen, recommended him for the regular army because of his "soldier qualities," "demonstrated proof of his bravery and courage in action," "upright character, temperate habits and considerable talent." Claassen further stated that "his retention in the military service of the Government would be for the interest of the Country."[21] These early efforts at securing a commission failed; the next year, however, Cusick secured the backing of prominent politicos, who facilitated his securing of a commission. E. L. Porter, the son of General Peter B. Porter, hero of the War of 1812 and former secretary of war, wrote on Cusick's behalf, describing him as "an hereditary chief of the Tuscarora and the grand-son of a brave man who fought under Washington."[22]

On June 22, 1866, the Tuscarora soldier, who had been mustered out of Civil War service almost exactly a year earlier, received a commission as second lieutenant in the 13th U.S. Infantry. On August 24, Cusick took the oath of allegiance to "support and defend" the Constitution of the United States and bear "true Faith and Allegiance to the same." Less than a week later, he was on duty in Kentucky. Eight months later, he was transferred to the 31st U.S. Infantry and sent with his regiment to fight Red Cloud's Lakota warriors in Dakota Territory.[23]

For most of the next quarter-century, Cusick was stationed on the trans-Mississippi frontier. His assignments read like a road map of the Indian wars: Forts Buford, Randall, Rice, Stevenson, Sully, Dakota Territory; Lower Brule Indian Agency; Fort Gibson, Indian Territory; Fort Keogh and Tongue River, Montana Territory; Forts Clark and Duncan, Texas; Fort Lyon, Colorado. As an officer in the frontier army, he was involved in campaigns of conquest and pacification against Plains Indians. Some of his own Tuscarora people resented Cusick's action in fighting other Indian nations. Others perceived him as a great warrior in the Iroquoian tradition. His frontier military service was not without risk. In August 1868 he was wounded in the right shoulder by a Plains Indian war club while fighting the Sioux.[24]

Eight months later, Cusick was transferred to the 22nd U.S. Infantry, rising to the rank of first lieutenant in August 1872 and captain of Company E in January 1888. He served under Nelson A. Miles's command, fighting in the Sioux War of 1876–77 in Montana and Dakota Territory, and, once again, was cited for heroism; he also was a participant in the Ute War of the late 1870s. Despite recurring medical problems—gastrointestinal and eye disorders—Cusick served with distinction until his retirement from military service on January 14, 1892.[25] In 1890 his commanding officer, Lieutenant Colonel J. S. Conrad, wrote a summary report of his military service performance in which he described Cusick as "generally conversant with his profession," rating "good" in "attention to duty, conduct and habits, discipline and care of men."[26]

Cusick died of hepatic disease "biliary obstruction," considered to be a service-related gastrointestinal disorder, on January 2, 1904, and was buried with military honors at Old Fort Niagara, only a few miles from his birthplace on the Tuscarora Indian Reservation. He was survived by his widow, Lizzie Barnes, whom he had married in 1879, and at least one child, Alton.[27] His career had led him far from his Tuscarora community, yet his path was not altogether strange to Iroquois warriors who had traveled sizable distances to fight Hurons and Ojibwas in the seventeenth century or Cherokees and Catawbas in the eighteenth century. However paradoxical his career, Cusick had followed a time-honored route to fame: the warpath. Ely S. Parker, a Seneca, was to choose a similar route and achieve even greater fame as a result of his Civil War service and his association with General Ulysses S. Grant.

PART FIVE   The Voices
of Nationhood

Introduction

The three chapters in part five focus on the Iroquois concept of nationhood. The individuals described came from three different Iroquois communities: Levi General, a Cayuga from the Six Nations Reserve; Laura Minnie Cornelius Kellogg, an Oneida from her Wisconsin reservation; and Ernest Benedict, a Mohawk from Akwesasne. Each saw/sees nationhood in a distinct way: (1) General—Iroquois political autonomy apart from Canadian and British colonialism; (2) Kellogg—Iroquois land claims in their homeland; and (3) Benedict—Iroquois sovereignty and nationhood based on free and unlimited passage across the U.S.-Canadian international boundary line. Although one of the three—Laura Minnie Cornelius Kellogg—was and is much more controversial than the others, she is nevertheless included because of her great significance in modern Iroquois history.

Much of my thinking on this subject emanates from an interview with the late Chief Julius Cook (Ernest Benedict's brother-in-law). An internationally renowned silversmith and incredibly skilled ironworker who led the Iroquois high-steel workers from the 1950s to the early 1970s, Cook, an Akwesasne Mohawk, told me of the great exploits of his workers/warriors on projects that included building the World Trade Center. While talking about one project, the construction of Buckminster Fuller's Geodesic Dome for the 1964 World's Fair in Flushing Meadows, Queens, New York, he mentioned a detail that I had not heard before: "The dome contains an extra light." To this day, I don't know whether Cook was telling a "tall tale" or revealing a secret. Curiously, I asked what he meant by the statement. The Mohawk replied, "Fuller's dome symbolized the world and each light signified a different nation. By adding an extra light in the dome, we were recognizing the nationhood of the Iroquois Confederacy."[1]

Indeed, nationhood is reinforced by the cosmology of the Iroquois. According to Iroquois beliefs, the League, symbolized by the rafters of the longhouse, was to be inevitably extended and limitless when the message of the Peacemaker was accepted by other peoples.[2] Thus the Iroquois Indians were to show the way. Their special role in the Native world was ingrained, although at times during the seventeenth and early eighteenth centuries, their methods of "extending the rafters" were not always peaceful ones.

As a result of their unique views based on their cosmology and their reading of past history, the Iroquois see themselves in a leadership role in the Native American world. The first three Native Americans to become commissioners of Indian affairs were Iroquois Indians: Ely Parker (Seneca), Robert Bennett (Oneida), and Louis Bruce, Jr. (Mohawk). Additionally, Iroquois were among the founders of the following national Indian organizations: Society of American Indians, American Indian Federation, National Congress of American Indians, National Indian Youth Council, Assembly of First Nations, and others.[3]

All three chapters included in part five reveal Iroquois involvement outside of their immediate communities. The first essay is on Levi General, better known by his Confederacy title "Deskaheh," a Cayuga chief from the Six Nations Reserve in Canada, among the most revered Iroquois patriots. He was a fearless individual who was willing to sacrifice everything for a principle, namely the maintenance of Six Nations autonomy.

Following the American Revolution, Joseph Brant, a Mohawk war chief, brought more than eighteen hundred Iroquois Loyalists to lands along the Grand River in Canada granted them by their British allies. The Haldimand Proclamation, also known as the Haldimand Deed, Patent, or Treaty, awarded six miles on each side of the river in partial recognition of the Iroquois' loss of millions of acres in their New York homeland in the aftermath of their alliance to the British Crown during the American War of Independence. The status of the Iroquois in Canada, the nature of Iroquois title, and the exact boundary of this Six Nations Reserve has been in dispute almost from the beginning.[4] Today the Six Nations Reserve has approximately forty-six thousand acres left out of the original lands set forth in the Haldimand Proclamation. The land loss of hundreds of thousands of acres has spawned land claims litigation and, more recently, an occupation of Iroquois-claimed territory in Caledonia, Ontario, an area surrounding the forty-six-thouand-acre tract.[5]

Until 1830, the British military administered Indian affairs on the reserve. Outside white administrators followed who urged a transformation of the Natives through education and Christian conversion. Even though Canada became a confederation in 1867, the overbearing British model of administration and regulation continued with the passage of the Indian Act of 1876 and its subsequent amendments right through the post–World War I period.[6] The pressure on the Six Nations Confederacy Council at Grand River during this period is clearly described by anthropologist Sally M. Weaver:

> Political pressures intensified on the chiefs in the 1880s [and onward through the 1920s] with the passage of many amendments to the Indian Act, designed to expand the duties of local band councils and to encourage elected governments on reserves. These years witnessed the council struggling to clarify its domain of power and traditional procedures of decision making. The old ideal of consensus proved impossible to achieve in some of the heated issues of the day, the major one being whether the council would agree to abide by the Indian Act in making its decisions. Discussions repeatedly occurred in council over whether the Confederacy was an autonomous local government or whether it should operate within the constraints of the Indian Act. Many chiefs argued that the act did not apply to the Six Nations because they were a sovereign nation with their own political constitution in the teachings of Deganawida[h]. Although many council decisions were made in accordance with its provisions, the council's ideological posture would remain one of denying the validity of the act.[7]

As the chapter on Deskaheh shows, Canadian efforts to push for a change in the Iroquois governing system, namely to overthrow the Six Nations Council and to suppress Indian criticism of Ottawa policies, led him to bring his cause to the international arena. Although not universally supported at Grand River, Deskaheh expressed the views of many Iroquois conservatives, namely that the Six Nations were sovereign nations that had existed before Canada had been established and that Great Britain had to abide by their commitment made in the Haldimand Treaty. Although Deskaheh's efforts were quixotic, having no chance to succeed against the overwhelming power of the British colonial system of the time, he nevertheless influenced future generations by his idealism and dogged determination to maintain Iroquois nationhood.

Deskaheh's crusade still inspires the Iroquois efforts to win international recognition to protect their autonomy and that of other indigenous peoples around the globe. The editors of *Akwesasne Notes,* founded in 1969, took Deskaheh as their role model and used his life story to bring attention to the crimes perpetrated on Native peoples. His fame was also spread by the White Roots of Peace, a largely Mohawk contingent of youngsters influenced by Ernest Benedict (see chapter 10), who toured the Americas teaching and inculcating the Peacemaker's message and Iroquois traditional values. From the early 1970s onward, delegates from Onondaga, such as the late John Mohawk, journeyed to Geneva, Switzerland, and became directly involved in the United Nations efforts to protect indigenous peoples around the world. Carrying forth the tradition of Deskaheh described in chapter 8, they helped draft the *United Nations Declaration on the Rights of Indigenous Peoples* that has been recently adopted. Moreover, the Iroquois Confederacy Council sent a delegation to support the takeover of Wounded Knee in 1973 and to help the Miskito Indians who were caught in the middle of the Contra-Sandinista War in Nicaragua in the 1980s. In 1992, Iroquois leaders attended and were active participants in the Rio Conference, a major world meeting dealing with environmental issues worldwide.[8]

Other Iroquois, such as Laura Minnie Cornelius Kellogg, voiced nationhood in other ways. To some, Kellogg was a charlatan or outlaw who fomented divisions within all of the Six Nations communities and swindled poor Indians out of hundreds of thousands of dollars in her abortive efforts to litigate their land claims. To others, Kellogg was a spellbinding orator who taught the lessons of Indian elders and told of the glory of the ancient League of the Iroquois; she pushed for tribal economic development and improvements in Indian education, and was a precursor of the contemporary Iroquois land claims movement.[9]

Kellogg was born Laura Cornelius on September 10, 1880, on the Wisconsin Oneida Indian reservation. Kellogg managed to avoid attending distant Indian boarding schools. She was educated in the 1890s at Grafton Hall, an Episcopal boarding school largely for non-Indians located at Fond du Lac, Wisconsin. In the first decade of the twentieth century, she studied at Barnard College, Cornell University, the New York School of Philanthropy (later the Columbia University School of Social Work), Stanford University, and the University of Wisconsin; however, she never received degrees from any of these institutions. One of the best Indian linguists of her generation, with a superior command of Oneida and Mohawk as well as English, Kellogg had gained national attention by 1911 because of her spellbinding oratory before Indian and non-Indian audiences. She was equally accomplished with a pen, devoting herself to writing on behalf of Progressive Era reform causes such as women's rights as well as writing political tracts on Indian issues, plays, and short stories.

In 1911 Kellogg was one of the founders of the Society of American Indians (SAI), a national reform-minded organization largely composed of highly educated Indian professionals. Later she served variously as secretary of the organization's executive committee and as vice president for education. Kellogg, however, differed from the majority of the SAI in her vehement opposition to the economic and educational policies of the Bureau of Indian Affairs (BIA). She was more confident than other organization members that Native Americans could, without assistance, transform their reservations into self-sustaining communities. After her marriage on April 22, 1912, to Orrin Joseph Kellogg, a non-Indian attorney from Minneapolis, she became more isolated from the SAI. Eventually she broke with the organization, outlining her views in *Our Democracy and the American Indian* (1920), which drew significant inspiration from the Mormon economic model of community development and survival.[10]

Kellogg and her husband spent much of the time before, during, and after World War I organizing a massive Iroquois land-claims suit. Their collection methods led to their arrests in Oklahoma (1913) and Montreal (1925), although they were never actually convicted of fraud. In 1927 the U.S. District Court dismissed their Iroquois land-claims suit, *Deere v. St. Lawrence River Power Company,* because of a lack of jurisdiction.[11] Kellogg continued to exercise influence in Indian affairs into the 1930s, but her insistence on self-sufficiency became less appealing during the New Deal era, when the government provided tribes with economic assistance and promoted Indian languages and cultural traditions. By the 1940s she was a forgotten woman who had outlived her time. According to Oneida tribal sources, she died in obscurity sometime in the late 1940s.

The Iroquois people are on both sides of what non-Indians call the U.S.-Canadian boundary, one that was formally created with their approval in 1822 by an Anglo-American commission.[12] The Akwesasne Mohawk (St. Regis) community was thus permanently divided into two—Canada and the United States—and these two outside jurisdictions have circumscribed Iroquois life ever since. Despite what the Mohawks and other Iroquois interpret as their right of free and unlimited passage across this line—they don't use the word *boundary*—one which they insist was set forth in Article III of the Jay Treaty between Great Britain and the United States, this guarantee has been ignored or rejected right up to the present time, especially by the Canadian government. Moreover, they insist that their Jay Treaty rights were reaffirmed in the Treaty of Ghent in 1814.[13]

The third portrait in part five focuses on the life of Ernest Benedict, a contemporary Mohawk who has taught two generations of youngsters about Iroquois history, sovereignty, and treaty rights. As a leading Native American journalist, educator, and activist, Benedict himself was inspired by Levi General and by Deskaheh's disciple, Chief Clinton Rickard. Benedict's life and educational efforts have been strongly motivated by where he lives, namely in the St. Lawrence River Valley, on a reservation that straddles the U.S.-Canadian boundary. Indeed, today Benedict lives on Cornwall Island in the middle of the St. Lawrence River, Mohawk territory occupied by intrusive non-Indian customs officials. From the time of the Jay Treaty in 1794 to today's era of "Homeland Security," the Mohawks have had to deal with the reality of outside powers affecting their lives: Great Britain, the United States, and Canada.

From the 1930s onward, partly as a result of Benedict's efforts as a journalist, educator, and activist, the Akwesasne Reservation has become a major communications center for Native Americans throughout the hemisphere. Akwesasne, which means "where the partridge drums," was an appropriate place to make noise and shout out signals, just as the partridge does by beating its feathers to warn of approaching danger. Benedict, as editor and publisher of a series of newspapers and the intellectual force behind the founding of *Akwesasne Notes* in 1969, warned Indian peoples in Canada and the United States of policy changes that were to affect their lives: infringements of Jay Treaty rights, plans to build the St. Lawrence Seaway, efforts to terminate the Iroquois existence and to shift federal jurisdiction to New York State control, and Canadian designs to end Indian status in the so-called "White Paper" of 1969.

As an educator, Benedict inspired Iroquois youth to learn their great history. He was the force behind the traditional troupe White Roots of Peace (although he did not direct it). Even more significantly, he was the founder of and inspiration for the North American Indian Travelling College that has taught Native American youth (not just Iroquois) traditional learning since its founding thirty-seven years ago. It is little wonder that the Assembly of First Nations, the Canadian Indian rights group that Benedict helped found, designated him as their special envoy to present Pope John Paul II with an eagle feather on his visit to North America in 1983.[14]

8

The Idealist and the Realist

Chief Deskaheh, Attorney George Decker,
and the Six Nations' Struggle to Get
to the World Court, 1921–1925

> ... and she [Rachel General, Deskaheh's daughter] tell's [*sic*] me when
> I return home, the mounties are going to put me in a jail[;] so it looks
> to me I will be treated just like Gandhi the India[n][;] they sent him to
> jail for 12 years, but they release[d] him and now he is free, because
> his people had the power stronger than the British colonies, so they
> discharged him.
>
> —Chief Deskaheh to George Decker, June 6, 1924

Scholars and popular writers in the United States, Canada, and Europe have long been fascinated by Levi General, the Cayuga chief who brought Six Nations' concerns before the League of Nations in the 1920s. General, a charismatic figure in Iroquois history, was a member of the Bear Clan. He was better known by his Cayuga chiefly title, Deskaheh (Deskáhe?), meaning "more than eleven."[1] Today many Iroquois consider Deskaheh one of the great patriots of their modern history.[2] Yet some at the Six Nations Reserve blame him for the increase in factionalism brought on by his crusade and by the severe repercussions imposed on his people by the administration of Canadian Prime Minister Mackenzie King.[3]

Levi General was born to Oneida-Cayuga parents on the Six Nations Reserve around 1873. Growing up along the Grand River, he attended grammar school there. Later he worked as a lumberjack in western New York and Pennsylvania. After hurting himself in an accident, he returned to the Six Nations Reserve to take up farming; he later married and raised four daughters. As a member of the Sour Springs Longhouse, he was known as a devout communicant and leader, and for his ability as an orator in the Cayuga language.[4]

Previous studies largely focus on Deskaheh alone and on his tireless but unsuccessful efforts to win international recognition for the Six Nations and indigenous people worldwide.[5] Not enough attention has been devoted to his attorney, George Decker, and their collaboration on the ultimate goal, namely bringing the Six Nations' legal case before the World Court, the Permanent Court of International Justice in the Hague.[6] In order to accomplish that objective, these two extraordinary men had to make their way to Geneva, Switzerland, and take the plight of the Six Nations to the international arena, to the halls of the League of Nations, an organization largely dominated by British imperial interests in the early 1920s. Although Decker stayed only a few weeks in Geneva while Deskaheh resided there for eighteen months, this effort was truly a cooperative venture between the idealistic chief and his realist "mouthpiece."

The Six Nations in Canada have had a long and illustrious history. Today six Iroquois reserves exist in Canada. A second Iroquois Confederacy (the first one centered at Onondaga near Syracuse, New York) was planted on the Grand River at Ohsweken, Ontario, by British-allied Indian refugees at the end of the American Revolution. Loyalist Iroquois led by the Mohawk war chief Joseph Brant were resettled on a vast tract of land along the Grand River recognized by the Crown in the Haldimand Grant/Patent/Treaty of 1784 and the Simcoe Deed of 1793.[7] Unlike the Iroquois Confederacy in the United States after 1783, the Iroquois Confederacy in Canada had to contend with more than one national reality: (1) the British Empire and its rigid colonial framework; and (2) Canada, which sought its independence from the British and gradually achieved it. Although Canada created its own confederation government in 1867 and received League of Nations membership in 1920, both its military and foreign policy were subject to British supervision and control until the end of Dominion status in 1949. Hence the Six Nations were faced with two levels of colonial administration that made their separate political and legal existence tenuous.[8]

Despite this dual colonial relationship, Frank Oliver, then minister of the Interior for the Canadian government, reassured the Six Nations

Council of their unique status in a memorandum dated April 5, 1909, and presented by Deskaheh to the British Colonial Office headed by Winston Churchill in 1921:

> It is the policy of the Canadian Government, as I understand it to recognize its relations with the Six Nations Indians of the Grand River as being on [a] different footing from those with any of the other Indians of Canada. The Six Nations Indians of the Grand River came to Canada under special treaty as allies of Britain, and the policy of the Canadian Government is to deal with them having that fact always in view. The system of tribal government which prevailed among the Six Nations on their coming to Canada was satisfactory to the Government at that time, and, so long as it is satisfactory to the Six Nations themselves, so long it will remain satisfactory to the Government of Canada.[9]

Unfortunately for the Six Nations, Oliver's interpretation was quickly repudiated after the conclusion of World War I. Taking advantage of growing internal dissatisfaction by Grand River community members about the conservative nature and slow decision making of the Confederacy Council, as well as other grievances, Canadian government officials pushed their policy of "Indian Advancement," one that included the replacement of the traditional government with an elected system and the extension of Canadian citizenship to the Indians on the reserve.[10]

As loyal subjects of the British Empire, the Six Nations reacted strongly to policies initiated by the Canadian Confederation in the postwar period. After all, they had recently faced the horrors of trench warfare and poison gas. In all, 292 men from Grand River served the British military effort between 1914 and 1918. Captain A. G. E. Smith, a Mohawk from the reserve and father of Jay Silverheels, the famous Hollywood actor, was the most decorated Indian soldier from Canada in World War I. Of those who enlisted, twenty-nine were killed in combat, five died of illness, and one was listed as missing in action.[11] Although some of the veterans petitioned for Canadian citizenship, others at Grand River were opposed to this move. They insisted that the Six Nations were a separate national entity allied to the British and that Canada's parliament had no right to foster citizenship on the Indians, extend its jurisdiction over reserves, and interfere with the traditional workings of Indian councils.

In a pamphlet written by Deskaheh and published in London in 1923, the chief outlined the Six Nations Confederacy Council's concerns. According to the Cayuga, the chiefs opposed the Canadian Enfranchisement Act of 1919 that was "imposing or purporting to improve Dominion rule upon neighboring Redmen"; the Royal Canadian Mounted Police invasion of Six Nations territory in December 1922 that led to the establishment of a constabulary/armed force at Grand River; the Canadian mishandling of the Six Nations' trust fund, which the Indians claimed had been "misappropriated and wasted without the consent of the Six Nations"; the Dominion government's attempts to "incite rebellion" to use as an excuse to overthrow the chiefs' council and impose a new band government "under a Dominion statute known as the Indian Act"; and the illegal seizing of personal property and, with it, the wrongful imprisonment of Six Nations residents under certain questionable Canadian penal laws.[12] The chiefs were also increasingly wary of the Canadian Indian Department's "increased scrutiny of council procedures" as well as of the application of the Dominion's Soldiers Settlement Act to the reserve. They saw the act, which provided World War I veterans low-interest loans to take up farming on assigned lands, as a major extension of Ottawa's jurisdiction over the Indians. They feared that if the Indians defaulted on these loans, the reserve's lands would be lost in foreclosures much like what was happening in the United States after the Burke Act of 1906.[13] In addition, the Iroquois objected to Canada's continuing policy of ignoring the Jay Treaty (1794) and the Treaty of Ghent (1814) between the United States and Great Britain that in their minds gave the Indians free and unlimited passage to cross the international boundary freely with their goods and belongings.[14]

On April 6, 1921, the Six Nations Confederacy Council at Grand River approved a preliminary resolution hiring George P. Decker "to accompany us [George Nash, David S. Hill, William Smith, Levi General (Deputy Speaker)] on a mission to lay our objections against enforcement of citizenship under Great Britain upon us as proposed and threatened by the Dominion of Canada." Decker was to consult about tribal rights and assist in securing "a recognition and respect for our tribal rights."[15] A month later, the full Six Nations Confederacy Council finalized its contract with the Rochester attorney. He was to accompany them to Ottawa in their "effort to secure recognition and respect at the hands of the British Government, for the right of sanctuary and independence of the Six Nations people."[16] When this mission to the Canadian capital failed to bring results, the council, at Decker's urging, sought to bring their case before the Permanent Court of International Justice. As payment, Decker was to receive a retainer of $100 and receive $25 a day plus expenses.[17]

The lawyer was no stranger to Iroquoia, an attorney with vast experience in Indian legal matters dating from the early 1890s. Decker was born in Clarkson, New York, in 1861. He read law in his father's law office in nearby Brockport and was admitted to the bar in 1884. Subsequently he moved to Rochester to practice law. There he entered Democrat politics and was rewarded by being named collector of the Port of Rochester and, shortly thereafter, first deputy attorney general of New York State and counsel for the Old Forest Fish and Game Commission. As the counsel, he helped codify the game laws of New York State, conservation regulations that severely affected Iroquois residual rights to hunt and fish on reservation and previously "ceded" lands. This role he came to regret, given that he later became the chief counsel for the Seneca Nation challenging these very laws.[18]

In 1903, Decker went into private practice in Rochester, where he worked as an attorney until his death in 1936. Around 1906, he succeeded John Van Voorhis, a former congressman from Rochester, as the attorney for the Seneca Nation. Besides fishing rights cases, Decker served the Seneca Nation and Tonawanda Senecas as counsel for their claims to Grand Island and the other smaller islands in the Niagara River; for the Cayugas in New York pushing their claims to land taken from them after the American Revolution; for Cayugas in Canada seeking international arbitration and pushing for their treaty annuities denied them from the time of the War of 1812; and the Oneidas seeking to regain much of their tribal lands and protect their remaining thirty-two-acre land base.

In 1920 Decker won *United States v. Boylan,* a major precedent-setting federal appeals court case that recognized continued Oneida tribal existence in New York and dismissed an ejectment proceeding filed against

Indian families occupying their thirty-two–acre tract in central New York.[19] Hence it was no coincidence that the Six Nations Iroquois Confederacy in Canada hired Decker as counsel less than one year after the *Boylan* decision. An attorney with ties on both sides of the border and with thirty years of experience reading treaties and statutes, Decker was extremely well informed about the Six Nations and their history.[20]

Because of his legal commitment to other Iroquois communities, Decker was to spend little time in Europe with Deskaheh; nevertheless, he cautioned his client and influenced Deskaheh. Yet the idealistic Cayuga chief frequently went off in directions that on occasions made his Rochester attorney shake his head. It should be noted that many but not all of Deskaheh's writings were either edited or penned by Decker, although the lawyer frequently checked things out with the chiefs of the Six Nations Confederacy Council when they visited Rochester, or with Deskaheh himself.[21]

Because of Deskaheh's reputation as a leader, the respect engendered by his straightforwardness, and his facility in English and in the languages of the Six Nations, he was chosen in 1921 as "Speaker of the Six Nations Council." Thus he was perceived by his people as an official ambassador, much like Indian envoys in the forest diplomacy of the eighteenth century. Despite his schooling in the ways of his people, the Cayuga chief nevertheless heavily relied on his Rochester "mouthpiece" for advice and editing abilities because his formal education was limited. With Six Nations in open rebellion against Ottawa's policies and knowing full well that Canadian officials would attempt to prevent Deskaheh's passage by withholding his Canadian passport, the Six Nations Confederacy, at Decker's suggestion, issued its own passport, a one-page document indicating that Chief Deskaheh was a member of the Six Nations, and stating his place and date of birth, physical description, and destination. Accompanied by Decker, Ambassador Deskaheh arrived in London in August 1921. Soon after, Deskaheh appeared at London's famous Hippodrome in full regalia. He also distributed a pamphlet, "Petition and Case of the Six Nations of the Grand River," addressed to King George V; however, these efforts failed.[22] On September 23, 1921, Winston Churchill, then the British undersecretary for the colonies, wrote, "as the matters submitted within the petition lie

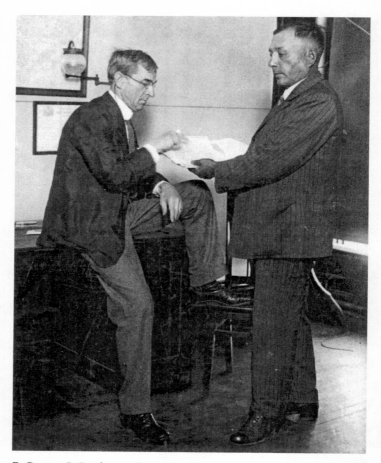

7. George P. Decker and Cayuga Chief Levi General [Deskaheh] in Decker's law office in Rochester, New York, c. early 1920s. Courtesy of Lavery Library, Special Collections, St. John Fisher College, Rochester, New York.

within the exclusive competency of the Canadian Government, it should be referred to them."[23]

Returning to North America in the fall of 1921, neither Deskaheh nor Decker was willing to abandon their crusade. Throughout the following year and into the first half of 1923, they prepared for a full-blown effort to take their legal fight before the Permanent Court of International Justice.

Before they could do that, the Six Nations had to be recognized as a nation-state by the League of Nations, as was required for any case to be brought before this world court. In December 1922, the two men traveled to Washington, D.C., and made appeals to Dutch officials for support. At the Netherlands embassy, Deskaheh, in traditional manner, made reference to the Two Row Wampum and the long relationship between the Iroquois and Hollanders that had started in the Hudson Valley in the early seventeenth century. Subsequently, the Netherlands' minister of foreign affairs, H. A. van Karnebeck, who had been president of the Assembly of the League of Nations, transmitted the Six Nations petition to the Secretary-General's office in Geneva.[24] At the same time, Deskaheh and Decker also made contact with prominent reformers in England, Scotland, France, and Switzerland, including Mrs. S. Robertson Matheson and Miss Rica Flemyng-Gill of the Aborigines Protection Society as well as members of the Swiss-based Bureau International pour la Défense des Indigenes (BIDI).[25]

Throughout 1923, Ottawa's policies intensified. Canadian officials ordered the building of Royal Canadian Mounted Police (RCMP) barracks on the Six Nations' Grand River lands. They prohibited the Indians from cutting wood for fuel while allowing non-Indians that right. The RCMPs entered and searched private homes on the reserve on the pretense that they were searching for illegal stills producing and distributing alcohol. Even Deskaheh's home on the reserve was searched and, according to Canadian officials, alcohol was seized. On several occasions the actions led to physical confrontations that resulted in beatings of several of the Indians. The Canadian government also established a one-man "commission" and sent Colonel A. L. Thompson, who had commanded Iroquois troops in the war, to investigate conditions on the reserve.[26]

The Canadian Ministry of the Interior also prevented the Six Nations Confederacy Council from receiving moneys entitled to it but held in trust by Ottawa. The Indians needed this money to mount an international campaign, provide for Deskaheh's travels, and pay Decker for his counsel. As a result, in February 1923, the Six Nations issued a bond to raise money. This $10,000 bond issue, in two denominations—one of fifty $100 bonds and one of a hundred $50 bonds—was to be paid off at 6 percent interest in Canadian legal tender in 1928 with moneys from the Indian trust fund held by Ottawa or with moneys raised by the Six Nations Council's imposition of taxes on its people at Grand River.[27]

Fearing reprisals, Deskaheh spent part of the first half of 1923 in Rochester plotting strategy with Decker. This separation from his family and from his community occurred precisely at a critical time when Ottawa was increasing pressures. There were also real Indian concerns about the Confederacy Council. To some, the chiefs were seen as out of touch with the realities of the postwar period and the daily economic needs of the community. Others saw Deskaheh's activities as a waste of time and money; they viewed the Six Nations' bond issue as a nefarious scheme to enrich the chiefs, whose council already faced allegations of corruption.[28]

By the first days of 1923, Deskaheh was now adamant about pursuing the case beyond Ottawa or London. In the popular optimism that followed the creation of the League of Nations after the Treaty of Versailles, the Iroquois, as other oppressed peoples around the world, began to see a ray of hope opening up on the international stage. Consequently, on January 24, 1923, the Cayuga chief wrote Charles Stewart, the Canadian superintendent of Indian Affairs, defiantly stating that the Six Nations would "seek elsewhere for the protection promised them by the British Crown and now denied them in its name by your government," given that Ottawa had quartered an armed force at Grand River and violated treaty rights.[29]

Decker advised Deskaheh on a variety of matters related to the Six Nations case. After carefully reading and underlining key passages of the Covenant of the League of Nations, he soon advised the chief not to seek membership in the League of Nations under Article 1 because attempting to enter as a nation-state through the front door of this international organization would be impossible, an effort that would require a greater financial commitment than the Six Nations could provide for; he added that the Iroquois would be inevitably blocked by the British and Canadian governments. He also dismissed the Covenant's Articles 10, 12, and 16 as not being applicable or realistic.[30] Instead, he focused on a backdoor strategy, namely Article 17:

> In the event of a dispute between a Member of the League and a State which is not a Member of the League, or between States not Members of

the League, the State or States not Members of the League shall be invited
to accept the obligations of membership in the League for the purposes
of such dispute, upon such conditions as the Council may deem just. If
such invitation is accepted, the provisions of Articles 12 and 16 inclusive
shall be applied with such modifications as may be deemed necessary by
the Council.[31]

In doing so, Decker hoped to get sanctions (provided for under Article 16
of the Covenant) placed on the Canadian government by the League of
Nations, which would then give the Six Nations a clear path to the Permanent Court of International Justice at the Hague.[32]

Decker had other suggestions for Deskaheh before they both set sail for
Europe. On January 2, 1923, he recommended, as a good lawyer would do,
that Deskaheh get everything in writing. Two weeks later, he urged the chief
to insist on real arbitration.[33] In a revealing letter on April 23, the vigilant
Decker, nervous about the Six Nations bond issue, urged the Cayuga chief
and the council at Grand River to keep detailed financial records with the
names and addresses of parties who bought bonds. The Rochester attorney
indicated that he expected the Dominion government to counter the Six
Nations' efforts at Geneva and that once Deskaheh reached Switzerland,
he should bring up the valuable military record of the Grand River Indians
in World War I. He also strongly recommended to Deskaheh and to the Six
Nations Council that they boycott the hearings of the Thompson commission sent by Ottawa to Grand River because the Indians were better off not
playing by Canadian officials' rules.[34]

A week later, Decker, in response to the growing complaints against
the Canadian policies brought to him by the chiefs at Grand River, wrote
Deskaheh, clearly defining the importance of the Cayuga Indian's mission
and seeing the crisis as a watershed event:

> In that same contemptuous light the [Canadian] Indian Office has for years
> looked up your [Six Nations Confederacy] Council. Sitting in its solemn
> sessions at Ohsweken, the Indian Office has considered your Chiefs as play-
> ing (by their leave) at the business of government because the Indian Office
> has paid no attention to your decisions, being content that you, as so many

children, were thus occupied. . . . If your people now yield the ground they have taken as their natural right of home and rule in their own domain, a right recognized and guaranteed by treaty with the British Crown, they will never regain that ground or be able to recall the fatal step.[35]

While advising Deskaheh, Decker also cultivated a relationship with Robert P. Skinner, the U.S. Department of State consul stationed in Paris, informing him that the chief was a political émigré intent on bringing the Six Nations' plight before the League of Nations.[36]

Even before Deskaheh and Decker sailed for Europe, Prime Minister King's government in Ottawa and the British Foreign Office attempted to discredit their efforts. On May 25, 1923, Joseph Pope, the Canadian undersecretary of state for external affairs, wrote the secretary-general of the League of Nations that the "claim" that the Six Nations were "an organized and self-governing people so as to form a political unit apart from Canada" was an "absurd one."[37] By the late summer of 1923, the British protested the Netherlands' "uncalled for interference" in the "internal affairs of Canada."[38] Later, in March 1924, in the most detailed brief filed by the Canadian government to stymie Deskaheh's crusade at Geneva, Undersecretary Pope wrote, "The Six Nations are not a state within the purview or meaning of Article 17 of the Covenant of the League of Nations" because they are "subjects" of the "British Crown domiciled within the Dominion of Canada" and thus owe a "natural debt of allegiance to His Majesty's Government." Pope added that the Six Nations are "not competent to apply for membership in the League" and that for centuries the Six Nations have not been recognized as a "self-governing people." In a clear cover-up of Ottawa's actions, the undersecretary denied that the Dominion was anti-Indian and said that it had only their welfare in mind. Labeling the Six Nations Council of Chiefs a "primitive matriarchal form of Government" that was "antiquated" at best, Pope noted that the Indians were given a certain level of local autonomy, but the ultimate supervision was with Ottawa officials. He denied that the Dominion police were placed on the reserve to harass the Indians but "for the purpose of suppressing illicit distilling and maintaining law and order generally for the protection of the law-abiding Indian populace."[39]

On July 14, 1923, Decker and Deskaheh sailed for Europe. Decker was to remain a brief time before returning to Rochester. Despite their separation, the two men frequently communicated by mail, with Decker providing advice about strategy and news of the turmoil happening at the Six Nations Reserve. Deskaheh, from his hotel room in the Hôtel des Familles in Geneva, set up the "Six Nations Bureau," printing stationery marked "The Ho-De-No-Sau-Nee Confederation of the Grand River [North America]."[40]

In the fall of 1923, Deskaheh made his first formal push for acceptance of the Six Nations' cause at Geneva. He began lecturing before a wide variety of audiences, including before five hundred devotees of Esperanto at Geneva's YMCA, the Theosophical Society, and the Swiss English Conversation Club. Working closely with journalist René Claparède of the *Bulletin pour la Defense des Indigenes* and his associate Henri A. Junot, both Christian Socialists who headed the BIDI (later renamed the "International Office for the Protection of Native Races [Colored Races])," Deskaheh generated larger and larger audiences to his talks.[41] He wrote Decker that at Geneva "these meetings at which I lectured were most successful and the halls were as crowded as possible, hundreds of people not being able to get in at all."[42] He soon began a tour of Swiss cities well beyond Geneva: Berne, Lausanne, Lucerne, Winterthur, and Zurich. In a letter to Decker on October 16, he reported that three thousand Swiss attended his presentation. Writing eighteen days later, the chief reported that his audience at Berne was "one of the biggest public meetings ever held in that city."[43]

Spurred on by these large crowds and by support from representatives of several nations—Estonia, Ireland, Panama, and Persia—the Cayuga chief resolved to push himself even more in his crusade.[44] Encouraged by the courtesies extended to him by the delegate from Norway, by the League president of the Swiss Confederation, and by Hjalmar Branting of Sweden, the president of the League of Nations' Assembly Council, Deskaheh began to believe that he was making some headway.[45] He wrote to Decker asking the attorney for copies of the Haldimand Treaty and the Simcoe Deed, as well as for Iroquois wampum belts and a peace pipe. Later he requested slides of the reserve, including a map, agricultural and dairy scenes, the schoolhouse, the baseball field, the Six Nations Council of Chiefs and Council building, and the Dominion (RCMP) barracks.

When Chief Garlow was informed by Decker about Deskaheh's request for the slides, he commented to Decker that to do so was impractical. The Rochester attorney then added that "neither of us could convince ourselves that a platform speaking campaign would be of immediate benefit within any reasonable length of time."[46]

Deskaheh misread the hoopla surrounding his presence in Switzerland. The British and Canadians had no intention of allowing him to succeed and they followed his movements at every turn. Moreover, the warm reception given to Deskaheh by the Swiss did not reflect the *real politique* of the times. The idealistic Deskaheh was now in an arena quite foreign to the Chiefs' Council at Ohsweken along the Grand River.

Throughout, Decker tried to bring Deskaheh back to reality and focus on securing Six Nations standing before the Permanent Court for International Justice under Article 17 of the Covenant of the League of Nations.[47] On October 6, 1923, he urged Deskaheh to explain to League delegates why the Six Nations had the proper status as a state and that the Indians' plight was not a domestic question.

In a letter to King Victor Emmanuel III written on December 12, 1923, Deskaheh appealed to the Italian monarch, largely a figurehead, to take up the Six Nations' cause, after receiving no reply from Prime Minister Benito Mussolini. The Cayuga chief urged the monarch to stand up to the "British lion" by joining with other nations such as Brazil, Estonia, Ireland, Panama, and Persia in allowing the Six Nations' case to be heard in the League's Assembly. Praising Mussolini's Italy as a "true democracy" with "an impartial and just attitude in international relations," Deskaheh hoped to convince Victor Emmanuel of the merits of the Iroquois' case against Canada and Great Britain. Turned away in a brief interview with Italian League envoy Bonin Longare, Deskaheh implied in that letter that such impudent action was worthy of "Japan, but never the style of Italy or France." Thus, in the manner of the forest diplomacy of the eighteenth century that the Iroquois had used to survive in the wars between England and France, a chief resorted to playing off the Great Powers—this time France and Italy against England and Japan![48]

But the world had changed, and decisions were now being made not at Onondaga, Albany, or Montreal, but by the British Foreign Office in

London and its colonial surrogates in Ottawa. Nine days earlier, the Rochester attorney informed the chief that the "Redcoats," namely the RCMPs, were surrounding the council house at Ohsweken.[49] Exactly three weeks later, he bluntly wrote that Deskaheh's extensive lecturing throughout Switzerland had proven "of little immediate effectiveness."[50]

On January 10, 1924, Deskaheh wrote the foreign ministers of Panama, Estonia, and Ireland, thanking them for their support. A separate letter was sent to Prince Arfa-ad-Dovleh, the Persian first delegate to the League of Nations, who was the Six Nations' most ardent supporter in Geneva.[51] On the same day, the chief appealed to Council President Branting of Sweden: "In the name of the Six Nations Indian Confederation (Iroquois) of the Grand River in North America. I have the honour to respectfully ask the Council of the League of Nations to give me an opportunity of being heard on the subject of sovereignty of our country, recognized and confirmed by treaty."[52] Despite Deskaheh's optimism that Branting would be powerful enough with Prince Arfa's support to bring the Six Nations' case under Article 17 before the League of Nations in March 1924, the British officials in the Foreign Office torpedoed this hearing by behind-the-scenes pressure on the governments of Estonia, Panama, and Persia, calling these nations' actions on behalf of the Six Nations "impertinent interference" in the internal affairs of the British Empire.[53]

Naïve about the Great Powers in the postwar period, the Cayuga chief was also clearly a poor judge of character. He viewed the kindness of strangers as their commitment to the Six Nations cause. Indeed, after moving into the Hôtel des Familles, he was soon surrounded by an entourage of hangers-on. Some were utopians, believing in the stated ideals of the League of Nations and looking at Deskaheh as the epitome of the "noble savage," the victim that had to be shown the way by whites in paternalistic fashion in order to attain Western justice. Intrigued by the "Red Man" of the North American forest, they had read too much of Rousseau's writings. Others espoused a political cause and hitched their wagon to the Six Nations' crusade. Still others sought their own fame and fortune by attempting to con the chief and hijack his cause.

Determined reformers with high ideals, his faithful supporters in the United Kingdom—Mrs. S. Robertson Matheson in Scotland and Miss Rica

Flemyng-Gill in England—were also naïve, simply believing that appeals
to King George V or to Prime Ministers J. Ramsay McDonald in England
or Mackenzie King in Canada would work. Mrs. Matheson, just before
Deskaheh's visit to Geneva, recommended that the Six Nations Council
request that Prime Minister McDonald put the issue before the British
cabinet and investigate Canada's treatment of the Indians. This strategy
had already failed in 1921, when Decker and Deskaheh visited London.[54]
Largely unaware of Six Nations history and worldview, W. H. Stoker, a
"bossy" British attorney working for these two women and for the Aborigines Protection Society in London, suggested in October 1923 that the Six
Nations apply to the League as a "minority," because he and an associate
viewed the Six Nations' plight as a "domestic question" for Great Britain and Canada, not as "an international question." Because the Iroquois
view themselves as nation(s), not minorities, the Cayuga chief was offended
by the attorney's comments. From then on, Deskaheh discounted Stoker's
opinion.[55] Even though Stoker made an attempt to stop the RCMP actions
at Grand River by corresponding with Prime Minister King, Deskaheh
never again trusted him and viewed the British attorney as a political spy.
Nearly a year later he wrote, "I do realy [sic] think that Mr. Stoker is 99
percent no good. I have no faith in him nor a hair of it."[56]

Although deeply involved in Deskaheh's crusade and sincere in help-
ing the chief foster the Six Nations cause, the BIDI, led by Claparède and
Junot, had another agenda as well. As Christian Socialists, they were committed to limiting the influence of the League Against Imperialism and
Colonial Oppression, what they labeled as a "Bolshevik" organization, at
Geneva.[57] Another Deskaheh "adviser" was Professor Gilbert Murray, who
wrote articles for *Headway,* the journal of the League of Nations Union in
London. Murray was a defender of the mandates system, the neocolonial
administration installed by the Great Powers after World War I.[58]

Then there was Dr. Scott Huntington, an eye specialist who claimed to
be an attorney from Seattle, who met the chief at Basel. Huntington knew
little about the Six Nations, yet he served as Deskaheh's adviser and trans-
lator in December 1923 and January 1924, and sought power of attorney
to legally represent the Six Nations case! In a series of letters from December 1923 to January 14, 1924, Decker went after Huntington, suggesting

that Deskaheh hire a Dutch lawyer in his place, because a Hollander could be of more valuable service at the Hague.[59] Huntington had suggested to Deskaheh that the chief appeal to the Vatican. Decker responded, calling the suggestion "absurd," one that might even "offend your own people [Longhouse traditionalists]" back at Grand River. The Rochester attorney apologized for being so frank about Huntington and hoped for success in Geneva. He reiterated his concern about Huntington, telling Deskaheh not to mistake the eye doctor's great language abilities (he was fluent in several languages) for true friendship. Decker urged the chief to write him "over your own signature, and if you must write me confidentially, without his [Huntington's] assisting on the typewriter, I wish you would."[60]

In the same letter, Decker, at the urging of Chief David Hill, warned Deskaheh about mailing his correspondence home, fearing that the Canadians were intercepting and opening letters. He also cautioned Deskaheh not to travel to England because the Cayuga could be arrested, according to a message sent to him by Chief Chauncey Garlow. The attorney was also taken aback by what appeared to be Deskaheh's abandonment of seeking justice under Article 17 and filing under Article 1 of the League Covenant, namely a direct Six Nations request for admission to the League.[61]

Preparing for the March 1924 meeting of the League of Nations Assembly in Paris, the two men corresponded about strategies. Deskaheh attempted to secure Decker's legal services in Geneva, but the Rochester attorney was busy with Seneca legal matters. Decker discussed the approaching meeting of the Anglo-American arbitration commission that was set to meet in Washington in January 1925 to focus on the failure of New York State to pay Canadian Cayugas' annuity moneys since 1811; he urged the chief to recommend that the Cayugas "withdraw all authority of Great Britain to go on with the claims" given that the British would probably not allow any moneys awarded to be released to the Indians.[62]

When the League refused to put the Six Nations' complaint on the March agenda, Decker consoled the chief, suggesting that a new government in England might eventually change things. By this time Deskaheh was suffering from a heavy cold that would later worsen, become bronchitis, and eventually lead to pneumonia. Although now informed by Stoker and others that his cause was hopeless, he continued to push onward.

Working with Claparède, he distributed a second pamphlet, "Chief Des-kaheh: Tells Why He Is Over Here Again," a further indictment of the policies of the Canadian Indian Office and the lack of response by the British colonial secretary to previous Six Nations' protests. Decker helped Deskaheh prepare and edit a new manuscript, "The Six Nations: A Sovereign State," that he hoped to present to the League at its next session. Chief Garlow provided Decker with $500 that the attorney forwarded to Geneva.[63] Hoping to comfort his client-friend, Decker sent Deskaheh a copy of Mohandas Gandhi's writings.[64]

On August 13, 1924, Decker, concerned with events transpiring at Grand River, admitted that the effort to go before the Permanent Court of International Justice had failed. Indeed, the attorney feared for Deskaheh's safety. Five days later, Decker wrote Deskaheh that his return through England would lead to his arrest, that he should not sail directly to a Canadian port, and that his safety depended on his disembarking in New York City and then making his way across the state into Canada. As a diversion, Decker wrote about his attendance at the Seneca picnic at Allegany. To cheer up his client-friend, he reported that Chief Hill and the Confederacy Council of Chiefs were unanimously behind Deskaheh's efforts, however unsuccessful they were. He suggested that Canada was like a stupid calf: "If a calf is given enough rope it hangs itself." He then went on to provide a laundry list of Canadian failures in its Indian policies, including squandering of the Six Nations' trust fund and providing abysmal schooling for Indian children. He reiterated his belief that the Six Nations were unlike any other community in Canada, given that they had always maintained a degree of self-government since 1784.[65]

Increasingly ill and fearful of Canadian intentions at Grand River, Deskaheh made last-ditch efforts in the fall and early winter of 1924 to bring the Six Nations cause into the world arena at Geneva. In hearing of his people's troubles on the reserve, he became even more outspoken; however, his was a lost cause. On September 17, 1924, Prime Minister King and Governor-General Lord Byng of Vimy signed an Order-in-Council mandating the replacement of the Six Nations Confederacy Council at Ohsweken with an elected band council under Canada's Indian Act. The RCMPs invaded the council house, seized the sacred wampum belts, and dissolved the traditional government, replacing it with an elective system, although the Six Nations Confederacy Council of Chiefs continued to operate outside of the Canadian government's purview.[66] Deskaheh also rejected a proposal made by a Swiss attorney who urged him to accept one Canadian jurist, not British, to arbitrate, and that the Six Nations choose another jurist. In reply, Deskaheh insisted that he could not negotiate the point because he had to have the full consent of the Six Nations Confederacy Council.[67] Deskaheh made one last appeal directly to King George V. Documenting the Canadian efforts at undermining self-rule at the reserve, Deskaheh assured the king of Six Nations loyalty to the Crown and urged the monarch to intervene on his people's behalf.[68]

Before Deskaheh departed, he left a copy of the following proclamation at the League of Nations' offices in Geneva:

> And whereas the said Six Nations as a peace-loving and law-abiding, autonomous and independent state are desirous of availing themselves of the Hague Convention of 1899 and 1907 for the pacific settlement of international disputes, now therefore I do by these presents proclaim and it is witnessed by my signature and seal hereunto duly fixed that the people of the Six Nations hereby adhere and by this Act will hereafter adhere to all the rules and regulations now made or to be made under the auspices of, and by virtue of, the said conventions and will do all things necessary in order to further the undertakings of such conventions for the purpose of the pacific settlement of international disputes, and the due execution of any award made thereunder.[69]

Decker then wrote to Robert Skinner, his old contact in the U.S. State Department, notifying him that Deskaheh needed to be provided a visa to land at a U.S. port, because he had no valid Canadian passport and "has political reasons for not desiring to land at a Canadian port." Because the chief was scheduled to appear before an Anglo-American Cayuga Arbitration hearing in Washington in January 1925. Decker made clear to the consul general the urgency of bypassing standard procedures.[70]

On January 3, 1925, Deskaheh, in broken health and spirit, left Geneva. He had become a political émigré across an international line that intruded on his people's lives. Much like Gandhi, he had created a problem for the mighty British Empire. Although not martyred by an assassin's bullet as was the case of the Mahatma, his crusade for self-determination for Six Nations people had weakened him, contributing to his death from pneumonia on June 27, 1925. Much like Gandhi, Deskaheh was a nonviolent advocate of the peaceful resolution of conflicts between nations.[71] He idealistically looked to the international arena for justice, much like his more famous contemporary in India.

On his return, Deskaheh went to live in Rochester, no coincidence given that his attorney-friend was nearby. Decker previously had found his Oneida clients work in the city after the case of *United States v. Boylan*.[72] Deskaheh frequently consulted with Decker and spoke before two Masonic lodges in western New York. In full regalia and holding the original Haldimand Treaty on parchment, he kept pressing the cause that had led him to the League of Nations.[73] On March 10, 1925, he made his last speech, one made on the local Rochester radio station. In words that are frequently reprinted by the Iroquois, he said, "Over in Ottawa, they call that Policy 'Indian Advancement.' Over in Washington, they call it 'Assimilation.' We who would be the helpless victims say it is tyranny."[74]

Deskaheh's health worsened and he soon afterward moved into Chief Rickard's home on the Tuscarora Reservation near Lewiston, New York.[75] On June 27, the chief died. His body was transported to the Six Nations Reserve and his funeral was held on June 30. A one-mile funeral cortege of two thousand mourners followed his casket to the cemetery after Sour Spring Longhouse ceremonies. Two days later, Chief Rickard wrote to Decker, "He was one of the bravest men I ever saw. . . . There wasn't a dry eye in the funeral service."[76]

9

Designing Woman

Minnie Kellogg

Minnie Kellogg, born Laura Miriam Cornelius, was one of the most important and tragic figures in recent American Indian history. She influenced important events in the national arena as well as in the local Iroquois communities in Canada and the United States. Kellogg was one of the founders of the Society of American Indians and of the modern Iroquois land-claims movement. Every scholar doing fieldwork among the Iroquois, from the time of J. N. B. Hewitt onward, encounters her name and her legacy in documents on Iroquois politics, land claims, religion and revitalization movements, and Indian views of Washington and Ottawa policies.[1]

Kellogg was a dynamic speaker who could sway large audiences. She was the dominant personality in a major Iroquois secular movement that had revitalizationist overtones. She conformed to what the anthropologist William N. Fenton has observed about Iroquois leadership:

> The prophet who would succeed among the Iroquois must speak in ancient tongues, he must use the old words, and he must relate his program to the old ways. He is a conservator at the same time he is a reformer. All of the Iroquois reformers have been traditionalists. This is one of the reasons that Iroquois culture has endured so long.[2]

In an extraordinary way, Kellogg could transcend her highly educated background to convey her ideas to largely rural and uneducated Indians. To white audiences and to her well-educated colleagues in the Society of American Indians, she frequently quoted Franz Boas, G. Stanley Hall, and

William James to support her points about Indian race equality and mental capacities. To reservation communities, she spoke in "ancient tongues," and with traditional metaphors, of the glory of the eighteenth-century League of the Iroquois, which she attempted to reconstruct; of the lessons of Indian elders and their wisdom; and, of course, of the overriding concerns of Indian people to win back their lands.

Despite her exceptional gifts—a brilliant mind, beauty, self-confidence, unusual oratorical abilities, and her educational attainments—Kellogg is also the most controversial Iroquois leader of the twentieth century. It is clear from her many bizarre involvements that either she misused her prodigious talents or was incapable of carrying out all the extraordinary designs she had for her people's betterment. Although acknowledged today as a major force and as a brilliant person, she is accused by Iroquois elders of swindling them out of hundreds of thousands of dollars in her abortive efforts to bring their land claims to fruition; of creating debilitating divisions that impeded tribal development for decades; and even of contributing to the loss of her own tribal land base at Oneida, Wisconsin, through her schemes that ultimately impoverished Indians.[3] Moreover, though never convicted of a felony, she was arrested on at least four separate occasions on a series of charges relating to her activities. Unfortunately, because of her questionable ethics and her inability to carry out what she espoused, Kellogg is blamed today for all that went wrong in Iroquois history during the interwar period from 1919 to 1941. Consequently, her life has the sense of tragedy; she wanted to use her extraordinary abilities to help her people but ended up being accused by them as a common outlaw.[4]

Kellogg's family was, in part, a major reason for her leadership in Iroquois affairs. Laura Miriam Cornelius, the daughter of Adam Poe and Cecilia Bread Cornelius, was born on the Oneida Indian Reservation in Wisconsin on September 10, 1880. She was a descendant of those Indians who had left New York in the 1820s and 1830s. She was related to both Chief Daniel Bread and Elijah Skenandore, two of the major Oneida political leaders of the nineteenth century.[5]

Kellogg was born into a society in cultural flux, people crying out for a prophet. The uprooting of the Oneidas from New York contributed to structural changes in politics and society. Politically divided into three

8. Laura Minnie Cornelius Kellogg, Oneida activist, 1911. From *Report of the Executive Council of the Proceedings of the First Annual Conference of the Society of American Indians*, Washington, D.C., 1912.

separate parties since their days in New York—the First and Second Christian and Orchard parties—the Oneidas replicated their divisive history on arriving in Wisconsin in the 1820s and 1830s. Other changes were also evident. By the end of the nineteenth century, clan affiliation had become a less important factor in Oneida politics. In the same period, encouraged by outside white influences and missionaries especially, the Oneida social structure became patrilineal, evolving from the traditional Iroquois matrilineal model.[6]

Even before the Dawes General Allotment Act of 1887, the Wisconsin Oneidas were faced with uncontrolled timber stripping of their lands, serious soil erosion, low leasing arrangements, and nearby off-reservation taverns plying the Indians with alcohol. On June 13, 1892, the 65,000-acre Oneida Reservation was finally allotted. In 1906, after the Burke Act, Oneidas began receiving fee patents, and their lands soon became subject to taxation, resulting in new and impossible tax burdens, foreclosures, and subsequent tax sales of property. Land speculators, sometimes in collusion with a few tribal members, encouraged Oneidas, largely uneducated rural people, to fall into debt by borrowing money or by mortgaging their homesteads to buy musical instruments, carriages, and livestock—all of which they generally did not need. Wisconsin Oneida homes were subsequently lost through their inability to pay back loans and in outright swindles, some perpetuated by a few unscrupulous Oneidas themselves.[7] Hence, by 1934, the Oneidas owned less than ninety acres; they had lost more than 95 percent of their lands under the allotment policies of the United States.[8]

Although Kellogg's upbringing occurred in a society in which clan importance and gender roles had been significantly transformed by outside pressures, her self-assuredness was based, in part, on ancient Iroquois respect for clan mothers and women's overall major involvement in behind-the-scenes political activities. Iroquois women traditionally did not generally make their mark through oratory, and they did not usually address meetings of the League as Kellogg did later in her life. Nevertheless, women could and did speak at local councils. According to one anthropologist, "the strength of the League and of the women in it also depended on its local character." She added, "That is, although intertribal meetings were held and were occasions of great importance and solemnity, decisions were made and approved on a local basis, thus allowing for the influence of women who tended to remain in the villages."[9] As a highly educated woman and one familiar with Iroquois history, she used traditionalism at all stages of her remarkable career to establish her right to speak, to win over audiences, and to generate political influence and power.

Unlike many of her contemporaries on the reservation, Cornelius managed to avoid the usual educational route to distant Indian boarding schools at Carlisle and Hampton. She was educated at Grafton Hall, a private boarding school at Fond du Lac administered by the Episcopal Diocese. The school was within sixty miles of her home at Seymour, Wisconsin, and provided a setting that included mostly non-Indian women, which was far different from the segregated regimen of military discipline in far-off Indian boarding schools.[10] Later in her life, in condemning Indian education under the auspices of the Bureau of Indian Affairs, Cornelius reflected on her education and credited her father for his "wonderful foresight" in sending her to Grafton Hall.

> I had been preserved from the spirit-breaking Indian schools. . . . My psychology, therefore, had not been shot to pieces by that cheap attitude of the Indian Service, whose one aim was to 'civilize' the race youth, by denouncing his parents, his customs, his people wholesale, and filling the vacuum they had created with their vulgar notions of what constituted civilization. I had none of those processes of the Bureaucratic mill in my tender years, to make me into a 'pinch-back white man.' Had it been imposed upon me, I am certain something would have happened to it then.[11]

After receiving a classical education, she was graduated with honors in 1898. Interestingly, her graduation essay, "The Romans of America," was a study that traced the "analogy between the Iroquois Confederacy, or Six Nations, to the ancient Roman Empire."[12] One writer has commented that her abilities were inherited and that her success at Grafton was attributable to her noteworthy ancestry. An equally important conclusion is that her pride in her Iroquois roots provided her with a strong measure of self-confidence that served her well all her life.

This pride in her Indian upbringing was frequently revealed. She was unquestionably one of the best orators among the Iroquois of her generation, speaking effectively in both English and Oneida. She is credited with being the best native speaker of her generation.[13] The ability to converse in proper syntax bestows an Iroquois with the power to influence and to impress audiences that is still used for political advantages among the Six Nations. This was especially true at Oneida, Wisconsin.[14] It is evident in early observations of Kellogg made by others as well as in her own writings that she was both aware of Iroquois oral traditions and proud of her Iroquois heritage.[15]

Her later education included two years in Europe, funded in part by her own performances as a "show Indian," and study at a series of major institutions of higher education: Stanford University, Barnard College, the New York School of Philanthropy (later the Columbia University School of Social Work), Cornell University, and the University of Wisconsin. She attended Barnard for no more than a year and a half but made a distinct mark on her colleagues. Kellogg wrote a short story for the college's literary magazine.[16] She also inspired the following comment in the *Mortarboard,* the college yearbook: "Her heart's desire, to uphold the honor of her ancient race."[17] Hence it is clear that during these years she had already determined to work on behalf of her people. Whether as a result of an unstable personality, her strong Progressive muckraking style, or her fervent advocacy of women's rights that led on one occasion to an arrest during a protest demonstration, Kellogg drifted from one college to another in the twelve years following her graduation from Grafton Hall.[18]

Like many Iroquois before and after her, Kellogg attempted to speak for indigenous peoples as a whole. This ethnocentric characteristic of expression has frequently led Iroquois to presume to voice the concerns of all Native Americans in international convocations from New York to Geneva, Switzerland. Consequently, during her career, she became involved not only in the affairs of the Six Nations but also in those of the Blackfeet, Brothertown, Cherokee, Crow, Delaware, Huron, Osage, and Stockbridge Indians.[19] Her crusading and relentless agitation, which led to trouble with the law and to arrests in Oklahoma in 1913 and in Colorado in 1916, also prompted her to assist reform-minded Indians in founding the Society of American Indians in 1911. It may be suggested that Kellogg's role was no mere coincidence but a cultural manifestation given that Iroquois on both sides of the United States–Canadian border frequently have been at the forefront of new Indian nationalist movements in the twentieth century.[20]

As politically savvy people with strong beliefs in tribal sovereignty and treaty rights inculcated from childhood, the Iroquois became involved in nationalist organizations very early. Among the original theorists behind the Society of American Indians were three Iroquois: Arthur C. Parker, Dennison Wheelock, and Laura Miriam Cornelius Kellogg.

The Society of American Indians, originally called the American Indian Association, held the second organizing meeting of its executive committee at the Kellogg home in Seymour, Wisconsin, on June 20 and 21, 1911. The meeting was attended by two prominent Oneida attorneys, Chester P. Cornelius and Dennison Wheelock, as well as by four other members of the organization. The participants discussed general rules of the organization; planned their first national convention at Columbus, Ohio, in October; arranged for publicity and invitations to tribal delegates; established a constitution and bylaws committee; and issued a statement outlining the objectives of the society.[21]

Although she served as secretary of the executive committee and later as vice president on education, Kellogg's views of Indian progress apparently were incompatible with those of the American Indian Association as a whole. Although she was in total agreement with the association's belief in the Indians' ability and inherent right to "defend all rights and just claims of the race" and to promote Indian dignity through self-help, she disagreed completely with the paternalistic expression drafted at her home: "While the Association and its founders most sincerely appreciate the splendid elements and achievements of the old-time Indian culture and the methods by which early conditions were met, it realizes most keenly the inefficacy of these methods in meeting the conditions of modern times."[22] Kellogg's speeches indicate that she broke with the society over this point. Unlike white reformers and even many members of the Society of American Indians, she wanted to blend the wisdom of the elders of the reservation into the education of Indian children. Writing in the *Quarterly Journal* of the Society of American Indians in 1913, she insisted, in language that is quite modern in tone, that

> culture is but the fine flowering of real education, and it is the training
> of the feeling, the tastes and the manners that make it so. When we stop

to think a little, old Indian training is not to be despised. The general tendency in the average Indian schools is to take away the child's set of Indian notions altogether, and to supplant them with the paleface's. There is no discrimination in that. Why should he not justly know his race's own heroes rather than through false teaching think them wrong? Have they not as much claim to valor as Hercules or Achilles? Now I do not say here that everything he has natively is right or better than the Caucasian's. Not at all, but I do say that there are noble qualities and traits and a set of literary traditions he had which are just as fine and finer, and when he has these for the sake of keeping a fine spirit of self-respect and pride in himself, let us preserve them.[23]

After citing the anthropologist Franz Boas as her authority on the equal mental capacity of Indian and Caucasian, she added that the Indians' power of abstraction, oratorical abilities, and sense of humor were three areas that could be incorporated into current Indian education in the United States. Unlike many of her Indian contemporaries in the Progressive Era, she honored the wisdom of ancient tribal leaders and their lessons inculcated in childhood as a vital reality in her life.[24]

By 1911, the white press compared Cornelius and other early leaders of the society to Booker T. Washington in their calls for self-help and the uplift of the "Indian race." After the society's Columbus meeting in 1911, the *New York Tribune* hailed Cornelius as a scholar, a social worker, "one of the moving spirits in the new American Indian Association," and "a woman of rare intellectual gifts."[25] Yet, because of her sharp break with the organization's leadership, her role in the Society of American Indians was peripheral at best. She emphasized the need for self-sufficiency and independence—much like the view from the modern-day Onondaga Longhouse—although her own model for this endeavor was based on the Mormons. Much of her rhetoric paralleled the self-help plans of the age; however, Kellogg went against the grain in her elaborate designs for reservation development and in her view of reservations and reservation Indians as generally positive.

To Kellogg, the ideal for the Indian was not simply the imitation of white society but the creation of planned industrial villages, which she considered a "hard-headed, practical scheme which is not dependent upon charity to carry it out."[26] Why should Indians, she asked, model themselves on a white society that produced child labor, sweatshops, unsanitary and unsafe working conditions, and concentration of capital and political power in the hands of a few? In her speech at the society's first convention in 1911, she advocated transforming reservations into self-governing industrial villages (based on the Garden City idea) by using the Mormon concept of communal cooperation for economic development and organizing along Rochdale lines with a provision prohibiting any individual from obtaining 51 percent of the voting stock. What Kellogg meant was that Indians, through their own hands, would contribute their labor to the community's improvement. Just as the Mormons bypassed the rake-off of "the contractor, the banker, the bonding company and the promoter," the Indians would also succeed without money because they would also capitalize labor. The community itself would set the rules and ensure against laziness by fixing the amount of labor required of its tribal members.[27]

Kellogg insisted that industrial organization for the Indians should be designed "along the lines of organization for himself and by himself—organization of those things which shall control his livelihood and which shall be based on a special consideration for his needs."[28] Instead of forcing him to become a white man, give the Indian the skills and opportunity to transform his reservation into a self-sustaining community. After all, she maintained, "I cannot see that everything the white man does is to be copied."[29] The key was to "reorganize the opportunities of the Indian at *home* [her emphasis]." The Indian possessed many assets—land, labor, the devotion to outdoor life. The conditions of labor in the outside world were inferior to those conditions that the Indian could establish for himself. As a Progressive Era reformer, Kellogg insisted that with the help of experts, development of Indian reservations could be achieved. They would design the best industry adapted for each reservation, which would take into account Indian diversity. The townsite for the "industrial village" would be chosen next and would serve all the people equitably. In a rather typical Iroquois way, Cornelius concluded that the Indian could teach the white man a thing or two and "avoid the things that are killing off the majority of the laboring population in the country among the whites."[30]

Kellogg's designs for the Iroquois were equally intriguing. In one of her first plans, the "Cherry Garden" experiment, she developed what she claimed was a strategy of self-sufficiency for her Oneida tribesmen. The rich cherry-growing area of their Wisconsin homeland was to be the economic salvation of those poor Indians. Through the hard work and cooperative efforts of the Oneidas, who rarely agreed on anything because of serious factional discord, Kellogg hoped to develop a large tract that would transform her people into "self-supporting and prosperous" members of society.[31] Despite her significant work, Kellogg's role in the society ended abruptly, and after 1913 she was no longer listed as a member of the organization.[32] The historian Hazel W. Hertzberg has perceptively observed that her ideas about reservation development at the 1911 convention may have disturbed those Indians in the society who believed that the reservation was a "transitional stage in Indian development."[33]

Her marriage in 1912 to Orrin Joseph Kellogg, a Minneapolis attorney, appears to have further alienated her from the society's leadership, although little information is available about her husband except his claim to distant Seneca ancestry and his relationship to his wife's Indian concerns. In 1913, the Kelloggs were arrested in Oklahoma on charges of fraud and for impersonating federal officials in their investigations of the Osage oil leases and the Indian school at Pawhuska. At the time, they had the support of Thomas Sloan, the noted attorney and officer of the Society of American Indians, who had asked them to help him in his capacity as a special examiner hired by a congressional committee.[34] Although not convicted in Oklahoma, the Kelloggs' overall political activism and involvement seem to have generated scorn from society members employed in the Indian service and from conservatives in the society. It is also apparent that Minnie Kellogg, as she was known, was never a follower and had difficulty working with other vocal members in the society whose programs she questioned. Although she remained active in Indian affairs, lobbying before Congress during the Wilson administration, her involvement in Indian nationalist organizations ended by World War I.[35]

In 1920, Kellogg published her major work, *Our Democracy and the American Indian: A Comprehensive Presentation of the Indian Situation as It Is Today*. Here she once again revealed her sharp differences with other Indian critics of Indian policy. The so-called "Lolomi plan," which had been outlined as early as 1916 in testimony before Congress, suggests that Indian affairs be separated from the everyday seedy side of hack politicians and their politics as well as from the corrupt and inefficient administration of the BIA. The management of Indian affairs, she insisted, should be placed in the hands of a gigantic trust headed by men of national and international standing who would serve as experts and consultants in the administration, development, and protection of Indian wealth.[36] The reform sentiment of the Progressive Era, with its emphasis on city managers and the gospel of efficiency, was now applied to the development of Indian reservations.

In the book, she leveled her major criticism against the Indian Service in the United States. Yet she also worked out a plan of action, unlike her radical Indian contemporary Dr. Carlos Montezuma, an acculturated Yavapai who merely called for the abolition of the BIA. Although the plan called *Lolomi*—a Hopi word meaning "perfect goodness be upon you"—was largely a diatribe against the BIA, it built on her earlier designs for self-sufficiency. She blamed the Indian Bureau's "school for sycophants" for packing Indian tribal councils, "destroying natural leadership in the race," pauperizing Indians, and fostering dependence.[37] In using the Iroquois Confederacy, of course, as her model for pre-BIA Indian independence and self-sufficiency, she insisted that "Indians have been denied their appreciation of their *place in history,* their noble primitive stock and their advanced philosophy of life" by a "Bureau who wishes to create factions among the tribes" and whose "ware-house Indians" are its executors. "Our solidarity will be threatened by them just so long as you do not wake up and refuse to allow them to represent you."[38] She reserved most of her ammunition for her attacks on BIA-managed boarding schools, which she insisted were injurious to Indians, destroying individuality, exploiting student labor, and producing a subservient type of Indian. In their place, the Lolomi plan would carry the "school to the field or the home. Not being dictated to by politics, it will secure only sympathetic instructors who know what they are about and whose service terminates when they cannot produce the desired results."[39] Sycophants and employees of the Indian Service who managed to obtain their positions after losing their footing in other areas would be rooted out. Instead of pauperizing Indians and fostering dependence by "making a pinchback white-man of the Indian,"—one of her favorite phrases—the Lolomi plan would help create self-sufficiency among reservation communities by adopting her earlier plan of synthesizing the Mormon model of cooperative labor and organization, the capitalization of labor, and the Garden City plan.[40]

Kellogg reserved her greatest design of all for the Iroquois. It involved her efforts in the 1920s and 1930s to resurrect and reconstruct the structure and operation of the eighteenth-century League of the Iroquois. Again advocating the Lolomi policy, she envisioned the transformation of the Iroquois reservations into self-governing, thrifty, industrious, and self-sustaining settlements with comfortable houses. In the process, Indian self-respect would be achieved through a concerted effort to restore "the pride of the Indian heritage, and to instill in the red man the proud consciousness of his race."[41] At the heart of her plan was the effort to win back between six and fifteen million acres of land, which she insisted was taken fraudulently from the Iroquois by New York State and by land speculators between 1784 and 1838. Her strategy was to win a favorable decision in the courts, which would allow the Iroquois a sizable restored land base for economic development and for the political restoration of the League's ancient greatness.[42]

One of the more interesting sidelights of this episode was Kellogg's rather strange relationship with J. N. B. Hewitt, the Iroquois ethnologist of the Smithsonian Institution's Bureau of American Ethnology. From 1920 to 1932, although each distrusted the other, both sought information and other favors relating to their particular research. Hewitt, attempting to complete a manuscript on the laws and ritual of the League of the Iroquois, needed Kellogg's help in gaining access to informants and information on reservations. Kellogg viewed Hewitt as a valuable contact, asking him for manuscripts about the League and attempting to win his support for her plans by writing to him about her ideas for a comparative study of the Iroquois languages and for an Iroquois grammar and dictionary. She frequently invited him to use her homes at Oneida, Wisconsin, and later Nedrow, New York, as bases for his fieldwork; she even went so far as to suggest her willingness to take care of his living expenses while he was at Onondaga. To Kellogg, in need of legitimizing both her efforts and her power, Hewitt, the leading scholar on the Iroquois of his generation, was an essential ingredient in her schemes.[43]

Hewitt, of Tuscarora ancestry, "played her along" for twelve years and consciously tried to tread lightly as an anthropologist working among highly divided native societies. Nevertheless, he eventually dismissed her grand design to resurrect the Iroquois League. He insisted that her plan was impractical and was very critical of some of her efforts, which he thought bastardized the ancient traditions of the Six Nations. He took strong exception to her stationery listing George Thomas as "presiding sachem" of the "League of the Six Iroquois Nations" because, Hewitt informed her, the proper word for Thomas's title was *royae'r* and not the Algonquian word *sachem*.[44] He also objected to the listing of six tribal organizations within Kellogg's league, which he maintained could not "claim or be regarded as the source and repository of the organic laws and authority of each separate tribe. Without such tribal organizations it is a mockery of words to speak of the League of the Six Nations of New York at the present time." He also condemned her for using in her stationery the phrase "Grand Council Fire, Indian Village, Onondaga National Domain, North America"; he believed that the use of the word *domain* was incorrect because the federal-Iroquois Treaty of Canandaigua of 1794 made the land in question a reservation in accordance with the "harsh implications of the Treaty of Fort Stanwix." In conclusion, he insisted that her "illustrated letterhead has a sinister import to me because it portrays as a reality the mere phantom of what has been, is not now, and long ago had gone into perdition."[45]

Kellogg was able to win support for her plans for the Iroquois from diverse communities because her activities emphasized solidarity with traditionalist politics, culture, and values. Traditional approaches to Iroquois medicine and attempts to resurrect the clan system were also encouraged. Through her understanding of the symbols of Iroquois existence, she established her headquarters at the Onondaga Reservation, the historic capital, in order to reconstruct the old offices of the Confederacy League. Despite Hewitt's pessimism and scorn, Kellogg and her party were able to gain influence and power on every reservation from Oneida, Wisconsin, to Akwesasne. Kellogg went so far as to revive Oneida chiefly titles associated with matrilineal lineages, to bring Longhouse leaders from Onondaga to Wisconsin to conduct a council, and to "arrange" a visit to New York by Iroquois traditionalists for the purpose of overseeing the installation of nine sachems. Combined with these efforts were her strong emphasis on the purity of spoken Oneida and her able and highly respected oratorical skills.[46] Equally important was her keen ability to articulate the traditional Iroquois belief in sovereignty based on treaty. Later, in testimony before a Senate committee in March 1929, she clearly set forth this overwhelming Iroquois concern:

> Here are a group of Indians [Iroquois], 16,000 in all, occupying some 78,000 acres in reservations in New York or colonized in small groups in western states and Canada. Their legal status is peculiar to Indian relations. They have . . . the status of an independent protectorate of the United States under this treaty of 1784, confirmed and added to in the treaty of 1789. They are a protected autonomy, with the title of original territory vested in them. In specific language, the U.S. ceded all right and title to them the territory they reserved to themselves out of their Iroquois domain in return for their ceding all right and title in the Ohio Valley to the United States Government.[47]

Two events gave Kellogg the opportunity to think of reconstructing the League. On March 3, 1920, the U.S. Circuit Court of Appeals for the Second Circuit, in *United States v. Boylan* (an ejectment proceeding involving the removal of Oneidas living on a thirty-two-acre tract of land and the partition of the land for use by non-Indians), found that the Oneidas were a federally recognized tribe and that New York State courts had no jurisdiction to dispose of their property without the consent of the United States.[48] This hard-won Indian victory gave Kellogg and the Iroquois hopes for other victories in the courts.

In August 1920, the Everett Commission—a New York State Assembly committee formed in 1919 to examine "the history, the affairs and transactions had by the people of the state of New York with the Indian tribes resident in the state and to report to the legislature the status of the American Indian residing in . . . New York"—began holding hearings. After nineteen months, which included on-site inspections of Iroquois reservations in Canada and the United States, Chairman Edward A. Everett of Potsdam issued a report in 1922 that largely reflected his opinion and that of the commission's researcher and stenographer, Lulu G. Stillman. The report concluded that the Iroquois as Six Nations were legally entitled to six million acres of New York State, having illegally been dispossessed of their title after the Treaty of Fort Stanwix in 1784. This report, however unrepresentative of the entire commission, helped to stimulate Iroquois efforts to regain their lands by legal means, and these efforts brought Kellogg to the fore.[49]

In the 1920s, Kellogg took advantage of these stirrings. She, her husband, her brother, and her many followers collected money in every Iroquois community—in New York, Oklahoma, Wisconsin, Ontario, and Quebec—with the intention of using it for a great Iroquois claim of up to eighteen million acres of land in New York and Pennsylvania. Her husband's legal background notwithstanding, much of the money collected—a considerable sum especially given that much of it coming from economically hard-pressed Indians—was never used for the intended purpose and was never returned to the contributors. The Indians were told that if they did not contribute they would not be eligible for the claims when they were awarded. Kellogg and her followers had several methods of collection in the pursuit of such claims. They gave tax receipts or due bills, which indicated that the contributor was entitled to 10 percent interest and 40 percent bonus when the money was "recovered in our claim against the State of New York." They also formed clubs on nearly every Iroquois reservation in the United States and Canada, charging dues for membership or levying a tax on each person of approximately a dollar and a quarter per month. Long after the Kelloggs' final legal appeal in pursuit of the claim ended, she and her followers were still collecting money. Although the exact extent of their fund-raising cannot be ascertained—it was perhaps as high as several hundreds of thousands of dollars—the record of numerous Indian protests filed with the Interior and Justice departments about the Kelloggs' activities, as well as the bitter memories of the incident that survive with today's Iroquois elders, confirm that many contributors lost their savings and property.[50] In an interview conducted in 1970, Oscar Archiquette, the noted Wisconsin Oneida leader, provided a description of her activities:

Then Minnie Kellogg, in 1921, insisted: "Oh, she said, I am working on the New York claim now. You will have your money before the snow flies—give me $10. Oh, give me $25. You will make more than the other guy. Give me $25." You know that lady, she collected $60,000 cash. That's on record at the Bureau of Indian Affairs. Minnie Kellogg, she is perhaps a 7th cousin of mine. I figure she is the smartest Oneida woman that ever walked in a pair of shoes. Oh she was smart—but in the wrong way. Oh, she could have been a big help to us Indians . . . In 1921, an educated Oneida lady [Minnie Kellogg] called a general meeting of Oneidas near Duck Creek Bridge, Brown County, Town of Hobart. The meeting concerned the New York land claim which we Oneidas have and never were paid for. She told us that it was necessary for us to go back to the old Indian ways of having chiefs as legal representatives for the Oneida Nation. She did manage to have a good number of Oneidas to attend the meeting where she took the authority of installing chiefs, and, of course, she had to collect money for expenses traveling back and forth to New York while working on this claim. One of the appointed chiefs was her treasurer, and he could not read or write, although he was smart enough to have property. My brother said, "I could give sweet talk, too, and collect money from the Indians." Not only did she collect from Oneidas, but also from the Stockbridge Indians and the Brothertowns, and a number of white business people in Green Bay. She also collected money in Canada and gave Indian dances in Germany, getting money for the Indians. . . . Our highly educated Oneida lady called another general meeting, after the meeting in 1921, perhaps in 1923. I was present at this meeting. She opened the meeting in English and Oneida and told us she had made arrangements for the attorney who was from New York to Oneida and tell us about our claim. He was from Wise and Whitney law firm of New York. . . . But it did substantiate the Oneida lady's talk as to our claim in New York to a certain extent. She was also telling us that the Six Nations were never paid for the land taken by St. Lawrence Power, and that she was going to work on that claim, too. And, of course, she mentioned that we had a lot of money coming. She might have had three or four meetings in Oneida with her sweet talk, and she went around in a way re-registering Oneidas for so much payment to her, or more like an investment, and a printed receipt given to the victim, written on it: "10% Interest, plus 40% Bonus." Not all the Oneidas believed her. This lady without question had college education and it is claimed that her English was next to perfect. I can say that her Oneida language was perfect. . . . Her last haul of money from poor Oneidas in Oneida, Wisconsin was perhaps in 1928 or so when she told her victims that they would be getting lots of money before the snow falls. The snow has fallen many times, but not the money.[51]

Despite these and other accusations, Kellogg's role in bringing to court the momentous land-claims case, *James Deere v. St. Lawrence River Power,* initiated in 1925, makes her a significant person worthy of study, for she helped to define one of the Iroquois positions in this matter well into the future.[52] In November 1922, Kellogg attended a meeting of the Indian Welfare League in Albany, in which Assemblyman Everett was chastised by both Indian and non-Indian reformers for his report, including his actions which allegedly stirred up false hopes among Indians about the land-claims issue. In a column in the *Knickerbocker Press,* Kellogg reacted to the meeting by defending Everett and claiming that she belonged to no welfare societies "because they seem to me to leave the Indians in a worse condition than they found them in." She added that the real question was not the workings of the Everett Commission but the legal status of the Six Nations. To her, the Treaty of Fort Stanwix of 1784 gave the Iroquois Confederacy independence; however, the "only way to put the Six Nations on an economic footing was to obtain the rights inherent" in that treaty.[53] Less than a week later, Kellogg, her brother, and the soon-to-be prominent James Deere sent Everett a letter endorsing his report, condemning the Indian Welfare League, and making an offer to retain his legal services in future litigation.[54]

The Deere case was brought before the U.S. District Court for the Northern District of New York. The litigation was a test case, a class-action suit, on behalf of the Iroquois Confederacy. Everett and the New York City law firm of Wise, Whitney, and Parker (Carl Whitney was Everett's nephew) represented James Deere, a Mohawk, in his ejectment proceedings against the St. Lawrence River Power Company, a subsidiary of Alcoa, and seventeen other occupants of this one-square-mile parcel of land. The power company hired the eminent statesman Charles Evans Hughes to argue the motion. Hughes soon maintained that the case should be dismissed on technical grounds, claiming that there was no federal question involved and consequently the court had no jurisdiction in the matter. The plaintiffs insisted that an 1824 treaty between the St. Regis Mohawks and New York State, which allowed for the sale of the disputed land to the state, was null and void because no single tribe of the Six Nations Confederacy had such authority and because only the federal government and the Six Nations Confederacy could write such agreements at that time.[55] Although the case was an outgrowth of efforts by Everett and Stillman, the Deere case was also part of Kellogg's attempt to win recognition for her reconstituted version of the League.[56]

During the lengthy deliberations in the Deere case, Kellogg, her husband, and Wilson K. Cornelius were arrested in Canada in 1925. They were charged with alleged conspiracy to defraud and with obtaining fifteen thousand dollars by false pretenses from members of the Iroquois living on reserves in Quebec and Ontario. At the trial in Montreal, the Kelloggs argued that the money was collected to help rehabilitate the Indian, to gain his independence, and to create "a sense of nationhood" through plans to recover millions of acres of land in New York and Pennsylvania. The Royal Canadian Mounted Police, on the other hand, accused them of obtaining subscriptions by false pretenses at Kanasatake, Kahnawake, Akwesasne, and other Canadian reserves.[57] Despite the apparent cooperation of the BIA—the Indian Bureau sent an expert witness to testify against the Kelloggs—the defendants were cleared on all charges by the court; nevertheless, they were deported from Canada.[58]

During the proceedings of the trial, the U.S. district court dismissed the Deere case because of what it insisted was the court's lack of jurisdiction in the matter.[59] Everett's death in 1928 and later fruitless appeals in the Deere case proved fatal to Kellogg's grand design. Her last major thrust toward reconstitution of the League came in 1929 when she testified at a major hearing of the U.S. Senate. Once again she spoke in proud terms of the Six Nations; of her reconstruction plans for their economic, political, and spiritual revival; of her hatred for the BIA, whom she now accused of spreading "propaganda, pernicious propaganda, criminal propaganda" against her as well as against the Iroquois as a whole; of her claims to lands in New York and Pennsylvania; and of her opposition to the building of a dam at Onondaga that would condemn part of the reservation. In packing the hearing with her supporters, her aim was to lobby for Senate pressure on the Justice Department to intervene on the side of the Indians in the Deere case. At the hearing Orrin Kellogg maintained, "We are here to get the Senate committee to look into the wrongs that have been done to the Six Nations of New York. We want them to make a survey of conditions up there and recommend to the United States Government . . . that they intervene and settle this question for all time to come."⁶⁰ Despite the Kelloggs' appeals, the Senate refused to act.

The land claims issue and the Kelloggs' efforts to reconstitute their version of the League led to increased divisions within the Iroquois. Every Iroquois reservation in the United States and Canada was affected. Onondaga was a case in point. For over a decade, two rival councils, one a Kellogg council headed by George Thomas and the other the traditional existing hereditary council headed by Joshua Jones, vied with each other for power. In reality, the major issue was Minnie Kellogg herself and whether she had a right to speak for the Six Nations. Her enemies maintained that she had no right to a voice in Iroquois affairs because her people, the Oneidas, had lost their place when they migrated to Wisconsin; she claimed, however, that the Six Nations remained intact and that the Oneidas had been forced out of their territory in New York and consequently their status as a member of the Six Nations remained unchanged. Eventually, in 1927, she lost a suit for control of the tribal funds of the Onondaga Nation. Nevertheless, Kellogg's rival council attempted to operate, however secretively, well into the 1930s.⁶¹ One Oneida described Kellogg's activities in 1930: "She does not hold her councils on any other reservation in New York State at the present time; she holds her councils in Syracuse's Onondaga Hotel, or some place like that. She selects her own officers, secretaries, treasurers, and field agents who go about the reservation."⁶²

The New Deal Era was the final death knell of the Kellogg Party. For better or worse, the federal government's work-relief programs increasingly tied the Indian to far-off Washington. Instead of a few thousand dollars, as was true in the 1920s, the federal government poured hundreds of thousands of dollars into Iroquoia. The Kellogg vision of self-help and self-sufficiency went out the window, along with the views of rugged individualism of Herbert Clark Hoover. The community action programs of the New Deal, though not accepted universally, had the blessing of the majority of the Iroquois. Pie-in-the-sky grand designs about reconstructing the ancient League or winning back eighteen million acres meant less to the Iroquois when they had an administration in Washington providing them with employment and allowing them to revive their arts, their language, and their pride in being Iroquois. By taking care of their immediate needs, the federal government actually contributed to the co-optation of the claims movement.[63]

Although Kellogg continued to operate throughout the 1930s in opposing Commissioner John Collier's policies and holding fast to her own rehabilitation program, few Iroquois listened.[64] By the 1940s, she was a broken woman who had outlived her time in history and dissipated both her fame and the money that had come with it. Ironically, the woman who had pushed for self-help and self-sufficiency was living by 1947 on welfare in New York City; she died in obscurity soon after.[65]

Kellogg's apparent obsession with elaborate master plans to rehabilitate the economic and political systems of Indian societies led her to believe that she was the only one capable of achieving these goals. As a secular leader of a mass movement with a messianic message of redemption, she could win large numbers of Indian people to her causes, but only at a price to her well-being. She drove herself relentlessly, and on at least one occasion she was institutionalized for depression. In her early life, her uncompromising style was reflected in her inability to stay at any one university for any length of time. Moreover, in the last two decades of her life, long after she had been repudiated by the Indian and non-Indian worlds, she lost touch with reality, clinging to ideas that had no hope of materializing.[66]

Minnie Kellogg, however, was not simply a neurotic accident in Iroquois history. Although she never fulfilled the expectations of her followers, she was a leader in the context of Iroquois culture and history. In the intense world of Indian politics, she promised her followers the political offices of her version of the League of the Iroquois. She also promised land that would be won through Indian claims assertions in the courts. In return, she received significant amounts of money and political support and power. The mutual interaction of Kellogg and her followers lay not simply in the power arena but also in other areas. Despite her sophistry and her inability to provide both moral stewardship and the total transformation of the Iroquois polity, she dealt with questions of Iroquois treaty rights and sovereignty as well as with other fundamental aspirations, needs, and values of her people.[67]

The Kellogg movement was no mere scam, nor was it a fleeting episode in Iroquois history. It was a revolution. Writing in the context of Oneida ethnohistory, which can be broadly extended to the Iroquois as a whole, anthropologist Jack Campisi has perceptively observed,

> Nonetheless, the actions of the Kelloggs encouraged Oneida identity and a sense that the various bands were one people, different in culture, history, and language from the other Indian groups. The Kelloggs encouraged communication among the Oneida bands and increased the awareness of their common heritage. And lastly, the Kelloggs kept active a series of contacts with the state and national governments relative to the status of the Oneidas. The Oneidas existed as a problem because they made themselves one.[68]

The Kellogg movement, and more particularly Minnie Kellogg, fooled too many Iroquois for too long a period to be dismissed too quickly. Despite chicanery, Kellogg helped transform the modern Iroquois, not back into their ancient League, but into major actors, activists, and litigants in the modern world of twentieth-century Indian politics.

10

Where the Partridge Drums

Ernest Benedict, Mohawk Intellectual as Activist

> It is the purpose of this paper to give everyone a chance to have his
> opinions printed and placed in the hands of every thinking Indian. . . .
> In order for people to think, they need some facts to help them. In
> order to govern themselves well, they must know their own history,
> laws and court cases and decisions. Not very many Indians know these
> well; every one realizes this. If it is worth anything to you to be a St.
> Regis Mohawk Indian, you will learn your history and laws so that
> you can help govern yourselves. If you cannot govern yourselves to
> your own satisfaction, there are always those who are willing to govern
> *you* to *their* own satisfaction.
> —Ernest Benedict, "A New Idea—A Reservation
> Newspaper-Magazine," *War Hoop,* May 1, 1941

Every single day of their existence, the Akwesasne Mohawks face the reality of crossing over what non-Indians call the international boundary between the United States and Canada. For the Mohawks of this community, one founded long before Canada and the United States were established, this boundary, which they refer to as "the line," was and is more than a simple inconvenience, the widely held view of non-Indians who cross every day into one of the two countries. To Mohawks and to many First Nations in Canada, it is a symbol of colonialism, much as the Panama Canal was seen by Latin Americans prior to the Carter administration. The reason is quite clear to anyone who spends time visiting Akwesasne: The Mohawk reservation straddles both sides of the United States–Canada boundary line, one formally set by outsiders, an Anglo-American commission in 1822.[1] Indeed, today three Mohawk governmental entities have to deal with five

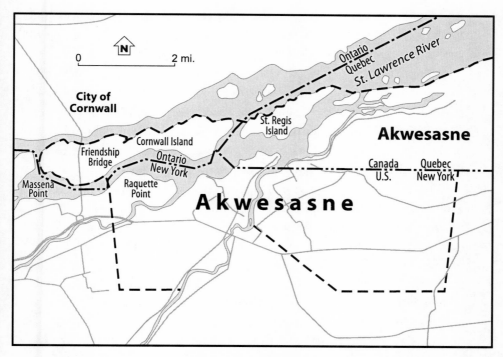

Map 5. Akwesasne (St. Regis) Mohawk Reservation Today. Map by Joe Stoll.

major jurisdictions that impinge on Mohawk life: the United States, Canada, New York State, Ontario, and Quebec.

Despite Iroquois assertions that they were guaranteed "free and unlimited passage" across the line under Article 3 of the Jay Treaty (1794), reaffirmed in the Treaty of Ghent (1814), they have been frequently denied this right, especially by Canadian officials over the years. Canadian customs and immigration facilities occupy Mohawk lands on Cornwall Island, and Canadian officials collect duties on Indians crossing into their own territory, which is a constant thorn within Mohawk existence. As late as 2001, Canadian courts have rejected Iroquois attempts to win recognition of their rights under the Jay and Ghent Treaties.[2] Although American officials since the late 1920s have been generally more respectful of the Indians' rights to cross over the line into the United States, new concerns about terrorism and the need for "homeland security" have impinged on Mohawk life and made daily life exasperating. Hence today, Mohawks traveling back and forth in their own territory face long delays, even when they are going to church, the longhouse, school, shopping, or work, or seeking medical care, including emergency services. They face the daily humiliation of having to deal with this intrusion on their sovereignty.[3] To add to the confusion, frustration, and anger of Mohawks at Akwesasne, a Mohawk woman on the "Canadian" side who married a Mohawk man from the opposite side of the line was to lose her status as an "Indian" under Canadian law that until two decades ago recognized only patrilineal descent.

For nearly three-quarters of a century, Ernest Benedict has articulated Mohawk concerns and led nonviolent resistance to both Ottawa and Washington about this and other problems. Since his teenage years, Benedict has been a leading voice challenging policies that restrict his people's right to cross "the line" freely. A well-respected intellectual, he has influenced generations of Iroquois youngsters with his writings and his teachings. Although not a great orator, his influence has been widespread in Iroquoia. Many an Indian or non-Indian activist or scholar has made the journey to his home on Cornwall Island on the "Canadian side" of the Akwesasne Mohawk Territory. In many ways he symbolizes the Mohawk word *Akwesasne,* "where the partridge drums"; his home there has been a communications center of Native America. There, he founded Indian newspapers that carefully analyzed policies emanating from Washington, Albany, and Ottawa and helped develop strategies to counter or delay what he viewed as policies harmful to his people.

Ernest Benedict was born into the Wolf Clan at Hogansburg on the Akwesasne (then known as the St. Regis) Mohawk Reservation on July 14, 1918. He was given the Mohawk name Kaientaronkwen, meaning "gathering the goods," associated with the Iroquois peach stone game. Importantly, his maternal grandparents were Sarah Claus, a Six Nations Reserve Mohawk, and Andrew Jandrew, a Kahnawake Mohawk, thus tying his family to two other major Mohawk communities. Ernest's mother, Julia Jandrew, married Charles Benedict, an Akwesasne Mohawk enrolled on the "Canadian side of the line." Despite being a so-called "Canadian Mohawk," Ernest and his two brothers and five sisters were raised at Hogansburg on the so-called "American side of the line." Hence, from the

9. Ernest Benedict, Mohawk chief, with Pope John Paul II, 1983. Midlands, Ontario, Canada. Courtesy of Salli Benedict.

first, the Benedict family's existence was affected by the United States–Canadian international boundary.[4]

With seven children to feed, Charles Benedict worked at a variety of jobs to make ends meet. He was employed seasonally in Adirondack logging camps and sold fish he caught in the St. Lawrence River and its tributaries. Although the fish today in the waters of the reservation is inedible owing to mercury and fluoride pollution, Mohawks in the 1920s and 1930s depended on the sustenance of the river, selling sturgeon and other fish that they caught in its waters. Other Mohawks depended on dairy farming, another major part of the tribal economy, which has since disappeared as a result of fluoride contamination.[5]

Major stirrings in Iroquoia in the 1920s influenced young Ernest's life. On April 22, 1922, Assemblyman Edward Everett of Potsdam presented a report to the New York State Legislature, concluding that the Iroquois Indians were entitled to six million acres of land that had been illegally taken from them from 1784 onward (see chap. 9).[6] Besides fueling major land claims cases up to the present time, the Everett Report had a more direct impact on Ernest Benedict's life. Lulu Stillman, Everett's assistant and the commission's stenographer, became the major adviser to the Six Nations Confederacies at Onondaga and Ohsweken through the 1960s. She also worked with Chief Clinton Rickard and the Indian Defense League of America (ILDA) from the 1920s onward, pushing for recognition of Indian border crossing rights under the Jay and Ghent Treaties. By the 1940s, Stillman, Rickard, Mohawk chiefs at Kahnawake and Akwesasne, and the Iroquois Tadodaho, Onondaga Chief George Thomas, Jr. were including Benedict in their strategy sessions.[7] Stillman in effect, as Benedict insists today, became one of his teachers, educating the young man about the unique legal and treaty status of the Six Nations in American, British, and Canadian law. This relationship had far-reaching consequences because Benedict passed this learning on to numerous Iroquois youngsters, including Tom Porter, Ron La France, John Mohawk, and Mike Mitchell.[8]

Other major developments in Washington and Ottawa after World War I were to shape Benedict's life. Despite strenuous objections by the Iroquois Confederacy, the U.S. Congress passed the Indian Citizenship Act in 1924. To the chiefs, the Iroquois had separate nationhood status, and therefore they believed that Congress had no right to make laws affecting them without their permission.[9] More egregious was the Canadian policy of 1924, which went beyond simply making Iroquois Canadian citizens. RCMPs invaded the Six Nations Council House, read an order excluding the hereditary chiefs, and then held a vote that replaced the chiefs with an elected council. Levi General (Deskaheh), who journeyed to Great Britain and Switzerland to protest Canadian postwar policies, became a hero to the young Benedict and other Mohawks growing up at Akwesasne.[10]

Iroquois' defense of their rights under the Jay Treaty also spurred the precocious Mohawk to action. The formation of the Indian Defense League of America (IDLA) by Chief Clinton Rickard in the mid-1920s in response to the all-too-frequent harassment of native peoples by Canadian and U.S. customs and immigration officials was to make a lasting impression on the young boy. The mobilization of the Iroquois was largely the result of Deska-heh's and Rickard's efforts and of the arrest of Paul Diabo, a Kahnawake ironworker. Diabo, who had been working in construction on the Dela-ware River Bridge, had been arrested in 1925 as an illegal alien for failing to secure a work permit and was subsequently taken before the federal district court in Philadelphia. He argued that the Jay Treaty recognized his right to pass freely across the border and negated the Immigration Act of 1924 under which he was being prosecuted. Diabo eventually won his case against deportation. As sociologist Gerald Reid has observed, the Diabo case "energized" the Kahnawake community and fueled a traditionalist revival there.[11] It was no coincidence that within a decade, a longhouse was established at Akwesasne and the *Gaiwiio,* the Code of Handsome Lake, was being preached for the first time in Benedict's own community.

These legal struggles influenced Mohawk life and shaped Benedict's world. As a boy growing up on the reservation, he was not immune from these forces swirling around him, given that his father, Charles, was active in tribal politics. Attending the Mohawk district school at Hogansburg, the inquisitive Mohawk boy was a stellar student. Skipping several grades, he advanced so quickly that by the age of fifteen he had completed the equiva-lency of high school, but he was too young and too poor to go on further with his schooling. As a result, Benedict stayed on an extra year in high school to sharpen his skills and pursue other intellectual endeavors.[12]

One turning point in the young Mohawk's life came about in the mid-1930s. The teenager was enraged by the arrest of Anna Garrow, a Mohawk basketmaker. In 1935, Garrow, who resided on the "Canadian side" at Akwesasne, crossed into the "American side," transporting twenty-four black ash splint baskets that she intended to sell. The American customs official imposed a duty under the U.S. Tariff Act of 1930, but Garrow claimed exemption under the Jay Treaty. On March 1, 1937, the U.S. Court of Customs and Patent Appeals held against Garrow, staring "that the provision of the Jay Treaty now under consideration was brought to an end by the War of 1812, leaving the contracting powers [the United States and Great Britain] discharged from all obligation in respect thereto."[13] Although Garrow lost the case and eventually had to pay a fine, the case inspired Benedict to become an active member of Chief Rickard's IDLA. The teenager resolved to help mobilize his people for collective action. The way to do it was to fight back with words, become a writer, editor, and publisher in order to educate and inspire Mohawks to overcome their colonial relationship with Ottawa and Washington.

Just prior to going off to Syracuse University, Benedict was also strongly influenced by Ray Fadden, a science teacher who had previously taught at the Tuscarora Reservation. Fadden established the Akwesasne Mohawk Counsellor Organization to encourage Indian youth to participate in outdoor recreation, learn wilderness survival skills, teach Indian history and lore as well as arts and crafts, and, most importantly, to inculcate a sense of pride in being Mohawk. Through rigorous outdoor conditioning that required youngsters to hike and climb through rugged parts of the Adirondacks, and by encouraging these youngsters to collect stories and learn crafts by listening to and watching their Indian elders, the boys soon began to be hired as camp counselors. The program trained Indians for leadership, instilling a sense of self-worth in these Indian youths at the crossroads of their lives. The successful program became the model for the National Youth Administration's Indian programs throughout the state administered by Benedict's second cousin, Louis R. Bruce, Jr., who in 1969 became the U.S. Commissioner of Indian Affairs.[14]

In August 1938, Benedict transferred to St. Lawrence University in Canton, New York. Intending to study theology with an eye on becoming a Universalist minister, Benedict soon changed his mind. By this time, he had begun attending ceremonies at the Mohawk Longhouse, which had been established by Alec Clute, an Onondaga, in the mid-1930s.[15] The St. Lawrence student soon took an interest in the humanities classes and excelled in anthropology courses taught by Dr. William N. Fenton, then a young instructor who had previously spent much time in Mohawk Country while serving as a community worker for the Bureau of Indian Affairs. Inculcated with certain values and trained from the earliest to listen carefully to the words of chiefs in council, Benedict became Fenton's prized pupil. Later, the prominent anthropologist evaluated Benedict's performance in his classes: "He never took notes, listening to my every word. He excelled in my class."[16] Benedict successfully completed his education, graduating in June 1940.

By this time, Benedict had established *War Whoop,* the first Mohawk newspaper on the reserve. The publication, which Benedict labeled a "newspaper-magazine," reveals much about Benedict as well as the concerns that Mohawks had at this time. In his first issue, he announced his goals in funding *War Whoop*:

> There are plenty of things happening on the reservation. Indians are born, get married, get sick, and die, the same as any one else and their neighbors, relatives and friends are concerned about such things. They have a right to an accurate account of these important events rather than an uncertain story. Church activities, social events, court cases, "big doings" of all kinds, should be printed somewhere, where people will be sure to see. In this paper, you will read more local news than anywhere else and more about each story.[17]

Benedict conducted interviews with reservation personalities such as Peter Cook, a Mohawk circus acrobat who had worked in Buffalo Bill's "Wild West" shows. He allowed others to write and submit articles for *War Whoop,* and he provided history lessons about the Iroquois Indian land claims, the Jay and federal Indian treaties, state legislative commissions, the Carlisle Indian School, and so forth. *War Whoop* provided information about Akwesasne Mohawk Counsellor activities, reservation sports events, happenings at school, and notices of funerals. In one editorial, Benedict warned about the harmful effects of tribal factionalism. In another, he called the Mohawks' attention to a crisis looming, namely the U.S. Congress's passage of the Selective Service Act.[18]

In June 1940, Congress passed this act, the first one in American history that required Native Americans to register for the draft and to be eligible for conscription. The Iroquois insisted that this act did not apply to them because they had never accepted the 1924 American Indian Citizenship Act and considered themselves allies, not U.S. citizens. Although not against participation in war on moral or patriotic grounds, the Iroquois clung to traditional beliefs about their sovereignty. Consequently, many were arrested and some were prosecuted as draft evaders, even after the United States gave them warnings.[19] It should be noted that the Iroquois lost three test cases when federal courts rejected their arguments and upheld the Selective Service Act's application to them.[20] In order to prevent further arrests, some prominent Iroquois, not the Confederacy Council at Onondaga, dramatically declared war against the Axis Powers in June 1942.[21]

In a protest against the Indian Citizenship Act of 1924, the Selective Service Act of 1940, and United States–Canada joint efforts to plan a future St. Lawrence Seaway, Benedict made an impassioned appeal in March 1941, two months prior to his graduation from St. Lawrence University. Writing to the American Civil Liberties Union (ACLU), he carefully outlined the opinion "of the great majority of the Six Nations Indians." He wrote that the Indian Citizenship Act could not apply to the Indians of the Six Nations "within the reservation since they are independent Nations. Congress may as well pass a law making Mexicans citizens." He then questioned the right of the United States to conscript Indians and notified the ACLU that Iroquois were being arrested and jailed for noncompliance. Importantly, he pointed out the provisions of the Jay Treaty, that "the boundary was not to affect the Indian but would be 'lifted into the sky' and would be only for the white citizens of the countries making the border." He informed the ACLU that Indian goods had been seized as "contraband" and that customs and immigration officers had arrested the Indians. He added that New York State had long ago imposed a system of chiefs that was unrepresentative of Mohawk interests and was inefficient and even corrupt.[22]

In the same letter, Benedict also called the ACLU's attention to the plans for the massive St. Lawrence Seaway project that would permanently transform his people's lives by devastating the environment and bringing ALCOA, Reynolds, and General Motors to the borders of Mohawk Territory. In poignant fashion, the Mohawk wordsmith wrote an explanation of why he was so determined to maintain the struggle:

> Many wonder why we hold to our reservation so tenaciously. They advise
> us to stop our weak struggling and give in to the State and National

governments and lose our racial identity in competition with the outside world. We answer that one cannot do that so easily. Why does not the United States join itself with the Soviet Republic whose numbers and territory are gr[e]ater than its own? Because Americans feel that their social system is so much superior to that of Russia. Similarly, we Six Nations Indians feel we have potentially a superior social system to that of the United States. If only we were left alone, we could redevelop our society to part of its original form which was solid in democracy when Europe knew only monarchs. In it was the real equality for all, and Religion had the strength of daily practice. At one time, the great nations awaited with anxiety the decisions of the Six Nations councils, today our death cries are lost in the clamor for power.[23]

As a postscript, he advised the ACLU that seven thousand Indians' lives were in the balance and that the organization should contact Chief Rickard and Lulu Stillman, as well as Mohawk Chief Frank Terrance, Tonawanda Seneca Chief Edward Black, and Onondaga Chief Jesse Lyons, all active members of the IDLA.[24]

In late 1941 and early 1942, Benedict went to prison for four months to challenge whether the federal government could draft the Iroquois. Because of the behind-the-scenes intervention of Louis R. Bruce, Jr., who had the ear of Eleanor Roosevelt, the U.S. Attorney in Albany released Benedict from jail in 1942, but only after a meeting in which the Mohawk agreed to enlist in the war effort.[25] The U.S. army soon shuttled him off to fight the Japanese in New Guinea and other areas of the South Pacific. Assigned to the 41st Signal Corps, Benedict served from March 1942 through November 1945, taking part in campaigns in New Guinea and the Philippines. He distinguished himself by being awarded several military medals, including the Asiatic Pacific Medal, the Philippines Liberation Ribbon, and the Bronze Star.[26]

After the war, in the fall of 1945, Benedict returned to Akwesasne. Returning somewhat later than other Mohawk veterans, he found postwar opportunities limited. Subsequently, he was hired by the Canadian Indian agent to teach manual trades at St. Regis Village. He worked and later resided on Cornwall Island, which Ottawa calls Ontario.[27]

In the postwar period, Mohawk attention was increasingly focused on stopping New York State efforts to extend its civil and criminal jurisdiction over Indian affairs, much to the opposition of most Iroquois. Indeed, the transfer of jurisdiction that soon followed became the model for four other states seeking similar control over its Indian populations in federal legislation known as PL 280.[28] In response, Benedict once again established a Mohawk newspaper, *Kahwehras*—which translates as "It Thunders"—in 1947. As with *War Whoop*, this new newspaper contained notices of community events, obituaries, tribal council meetings, background pieces on Canada's Indian Act and its planned revisions, fund-raising efforts by the IDLA, and excerpts from books that focused on the great achievements of native peoples of the hemisphere. In 1948, much of the news focused on Bill 1683 that dealt with the transfer of criminal jurisdiction to New York State. Tied to both proposed pieces of legislation was Bill 1686, "A Bill to Provide for the Settlement of Certain Obligations of the United States to the Indians of New York," a termination-era bill attempting to buy out and end the federal treaty relationship with the Iroquois.[29]

Working with his future brother-in-law, Julius Cook, Benedict brought the news of the crisis to his Akwesasne community.[30] Benedict saw these bills transferring jurisdiction not as an attempt to "liberate the Indian, but rather as a not-so-veiled effort to get at Indian land; natural resource(s), money, or claim(s)."[31] Chosen as a member of the Mohawk delegation to Washington headed by the well-respected Philip Cook, Benedict set off to the Capitol in early March 1948.[32]

Working with Lulu Stillman and Chief Rickard as well as the Grand Council of the Six Nations at Onondaga, Benedict presented a Mohawk petition strongly opposing the bills. In testimony before the U.S. Senate Subcommittee on Interior and Insular Affairs, Benedict insisted that the Indians were law-abiding people and that New York State jurisdiction would be an intrusion on Indian sovereignty and lead to further interference in the future that might then lead to the alienation of Indian lands. In concluding his remarks, he insisted that he was not a "New York Indian" but a citizen of the Six Nations. He reiterated the Mohawk traditionalist belief that the Six Nations Confederacy was not subject to "the laws of the State of New York, and as such this Congress had no right to regulate the internal affairs of the Six Nations Indians."[33] Despite the protest, the U.S. Congress passed the criminal jurisdiction transfer bill in 1948 and the civil jurisdiction transfer bill in 1950.[34]

The greatest modern challenge to Mohawk life occurred in the early 1950s as a result of the joint Canadian-American St. Lawrence Seaway project. Sleepy little hamlets, Indian and non-Indian, now were rudely awakened and transformed forever by gigantic "cats" that were used to bulldoze tons of earth to build cofferdams and permanent dams, shift the course of the river, widen the waterway, and construct immense powerhouses. One hundred thirty acres of Mohawk Territory at Akwesasne were condemned and expropriated for highway approaches to the Cornwall-Massena International Bridge. Other Mohawk lands were taken for the project at the Kahnawake Reserve. Despite assurances from the Canadian government that the Indians at Akwesasne would not be charged tolls, the promise was broken. Instead, the Ottawa government soon installed tollgates, a customs house, garages, and offices on Mohawk Territory at Cornwall Island, approximately two kilometers from Benedict's home. Moreover, on the "American side," Mohawk land claims to Barnhart Island dating back to 1822 were swept aside by the actions of Robert Moses and the New York State Power Authority, with the building of two major powerhouses, high voltage power lines, two ship locks, and a major beach camp recreation area constructed on the island.[35]

The St. Lawrence Seaway became a reality in 1954. A new industrial corridor soon was created just off the reservation with giant plants established by General Motors and Reynolds Aluminum. Although there were short-term benefits—jobs for Mohawks at these plants—there were devastating long-term results, namely that the nearby reservation was being contaminated by mercury, fluoride, and heavy metals from these two plants and others at Massena, New York, and Cornwall, Ontario.[36]

By the mid-1950s, Benedict largely centered on the everyday concerns of providing for his growing family on Cornwall Island. After World War II, his wife, Florence, gave birth to four children—Salli, Rebecca, Lloyd, and Daniel. Consequently, Ernest left his job teaching at the Canadian government school and entered the workforce at Reynolds Aluminum. Yet he never abandoned his responsibilities to his people, attempting to ameliorate the conditions brought on by the seaway and its new industrial corridor. In 1956 he was elected to the St. Regis Band Council, now called the Mohawk Council of Akwesasne, and subsequently was reelected seven times as a councilor. A member of the Wolf clan, Benedict was to carry out the obligations associated with being a member of that clan. Wolf clan members are traditionally "ones who make the path" so others can follow. Such was the case with Benedict. His wife, Florence, herself a noted Mohawk basketmaker involved in numerous community efforts, and their growing family clearly sacrificed to allow Ernest to pursue his goals.[37]

Benedict had served his apprenticeship as a "runner," just as in olden days, bringing news of far-off campaigns, albeit political battles with Albany, Washington, D.C., and Ottawa, back to his community. As a journalist, he had warned of approaching dangers and prepared his people for the challenges. Because of the respect for his service to the community, Onondaga Chief George Thomas, Jr., the Tadodaho of the Iroquois Confederacy, condoled him as Life Chief (*Rotinonkiseres,* or "Longhair"), thus recognizing his contributions and service to his community's welfare.[38]

While serving as counselor for the Band Council (1956–82), Chief Benedict supported the efforts of Louis Francis, who challenged Canada's policies restricting Mohawk rights under the Jay Treaty.[39] Francis, who lived on the Canadian side, had purchased a washing machine, refrigerator, and stove from his brother-in-law who lived on the U.S. side of the international boundary. The purchases were seized by Canadian authorities who also imposed a $123 fine. Francis paid the fine and the purchased items were returned. Then he sued the Canadian government to obtain return of the moneys from the fine as a test case of Iroquois rights under the Jay and Ghent treaties. Eventually the court dismissed the action, maintaining that Indian rights under the two Anglo-American treaties were never implemented or sanctioned by the Canadian Parliament and therefore could not provide the plaintiff exemption from customs duties.[40]

Athough there had been previous incidents, the Francis case helped bring Canadian Indian policies to the forefront, and not just among Iroquois Indians. Mohawk traditionalists had long memories of 1924, when RCMPs invaded the Six Nations Confederacy Council House and imposed an elected system of government at Grand River. Ten years later,

Ottawa officials helped "institute" a similar elected band council system at the Oneida reserve at Southwold, Ontario.[41] Both Ernest and his father, Charles, had taken an active interest in the Francis case. Charles Benedict had been involved in native concerns in Canada for several decades. During the Francis case, Charles journeyed to Ottawa to protest outside of Parliament along with other members of the decade-old North American Indian Brotherhood, later known as the National Indian Brotherhood.[42]

From the 1950s onward, Benedict was also involved in pursuing Mohawk land claims on both sides of "the line." The claim on the American side of the line centered on Barnhart Island. In the St. Lawrence Seaway project, eighty-eight acres of Raquette Point on the American side of the reserve were expropriated, while Mohawk claims to Barnhart Island were ignored when a dam, seaway locks, and a state park were established on the island. Although the Mohawks sued for compensation, the courts denied the claim.[43]

Benedict's land claims efforts were more successful on the Canadian side of the reserve. In 1970, a group of Mohawks that included Tom Porter, who had been mentored by Benedict, initiated an occupation for several months of Stanley Island in the St. Lawrence River. Their peaceful demonstration, initiated with the full support of the Longhouse, led to Canadian authorities recognizing the Mohawk claim to the island.[44] Subsequently, Benedict, working with the Assembly of First Nations, the leading native organization in Canada, pushed for the creation of Canada's Indian Claims Commission.[45]

In the late 1950s, Benedict and other Mohawks were also strongly affected by the actions of Francis Johnson, known as Standing Arrow and later as Frank Thomas.[46] In August 1957, this muscular twenty-four-year-old Mohawk ironworker from Akwesasne began occupying lands off Route 5S on Schoharie Creek near Fort Hunter, claiming the site as Indian territory that had been illegally taken by the New York State officials after the American Revolution. Standing Arrow, a charismatic figure, brought the plight of the Mohawk people to the attention of the American public. He insisted that more than two thousand Mohawks from reservations in Quebec, at Kahnawake, Kahnesatake, and Akwesasne, had their life changed by the St. Lawrence Seaway's construction. He suggested that the

Hotinoshsyóni⁷ establish tollbooths on the newly opened New York State Thruway, which had been built through Indian-claimed lands or through Seneca Territory that had been expropriated.⁴⁷

Although Standing Arrow's peaceful protest was a temporary one, he had struck a chord with Benedict. Even though Standing Arrow's actions were seen by many, including some Mohawks, as outrageous behavior, others such as Benedict saw something else. Benedict respected Standing Arrow for his knowledge of Mohawk history, language, and traditions and thus did not view him as merely a media hound or political opponent.⁴⁸ Benedict clearly learned a lesson from Standing Arrow, namely that in order to counter threats to tribal existence, the Iroquois needed to bring their cause before a wider audience.

With talk of "captive nations" behind the Soviet's Iron Curtain and with increasing concern over civil rights in the United States, the time was ripe. At precisely this moment in history, the renowned writer Edmund Wilson was to arrive at Benedict's home on Cornwall Island, seeking to understand this "Iroquois national movement—not unlike Scottish nationalism and Zionism—with a revival of the old religion and claims for territory of their own."⁴⁹ Accompanied by William Fenton, Benedict's former college professor and then New York State deputy commissioner of education and director of the New York State Museum in Albany, Wilson, the pudgy, stammering enfant terrible, made his way to Mohawk Territory. There, in 1958, he was introduced to the forty-year-old Mohawk chief. Wilson was impressed by Benedict's education at St. Lawrence University and by the Mohawk's making "himself a test case of Iroquois non-citizenship at the time of the last war, by going to jail" for resisting the Selective Service Act. The member of the literati then added, "Today he [Benedict] is an active collaborator in the effort to restore the Confederacy."⁵⁰ To Wilson, Benedict was a Six Nations traditionalist, challenging assumptions of the modern world of the late 1950s. The result was one of Wilson's greatest pieces of literature, *Apologies to the Iroquois,* which was excerpted in the *New Yorker* and published in book form in 1959.⁵¹

Throughout the decade of the 1960s, Benedict developed a plan to promote Native American culture, history, and values. Eventually his far-reaching experiment became a reality with the establishment of the North

American Indian Travelling College (NAITC). Looking at a map of the locations of reserves in Canada, he concluded that many of the Native communities in Canada could be reached by rail easier than by unpaved roads. His original idea was to establish a traveling college, a mobile heritage center on a railroad car that could carry teachers of Indian traditions to far-off communities. The teachers would be responsible for inculcating traditional values and fostering pride and unity among Native peoples. This mobile railroad car would carry the teachers from one reserve to another, network Canadian Indian communities, and foster pride as well as unity among Native peoples. Working with the young Mohawk Mike Mitchell, later a Mohawk chief, and Jerry Gambill (Rarihokwats), a young non-Indian employee of the Canadian Department of Indian Affairs (DIA) and a community development worker, Benedict carefully planned the project, raising money from private sources, quitting his job at Reynolds to devote full time to the effort. The project never got off the ground because railroad charges were excessive for down time, namely for the fees for a rail car stored on the track. Nevertheless, the North American Travelling College, now the Native North American Travelling College, became a reality in 1974 and continues to this day as the Ronathahon:ni Cultural Center, an institution of traditional learning at Cornwall Island at Akwesasne.[52]

In its early days of operation, the NAITC, with its enthusiastic and idealistic staff of Iroquois youth, also brought their programs by van to audiences of Indian and non-Indian people throughout North America. Inspired by Benedict's teachings, an offshoot of the NAITC was formed by Jerry Gambill that was named "the White Roots of Peace." A new generation of Mohawk youngsters comprising Tom Porter, Ron La France, Mike Mitchell, and Francis Boots went to Indian communities, urban Indian centers, and high school and college campuses, presenting talks about traditional values, inculcating a sense of pride in being "Indian," and, at times, motivating their audience with a call to action. Among those inspired was Richard Oakes, an urban-raised Mohawk, who later became known for his involvement at the Alcatraz takeover in November 1969.[53]

By the late 1960s, Jay Treaty rights once again took center stage at Akwesasne. In the fall of 1968, Indians at Cornwall Island were required to pay customs duties on all goods, including food, of more than five dollars in value. On the eighteenth of December, after careful planning, approximately one hundred Mohawks, mostly women and teenagers, blocked the International Bridge with twenty-five automobiles in protest against these Canadian levies. The demonstration was planned from early November onward in Benedict's home on Cornwall Island. The fifty-year-old head of the North American Indian College had, as one Iroquois newspaper stated, "put aside his school work to assist the distraught St. Regis Indians" in protest against the Francis decision and Canadian violations of the Jay Treaty.[54] Charging that the Mohawk agreement with the St. Lawrence Seaway Authority had been violated by the imposition of tolls and by the presence of a customs office, the Indians sat down or threw their bodies in front of tow trucks sent to clear away the wall of Mohawks and their automobiles. Letting the air out of the tires of their automobiles and carrying placards reading "This is an Indian Reservation, No Trespassing," they confronted the RCMPs and the Ontario Provincial Police. The police seized and arrested forty-one Mohawks, including Kahn-Tineta Horn, a colorful Mohawk activist and former fashion model from Kahnawake. Eventually, after another sitdown in February 1969 and a prolonged series of negotiations, the Canadian government agreed to the creation of a separate lane of entry for Cornwall Island Mohawks returning from the American side of the line.[55]

During this maelstrom of protest, in strategy sessions in Benedict's kitchen, Gambill, inspired by Benedict, founded *Akwesasne News,* later renamed *Akwesasne Notes,* in December 1968, which he edited until the mid-1970s. Both the White Roots of Peace and *Akwesasne Notes* were conceived as community development projects, and both helped shape the Iroquois polity and Indian movements nationwide for two decades. Originally the newspaper focused on informing reservation readers about immediate concerns. Later, Gambill started reaching an international audience with *Akwesasne Notes,* focusing on the crimes committed against indigenous peoples worldwide. *Akwesasne Notes* included graphic depictions of injustices on the Indians of Brazil, Canada, Guatemala, and the United States; circumpolar peoples of the Arctic in Scandinavia and the Soviet Union; aborigines and Polynesian natives of the South Pacific; and Montagnards caught in the middle of the Vietnam War. Indeed, inspired by Benedict's early efforts, Akwesasne, "Where the Partridge Drums," had become a communications center for indigenous peoples throughout the planet, documenting their plight.[56]

Almost precisely at this same time, many First Nations in Canada were openly resisting Ottawa, challenging the Trudeau-Chretíen policies of termination, the so-called "White Paper." Consequently, Canadian Indian agents, seen as the vestiges of colonial rule, were being barred from access to council meetings. Benedict joined with Chief Burton Jacobs of the Walpole Island Band (the Three Fires People—Odawa, Ojibwe, Potawatomi) and others from as far away as British Columbia in the nationwide drive to remove these agents from reserves in Canada; they succeeded by the early 1970s.[57]

Benedict continued his educational efforts after he turned over the reins of the Mohawk Travelling College to Mike Mitchell. By this time, Benedict was largely focused on teaching, lecturing at conferences, and organizing First Nations' efforts to change the Canadian policies. He spent the first years of that decade teaching at Trent University, later receiving an honorary doctorate of letters from that Ontario university. His frequent travels and speaking engagements led his daughter Salli to affectionately refer to him as "my father, the conference Indian."[58]

Subsequently, throughout the 1970s Benedict was directly involved in establishing the Assembly of First Nations (AFN), formally founded in Ottawa in 1980. The AFN resulted from a national movement to restore the direct voices of the chiefs in matters of Canada-wide concern since the National Indian Brotherhood (NIB) centered on representation through provincial organizations such as the Union of Ontario Indians. Today the AFN also operates as a deliberative body not subject to regulation by the Ottawa government, unlike the NIB, which is an incorporated body entering into contractual agreements subject to Canadian officials' scrutiny. Yet the "conference Indian" was actually working with prominent First Nations representatives throughout Canada, networking to produce fundamental changes in policy. Galvanized by Harold Cardinal of the Fox Lake Band and his writings and by the work of Stan Daniels of the Slave Lake Band, who had exposed that the Hudson Bay's stores were charging Native peoples 800 percent more on some basic food items than non-Indians,

Benedict saw the need for more effective Native organizations nationwide. Canada at that time recognized only the sons and daughters of an enrolled father as "Indian," while Mohawk people traditionally traced their enrollment through matrilineal descent. Hence, Benedict worked with Jeanette Lavell-Corbier on Bill C31, the successful attempt to put First Nations children whose mothers were Indian and whose fathers were non-Indian back on the band rolls; or restored Indian women or "American side" Indians who had been thrown off for marrying non-Indians.[59]

Changes came slowly after the creation by the Canadian Parliament of the Penner Commission for constitutional reform of Indian policies. Working with Jerry Gambill, then a researcher for the commission, and Roberta Jamieson, a Mohawk attorney from Grand River who served as an ex officio member of the commission, Benedict pushed for changes in Ottawa that eventually led to the passage by the Canadian Parliament of Bill C31 in the mid-1980s, as well as to a recognition of the aboriginal rights of Métis, descendants of Franco-Indians who make up a significant portion of the Indian population of Canada. Eventually these efforts also resulted in the creation of a Canadian Indian Claims Commission.[60]

For his work on behalf of the AFN and later for promoting the idea of what became Canada's Indian Claims Commission, Benedict was chosen as the representative elder of all First Nations of Canada to meet with and honor Pope John Paul II on his historic visit to Canada in 1983. At Midland, Ontario, the pope officially apologized to Native peoples for the past policies and insensitivities of Roman Catholic clergymen. The pontiff emphasized the need "to heal the divisions which had kept Aboriginal and Non-Aboriginal apart." The pope also elevated Kateri Tekakwitha, an Algonquian adopted by the Mohawks, to beatification status, just below sainthood in the Roman Catholic church. At the ceremony on September 30, 1983, Benedict offered a prayer and presented an eagle feather to the globe-trotting "People's Pope."[61]

Despite his efforts to change Ottawa's national policies, Benedict never lost touch with Mohawk concerns. By the mid- and late 1970s, Benedict and his wife, Florence, were actively promoting the establishment of the Akwesasne Mohawk Freedom School, and both taught language immersion classes there. During this same period, he lent his land on Cornwall

Island to establish the first Mohawk radio station, which helped promote Indian language instruction and, as was true of his newspapers, kept his community informed of what transpired on and off the reserve.[62]

Meanwhile, at Akwesasne, internal divisions had intensified in 1979–80, especially on the American side of the line, between the Longhouse and the tribal government of three elected chiefs. At this time, on the Canadian side, Benedict was elected as a councilor and made head chief of the Mohawk Council of Akwesasne from 1980 to 1982; however, he could not heal the splits that were becoming chasms in the Mohawk community. His quiet voice was unacceptable to many, and the council was completely divided, with a rival head chief chosen to counter his influence.[63]

By 1990, things had changed for the worse and had even turned violent. The Longhouse had split apart. Mohawk entrepreneurs began to sell tax-free cigarettes and gasoline at one-stops along State Route 37 that traverses the reservation on the American side. Mohawks quarreled and even shot at each other over whether high-stakes bingo and later casinos should be opened on the reservation. Because of the physical geography of the community, international smuggling networks began to operate on the roads and waterways throughout the reservation. Generations of feuding between rival political families were exacerbated by the new materialistic pulls of the times.[64] Benedict's efforts to bring people together and foster Mohawk nationhood across both sides of the line were largely lost.

Attempting to shift the debate away from internal political feuding over Indian gaming operations, Benedict, now an elder in his seventies, pointed his finger once again southward toward Albany, accusing New York State of being the ruination of his people's livelihood. Extremely agitated by the growing environmental crisis, one that severely affected his own family's health on Cornwall Island, and the lack of response for two decades from non-Indian officials, Benedict spoke out against the despoliation of Mohawk Country by General Motors and Reynolds Aluminum. On July 24, 1990, the Mohawk elder testified before a New York Assembly hearing held at Fort Covington, New York, focusing on the environmental crisis, suggesting that his people had been sensitive to their natural surroundings but that "all of a sudden, the rug is pulled out from under you." Sadly, he observed that although his people were "expected to survive," they didn't "have the tools to survive [this disaster] in this contemporary time."[65] By this time, all of Iroquoia on the American side was soon diverted, not by Benedict's efforts, but by fighting off Albany's imposition of the state sales tax on reservations. On the Canadian side, Mohawks' attentions became diverted to a major conflict at Oka (Kahnesatake) that led to an armed confrontation between the Canadian military and Mohawk residents of this reserve outside Montreal, which started over local non-Indians' plans to develop Indian-claimed lands for a golf course.

Benedict's long effort to fight for Jay Treaty rights suffered a major setback in a Canadian Supreme Court ruling in 2001. On March 22, 1988, Mike Mitchell, Benedict's prized student and then grand chief of the Mohawk Council of Akwesasne, entered Canada from New York at the International Bridge at Cornwall with a washing machine, ten blankets, twenty Bibles, used clothing, one case of motor oil, ten loaves of bread, two pounds of butter, four gallons of milk, six bags of cookies, and twelve cans of soup. Mitchell, a resident of Cornwall Island, intended to take all of the items to the Mohawk reserve of Tyendinaga in Canada, except for the motor oil, which he was bringing to a store at Akwesasne. Most of the goods intended for Tyendinaga were, according to Mitchell, gifts for community residents to renew the connections between the two Mohawk communities; other items were for trade. Although Mitchell was allowed to cross the border with these items, he was charged a duty of $361.64, which he refused to pay, insisting that the Jay Treaty allowed him to bring in these goods.[66]

Previously, on June 13, 1991, Canada's governor general in Council had issued the "Akwesasne Residents Remission Order." Because of the unique geography of the reserve, this order applied to "goods acquired in the United States and imported into Canada by Akwesasne residents, by owners or operators of duly authorized community stores and by the Mohawk Council of Akwesasne or an entity authorized by that council." The order exempted Akwesasne residents from duties "in respect of goods, other than alcoholic beverages, cigars, cigarettes and manufactured tobacco" for "use in connection with educational, hospital or social services provided to residents of the Akwesasne Reserve."[67] Although this order issued by Canada's Department of Justice did not carry the power of a parliamentary statute, it did give the Mohawks at Akwesasne the hope that their Indian border crossing rights would be respected in the future.

Benedict and the Mohawk community at Akwesasne also were encouraged by how the Canadian federal courts dealt with the Mitchell case as it made its way up the judicial ladder. The Mitchell case went through three stages of the Canadian federal court system. At the lower court, the federal judge held that the Mohawks had a right to enter Canada duty-free if they brought items purchased in the United States for personal use, for community benefit, or even to trade. At the appellate level, a court of three federal judges recognized the Mohawks' right to enter Canada duty-free if they brought items strictly for personal use or community benefit, but only for local trade with other reserves in Ontario and Quebec, not in other provinces or throughout Canada.[68]

When the case reached the highest court in 2001, the justices recognized that the "crisscrossing of borders through the Mohawk community goes beyond inconvenience and does constitute a significant burden on everyday living." Nevertheless, they denied Mitchell's argument, once again rejecting Indian border crossing rights:

With the creation of the international boundary in 1783 [actually 1822], Akwesasne became the point at which British (and later Canadian) sovereignty came face to face with the sovereignty of the U.S. Control over the mobility of persons and goods across a border has always been a fundamental attribute and incident of sovereignty. States are expected to exercise their authority over borders in the public interest. The duty cannot be abdicated to the vagaries of an earlier regime whose sovereignty has been eclipsed. Therefore, the international trading/mobility right claimed by the respondent is incompatible with the historical attributes of Canadian sovereignty.[69]

Despite this recent major setback, Benedict's legacy is clear today at Akwesasne. The North American Indian Travelling College has an established home on Cornwall Island and includes a cultural center, library, and museum. Importantly, Benedict instilled in his children—Salli, Rebecca, Lloyd, and Daniel—a sense of noblesse oblige, serving the Mohawk community in a variety of capacities: Salli, one of the first directors of the Akwesasne Museum, former editor of *Akwesasne Notes,* founder of the Mohawk newspaper *Indian Time,* and manager of the aboriginal research office of the Mohawk Council of Akwesasne; Rebecca, former manager of the Mohawk radio station and currently manager of the St. Regis Mohawk Tribal Health Service Dental Clinic; Lloyd, the founder of the Mohawk radio station and former councilor and district chief of the Mohawk Council of Akwesasne; and Daniel, past director of the Akwesasne Freedom School and currently computer technician for the St. Regis Mohawk environmental division.[70]

Over the past decade and a half, Ernest Benedict, that young Mohawk teenager incensed by the Anna Garrow case, was still inspiring others to think and act collectively for the common good. The official publication of Canada's Indian Claims Commission quotes his poetic wisdom on its very masthead:

> I have heard the elders say that when the terms of the treaties were deliberated the smoke from the pipe carried that agreement to the Creator binding it forever. An agreement can be written in stone, stone can be chipped away, but the smoke from the sacred pipe signified to the First Nations peoples that the treaties could not be undone.[71]

Even today, when students or officials from overseas seek information about Native American concerns and indigenous rights, they consult with Benedict. For example, in 1997, when Dr. Alicia P. Magos, an official of SEAMO, a Southeast Asian organization that formulates cultural, educational, and scientific policies, wanted to learn more about Canada's Native populations, she and her colleagues visited Benedict, "a respected Indian Chieftain" who "accommodated us and talked about an hour on varied topics which touched on present state/problems of the Six Nations." To Dr. Magos's surprise, Benedict greeted the delegation in Tagalog, one of the languages of the Philippines, which the Mohawk intellectual had picked up in the Philippines while serving in World War II.[72]

It is little wonder that the brilliance of this Mohawk educator has been recognized on both sides of "the line." Besides his honorary doctorate from

Trent University, in 1994 he received the National Aboriginal Achievement Award for his work promoting education throughout the Canadian land-scape. He also received the Sol Feinstone Service Award from St. Lawrence University, moneys that he donated to the Akwesasne Freedom School.[73] Yet one award, much more important to him than trophies and certificates on the wall, has eluded him, namely recognition by Canada and the United States that his people, the Mohawks (the Rotinonsónni), one of the original members of the Iroquois League of Peace and Power, are a distinct nation-state with a unique history, and that their sovereignty, guaranteed by treaty, must be respected. Although he and the partridge have drummed those ideas, Ottawa and Washington officials have worn earplugs for decades.

PART SIX Women's Leadership,
A Memoir

Introduction

Unlike the chapters in the previous five parts, chapter 11 is a memoir based on my fieldwork at three of the Seneca reservations in New York—Allegany, Cattaraugus, and Tonawanda Reservations—that began in 1971. The chapter also differs from the preceding eleven because it is not a biography of a single Iroquois male or female leader but rather encompasses the extraordinary achievements of thirty-five Seneca (and Cayuga women married to Seneca men) who played a vital role in the rebuilding of the Seneca Nation of Indians in the wake of their greatest tragedy of the twentieth century, namely the building of the Kinzua Dam that led to substantial tribal land loss and the near-total disruption of Indian life.

The original motivation to write this essay started when in 2002 the Board of Trustees of the Seneca-Iroquois National Museum in Salamanca asked me to speak at the twenty-fifth anniversary of the institution's founding. I began to reflect on my experiences over the years and on the numerous Iroquois Indians I had known. What came to mind almost immediately were the changes I had witnessed as an invited scholar into the Seneca Territory. I began to reflect on what I had learned and soon came to what now appears to be an obvious conclusion. Seneca (and Cayuga women married to Seneca men) played a key role in yet another rebirth of the Seneca Nation. As brought out in part two, "Keepers of the Kettle/Mothers of the Nation," women were protectors of the tribal estate in days past. Once again, women's groups sprang up, and this time to spur recovery. Their efforts began almost precisely at the same time (1964) that Seneca women were receiving the right to vote in tribal elections and hold office within the nation, largely as a result of the work of Martha Bucktooth, Reva Barse, and Genevieve Plummer.[1]

These women were not the same nor did all of them have the same level of education. Some had remained on the reservation and had long become involved in daily life of the communities. Others returned after years away from the reservations. Some were products of the Thomas Indian School, the educational institution that operated for a century from 1856 onward, and a few were educated at local colleges or at Haskell.

To me, one of those ladies stood out more than the rest: Pauline Lay Seneca, the Cayuga wife of Cornelius Seneca, the late Seneca Nation president. She had never had children of her own, but she was known to the reservation community as "Aunt Polly," although I never addressed her as that. Educated as a young girl by the Quakers at their Tunessassa School, Pauline Seneca had a magnetic personality and was full of spunk, even in her advanced years. She was ready at any time to go on the hunt for garage sales or to help out at the United Mission Church (Wright Memorial Church). Eventually she would go blind because of advancing diabetes, the scourge of modern Iroquoia.

I would always carefully listen to every word she said. Most of the time, I would show up at Cattaraugus in June when the Iroquois were celebrating the strawberry ceremonial or in early September at the Seneca Fall Festival, both times to find good things to eat. At each visit, I would learn something new from Mrs. Seneca. I was not the first scholar to visit her. Arthur C. Parker frequented her home, as did William N. Fenton. To me, it was no accident that my path led to her home on Route 438.

Mrs. Seneca told me that she had gone back to school later in life to secure a master's degree, one of the first Seneca women to get an advanced degree. She described her relatives who had attended boarding school such as Hampton and Carlisle or had become prominent bandleaders and musicians. She helped me understand the life of her niece, Alice Lee Jemison, who had been terribly slandered by previous historians. On a beautiful late spring or early summer evening, I would read to her in what this Cayuga elder called her "bug house," a screened-in portable area outside her home. There I would read from her personal archives, including the poignant letters of Iroquois GIs serving in combat in the Pacific during World War II.[2]

As a historian of the Iroquois, I realized her significance as a leader, but not in the same way that her Cayuga and Seneca women neighbors saw her.

In an interview at the Seneca Nation library at the Allegany Indian Reservation that I conducted on August 15, 2001, Marlene Johnson, a noted Seneca and former member of the President's Commission on Indian Higher Education, told me,

> In the 1940s and 1950s, we as Indians were told we couldn't succeed and were discouraged from entering the educational field. Yet, I saw Mrs. Seneca [Pauline Lay Seneca] teaching at the time. I realized I could pursue this dream. When I returned to the Cattaraugus Reservation in the 1970s, Mrs. Seneca became my role model.[3]

Although her husband, Cornelius, and other male Seneca leaders fought the good battle to stop the building of the Kinzua Dam, it was women such as Pauline Seneca who inspired other women to take charge and rebuild after that disaster.

11

Women's Leadership and the Rebuilding of the Seneca Nation in the Wake of Kinzua, 1966–1990

For nearly four decades, I have had the privilege of being invited into the Seneca communities at Allegany and Cattaraugus, as well as into the Tonawanda Seneca's community near Akron/Basom, New York. Consequently, I have spent much time with elders, especially many remarkable Seneca and Cayuga women. Starting as a rather shy young man of twenty-five, I made it my point to come almost every year (from the 1970s onward) to the Peter Doctor Dinner and to the Cattaraugus Fall Festival.

Early in my academic career, I was taken before a three-member women's committee headed by Wini Kettle at the Women's, Infants' and Children's (WIC) Center at the Cattaraugus Reservation, where I was questioned/grilled for two and a half hours about my research on Seneca history, then focused on the life of Alice Lee Jemison, the outspoken critic of the BIA in the 1930s until her death in 1964. I apparently passed the test given that Wini, at the end of the "interview," gave me the address of Alice's daughter, Jeanne Marie Jemison, later the surrogate judge of the Seneca Nation and a person who became my dear friend until her death several years ago.

I gained an even greater appreciation of the role of women within the Seneca Nation while testifying on the Seneca Nation Settlement Bill in September 1990. Senecas Loretta Crane, Marlene Johnson, Rovena Abrams, and Mae Chambers made sure that this "nerdy" historian from New Paltz was not stagestruck before I testified before two congressional committees about the history of the Salamanca leases. Working with Congressman

Amory Houghton of Corning and his staff, I was the expert witness for what became the Seneca Nation Settlement Act, passed by Congress and signed into law by President George Herbert Walker Bush in November 1990. Public Law 101-503, the Seneca Nation Settlement Act, provided $60 million in compensation to the Seneca Nation of Indians for federal failures to carry out trust responsibilities and properly protect Indian interests under leasing arrangements made in the second half of the nineteenth century. Before the Seneca Nation signed two long-term leases of forty years each with the City of Salamanca, New York—85 percent of which is on the Seneca Nation's Allegany Indian Reservation—and other "congressional villages" established in 1875, the Seneca Nation insisted on compensatory justice. Although no amount of money could fully pay them for the intrusion of outsiders into their territory, Seneca representatives nevertheless agreed to work with delegates from Salamanca and the congressional villages. Encouraged by Congressman Houghton, they attempted to repair the damage caused by nearly a century and a half of inequitable leasing, injustices, and racism.[1]

I first showed up in Seneca Country in 1971, in the shadow of the Kinzua Dam tragedy that Dr. Joy Bilharz has so well documented in her book.[2] The building of the Kinzua Dam shattered Seneca existence, and this sad event is commemorated every September to remind tribal members of this most traumatic episode in their modern history. The $125 million Kinzua Dam broke the most revered federal-Iroquois treaty, the Canandaigua Treaty (Pickering Treaty) of 1794; flooded more than nine thousand acres of Seneca lands (all acreage below 1,365 feet elevation, including the entire Cornplanter Tract); destroyed the old Cold Spring Longhouse, the ceremonial center of Seneca traditional life; caused the removal of 130 Indian families from the "take area"; and resulted in the relocation of these same families from widely spaced rural surroundings to two suburban-styled housing clusters, one at Steamburg and the other at Jimersontown adjacent to the city of Salamanca. In compensation, Congress awarded the Seneca Nation $15,000,573 by a law passed, belatedly, in 1964. This act provided $1,289,060 for direct damages caused by land loss; $945,573 for indirect damages, compensating the Indians for relocation expenses, loss of timber, and destruction of wildlife; $387,023 for "cemetery relocation"; $250,000 for Indian legal and appraisal fees; and $12,128,917 for "rehabilitation," which was directed at meeting the Senecas' urgent need for community buildings, economic development, education, and housing. Going against Iroquois customary decorum, Seneca elders break down and cry, expressing their anguish in recalling the years 1957 to 1964. To them, the relocation and removal of Seneca families from the "take area" was their second "Trail of Tears," comparable only to these same Indians' loss of and removal from the Buffalo Creek Reservation in the first half of the nineteenth century.[3]

As I began collecting and researching about the origins of the Seneca Nation Libraries, I came to the conclusion that the great impetus for the rebuilding of the Seneca Nation after the Kinzua crisis, namely the creation of the Seneca Nation Libraries, the Seneca-Iroquois National Museum, and the Seneca Nation Health Clinics, came directly from Indian women's groups on the two reservations. Taking advantage of the favorable political climate in the 1970s, these women often operated behind the scenes as in their traditional manner of the past. Although Seneca presidents Bob Hoag and Lionel John and other Seneca men were much more visible and received the outside attention, these modern "mothers of the nation" determined to rebuild the Seneca communities after the horror of Kinzua, and carefully and methodically set about to carry out their agenda. They built on the work of other extraordinary women such as Senecas Genevieve Plummer and Martha Bucktooth, as well as of Cayugas such as Pauline Seneca.[4]

This memoir focuses on two specific areas: (1) the creation of the Seneca Nation Libraries, and (2) the establishment of the Seneca Nation Health Clinics at Cattaraugus and Allegany Indian Reservations. The impetus for the Seneca-Iroquois National Museum is directly related to these events, and many of the women mentioned in this chapter were also the "founding mothers" of the museum project. Both the library and museum projects were interrelated, and the proximity of the two facilities today is no accident. Although there was opposition to placing the library on Salamanca's main commercial thoroughfare, and there was talk of placing the library building behind the Haley Building, the library board and its supporters pushed for the present location of the library next door to the museum. According to several members of the library committee, it was placed on

10. Pauline Seneca, Cayuga elder, c. early 1980s. Photograph by Laurence M. Hauptman.

the main thoroughfare intentionally to "show *all* that the city was on Indian land."[5] Thus the individual Senecas and Cayugas involved in the lobbying were in their own way championing Indian sovereignty.

The creation of the Seneca Nation Libraries and the Seneca-Iroquois National Museum must be understood in the context of the times. New York State had ignored the securing of Johnson-O'Malley federal funds for nearly forty years, thus losing millions of dollars that could have been used for the improvement of Indian education. The policy of the New York State Department of Education was not to encourage the teaching of Native American history, culture, and languages. As a result of two major protests—by the Mohawks in 1968 and the Onondagas in 1971—that led to temporary boycotts of the public schools that Indian youth attended, the New York State Education Department (SED) was forced to respond.[6] The determined efforts of Ann Lewis of the Native American Indian Education Unit of SED, and the annual Iroquois Conference of concerned Native Americans held throughout the decade of the 1970s, helped lead women throughout Iroquoia to organize. They came together, networking as advocates of their communities. News of what was happening at one reservation community soon spread to others as these women came and went from these annual gatherings, first held at St. Lawrence University in 1971. Two of the Seneca women involved in this initial gathering included museum trustee Maribel Printup and Arliss Barse, whose mother, Reva, was a most vocal advocate of Seneca woman suffrage.[7]

A friendly rivalry with the Mohawk women at these Iroquois Conferences spurred on these Seneca women. There was a real feeling that if the Mohawks could get a library, then the Seneca Nation could do even better and get two. This competitive spirit motivated these goal-oriented women.[8] With New York State officials constantly doing battle with the Mohawks, Oneidas, and Onondagas on a variety of fronts—education, Ganienkeh, highway construction, jurisdiction, and land claims—these Senecas plotted a slightly different course of action.

Many prominent Seneca and Cayuga women attended these meetings and learned of Minerva White's and Margaret Jacobs' determined efforts to establish a Mohawk Nation Library at the Akwesasne Cultural Center.[9] Learning from the Mohawk example, the women formed committees on both the Allegany and Cattaraugus Reservations. These determined women and the early staff of the libraries included Pauline Seneca, Virginia Snow, Marlene Johnson, Alice Waterman, Dorothy Cox, Tessie Snow, Wini Kettle, and Marjorie Curry. Lana Redeye, hired as head of the Seneca Education Committee, served as liaison to the Seneca Nation Tribal Council and reported on these women's efforts. She also served as the major contact person from the Seneca Nation government to the New York State Education Department's Office of Library Development in Albany. Rae Snyder, the Seneca Nation's Comprehensive Employment and Training Act of 1973 (CETA) director, was also directly involved in the planning and hiring of Peggy Bray and Eleanor Bowen, Dorothy Cox, and Merrill Bowen as library staff. George Abrams, Martha Symes, and other members of the Seneca-Iroquois Museum helped push for the present Allegany Library's location, drew up the necessary legal incorporation, helped with the inner and outer design of the library, and coordinated the essential effort of making the two libraries part of the Cattaraugus-Chautauqua Library network.[10]

The women of the Seneca communities at Allegany and Cattaraugus (and their highly able ally Ramona Charles at Tonawanda) carefully cultivated a relationship with New York State Board of Regents Laura Chodos; with Joseph Shubert, assistant commissioner of education and head of the New York State Library, who had formerly lived at North Collins, New York, near the Cattaraugus Indian Reservation; and with SED personnel such as Bernard Finney of the New York State Library's Office of Library Development. Both Shubert and Finney visited the reservations, where the women helped sell the idea for two libraries.[11] Exploiting the tenor of the times with its call to provide access to library services, these women secured the support of the New York State Library Association, the American Library Association, and the National Indian Education Association. These women took advantage of the spadework done by the Mohawks as well as by Dr. Lotsee Patterson, a librarian of Chickasaw-Comanche ancestry at the University of Oklahoma, and Dr. Charles Townley, a librarian at the University of Minnesota who had a major four-year federal grant to promote Indian libraries nationwide. Patterson and Townley were both associated with the American Library Association and the National Indian Education Association and accomplished much in their push for Indian tribal libraries.[12]

These determined women's actions (and those of their male supporters) were a reaction to the colonial mind-set of Albany officials. Until the last three decades, the entire educational philosophy of SED was largely to assimilate American Indians into American life. With the rise of Red Power activism in the late 1960s and early 1970s, SED was forced to reconsider its historic educational policies vis-à-vis American Indians.

In 1975, the New York Board of Regents announced a position paper, "Native American Education," which significantly altered SED's past educational policies with respect to American Indians in New York State. This position paper, number twenty-two in the Board of Regents series, explained the reasons for this major policy shift in the following manner:

> The formal educational programs provided for Native Americans in New York State assumed that they desired to become assimilated into the dominant society, while forsaking their tribal heritages. The Regents now

recognize that these people prefer to retain their specific tribal cultural identities and life styles and that they wish to exercise the prerogatives of adopting only those components of the dominant American culture that meet their needs. In American history, the State and Federal attempts to terminate tribes, to dissolve their reservation status, and to relocate their people into urban settings have been unsuccessful.[13]

Hence a favorable climate was there for the Senecas to pursue the goal of creating tribal libraries as well as the Seneca-Iroquois National Museum.

In a move promoted by the Board of Regents, the New York State legislature passed a bill in 1977 creating and appropriating $175,000 for an Indian public library system, the first of its kind in the United States. The act also provided for specific means of acquiring and accepting surplus library books, a specific formula of apportionment of state aid to Indian libraries, and a mechanism for distribution of state aid to either the Indian library board of trustees or directly to the tribal government for a contract for library service.[14]

The women at Allegany and Cattaraugus now saw an opening and went through it to secure two tribal libraries. They took advantage of the national code words of the time: the need to provide access and cultural enrichment to all Americans, including so-called "disadvantaged" groups.[15]

These women won the support of Dadie Perlov, the head of the New York Library Association, who insisted that "this [library access to American Indians] service is still part of the unfinished business of this [New York] state" and consequently "is an embarrassment at a time when the country's conscience has been raised about the legitimate grievance of its Native Americans." She insisted that this "piece of progressive legislation will begin to redress a very old problem."[16] Using their "political smarts," these women even got State Senator James Donovan, an ultra-conservative legislator from Utica, to sponsor the bill. Donovan, who had a background in the building construction trades, was approached by Mohawks with a similar background. Donovan reached out in this fashion because he and his district were beset with the Eagle Bay (Ganienkeh) takeover and sought a way out of this Indian-white confrontation. The bill passed with only one dissenting vote in both houses of the New York State legislature in 1977.[17]

Ethel "Peggy" Bray was hired as a CETA worker in the Role Model Program of the federal government's Title IV-C. Importantly, she had been previously placed in the Silver Creek Junior-Senior High School library and worked there for five years after her children had grown up. Although not a certified librarian, Bray's work experience and abilities qualified her to serve as the first Seneca Nation librarian, and she was formally hired in the spring of 1979 to administer her staff, which included Merrill Bowen, Eleanor Bowen, and Dorothy Cox.[18] Joseph Shubert, in a 1990 paper on the Indian libraries, referred to Peggy Bray as "an expert on Native American libraries in New York State. She brought her library into being and into the Chautauqua-Cattaraugus Library System. She, Margaret Jacobs (who founded the Akwesasne Library and Cultural Center), and Ramona Charles of the Tonawanda Band of Senecas are the deans of Native American library services in our state."[19] Today these women's legacies live on in the operations of two well-used Seneca Nation libraries. The libraries are also community centers: over 250 programs—adult, young adult, and children's—are held at the two libraries.[20]

The women of the Allegany and Cattaraugus Indian reservations also played a key role in improving Indian health care in New York. In the early 1970s, conditions were scandalous. Policymakers at the state commissioner's level were even totally misinformed about the American Indians' legal status. In the early 1970s, New York State appropriations for Indian health were minimal, and statistics on Indian health were virtually nonexistent.[21] In 1971, a New York State Assembly report clearly showed that the state operated outdated, archaic, and inferior health facilities. At Cattaraugus, the "clinic" was housed in a dilapidated building of the Thomas Indian School.[22] Indian health care in New York was also characterized in one study prepared in 1972–73, but later published in *Clinical Pediatrics,* as being worse than health care in the ghetto areas of Rochester and New York City.[23] Furthermore, a Harvard University Public Health Study prepared in 1975 with the cooperation of the Seneca Nation documented among other things that Indian infant mortality rates were well over twice the national average.[24]

The Indian women of the Allegany and Cattaraugus Indian Reservations, including Wini Kettle, Hazel Dean John, Norma Kennedy, Betty Owl

Nephew, Marilyn Anderson, and many others came to the fore at this time, pushing male leaders, especially Lionel John, to take up this issue. Although Lionel John was the spokesman, becoming an advocate of improved health care both within the Seneca Nation and nationally, it was these women from behind the scenes—the traditional avenue of women—who helped organize the movement to build the clinics of the Seneca Nation.[25]

The impetus for improvement of these conditions was led by the Seneca Nation Health Action Group, not the New York State Department of Health, and it served as the major advocate group for better health services. Past experiences suggested the limitations of appealing directly for funds from the State Department of Health, so the Senecas worked informally and after work hours with their physicians and nurses, health care providers on the reservations, Karen Kalaijian of the Buffalo office of the New York State Department of Health, and the Harvard School of Public Health. They developed a health care proposal that was submitted to and approved by the U.S. Indian Health Service. After this and later proposals were funded, federal moneys were allocated for two new modern clinics that were built at the Allegany and Cattaraugus Indian Reservations. These health clinics, developed largely by the initiative of the Seneca people, became the model for the Mohawk Indian health program in New York and have even influenced some Indian health services nationwide.[26]

In this brief chapter, I have only touched on the work of some of the women of the era. There were many others who made their marks in the decade of the 1970s to help their people.[27] Some have been controversial figures in the Seneca world, while others have been mainstream types. All sought improvement, although they might have had different causes. Some eventually were elected to office and worked directly for the Seneca government. These "mothers of the nation" appear periodically in Iroquois history to show the way. They definitely arose at a most difficult time and rebuilt the Seneca Nation in the wake of Kinzua.

Conclusion

Iroquois Leadership into the Twenty-first Century

Whether looking at Iroquoia in 1800 or today, one might get the impression that there is no whole. The eminent anthropologist William N. Fenton once described to me his impressions of Iroquois politics. This leading scholar was in no way criticizing or making value judgments, but rather was assessing what he had uncovered in documents and in his fieldwork for over a half-century. To him, the rich diversity of opinion made locale central to Iroquoia and every villager significant. To ensure that their views were to be respected, villagers were expected to pull down leadership a notch or two or more. Consequently, chiefs were to have "skin seven thumbs thick" in order to be able to survive. Fenton concluded that at times this situation appeared to him to be "anarchic."[1]

In September 2007, Robert Odawi Porter, a major legal scholar at Syracuse University and senior policy advisor and counsel for the Seneca Nation, added to what Fenton had said to me more than twenty years earlier. "What appears to the outside as chaos," Porter insisted, "is what makes us who we are." Porter, a Seneca from Allegany, saw the variation of opinion and, at other times, explosive debate over leadership and its directions, as healthy. Porter, whose people were removed by the U.S. Army Corps of Engineers in the building of the Kinzua Dam, had put his finger on the pulse of Six Nations existence then and now.[2]

The Iroquois have been actively involved in finding ways to fend off the Euro-American intrusion since the sixteenth century. While they frequently do not reach the ideal of consensus as defined in their past, they nevertheless have used diverse strategies, sometimes in conflict with each other, that have allowed them to survive. From the era of forest diplomacy and beaver wars to the present age of casinos, they have come up with a variety of ideas and distinct, often competing, strategies and leadership styles to maintain their cultures and separate nationhood.

Modern Iroquois leadership in the United States and Canada was born in the years during and after World War II. The immediate postwar era was marked by continued land loss for non-Indian public works projects; armed confrontations between Indians and non-Indians over tribal lands, jurisdiction, and taxation; the rapid decline of the number of speakers of the Iroquoian languages as well as the passing of key elders with extensive knowledge of ritual and culture; and, most recently, Iroquois setbacks in the federal courts of the United States and Canada. The Iroquois Indians lost substantial acreage between 1954 and 1966 to power projects and transportation development favored by New York, Pennsylvania, Washington, D.C., and Ottawa officials. In building the Tuscarora Reservoir, the New York State Power Authority flooded 550 acres of the Tuscarora Reservation. The St. Lawrence Seaway, pushed by both American and Canadian officials, condemned 130 acres of land of the Akwesasne Mohawks and 1,260 acres of the Kahnawake Mohawks; it also furthered industrialization and environmentally contaminated both Mohawk territories and environs. The Kinzua Dam, largely pushed by Pennsylvania politicians but supported by local non-Indian officials in southwestern New York who feared an alternative plan, flooded over 9,000 acres, the entire Cornplanter Tract of the Seneca Nation; the dam's construction also led to the forced removal and resettlement of more than five hundred Senecas to new homesteads at Steamburg and Salamanca, New York.[3]

Outside intrusions into Iroquois existence took other forms besides land loss. Congress transferred criminal jurisdiction over the Iroquois to New York State in 1948 and to Wisconsin in 1954.[4] A major national relocation program was initiated to entice Indians off the reservations and into the cities during the 1950s. Moreover, efforts at federal withdrawal/termination of treaty obligations threatened Indian existence until 1970.[5] In Canada, until the late 1960s, Indian agents resided on Indian reservations, a carryover from the British colonial model of administration. As late as Pierre Trudeau's premiership in the 1960s and early 1970s, Canadian officials discussed their own version of termination, but failed to implement that after an outcry by Native peoples throughout the country.[6]

Iroquois leaders sought to transform their communities to meet these and other crises. One noticeable change was in the growth of Iroquois governments over the past half-century. In the 1950s, before the building of the Kinzua Dam, the council of the Seneca Nation of Indians would meet on an irregular basis in Leo Cooper's garage to handle the required affairs of the nation.[7] In the 1960s, with the growth of Great Society "remediation programs" to deal with problems caused by these disasters, Indian bureaucracies slowly developed on the reservations. With the Office of Economic Opportunity Great Society programs of the Johnson administration in the mid-1960s and later the Indian Self-Determination and Education Act of 1975 came increased federal programs. Consequently, Indian employment on reservations in the United States has mushroomed.[8]

The changes were not simply on the U.S. side of the "line." Canadian federal and provincial governments also poured money into Indian communities. At Akwesasne, tens of millions of dollars flowed into the community to build elders' residences, an arena, and a medical center, as well as to support the teaching of the Mohawk language, substance abuse programs, youth and women's shelters, and environmental initiatives.[9]

With the establishment of bingo operations from the early 1980s, casino gaming that followed after the Cabazon decision in 1987, and the passage of the American Indian Gaming Regulatory Act by Congress in 1988, moneys began to flow into some of the Iroquois communities, which led to a greater expansion of employment.[10] In New York, the Turning Stone Casino of the Oneida Nation of Indians of New York opened in 1993. Today the Oneida Nation of New York alone employs over four thousand people in their hotel-gaming complex in Verona, New York, offering Las Vegas–styled entertainment, championship boxing and billiards matches, and a first-class golf facility.[11] The Seneca Nation of Indians followed suit in developing gaming, but only after a decade-long bitter internal fight over whether to go in this direction. In 2001, the Senecas opened their Niagara Falls casino, followed in 2005 by the opening of a second gaming operation at Salamanca on the Allegany Reservation. A third temporary Seneca Nation casino opened in Buffalo on July 3, 2007, that will be replaced by a major gaming facility by 2010. In its first month alone, this new Buffalo gaming center drew 49,000 patrons. Moreover, both the Senecas' Allegany and Niagara Falls gaming operations have expanded significantly since their openings. As of February 2007, the Seneca gaming industry was employing five thousand employees and grossing $1.2 billion in revenues.[12]

Much less ambitious in scope or profitability than either the Oneidas' Turning Stone Casino or the three facilities run by the Seneca Nation is that of the Akwesasne Mohawks, who opened their casino in 2004 along State Road 37 near Hogansburg, New York. This gaming facility was developed on the reservation, but only after a decade and a half of internal conflict that on occasions spilled over into violent confrontations between pro-gaming and anti-gaming elements. In the last decade, the Mohawks have also pursued the possibility of opening up a casino in Sullivan County, New York.[13]

The Wisconsin Oneidas administer one of the most successful Indian casino operations in the United States. Indeed, two of its former tribal leaders—Richard Hill and Ernest Stevens Jr.—have served as the director of the National Indian Gaming Association, which represents the entire Indian gaming industry and promotes its development.[14] The Wisconsin Oneidas fully own and operate the Radisson Hotel and Conference Center, along with their Oneida Casino established in 1988, situated just across from Green Bay's Austin Straubel Airport; the Baybank, a full-service bank; the Oneida Industrial Park, a thirty-two-acre land development project with Wal-Mart as its major tenant and anchor store and with the Oneida Mason Street Casino adjacent to the site; Oneida Printing, a state-of-the-art printing business; Oneida Nation Farms, an agricultural operation on the reservation focusing on cattle and apple raising, that provides discounted food to tribal members; Oneida Retail Enterprise, a chain of four one-stops, four smokeshops, and one gift shop that sell Pendleton blankets as well as gas and discounted cigarettes and serve as mini-marts and mini-casinos; and Seven Generations Corporation, which leases a fifty-thousand-square-foot health facility to Belin Health Systems. Moreover, the Oneida Nation of Indians of Wisconsin is an investor, with three other Indian nations, in the Marriott Residence Inn Capitol in Washington, D.C., and is a major shareholder in the Native American Bank, N.A.

Recently, during the renovation of the Green Bay Packers' Lambeau Field, the Oneidas contributed moneys to the project, which led to the naming of part of the facility as the "Oneida Nation Entrance Gate."[15]

Any outsider can easily see the economic transformation of Iroquois life over the past half century. Although high-steel construction and other manual trades remain respected occupations, there are more economic alternatives for younger men and women growing up in the communities. Casino operations have also led to substantial purchases of land and helped capitalize vast economic development ventures while providing more employment, improved health care delivery, new housing, and varied efforts at cultural preservation. These efforts have also led to criticism of leadership, namely accusations of violating the *Gaiwiio,* charges of political patronage in the awarding of tribal employment and contracts, and suspicions of "selling out" to the non-Indian world and sacrificing Iroquois sovereignty by signing gaming compacts with the State of New York. Confrontations between pro-gaming and anti-gaming interests have led to violence and even deadly confrontations among the Mohawks and Senecas.[16]

In the Oneida communities in New York, Wisconsin, and Ontario, much of the conflict has centered on the views of one individual—Ray Halbritter— whose official title is "CEO and Nation Representative" of the Oneida Indian Nation in New York. To some, Halbritter, a graduate of Syracuse University and Harvard Law School, is a skillful entrepreneur who revived Oneida fortunes by his brilliant economic planning and his development of Turning Stone; he is also credited for his major philanthropic efforts that include funding veterans' organizations, aiding the developmentally challenged, and providing $10 million to the Smithsonian Institution to help establish the National Museum of the American Indian on the National Mall in Washington, D.C. To others, he is viewed as a power-hungry individual willing to sacrifice Iroquois concepts of sovereignty by separately negotiating with New York State governors; he is often accused of undermining traditional values by dictatorially governing through the Oneida Men's Council that is deemed alien to Oneida culture and history. Despite Halbritter's removal as the Oneida Wolf Clan designee on the Iroquois Grand Council at Onondaga in 1993, the federal government recognizes him as the official representative/voice of the Oneida Indian Nation of New York.[17]

These sudden economic changes have had other consequences as well. Iroquois attempts to buy back lands that had been taken from them in the past have led to a backlash, because extending the boundaries of "Indian Country" means to many local non-Indian communities the loss of vital tax revenues to maintain and operate their government services. This backlash has given further impetus to the activities of UCE (Upstate Citizens for Equality), an anti-Indian organization devoted to denying Indian land claims that brings pressure on state and federal officials to resist Iroquois efforts in the courts.[18]

Today's generation of leadership has been affected by other factors. Iroquois leadership has ardently pursued their land claims in New York State. These claims, as described by Arlinda Locklear, the attorney for the Oneida Nation of Indians of Wisconsin, are no "technical disputes hatched by clever lawyers" but are "long-standing pleas for justice by the tribes, pleas that are based on established legal principles well known to New York State, and have been asserted by the tribes for generations in every form available to them."[19] In 1974, the U.S. Supreme Court awarded three Oneida nations— in New York, Wisconsin, and Ontario—the right to sue in federal courts for land taken by New York in so-called state treaties after the adoption of the U.S. Constitution.[20] In 1985, the U.S. Supreme Court ruled in a test case, involving over seven hundred acres in the vast claim area, that New York had violated the federal Trade and Intercourse Act of 1790 and had negotiated a transfer of land title to the state without the presence of a federal commissioner, Senate ratification, or the president's proclamation.[21]

For the next two decades, any and all efforts to settle Indian land claims failed despite the efforts of tribal leaders of the Oneidas, Cayugas, Senecas, and Mohawks to press their claims. In 2005, the U.S. Supreme Court, in an eight-to-one decision, refused to recognize the Oneida Nation of Indians' reassertion of tribal jurisdiction and exemption from local and state taxes on lands repurchased within their original aboriginal territory.[22] The court held in this case, *The City of Sherrill v. Oneida Indian Nation*:

Today, we decline to project redress for the Tribe into the present and future, thereby disrupting the governance of central New York's counties and towns. Generations have passed during which non-Indians have

owned and developed the area that once composed the Tribe's historic
reservation. And at least since the middle years of the 19th century, most
of the Oneidas have resided elsewhere. Given the longstanding, distinctly
non-Indian character of the area and its inhabitants, the regulatory authority constantly exercised by New York State and its counties and towns,
and the Oneidas' long delay in seeking judicial relief against parties other
than the United States, we hold that the Tribe cannot unilaterally revive
its ancient sovereignty, in whole or in part, over the parcels at issue. The
Oneidas long ago relinquished the reins of government and cannot regain
them through open-market purchases from current titleholders.[23]

Several months later, on June 28, 2005, the Federal Court of Appeals for
the Second Circuit reversed a federal district court decision awarding the
Cayuga Indian Nation of New York and Seneca-Cayuga Tribe of Oklahoma $247.8 million in their land claim. The judges applied/misapplied
the *Sherrill* case to the Cayuga, insisting that both Cayuga nations had
waited too long, even though the Indians had no right to bring their case
in federal court before 1974.[24] The judges insisted, "Based on *Sherrill,* we
conclude that the possessory land claim alleged here is the type of claim to
which a laches defense can be applied. Taking into account the consider-
ations identified by the Supreme Court in *Sherrill* and the findings of the
District Court in the remedies stages of this case, we further conclude that
the plaintiffs' claim is barred by laches."[25] A third claim put forth by the
Seneca Nation of Indians for the 17,000-acre Grand Island in Erie County,
New York, was also denied at the federal district level in 2002 and on
appeal in 2005.[26]

While other Native Americans have secured sizable land settlements in
Connecticut, Maine, Massachusetts, Rhode Island, and South Carolina,
the Iroquois leadership has been stymied in this regard. The late Vine Deloria Jr. perceptively observed,

We do hear occasionally of the gigantic awards given to the tribes of the
Six Nations in their land claims against the state of New York, only to be
followed by appeals to higher courts, where tortured rhetoric and reason-
ing deprive the Indians of their hard-won victory. Indeed, if one follows

the litigation of the Oneida claim, it is like watching a tennis match, with one of the players having the right to determine for the other the boundary lines of the court. One expects rabbits to be pulled from hats as a case proceeds up the judicial structure, but sometimes the courts are pulling whole herds of cattle and buffalo from nowhere. Judgments often appear to be the first blush of contact between the tribes and their adversaries, and judges and justice are not a bit ashamed of their threadbare reasons for denying the Indian claims.[27]

These failures to secure justice in land claims settlements negotiated with New York State officials or by federal court decisions have also exacerbated tensions within Iroquois communities. The resulting "politics of blame" brought criticism of elected and traditional councils. Once again, as in the past, leaders had to have thick skin to deal with the brewing cauldron of discontent and the multitude of issues facing Iroquois communities.

This impatience, the long legal process of adjudication, and the belief that justice would not prevail in the "white man's world" have given rise to two other directions within Iroquoia, namely an age of activism and media-centered politics. Legitimate grievances over land loss, border crossing rights, economic and educational impoverishment, and environmental degradation in the Akwesasne Mohawk community influenced the origins and direction of Iroquois activism. These included the Tuscarora protest over the condemnation of their lands for the Niagara Power Project between 1958 and 1961; the boycotts of schools at Akwesasne in 1968 and at Onondaga in 1971; the Mohawk bridge sit-down protesting violations of their border crossing rights in 1968 and 1969; and the Onondaga protest over the expansion of Interstate 81 into their territory in 1971.[28]

Yet there was another side to activism: self-promoting opportunism. Unlike the idealistic Standing Arrow, others arose with less noble motives. Wallace "Mad Bear" Anderson, a Tuscarora "media hound," was one such self-styled "leader." By entertaining rather than educating, Mad Bear deflected attention away from real issues—land loss, jurisdictional concerns, poverty, treaty rights—expressed by recognized leaders, condoled chiefs, clan mothers, tribal presidents, and well-respected longtime advocates such as the Indian Defense League of America.[29] Anthropologist

Dean Snow has accurately described this phenomenon, one that unfortunately continues to the present day: "The popular press continues to be sympathetic but often misguided. In an effort to make sure that the voices of the Iroquois are heard, many non-Indians have failed to recognize that the Iroquois do not always speak with one voice." He added rightly, "Fortunately the lives of modern Iroquois are not defined by the sensational newspaper stories through which most non-Indians have come to know them [the Iroquois]."[30]

This type of "leadership" reached an apogee in the 1970s when a group of Kahnawake Mohawk activists, with little support from Iroquois communities in New York, seized and occupied lands in and around Eagle Bay in the Adirondacks. Instead of negotiating with the recognized Iroquois leadership, New York State officials negotiated with Ganienkeh activists and even agreed to give them a land base, near Plattsburgh, New York, for fear that rejecting their demands would lead to bad publicity and a violent confrontation. This sellout only undermined legitimate tribal leadership's efforts to negotiate settlements of existing land claims.[31]

The generation of Iroquois leaders today is clearly affected by a cultural crisis. Even though the Thomas Indian School as well as federal boarding schools housing Iroquois students are now closed, these institutions and past educational policies have had a damaging effect on Indian language retention. Perhaps 1 percent of the Six Nations population still speak one of the Iroquoian languages. Consequently, Handsome Lake's requirement about conducting the rituals of the *Gaiwiio* in one of the Native tongues is now threatened. Although there have been herculean Iroquois efforts to preserve the Oneida language in Wisconsin by Marie Hinton and Amos Christjohn, the Mohawk language by Tom Porter, and the Cayuga language by Jake Thomas and Reg Henry, these efforts have had limited success.[32]

This cultural crisis, as well as the increasing criticisms of elected systems or traditional councils of chiefs to meet the growing expectations of a rapidly expanding younger generation of Indians, has had other consequences. An Iroquois Warriors Movement has come to the fore in the last quarter-century. Inspired by the writings of Mohawk Louis Karoniaktajeh Hall, this movement was especially influential at Kahnawake,

Kahnesatake, and Akwesasne. Hall insisted that he was looking back to the pre–Handsome Lake Iroquois religious traditions. He rejected Handsome Lake and the *Gaiwiio* as being too much of an accommodation with the white world. Hall, a former Jesuit seminarian, also advocated the overthrow of all existing leadership—purging elected governments as well as traditional Confederacy chiefs.[33] To some, Hall was a needed revolutionary, a prophet expunging outside white influences, the leader necessary to stand up to Ottawa, Albany, and Washington. To others, Hall and his warriors were a threat to tranquility; they accused the movement of using intimidation and violent methods and promoting individual gain at the expense of community benefit. At times, the warriors were blamed for fostering illegal activities, a growing underground economy of smuggling cigarettes, drugs, and illegal aliens across the U.S.–Canadian international boundary.[34] Divisions intensified, especially within the three Mohawk communities of Akwesasne, Kahnesatake, and Kahnawake. One sign of this internecine conflict came at Akwesasne. In 1990, a civil war broke out between Mohawks pushing for casino gaming and those opposed to it.[35]

The same year, a major crisis occurred at Kahnesatake. The Town of Oka, Quebec, had decided to expand its municipal golf course. The Mohawks objected and put up barriers on the disputed land, arguing that the expansion would encroach on reservation land, including the site of Indian graves. The Quebec police moved in to remove the protesters, but on July 11, one member of the police was killed. Then, at the nearby Kahnawake reserve, Mohawks began blockading the heavily traveled Mercier Bridge that crosses the St. Lawrence River and is immediately adjacent to the reserve. The Quebec police began to blockade Kahnesatake, hoping to starve out the protesters. By this time, the premier of Quebec gave the Mohawks an ultimatum. Soon the United Nations Subcommission on Human Rights intervened in an attempt to quell further bloodshed. Indians from all over Canada, including the Iroquois Warriors Movement, came to support the protesters. Canada's prime minister, Brian Mulroney, ordered the Canadian army in, and more than three thousand troops surrounded the perimeter of the barricade. The situation was defused in September, when the Ottawa government relented and purchased the disputed ninety-two acres, which allowed the land to be transferred to Kahnesatake's council.[36]

Long-standing land claims disputes have continued in Canada. Besides raising to U.S. officials their claim to Barnhart Island as well as to the lands adjacent to the southeastern boundary of their reservation, the Akwesasne Mohawks frequently bring up to the Canadian government their Dundee claim to the islands in the St. Lawrence River.[37] In recent days, the Iroquois' most volatile land claim involves one centering around Caledonia, Ontario. The Six Nations at Ohsweken have long asserted that under the terms of the Haldimand Purchase/Treaty of 1784, their territory is the vast one-million-acre tract between Lakes Ontario, Erie, and Huron. They insist that through a series of outright frauds, their reserve was reduced by 95 percent. In 1793, Lord John Graves Simcoe, lieutenant governor of Upper Canada, drafted the Simcoe Patent, which required that all Six Nations land transactions be approved by the British Crown. Soon after, Joseph Brant illegally leased or sold over 350,000 acres to white farmers and merchants, which went directly against the Simcoe Patent. Other sources of contention over land boundaries included the vague language of the Haldimand Purchase/Treaty; in it there was no formal explicit mention of "lands draining into the headwaters of the Grand River above Nicoll Township."[38] In a similar vein to Levi General's protest in the early 1920s, the Iroquois claim that both the British and the Canadians in the post-Confederation period allowed the chipping away of Iroquois lands. They also accuse the British in particular of having invested and lost the Indians' trust money through poor investment in the Grand River Navigation Company.

In February 2006, with increased plans by non-Indian developers to build homesites, a small group of Iroquois protesters moved onto a small construction site at Caledonia, claiming this as "Haudenosaunee" by treaty and occupying it. As of August 2007, they still occupy the site. For the first time since 1924, in order to prevent another Oka disaster, the Canadian government is negotiating directly with the Confederacy chiefs at Ohsweken rather than with the elected band council established and recognized by Ottawa.[39]

Reminiscent of Levi General, the Six Nations Confederacy Council issued a statement on July 21, 2007, bringing up the British commitment to recognize their "land rights in the tract confirmed by Governor Frederick Haldimand on October 25, 1784." The council insisted,

> We seek to renew the existing relationship that we had with Crown prior
> to 1924. That relationship is symbolized by the Tehontatenentsonteron-
> tahkwa ("The thing by which they link arms") also known as the Silver
> Covenant Chain of Peace and Friendship. Our ancestors met repeatedly
> to polish that chain, to renew its commitments, to reaffirm our friend-
> ship and to make sure that the future generations could live in peace, and
> allow the land to provide its bounty for the well-being of all of the people.
> The Covenant Chain symbolizes our treaty relationship, also symbolized
> by Tekani Teyothata'tye Kaswénta (Two Row Wampum) which affirms
> the inherent sovereignty and distinctness of our governments. An essen-
> tial part of the relationship is our commitment to resolve matters through
> good-faith negotiation between our governments, including consultation
> on any plans which might affect the other government or its people.[40]

Hence, as this tense crisis shows, Iroquois leadership continues to draw
from the past to deal with the present. While outsiders impose conditions,
the Six Nations do not merely imitate other social protest movements. As
in the Condolence Council Ceremony, they draw inspiration from their
ancient antecedents to maintain their separation from others as well as
their sense of nationhood.

Other crisis situations are continuing at the present time. In the wake
of the Mitchell decision, the situation on the United States–Canada international boundary remains tense. The issue has been further complicated
by the tragedy of 9/11. Homeland security concerns about terrorists' entering both the United States and Canada have led to new border crossing
restrictions. Recently the Mohawk Council of Akwesasne has actually
recruited security officers on the reserve to monitor the actions of customs
officials. They have held numerous meetings with these officials, locally
and in Ottawa and Washington, in an attempt to sensitize them to Mohawk
concerns. Much like Levi General's efforts in the 1920s, the Mohawks at
Akwesasne have taken the issue before international organizations, including the Inter-American Commission on Human Rights.[41]

Tensions between the Iroquois and non-Indian governmental authorities have not been limited to Mohawk Country. The attempt by Albany
officials to apply the New York State sales tax to gas and cigarette sales

on Iroquois reservations led to two major "wars" in 1992 and 1997. In each instance, the Senecas closed down parts of major highways and forced Governors Cuomo and Pataki to back down from plans to enforce the state sales tax on Iroquois lands.[42] With a new governor in place, one cannot predict the future outcome of this continuing open sore.

In April 2007, much like Standing Arrow's protest in the 1950s, President Maurice John, Sr., and the council of the Seneca Nation of Indians threatened to put up a tollbooth on the New York State Thruway, on a three-mile strip of land that traverses the Cattaraugus Indian Reservation, claiming that no federal approval of the easement had been given to Albany officials. Subsequently, in defiance, John forwarded a bill to Governor Spitzer for $2,156,000 to cover the unpaid toll bill for buses, cars, and trucks traveling through Seneca territory. Besides the sales tax issue, the Senecas were clearly responding to state legal efforts, especially those of the Thruway Authority, that stymied their Grand Island land claim.[43]

Despite these crises, Iroquois leadership has achieved certain successes over the past quarter-century. The trustees of the Museum of the American Indian in New York City returned eleven wampum belts to the Onondaga chiefs at the Six Nations Reserve in 1988. The New York State Museum conveyed twelve wampum belts to the chiefs at Onondaga the following year.[44] The return of these and other ritual objects deemed sacred by the Iroquois ties their culture once again to the greatness of their people's past. It reinforces their separate views of nationhood, just as their ancestors had exchanged these belts with colonial powers to ensure reciprocal obligations.

On November 3, 1991, in the Seneca Nation Settlement Act, the U.S. Congress awarded the Seneca Nation of Indians $60 million in compensation for failure to carry out its trust responsibilities and to protect Indian interests in supervising leasing on the Allegany Indian Reservation. The act also provided for the renegotiation of two forty-year leases at a substantial increase in lease fees.[45] In addition, the Oneidas in both New York and Wisconsin have added substantially to their tribal land holdings, each acquiring more than 17,000 acres over the last decade and a half. In 2005, the Seneca Nation of Indians reached a final settlement on their land claim involving the Oil Spring Reservation, when New York State officials finally recognized that 51.3 acres should be returned to the nation. Other successes have been achieved outside of the New York homeland. In 2002–3, the Fox Valley & Western Railroad agreed to turn over a 130-acre abandoned right-of-way easement to the Oneida Nation of Indians of Wisconsin.[46]

DESPITE RECENT LEGAL SETBACKS in the courts, internal discord, and the loss of elders with vital knowledge, the Six Nations still demonstrate the cultural adaptability that has allowed them to maintain their individual and collective nationhood since before Euro-american contact. They have made great strides economically, reducing unemployment and repurchasing lands previously lost in dispossession; have achieved greater educational attainments; have lobbied successfully to secure some favorable outcomes of festering issues; and have made their mark culturally on the world scene in art, creative writing, and music. They have survived as a distinct people by tying their great past to the present. Their remarkable flexibility and adaptive skills have served them well. Their struggle to maintain their separate cultural identity and unique status as sovereign Indian nations continues today into the twenty-first century. Hopefully these strengths will allow the Hotinohsyóni⁷ to persevere into the future, or as they like to say, "for seven generations to come."

NOTES

BIBLIOGRAPHY

INDEX

Notes

ACLU	American Civil Liberties Union
ACP	Appointments, Commissions, Promotions (U.S. War Department Records, RG94, NA)
AFN	Assembly of First Nations
AIF	American Indian Federation
ANB	*American National Biography*
APS	American Philosophical Society, Philadelphia
App.	Appendixes
ARCIA	*Annual Reports of the Commissioner of Indian Affairs*
BECHS	Buffalo and Erie County Historical Society, Buffalo, N.Y.
BIA	Bureau of Indian Affairs
BIDI	Bureau International pour la Défense des Indigenes
Cong.	Congress
DAB	*Dictionary of American Biography*
CWPR	Civil War Pension Record
CCF	Central Classified Files
Coll.	Collection
CU	Columbia University
DMNA	[New York State] Division of Military and Naval Affairs
GBAR	Green Bay Agency Records
GU	Georgetown University
H.R.	U.S. House of Representatives
IDLA	Indian Defense League of America
IRA	Indian Reorganization Act (1934)
LC	Library of Congress, Washington, D.C.
M	Microcopy
MD	Manuscript Division
MR	Microfilm Reel

MSS.   Manuscript Collection
NA   National Archives, Washington, D.C.
NAA   National Anthropological Archives, Smithsonian Institution, Washington, D.C.
N.D.N.Y.   Northern District of New York
NIB   National Indian Brotherhood
NYAR   New York Agency Records
NYSA   New York State Archives, Albany
NYSL   New York State Library, Albany
OF   Official File (FDR Presidential Library, Hyde Park, N.Y.)
OHA   Onondaga Historical Association, Syracuse, N.Y.
OLD   Office of Library Development, New York State Library, Albany
OR   U.S. War Department, *The War of the Rebellion: A Compilation of the Official Records of the Union and Confederate Armies,* 128 vols. (Washington, D.C.: USGPO, 1880–1901).
PPF   President's Personal File (FDR Presidential Library, Hyde Park, N.Y.)
RG   Record Group
sess.   session
SHSW   Wisconsin Historical Society (formerly State Historical Society of Wisconsin), Madison; see also WHS
SJFC   St. John Fisher College, Rochester, N.Y.
Stat.   *United States Statutes at Large*
USGPO   U.S. Government Printing Office
VC   Vassar College
W.D.N.Y.   Western District of New York
WHC   Wisconsin Historical Collections
Whipple Report New York State Legislature, Assembly, *Report of the Special Committee to Investigate the Indian Problem of the State of New York, Appointed by the Assembly of 1888* (Albany: Troy Press, 1889)
WHS   Wisconsin Historical Society, Madison; see also SHSW
WPA   Works Progress Administration

PREFACE

1. David M. Ellis et al., *A History of New York State* (Ithaca, N.Y.: Cornell Univ. Press, 1973); Milton M. Klein, ed., *The Empire State: A History of New York* (Ithaca, N.Y.: Cornell Univ. Press, 2001).

2. William M. Beauchamp, *A History of the New York Iroquois,* Bulletin No. 78 (Albany: New York State Museum, 1906).

3. Dean R. Snow, *The Iroquois* (Oxford, U.K.: Blackwell, 1994).

4. Benjamin S. Cohn, "History and Anthropology: The State of Play," *Comparative Studies in Society and History* 22 (Apr. 1980): 198–221.

INTRODUCTION

1. Alvin M. Josephy, Jr., *The Patriot Chiefs: A Chronicle of American Indian Resistance* (New York: Viking, 1961); R. David Edmunds, ed., *American Indian Leaders: Studies in Diversity* (Lincoln: Univ. of Nebraska Press, 1980); R. David Edmunds, *The New Warriors: Native American Leaders Since 1900* (Lincoln: Univ. of Nebraska Press, 2001); L. George Moses and Raymond Wilson, eds., *Indian Lives: Essays on Nineteenth- and Twentieth-Century Native American Leaders* (Albuquerque: Univ. of New Mexico Press, 1985). For women's leadership, see Theda Perdue, ed., *Sifters: Native American Women's Lives* (New York: Oxford Univ. Press, 2001). For comparisons with other ethnic leadership in the United States, see Robert F. Berkhofer, "Native Leadership," in *Ethnic Leadership in America*, ed. John Higham (Baltimore: Johns Hopkins Univ. Press, 1978), 119–49.

2. Robert M. Utley, *The Lance and the Shield: The Life and Times of Sitting Bull* (New York: Henry Holt and Co., 1993); John Sugden, *Tecumseh: A Life* (New York: Henry Holt and Co., 1997).

3. James McGregor Burns, *Leadership* (New York: Harper and Row, 1978), 18–20. Burns continued to refine his thinking over the next three decades. See Burns, *Running Alone: Presidential Leadership—JFK to Bush II: Why It Has Failed and How We Can Fix It* (New York: Basic Books, 2006).

4. Anthony F. C. Wallace, *The Death and Rebirth of the Seneca* (New York: Alfred A. Knopf, 1970); William N. Fenton, *The Great Law and the Longhouse: A Political History of the Iroquois Confederacy* (Norman: Univ. of Oklahoma Press, 1998).

5. 7 *Stat.,* 44 (Nov. 11, 1794).

6. Lewis Henry Morgan, *League of the Ho-de-no-sau-nee, or Iroquois* (1851; reprinted as *League of the Haudenosaunee, or Iroquois* [New York: Corinth Books, 1962]).

7. J. N. B. Hewitt, *Iroquoian Cosmology,* part 1: *Annual Report of the Bureau of American Ethnology for the Years 1899–1900* (Washington, D.C., 1903), 21:127–339, and *Iroquoian Cosmology,* part 2: *Annual Report of the Bureau of American Ethnology for the years 1925–1926* (Washington, D.C., 1928), 43:449–818; Arthur C. Parker, *Parker on the Iroquois,* ed. William N. Fenton (Syracuse, N.Y.: Syracuse Univ. Press, 1968).

8. For a thorough discussion of this term, see William N. Fenton, "Northern Iroquoian Culture Patterns," in *Handbook of North American Indians,* vol. 15: *The Northeast,* ed. Bruce G. Trigger (Washington, D.C.: Smithsonian Institution, 1978), 319–21. Fenton was aided by Ives Goddard, Floyd Lounsbury, Hanni Woodbury, and Michael Foster in this endeavor.

9. For more on this aspect of Iroquois adaptability, see Wallace, *Death and Rebirth,* 111–14. See also Francis Jennings, *The Ambiguous Iroquois Empire* (New York: W. W. Norton,

1984); Daniel K. Richter, *The Ordeal of the Longhouse: The Peoples of the Iroquois League in the Era of European Colonization* (Chapel Hill: Univ. of North Carolina Press, 1992).

10. Edmund Wilson, *Apologies to the Iroquois* (1960; reprint, with a new introduction by William N. Fenton, Syracuse, N.Y.: Syracuse Univ. Press, 1991).

1. THE IROQUOIS IN 1800

1. See Barbara Graymont, *The Iroquois in the American Revolution* (Syracuse, N.Y.: Syracuse Univ. Press, 1972); Joseph Glatthaar and James Kirby Martin, *Forgotten Allies: The Oneida Indians and the American Revolution* (New York: Hill and Wang, 2006); Alan Taylor, *The Divided Ground: Indians, Settlers, and the Northern Borderland of the American Revolution* (New York: Alfred A. Knopf, 2006).

2. For more on the Jay Treaty, see chap. 10 of this book.

3. For the texts of these state treaties, see Whipple Report, appendix d, 190 passim. For the federal Treaty of Big Tree, see Wallace, *Death and Rebirth*, 179–83; Norman B. Wilkinson, "Robert Morris and the Treaty of Big Tree," *Mississippi Valley Historical Review* 40 (Sept. 1953): 257–78; Barbara A. Chernow, "Robert Moses: Genesee Land Speculator," *New York History* 58 (Apr. 1977): 195–220.

4. 1 *Stat.*, (July 22, 1790), 137–38. The federal requirements were clearly spelled out; see also William Bradford (U.S. attorney general) to Timothy Pickering, June 16, 1795, in *Iroquois Indians: A Documentary History of the Six Nations and Their League,* ed. Francis Jennings et al., MR 43, NYSL; Pickering to John Jay (governor of New York State), July 16 and Sept. 1, 1795, John Jay MSS., CU.

5. Whipple Report, 366–68.

6. Barbara Graymont, "New York State Indian Policy After the American Revolution," *New York History* 58 (Oct. 1976): 438–74. As Graymont brings out, the enabling legislation in 1795 that created the state commission to negotiate with the Iroquois set limits on profits to be made from the sale of these lands, a policy that was never followed.

7. For the federal Treaty of Fort Stanwix of 1784, see 7 *Stat.*, 15 (Oct. 22, 1784).

8. Whipple Report, 234–43.

9. For the federal Treaty of Canandaigua (also known as the Pickering Treaty or the Treaty with the Six Nations), see 7 *Stat.*, 44 (Nov. 11, 1794). By far the best account of this historic treaty and what led up to it, see Fenton, *Great Law and the Longhouse,* 622–706.

10. See Wallace, *Death and Rebirth,* 179–83.

11. For a fuller treatment of these forces, see Laurence M. Hauptman, *Conspiracy of Interests: Iroquois Dispossession and the Rise of New York State* (Syracuse, N.Y.: Syracuse Univ. Press, 1999).

12. Wallace, *Death and Rebirth,* 199–202.

13. For Friends-Seneca connections in the age of Handsome Lake, see Anthony F. C. Wallace, ed., "Halliday Jackson's Journal to the Seneca Indians, 1798–1800," *Pennsylvania History* 19 (1952): 117–46, 325–49; George Snyderman, ed., "Halliday Jackson's Journal of a Visit Paid to the Indians of New York (1806)," *Proceedings of the American Philosophical Society* 101 (Dec. 1957): 565–88; Halliday Jackson, *Civilization of the Indian Natives* (Philadelphia: Marcus Gould, 1830); Merle H. Deardorff and George Snyderman, "A Nineteenth-Century Journal of a Visit to the Indians of New York," *Proceedings of the American Philosophical Society* 100 (Dec. 1956): 582–612.

14. Wallace, *Death and Rebirth,* 308–9.

15. Ibid., 239–302. The literature on the origins of the Handsome Lake Religion is too vast to cite in its entirety. For a synopsis see Anthony F. C. Wallace, "Origins of the Longhouse Religion," in Trigger, *Handbook of North American Indians,* 442–48.

16. Wallace, *Death and Rebirth,* 149–236.

17. Elisabeth Tooker, "On the New Religion of Handsome Lake," *Anthropological Quarterly* 41 (1968): 187–200.

18. Graymont, *Iroquois in the American Revolution,* 291; Wallace, "Origins of the Longhouse Religion," 447.

19. For Handsome Lake's attempt to keep the Indians out of the War of 1812, see Erastus Granger to Jasper Parrish, Oct. 24, 1812, Jasper Parrish MSS., VC.

20. Wallace, "Origins of the Longhouse Religion," 447.

21. Wallace, *Death and Rebirth,* 327.

22. Walter Pilkington, ed., *The Journals of Samuel Kirkland* (Clinton, N.Y.: Hamilton College, 1980), 413.

23. Federal Census 1790–1860; New York State Census, 1825, 1835, 1845, 1855.

PART ONE — INTRODUCTION

1. Alan Taylor, *Divided Ground,* 404.

2. See Hauptman, *Conspiracy of Interests,* 191–220. For the later building of highways through Iroquoia, see Laurence M. Hauptman, *Formulating American Indian Policy in New York State, 1970–1986* (Albany: State Univ. of New York Press, 1988), 95–103.

3. Hauptman, *Formulating American Indian Policy,* 45–88.

4. Elisabeth Tooker, "On the Development of the Handsome Lake Religion," *Proceedings of the American Philosophical Society* 133 (1989): 36–37.

5. Tooker, "Development of the Handsome Lake Religion," 35–50.

6. Ibid., 48, 48nn. 11 and 12.

7. 7 *Stat.,* 44 (Nov. 11, 1794).

8. Carl Benn, *The Iroquois in the War of 1812* (Toronto: Univ. of Toronto Press, 1998), 24–25.

9. For more on these treaties, see Hauptman, *Conspiracy of Interests*, 144–61, 175–212.

10. Wallace, *Death and Rebirth*, 111–14.

11. See Richter, *Ordeal of the Longhouse*, 255–80.

2. GOVERNOR BLACKSNAKE AND THE OIL SPRING RESERVATION

1. Interview of Calvin "Kelly" John, May 4, 1997, Allegany Indian Reservation. The late Calvin John was the former president of the Seneca Nation of Indians. All interviews are by author unless otherwise noted.

2. Thomas S. Abler, ed., *Chainbreaker: The Revolutionary War Memoirs of Governor Blacksnake as Told to Benjamin Williams* (Lincoln: Univ. of Nebraska Press, 1989). For more on Governor Blacksnake, see Lyman C. Draper, "Visit to Coldspring, Cattaraugus County— Governor Blacksnake," Feb. 10–20, 1850, Lyman C. Draper Collection, 45, WHS.

3. See Tooker, "Development of the Handsome Lake Religion," 35–50; and her "New Religion of Handsome Lake," 187–200; and Anthony F. C. Wallace, "Origins of the Long-house Religion," 442–48.

4. Tooker, "Development of the Handsome Lake Religion," 36–37.

5. Abler, *Chainbreaker*, 2–3.

6. Laurence M. Hauptman, Seneca Field Notes, 1971–98, emphasis mine. I've attended five funerals at this cemetery over the past thirty-five years.

7. Abler, *Chainbreaker*, 16–43, 151–62, 203–6.

8. For the crises facing the Seneca Indians in this period, see Laurence M. Hauptman, "State's Men, Salvation Seekers and the Senecas: The Supplemental Treaty of Buffalo Creek, 1842," *New York History* 78 (Jan. 1997): 51–82; Laurence M. Hauptman, "Four Eastern New Yorkers and Seneca Lands: A Study in Treaty-Making," *Hudson Valley Regional Review* 13 (Mar. 1996): 1–19; Thomas S. Abler, "Factional Dispute and Party Conflict in the Political System of the Seneca Nation (1845–1895): An Ethnohistorical Analysis" (Ph. D. diss., Univ. of Toronto, 1969); and Henry S. Manley, "Buying Buffalo from the Indians," *New York History* 28 (July 1947): 313–29.

9. Wallace, *Death and Rebirth*, 308–9.

10. Abler, *Chainbreaker*, 216–25.

11. Draper, "Visit to Coldspring"; William Ketchum, *An Authentic and Comprehensive History of Buffalo* (Buffalo, N.Y.: Rockwell, Baker and Hill, 1864–65), 2:275, 2:326.

12. Diane B. Rothenberg, "Friends Like These: An Ethnohistorical Analysis of the Interaction between Allegheny Senecas and Quakers, 1798–1823" (Ph.D. diss., City Univ. of New York, 1976), 252–53.

13. Wallace, *Death and Rebirth*, 331–32.

14. Lois Barton, *A Quaker Promise Kept: Philadelphia Friends' Work with the Allegany Senecas, 1795–1960* (Eugene, Ore.: Spencer Butte Press, 1990), 20.

15. Orsamus Turner, *Pioneer History of the Holland Purchase of Western New York* (1850; reprint, Geneseo, N.Y.: James Brunner, 1974), 509–10.

16. Turner, *Holland Purchase,* 509–10; Wallace, *Death and Rebirth,* 332.

17. Fenton, *Great Law and the Longhouse,* 712.

18. Wallace, *Death and Rebirth,* 335.

19. See note 8 in this chapter.

20. For the Treaty of Big Tree, see Charles J. Kappler, *Indian Affairs: Laws and Treaties* (Washington, D.C.: USGPO, 1904–41), 1027–30; *Seneca Nation v. Philonus Pattison,* New York State Court of Appeals, vol. 487, case no. 1, 1860–61, NYSL. The special status of the Oil Spring Reservation has been misinterpreted ever since. See, for example: C. C. Royce, comp., *Indian Land Cessions in the United States, 18th Annual Report of the Bureau of American Ethnology, 1896–1897* (Washington, D.C.: USGPO, 1899), 660; Thomas Donaldson, comp., *The Six Nations of New York,* Extra Census Bulletin of the 11th Census (1890) of the United States (Washington, D.C.: U.S. Census Printing Office, 1892), 28; Wallace, *Death and Rebirth,* 183.

21. Wallace, *Death and Rebirth,* 182.

22. *Jesuit Relations* 43 (1656): 259–61.

23. Wallace, *Death and Rebirth,* 182, 266, 269, 280, 300, 324.

24. Robert Munro, "A Description of the Genesee Country," in *Documents Relative to the Colonial History of the State of New York,* ed. E. B. O'Callaghan and Berthold Fernow (New York: Weed Parsons, 1856–87), 2:1176.

25. William W. Campbell, ed., *The Life and Writings of De Witt Clinton* (New York: Baker and Scribner, 1849), 204.

26. Campbell, *Life and Writings of De Witt Clinton,* 194.

27. Blake McKelvey, *Rochester on the Genesee* (Syracuse, N.Y.: Syracuse Univ. Press, 1973), 44–50; and McKelvey's *Rochester: The Water-Power City, 1812–1854* (Cambridge, Mass.: Harvard Univ. Press, 1945), 6, 72, 112, 203; Neil Adams McNall, *An Agricultural History of the Genesee Valley, 1790–1860* (Philadelphia: Univ. of Pennsylvania Press, 1952), 124–27, 183–200; Ronald E. Shaw, *Erie Water West* (Lexington: Univ. of Kentucky Press, 1965), 123–30.

28. McKelvey, *Rochester on the Genesee,* 44–50; McKelvey, *Rochester: The Water-Power City,* 6, 72, 112, 203; Henry O'Reilly, *Sketches of Rochester* (Rochester, N.Y.: William Alling, 1838), 31.

29. Noble E. Whitford, *History of the Canal System of the State of New York* (Albany: Office of the Chief Engineer and Brandon Printing, 1906), 1:708–27.

30. Whitford, *History of the Canal System,* 1:708–27, 1010–15; 2:1030–36.

31. Ibid., 1:708–27, 1030–36; Robert J. Rayback, ed., *Richards Atlas of New York State,* rev. ed. (Phoenix, N.Y.: Frank E. Richards, 1965), 50.

32. Charles C. Congdon, *Allegany Oxbow* (Little Valley, N.Y.: privately printed, 1967), 205.

33. In 1927, New York State convinced Congress to retroactively confirm the state's take of Indian lands at Oil Spring between 1858 and 1865 in what is popularly known as the "Seneca Conservation Act." *Stat.*, 44, part 2 (Jan. 5, 1927), 932–33. The New York State Treasurer's records for May 12, 1866, indicate that the New York State "Canal Fund" paid out in 1865 to "D. Sherman Atty" $1,396.04, NYSA, series A0005, *Records of the New York State Treasurer, Register of Payments* 176 (Oct. 1864–Sept. 1865): 312. Yet "takes" of Seneca lands at Oil Spring occurred *after* 1865. See New York State Land Office, *Proceedings of the Commissioners of the Land Office for the Year 1924* (Albany: J. B. Lyon Co., 1924), 109–12; *Documents of the Convention of the State of New York, 1867–1868* (Albany: Weed, Parsons and Co., 1868), 5, Document No. 168, Jan. 21, 1868, 167–68; Charles Z. Lincoln, comp., *The Constitutional History of New York* (Rochester, N.Y.: Lawyers Cooperative Publishing Co., 1906), 2:389–90; New York State Legislature Senate Document No. 72, April 3, 1868; New York State Board of Canal Appraisers, *Digest of Claims . . . from 1866 to 1870, Inclusive* (Albany: Argus Co., 1870), 113; New York State Legislature, *Senate Journal for 1869* (Albany: Argus Co., 1869), 288–91, 442–43, 562–65, 604–5; New York State Legislature, *Assembly Journal for 1869* (Albany: Argus Co., 1869), 562–63, 634–35, 1180–81, 1414–15.

34. Albert E. Hoyt to Delbert F. Snyder (County Clerk, Allegany County, N.Y.), Aug. 13, 1914, Records of the Seneca Nation of Indians, Department of Justice, 4; Sen. Seneca Nation of Indians, 3.1D (4): Documents Produced by New York State Office of Parks, Recreation, etc. (loose), 000058, Genevieve Plummer Building, Allegany Indian Reservation. See also F. A. Gaylord, "Report on State Land in the Vicinity of Cuba Lake" (1913), a copy of which is also found in *Map Book: Indian Reservations,* Cattaraugus County Courthouse, Little Valley, N.Y., as well as in records of the Seneca Nation Department of Justice.

35. New York State Legislature, Assembly Document No. 168 (1836), 1–4.

36. Ibid.

37. Turner, *Holland Purchase,* 538–39; John S. Minard, *History of Allegany County* (New York: W. A. Ferguson, 1876), 813–15; John S. Minard, *The Indian Oil Spring* (Gowanda, N.Y., privately printed, 1901), 3.

38. Minard, *Indian Oil Spring,* 4.

39. For the briefs and court proceedings, see *Seneca Nation v. Philonus Pattison.* Transcript of the local court proceedings and testimony at the Cattaraugus County Court in 1857–58 can be found in *Map Book Indian Reservation,* Cattaraugus County Courthouse, Little Valley, N.Y. A copy of Blacksnake's map and papers are also filed there. For a discussion of this case and for the Horatio Seymour reference, see Congdon, 197–202; Donaldson, *Six Nations of New York,* 28–29; Daniel Sherman, "The Six Nations," a speech delivered before the Chautauqua Society, Jan. 29, 1885 (Cleveland, Ohio: W. W. Williams, 1885), 4–8.

40. See note 38 in this chapter.

41. Ibid.

42. Henry R. Howland, *The Old Caneadea Council House and Its Last Council Fire* (Perry, N.Y.: Comfort Craftsmen, 1932), 34–40 (supplement about Letchworth).

43. See the original edition of Howland's "The Old Caneadea Council House and Its Last Council," *Buffalo Historical Society Publications*, 1903, 6:97–123.

3. SAMUEL GEORGE

1. For a more even-handed treatment of the Iroquois, see Trigger, *Handbook of North American Indians*, 15:418–546.

2. Whipple Report, 390.

3. For the life of Albert Cusick, see William M. Beauchamp, Notebook: "Sketches of Onondagas of Note," 219–21, William M. Beauchamp MSS., box 3, NYSL, MD.

4. Frederick Houghton, *The History of the Buffalo Creek Reservation*, Publication No. 24 (Buffalo, N.Y.: Buffalo Historical Society, 1920), 1–181; Beauchamp, Notebook, 172–73; Samuel George's Pension Application, New York State DMNA, Adjutant General's Office, Claims, Applications and Awards for Service in the War of 1812, ca. 1857–1861, NYSA; Charles M. Snyder, ed., *Red and White on the New York Frontier: A Struggle for Survival—Insights from the Papers of Erastus Granger, Indian Agent, 1807–1819* (Harrison, N.Y.: Harbor Hill, 1978), 30; Kappler, *Laws and Treaties,* 2:515–16.

5. Wallace, *Death and Rebirth,* 239–337.

6. Wallace, "Origins of the Longhouse Religion," 447.

7. Harold Blau, Jack Campisi, and Elisabeth Tooker, "Onondaga," in Trigger, *Handbook of North American Indians,* 15:496. Interview of Ray Gonyea, Jan. 22, 1988, Albany, N.Y. Mr. Gonyea, an Onondaga Indian, was the specialist in Native American culture, New York State Museum.

8. See Benn, *Iroquois in the War of 1812.* For good source material, see Snyder, *Red and White on the New York Frontier*; and Arthur C. Parker, "The Senecas in the War of 1812," *Proceedings of the New York State Historical Association* 15 (1916): 78–90.

9. For the Iroquois on the British side, see Charles M. Johnston, ed., *The Valley of the Six Nations: A Collection of Documents on the Indian Lands of the Grand River* (Toronto: Champlain Society, 1964), 193–228; John Norton, *The Journal of Major John Norton,* ed. Carl F. Klinck and James J. Talman (Toronto: Champlain Society, 1970), 349–53; and G. F. G. Stanley, "The Significance of the Six Nations Participation in the War of 1812," *Ontario History* 55 (1963): 215–63.

10. See notes 8 and 9 in this chapter. See also William M. Beauchamp, Notebook, 159–60; Jasper Parrish to Peter B. Porter, July 27, 1814, and Asa Landforth to Peter B. Porter, Sept. 7, 1814, MR 2, Peter B. Porter MSS., BECHS; E. A. Cruikshank, ed., *The Documentary History of the Campaign Upon the Niagara Frontier, 1812–1814* (Welland, Ontario: Lundy's Lane Historical Society, 1896–1908), 2:338–89, 406, 448, and 3:145. For Indian casualties (at the Battle of Chippawa), see John Brannan, comp., *Official Letters of*

the Military and Naval Officers of the United States During the War with Great Britain . . . (Washington, D.C.: n.p., 1823), 368–73; "General Peter B. Porter's Description of the Battle of Chippawa," in *Public Papers of Daniel D. Tompkins: Governor of New York,* ed. Hugh Hastings (New York: n.p., 1898), 1:86–92; Snyder, *Red and White on the New York Frontier,* 80–81.

11. Beauchamp, Notebook, 173; "Clifton" letter to *Narragansett Weekly,* quoted in *Syracuse Standard,* July 26, 1858, news clipping in Sanford Thayer file (relative to portrait of Captain George), OHA.

12. Orlando Allen, "Personal Recollections of Captains Jones and Parrish," Buffalo Historical Society, *Publications* 6 (1903): 544.

13. Morgan, *League of the Haudenosaunee,* 441.

14. Interviews of Lee Lyons and Oren Lyons, Sept. 8, 1984, Syracuse. The late Lee Lyons, a Seneca Indian, served as a runner for the Grand Council of the Iroquois Confederacy; his brother Oren Lyons is a Seneca Indian by birth and an Onondaga chief who serves as an Iroquois faithkeeper. For the life of one modern-day runner, see "Joyondawde Lee A. Lyons, Wolf Clan, Seneca Nation," *Akwesasne Notes* 18 (Midwinter 1986): 3. In July 1984, I attended ceremonies at the Cattaraugus Indian Reservation, at which time Iroquois runners were sent cross-country to the site of the Olympic Games in Los Angeles. For more on Iroquois runners, see Morgan, *League of the Ho-de-no-sau-nee,* 109–10; and Peter Nabokov, *Indian Running: Native American History and Tradition* (Santa Fe, N.M.: Ancient City Press, 1981), 18, 84, 178.

15. New York State, Adjutant-General's Office, *Index of Awards: Soldiers of the War of 1812* (Baltimore: Genealogical Society, 1969), 571.

16. William N. Fenton, "The Iroquois in History," in *North American Indians in Historical Perspective,* ed. Eleanor Burke Leacock and Nancy Oestreich Lurie (New York: Random House, 1971), 161–62; Manley, 313–29. For the text of the Treaty of Buffalo Creek, see Kappler, *Laws and Treaties,* 2:502–16.

17. Sam George and David Smith to the Chiefs at Cattaraugus, June 8, 1850, Marius B. Pierce MSS., BECHS.

18. Jabez Backus Hyde, *A Teacher Among the Senecas: Historical and Personal Narrative of Jabez Backus Hyde,* Buffalo Historical Society Publication, 1903, 6:247; U.S. Bureau of the Census, *The Six Nations of New York,* Extra Census Bulletin of the 11th Census of the United States, 1890 (Washington, D.C.: USGPO, 1892), 6–9. See also Laurence M. Hauptman, foreword to *Onondaga: Portrait of a Native People,* by Fred R. Wolcott (Syracuse, N.Y.: Syracuse Univ. Press, 1986), 5–10.

19. For Captain Cold, sometimes referred to as Captain Cole (Tayatoaque or Uthawah), see Beauchamp, Notebook, 165–66; Elisabeth Tooker, "The League of the Iroquois: Its History, Politics and Ritual," in Trigger, *Handbook of North American Indians,* 5:436. In (Schoolcraft) Census of the State of New York, 1845, George is listed under "Senecas of Cattaraugus Reservation," entry No. 170, NYSL, MD; Beauchamp, Notebook, 172.

20. Annemarie Shimony, "Conflict and Continuity: An Analysis of an Iroquois Uprising," in *Extending the Rafters: Interdisciplinary Approaches to Iroquoian Studies,* ed. Michael K. Foster, Jack Campisi, and Marianne Mithun (Albany: State University of New York Press, for the Center for the History of the American Indian of the Newberry Library, 1984), 154. For the Great Wolf, see Morgan, *League of the Haudenosaunee,* 65; William N. Fenton, "The Roll Call of the Iroquois Chiefs: A Study of a Mnemonic Cane from the Six Nations Reserve," *Smithsonian Miscellaneous Collections* 111 (1950): 1–73; and Tooker, "League of the Iroquois," 424–25.

21. New York State, Superintendent of Common Schools, *Annual Report, 1849* (Albany, 1849), 17.

22. New York State, Superintendent of Public Instruction, *Eleventh Annual Report, 1865* (Albany, 1865), 94–95.

23. Onondaga Chiefs to Nathan Bristol, Apr. 3, 1853, Ely S. Parker MSS., APS.

24. Ibid.; David Hill to Ebenezer Meriam, Feb. 16, 1853, Nov. 17, 1854, Jan. 4, 1855; and Thomas LaFort to Meriam, May 31, 1853, Letters of Onondaga Indians, 1850–1855 MSS., APS.

25. Laurence M. Hauptman, "The Tuscarora Company: An Iroquois Unit in the American Civil War," *Turtle Quarterly* 1 (Spring 1987): 10–12; Laurence M. Hauptman, "Iroquois in Blue: From Reservation to Civil War Battlefield," *Northeast Indian Quarterly* 5 (Fall 1988): 35–39; William H. Armstrong, *Warrior in Two Camps: Ely S. Parker, Union General and Seneca Chief* (Syracuse, N.Y.: Syracuse Univ. Press, 1978), 71–121. See chap. 7 of this book.

26. For the draft in New York State, see Eugene C. Murdock, *Patriotism Limited, 1862–1865: The Civil War Draft and the Bounty System* (Kent, Ohio: Kent State Univ. Press, 1967), vii–41. For some modifications upon Murdock's work, see James W. Geary, "Civil War Conscription in the North: An Historiographical Review," *Civil War History* 32 (Sept. 1986): 208–28.

27. For Iroquois conscription in World War II and Vietnam, see Laurence M. Hauptman, *The Iroquois Struggle for Survival: World War II to Red Power* (Syracuse, N.Y.: Syracuse Univ. Press, 1986), 1–9.

28. "An Onondaga Chief at Washington" and "Affairs of the Six Nations," Nov. 25, 1863, news clipping in Samuel George File, OHA; Herman J. Viola, *Diplomats in Buckskin: A History of Indian Delegations in Washington City* (Washington, D.C.: Smithsonian Institution Press, 1981), 95–96.

29. Roy Basler, ed., *Collected Works of Abraham Lincoln* (New Brunswick, N.J.: Rutgers Univ. Press, 1953), 7:27; F. D. Townsend and C. S. Christinsen, Special Order No. 542, Dec. 7, 1863, Correspondence of the Office of Indian Affairs, Letters Received, 1824–1880, NYA, 1829–1880, MR 590, RG75, NA.

30. Quoted in Abstract, Muster Rolls: 13th New York Heavy Artillery—James Big Kettle (p. 242), Cornelius Fatty (p. 1058), James Halfwhite (p. 1381), Seth Jacob (p. 1669), Jesse Kenjockety (p. 1797), Wooster King (p. 1838), Young King (p. 1840), Murphy Longfinger (p.

1969), Stephen Ray (p. 2672), Martin Red Eye (p. 2678), Thomas Scrogg (p. 2879), Nathaniel Strong (p. 3165), and Dennis Titus (p. 3275); 86th New York Volunteers: John Thomas (p. 1939), series 13775, NYSDMNA, NYSA.

31. Seneca Residing at Cattaraugus Petition to Abraham Lincoln, June 4, 1864, NYAR 1829–1880, MR 590, RG75, NA.

32. Samuel George to William Dole, July 5, 1864, NYA, 1829–1880, MR 590, RG75, NA.

33. Ibid; E.R.S. Canby to J. P. Usher, Jan. 14, 1864; E. Townsend Special Order No. 126, Mar. 24, 1864; N. T. Strong to General Sprague, Apr. 12, 1864; J. Stonehouse to Edwin Stanton, Apr. 1, 1864; John Sprague to William P. Doyle, Apr. 13, 1864; Samuel George to President of the United States, June 16, 1864, N.Y. Agency, MR 590, RG75, NA; Abstract, Muster Rolls: 24th New York Cavalry: John Bennett (p. 122); 97th New York Volunteers: Titus Mohawk (p. 1616); and 14th New York Heavy Artillery: Oliver Silverheels (p. 374), series 13775, NYS DMNA, NYSA; Abstract, Muster Rolls: 24th New York Calvary: Ira Pierce (p. 1453); John B. Williams (p. 2046), series 13775, NYS DMNA, NYSA. For Williams's death at Andersonville Prison, see Daniel G. Kelley, *What I Saw and Suffered in Rebel Prisons* (Buffalo, N.Y.: Matthews and Warren, 1868), 30–43.

34. Laurence M. Hauptman, *The Iroquois and the New Deal* (Syracuse, N.Y.: Syracuse Univ. Press, 1981), 1–18; Hauptman, *Iroquois Struggle for Survival,* 205–43.

35. Samuel George to Governor John J. Hoffman, Mar. 5, June 18, 1870, MSS. Item Nos. 17605 and 17606, NYSL, MD.

36. Beauchamp, Notebook, 174.

37. "Captain George's Speech at the Fourth of July dinner," *Syracuse Journal,* July 6, 1865, news clipping found in Samuel George File, OHA; Beauchamp, Notebook, 173–74.

38. Morgan, *League of the Haudenosaunee,* 107.

39. Laurence M. Hauptman, Iroquois Field Notes, 1971–1988.

40. "Funeral of an Indian Chief," news clipping, Sept. 1873; and "Ho-no-we-yeach-te: Death of Capt. Samuel George, Head Chief of the Onondagas," *Syracuse Journal,* Sept. 25, 1873, Samuel George File, OHA.

41. Interview of John Fadden, Jan. 8, 1987, Albany, N.Y. Mr. Fadden, a Mohawk-Tuscarora Indian educator, directs the Six Nations Indian Museum in Onchiota, N.Y.

PART TWO — INTRODUCTION

1. Dr. Lloyd Elm, personal communication, May 6, 2005. The two-week symposium at St. Lawrence University in Canton, New York, was entitled "Teaching American History Through Hotinonshónni Eyes."

2. Elisabeth Tooker, "Women in Iroquois Society," in *Extending the Rafters: Interdisciplinary Approaches to Iroquoian Studies,* ed. Michael Foster et al. (Albany: State Univ. of New York Press, 1984), 109–23.

3. For a superb analysis of the Iroquois cosmology, see Fenton, *Great Law and the Longhouse*, 1–65.

4. For a critique of "declension studies" of Iroquoian women, see Nancy Shoemaker, "The Rise and Fall of Iroquois Women," *Journal of Women's History* 2 (Winter 1991): 39–57.

5. Theda Perdue, "Writing the Ethnohistory of Native Women," in *Rethinking American Indian History*, ed. Donald L. Fixico (Albuquerque: Univ. of New Mexico Press, 1997), 81.

6. Interview of Michael Tarbell, Sept. 2, 2005, Howe Caves, New York. Tarbell, a Mohawk who lived in Syracuse, remembered those Iroquois women who would make their daily journey from the reservation to sell baskets and sassafras in downtown Syracuse.

7. Kees-Jan Waterman, *"To Do Justice to Him and Myself": Evert Wendell's Account Book of the Fur Trade with the Indians in Albany, New York, 1695–1726* (Philadelphia: APS, forthcoming.)

8. Ray Jimerson to Congressman James Mead, Jan. 28, 1933, with attached resolution of the Seneca Nation of Indians Tribal Council and résumé of Alice Lee Jemison, Indian Collection, BECHS. Later I located a second letter of recommendation: Ray Jimerson to John Collier, Mar. 26, 1934, with attached resolutions of Seneca Nation Tribal Council dated Jan. 28, 1933 and Dec. 30, 1933, BIA CCF, 1907–1939, #19086-1934-162 New York, RG75, NA.

9. Alice Lee Jemison to President Franklin Delano Roosevelt, June 20, 1935, FDR MSS., OF 296, FDR Presidential Library, Hyde Park, New York.

10. See, for example, Harold L. Ickes, *The Secret Diary of Harold L. Ickes* (New York: Dutton, 1954), 2:506–7; House of Representatives, Committee on Indian Affairs, *Hearings on S. 2103: Wheeler-Howard Act—Exempt Certain Indians*, 76th Cong., 3rd sess. (Washington, D.C.: USGPO, 1940), 110, 165. For more on this smear campaign, see Hauptman, *Iroquois and the New Deal*, 34–55. It should be noted that Jemison also smeared members of the Roosevelt administration with charges of "communism." For a fuller treatment, see ibid.; and Laurence M. Hauptman, "The American Indian Federation and the Indian New Deal: A Reinterpretation," *Pacific Historical Review* 52 (Nov. 1983): 378–402.

11. Alice Lee Jemison FBI file, #60,431, released Aug. 17, 1978, to Jeanne Marie Jemison and to Laurence M. Hauptman (copy in author's possession). The file indicates that Jemison, the so-called "subversive," worked for the U.S. Department of Agriculture during World War II and even later applied for a position in the FBI. Her organization, the American Indian Federation, was never cited as subversive by the FBI or the House Committee on Un-American Activities. J. Edgar Hoover memorandum of May 13, 1948; Guy Hottel [a special agent of the FBI] to J. Edgar Hoover, June 4, 1948. Despite these conclusions, contemporary officials and even recent historians have repeated these slanderous charges. See O. John Rogge (assistant attorney general), *The Official German Report: Nazi Penetration, 1924–1942: Pan-Arabism, 1939–Today* (New York: Thomas Yoseloff, 1961), 315; John Roy Carlson (pseud. of Arthur Derounian, FBI agent), *Under Cover: My Four Years*

in the Nazi Underworld of America—The Amazing Revelation of How Axis Agents and Our Enemies Within Are Now Plotting to Destroy the United States (New York: American Book, 1943), 145–46, 150–52, 218; Jeré Franco, *Crossing the Pond: The Native American Effort in World War II* (Denton: Univ. of North Texas Press, 1999), 5–6, 11–12, 17, 25, 31–32; Kenneth William Townsend, *World War II and the American Indian* (Albuquerque: Univ. of New Mexico Press, 2000), 46–55.

12. Interview of Calvin "Kelly" John, May 4, 1997. The late Kelly John was the well-respected president of the Seneca Nation of Indians in 1948–49 and again in 1992–93, and a decorated veteran of the war in the Pacific during World War II. Cornelius Seneca was his political mentor. Interviews of Jeanne Marie Jemison, Aug. 26, 1977, Herndon, Va., and May 2–4, 1978, New Paltz, N.Y.; and Pauline Seneca, June 4, 1978, Cattaraugus Indian Reservation. The late Mrs. Seneca, a Cayuga elder, was Alice Lee Jemison's aunt. Interviews of Francis Kettle (former president of the Seneca Nation), July 27, 1977, June 4, 1978; and Wini Kettle, July 27, 1977, Cattaraugus Indian Reservation. It should be noted that Alice Lee Jemison had close contact with the leaders of all the Six Nations throughout the interwar period, including Clinton Rickard, Ray Jimerson, Aaron Poodry, Jesse Lyons, and Joshua Jones. Joshua Jones, Jesse Lyons, and Alice Lee Jemison to Senator Robert Wagner, June 10, 1934, Robert Wagner MSS., Legislative File, box 224, File 1544 "Indians," GU Library. Both Jones and Lyons were members of Jemison's American Indian Federation. Jones, Lyons, and Poodry held offices on the Six Nations Confederacy Council during the interwar years, while Jimerson and Rickard were tribal leaders among the Iroquois during the same period.

13. Hauptman, *Iroquois and the New Deal*, 56–69.

14. Hauptman, *Iroquois Struggle for Survival*, 148–49, 166, 207; Hauptman, Seneca Field Notes, 1971–2006.

4. THE TWO WORLDS OF AUNT DINAH JOHN

1. The term *Aunt* appears to have been applied affectionately to Dinah John as well as to many elderly white Americans. For its use as a pejorative term, see M. M. Manring, *Slave in a Box: The Strange Career of Aunt Jemima* (Charlottesville: Univ. Press of Virginia, 1998). For the Onondagas and the Two Row Wampum, see two of their nation's websites: <http://www.onondaganation.org/wampum.tworow.html>; <http://www.redhawkslaw.com/arena .html>. The latter website contains an image of the Two Row Wampum motif on the Onondaga Arena. The design is frequently used among the Iroquois in Canada as well. See Canadian Parliament, House of Commons, *Report No. 40: Indian Self-Government* [*Penner Report*] (Ottawa, Ontario, 1983), front and back cover.

2. For Dinah A. John's obituary and funeral, see "An Indian Burial," *Syracuse Journal,* May 28, 1883; "One Hundred and Nine," *Syracuse Herald,* May 26, 1883; "Burial of Aunt Dinah," *Syracuse Herald,* May 28, 1883, Aunt Dinah John Vertical File, OHA.

3. See illustration 3 accompanying this chapter. For the Ryder photograph, see Dwight H. Bruce, *Onondaga's Centennial* (Syracuse, N.Y.: Boston History Co., 1896), 2:1068; and Donaldson, *Six Nations of New York*, 58 (opposite). According to William M. Beauchamp's biographical sketch, the noted painter Sanford Thayer apparently also did a portrait of Dinah John around 1840. William M. Beauchamp, "Ta-wah-ta=whe·jah·quah or Aunt Dinah John," *Biographical Sketches of Onondaga Indians*, entry 398, 171–72, Beauchamp MSS., series 2, box 15, vol. 2, NYSL, MD. A mystery exists about whether a portrait in private hands of a so-called "Iroquois Mona Lisa" depicts Dinah John. See Richard G. Case, "Woman's Portrait Puzzles Historians," *Syracuse Herald Journal*, Apr. 30, 1975, Aunt Dinah Vertical File, OHA.

4. Donaldson, *Six Nations of New York*, 74.

5. Beauchamp, "Ta-wah-ta=whe·jah·quah"; Beauchamp notes on Philip Ryder photograph, OHA. The author would like to thank two noted Iroquoian linguists, Drs. Clifford Abbott and Hanni Woodbury, for confirming Beauchamp's definition of Dinah John's Onondaga name. Clifford Abbott to Laurence M. Hauptman, July 8, 2005, in author's possession.

6. Graymont, *Iroquois in the American Revolution*, 196.

7. Blau, Campisi, and Tooker, "Onondaga," 15:495–96.

8. Barbara S. Rivette, "Onondaga County," and Dennis J. Connors, "Syracuse," in *Encyclopedia of New York State*, ed. Peter Eisenstadt and Laura-Eve Moss (Syracuse, N.Y.: Syracuse Univ. Press, 2005), 1145–49, 1517–22.

9. Donaldson, *Six Nations of New York*, 14.

10. Whipple Report, 190–94.

11. Ibid., 195–204. For a full discussion of these "treaties," see Barbara Graymont, "New York State Indian Policy," 438–74.

12. For the role of salt in the dispossession of the Iroquois, see Hauptman, *Conspiracy of Interests*, 13–21, 77–84, 122–24, 239n. 68.

13. For descriptions of traditional Iroquoian marriage ceremonies, see Joseph-François Lafitau, *Customs of the American Indians Compared with the Customs of Primitive Times*, ed. and trans. William N. Fenton and Elizabeth L. Moore (1724; reprint, Toronto: Champlain Society, 1977), 1:342–49. See also Fenton, *Great Law and the Longhouse*, 40–41; and Morgan, *League of the Haudenosaunee*, 320–27.

14. See Benn, *The Iroquois in the War of 1812*.

15. William M. Beauchamp, "Thomas John," *Biographical Sketches of Onondaga Indians*, entry 397, 171, Beauchamp MSS., series 2, box 15, vol. 2, NYSL; Thomas John Abstract of Application [Aug. 20, 1857] for War of 1812 Pension, No. 7226, Records of the New York State Adjutant-General's Office, DMNA, NYSA; Thomas John's War of 1812 Pension File, Widow's Pension, No. 32.463, Records of the United States Department of War, RG94, NA.

16. Parker, "Senecas in the War of 1812," 85. Parker includes Brothertowns and Stockbridges in his list of fourteen Iroquoian women who served in the War of 1812. Pensions

234 | Notes to Pages 53-56

Applications of Polly Cooper, Julia John, Susan Jacob, Dolly Skanandoah, Records of the New York State Adjutant-General's Office, DMNA, Claims, Applications, and Awards for Service in the War of 1812, ca. 1857–1861, NYSA. See also New York State, Adjutant-General's Office, 563–73.

17. Beauchamp, "Ta-wah-ta-whe·jah·quah" ; William M. Beauchamp, "Ké·yuk-too-nes" [Elizabeth John Tallchief George], *Biographical Sketches of Onondaga Indians,* entry 399, 172, Beauchamp MSS., series 2, box 15, vol. 2, NYSL, MD.; "An Indian Burial," *Syracuse Journal,* May 28, 1883, Aunt Dinah John Vertical File, OHA.

18. See chap. 3 of this book.

19. For Iroquois land loss in this period, see Laurence M. Hauptman, "The Iroquois Indians and the Rise of the Empire State: Ditches, Defense and Dispossession," *New York History* 79 (Oct. 1998): 325–58.

20. Onondaga Enumeration List, May 1, 1847, New York State Comptroller, Indian Annuity Records, box 5, NYSA.

21. Henry Rowe Schoolcraft, *Six Nations Census of 1845, Onondaga Reservation,* entry No. 11: Thomas John *Ska·hon-don-yu* (Big Field) Head of Family, NYSL.

22. Ibid.

23. Most of the scholarship on Iroquoian women in this period focuses on the Senecas. Shoemaker, "Rise and Fall of Iroquois Women," 39–57. See also Shoemaker's "From Long-house to Longhouse: Household Structure Among the Senecas in 1900," *American Indian Quarterly* 15 (1991): 329–38; cf. Joy Bilharz, "First Among Equals? The Changing Status of Seneca Women," in *Women and Power in Native North America,* ed. Laura F. Klein and Lillian A. Ackerman (Norman: Univ. of Oklahoma Press, 1995), 101–12.

24. Wallace, *Death and Rebirth,* 239–54; Benn, *Iroquois in the War of 1812,* 25, 31, 63, 65, 132.

25. Christopher Densmore, *Red Jacket: Iroquois Diplomat and Orator* (Syracuse, N.Y.: Syracuse Univ. Press, 1999), 67–70, 73, 114–18, 135–42.

26. Diane Shaw, *City Building on the Eastern Frontier: Sorting the New Nineteenth-Century City* (Baltimore: Johns Hopkins Univ. Press, 2004), 102–7, 187–88n. 103.

27. See, for example, *Twentieth Annual Report* (Albany: New York State Superintendent of Public Instruction, 1874), 94–95, and *Twenty-First Annual Report* (Albany: New York State Superintendent of Public Instruction, 1875), 118–19.

28. See note 1 in this chapter. See also "Old Dinah," *Syracuse Journal,* Jan. 7, 1876; "Aunt Dinah," *Syracuse Journal,* June 5, 1879; "The Oldest Squaw: Aunt Dinah's Condition," *Syracuse Journal,* Oct. 9, 1880; "Aunt Dinah," *Syracuse Journal,* Apr. 21, 1877; "Aunt Dinah," *Syracuse Courier,* Oct. 11, 1880, all in Aunt Dinah Vertical File, OHA.

29. For Skenando[ah], see Hauptman, *Conspiracy of Interests,* 39–56, 72–75, 232n. 20, 232n. 26 (Skenandoah). For more on Governor Blacksnake, see chap. 2 of this book and Abler, *Chainbreaker.*

30. See note 1 in this chapter; and David Hackett Fischer, *Growing Old in America* (New York: Oxford Univ. Press, 1977), appendices. I have benefited by reading the work of Carole Haber and Brian Gratton that modifies Fischer's pioneering work about the history of old age: *Old Age and the Search for Security: An American Social History* (Bloomington: Indiana Univ. Press, 1994), 1–19.

31. See note 1 in this chapter. W. Andrew Achenbaum and Peggy Ann Kusnerz, *Images of Old Age in America, 1790 to the Present* (Detroit: Univ. of Michigan–Wayne State Univ. Institute of Gerontology, 1978), 7–29.

32. Thomas John Application for War of 1812 Pension, No. 7226, New York State, Adjutant-General's Office, 571.

33. 3 *Stat.*, 285, 394; William H. Glasson, *Federal Military Pensions in the United States*, ed. David Kinley (New York: Carnegie Endowment for International Peace and Oxford Univ. Press, 1918), 108–9.

34. The marriage was "according to the laws and usages and customs of the Onondaga Tribe of Indians." There are some discrepancies throughout the entire War of 1812 pension files about Dinah John's age, the date of her marriage, the dates of Thomas John's military service, and the date of his death. Affidavit of Dinah John [witnesses David Tall Chief and Phillip Jones], Aug. 1, 1857; Affidavit of Harry Webster [veteran of War of 1812] and Henry Jones, Nov. 1, 1858; Third Auditor's Report, Jan. 4, 1858, Thomas John's Pension Record, Widow's Pension, No. 32.463, War of 1812 Pension Records, RG94, NA (hereafter cited as Thomas John's Pension Record, NA). For traditional Iroquoian marriage customs, see Fenton, *Great Law and the Longhouse*, 40–41; Lafitau, 1:342–49; Morgan, *League of the Haudenosaunee*, 319–26.

35. 16 *Stat.*, 411; Glasson, *Federal Military Pensions*, 109–10.

36. Widow's Claim for Pension under Act of 1871, Thomas John's Pension Record; Lawyer's Contract [John C. Bennett], Mar. 24, 1871; Widow's Declaration for Pension under Act of 1871; Affidavit of Samuel George [age 77] and Mary Watersnake [age 103], Aug. 21, 1871; Affidavit of Samuel George and Anthony Jones, Jan. 2, 1872; Rejection of Widow's Pension under Act of 1871, Jan. 18, 1872, Mar. 7, 1872, Apr. 11, 1873, Thomas John's Pension Record, NA. For Samuel George, see chapter 3.

37. Widow's Claim for Pension under Act of 1871; Widow's Declaration for Pension, Mar. 4, 1871; Affidavit of Dinah John, Aug. 21, 1871, Thomas John's Pension Record, NA.

38. Rejection of Widow's Pension Application under Act of 1871, Mar. 7, 1872: "Rejection by reason of non citizenship, and in consequence of claimants inability to validly take an[d] subscribe an oath to support the Constitution of the United States," Thomas John's Pension Record, NA.

39. John S. Parker [special agent] to J. H. Baker [commissioner of pensions], July 14, 1873, Thomas John's Pension Record, NA.

40. Affidavit of Samuel George and Mary Watersnake, Aug. 21, 1871; Affidavit of Samuel George and Anthony Jones, Jan. 2, 1872; Samuel George and Hannah George

affidavit attached to Widow's Claim for Pension under Act of 1871, Thomas John's Pension Record, NA.

41. See note 39 of this chapter.

42. Annuity Receipts, June 12, 1878, New York State Comptroller, Indian Annuity Records, box 6, NYSA.

43. See notes 1 and 28 in this chapter.

44. M.E.B., "Among the Onondagas," Beauchamp MSS., box 32, Scrapbook, 11, NYSL.

45. Ibid., 44.

46. 20 *Stat.*, 27 (Mar. 9, 1878); Glasson, *Federal Military Pensions*, 110–11, 113.

47. Widow's Brief Service Pension of Thomas John Pension, War of 1812, Approved June 14, 1882, certificate No. 32.463, War of 1812 Pension Records, NA.

48. See note 1 in this chapter. According to Beauchamp, "she was buried by Methodist ministers, though she desired some of the customary pagan rites at the council house. According to the preacher's statement she claimed to be both Episcopalian and a Methodist." Beauchamp, "Ta-wah-ta-whe-jah-quah."

49. "One Hundred and Nine," *Syracuse Herald,* May 28, 1883.

50. "An Indian Burial," *Syracuse Journal,* May 28, 1883.

51. "Aunt Dinah's Monument," *Syracuse Standard,* July 9, 1883.

52. Whipple Report, 41–45.

53. See "Indian Lands," *Syracuse Journal,* Feb. 27, 1865. For Alvord, see "Albany: The Journal's Correspondence," *Syracuse Journal,* Mar. 26, 1880; "The Onondaga Reservation," *Syracuse Journal,* Mar. 28, 1880. Vertical File: Indian-Onondaga History, 1880–1889, OHA. For Sims's views, see his *Report to the Legislature of the State of New York Concerning the Onondaga Indians . . . , March 1883* (Albany, 1883).

54. See note 52 in this chapter.

55. Citing J. N. Sims, chancellor of Syracuse University, as his source, J. S. Whipple, assemblyman and committee chairman, spoke of Onondaga schoolchildren of 1888: "He contrasted their lack of intelligence with old Aunt Dinah's bright face, although she had never been to school a single day. She was pure blood; these children were not." Yet then Whipple went on to brand all "great Indians from King Philip to Pontiac and Tecumseh" as "savage and an advocate of savagery." Whipple Report, 447, 1225. For Sims' views, see ibid., 421 passim.

56. One of the disgruntled Onondagas listed in the Sims Report was Elizabeth Tallchief, Dinah John's daughter. Ibid., 48. We know little about her except for a Beauchamp thumbnail sketch: "Ké·yuk-too-nes."

5. ALICE LEE JEMISON

1. I have written about Alice Mae Lee Jemison before: Besides brief accounts in the *DAB, ANB,* and *Notable American Women,* see my "Alice Lee Jemison: Seneca Political

Activist, 1901–1964," *Indian Historian* 12 (June 1979): 15–22; *Iroquois and the New Deal,* chap. 3; "The American Indian Federation and the Indian New Deal: A Reinterpretation," *Pacific Historical Review* 52 (Nov. 1983): 378–402; *Iroquois Struggle for Survival;* "The First American," in *American Indian and Alaska Native Newspapers and Periodicals, 1925–1970,* ed. Daniel F. Littlefield, Jr., and James W. Parins (Westport, Conn.: Greenwood Press, 1986), 28.

2. For the accusations against Jemison, see House of Representatives, Committee on Indian Affairs, *Hearings on S. 2103: Wheeler-Howard Act—Exempt Certain Indians,* 76th Cong., 3rd sess. (Washington, D.C., 1940), 165; "Name-Calling Led by Ickes and Dies," *New York Times,* Nov. 24, 1938, 1; "Ickes Call Dies a Zany," *Baltimore Sun,* Nov. 24, 1938, found in Ickes MSS., Scrapbooks, box 491, LC, MD; Ickes, 2:306–7; U.S. Dept. of the Interior News Release, Nov. 23, 1938, Office File of Commissioner John Collier, box 6, File: "Alice Lee Jemison," RG75, NA; Alice Lee Jemison FBI File, Freedom of Information and Privacy Act request #60, 431, released Aug. 17, 1978.

3. Tooker, "Women in Iroquois Society," 109–23; Nancy Bonvillain, "Iroquoian Women," in *Studies on Iroquoian Culture,* ed. Nancy Bonvillain, Occasional Publications in Northeastern Anthropology No. 6, *Man in the Northeast* (Rindge, N.H.: Dept. of Anthropology, Franklin Pierce College, 1980), 47–58; Judith K. Brown, "Economic Organization and the Position of Women Among the Iroquois," *Ethnohistory* 17 (Summer–Fall 1970): 151–67.

4. Shoemaker, "Rise and Fall of Iroquois Women," 39–57; and Shoemaker's "From Longhouse to Loghouse," 329–38; Bilharz, "First Among Equals," 101–12; and Joy Bilharz, *The Allegany Senecas and Kinzua Dam: Forced Relocation Through Two Generations* (Lincoln: Univ. of Nebraska Press, 1998), 3–4, 73, 130–31, 147–48.

5. Diane Rothenberg, "The Mothers of the Nation: Seneca Resistance to Quaker Intervention," in *Women and Colonization,* ed. Mona Etienne and Eleanor Leacock (New York: J. F. Bergin Publishers, 1980), 63–87; Wallace, *Death and Rebirth,* 28–30, 182; Joan M. Jensen, "Native American Women and Agriculture" [reprint of 1977 article], in *Unequal Sisters: A Multicultural Reader in U.S. Women's History,* ed. Ellen Carol DuBois and Vicki L. Ruiz (New York: Routledge, 1991), 51–65.

6. Tooker, "Women in Iroquois Society," 109–23.

7. Hauptman, *Conspiracy of Interests,* chaps. 10–12.

8. Shoemaker, "Rise and Fall of Iroquois Women," 44.

9. Ibid., 43.

10. Ibid., 44–53.

11. Bilharz, "First Among Equals?" 109–10.

12. Bilharz, *Allegany Senecas and the Kinzua Dam,* 147–48.

13. Hauptman, Seneca Field Notes, 1971–99. Martha Bucktooth's granddaughter, the late Carol Moses, was my student at the State University of New York at New Paltz.

14. Hauptman, *Formulating American Indian Policy,* 54.

15. I was one of the honored speakers at "Remember the Removal Day," Sept. 29, 1964, Allegany Indian Reservation.

16. Hauptman, Seneca Field Notes, 1971–99. I was the expert witness testifying before both houses of Congress on the Seneca Nation–Salamanca lease controversy that led to federal legislation signed into law by President George H. W. Bush on Nov. 3, 1990.

17. Ibid. I attended the 1992 legislative hearing on the sales tax issue in Albany and was at certain Seneca Nation events and meetings in both 1992 and 1997 as an invited guest of the Seneca Nation Tribal Council. In every instance, I was keenly aware of the sizable influence of women in the political doings of the nation. Because of issues of privacy, I cannot reveal all of these women's names. See chap. 11 of this book.

18. Interviews of Francis Kettle, July 27, 1977, and June 4, 1978; Winifred Kettle, July 27, 1977; Florence Lay, June 4, 1978; Pauline Seneca, June 4, 1978; Jeanne Marie Jemison, Aug. 26, 1977; and Robert Galloway, June 3, 1978. The late Jeanne Marie Jemison was Alice Lee Jemison's daughter. Ray Jimerson to Congressman James Mead, Jan. 28, 1933, with attached résumé (Alice Lee Jemison's) and resolution of Seneca Nation Tribal Council, Indian Collection, BECHS.

19. Interviews of Pauline Seneca, June 4, 1978; Jeanne Marie Jemison, Aug. 26, 1977. The late Pauline Seneca was Alice Mae Lee Jemison's aunt and wife of the late Cornelius Seneca, former president of the Seneca Nation on several occasions in the 1940s and 1950s.

20. See four articles by Alice Lee Jemison in *Buffalo Evening News*: "Indians Want Some Voice in Selecting Commissioner," Apr. 20, 1933, 27; "Indians Plan United Drive for Their Racial Freedom," Apr. 18, 1933, 27; "Indian Freedom Set Forth as Real Economy Measure," Apr. 19, 1933, 6; "Indians Seek End of Bureau Control," Apr. 21, 1933, 38.

21. U.S. National Resources Board, Land Planning Committee, *Indian Land Tenure, Economic Status, and Population Trends* (Washington, D.C., 1935), 56–57; D. S. Otis, *The Dawes Act and the Allotment of Indian Lands,* ed. Francis Paul Prucha (Norman: Univ. of Oklahoma Press, 1973), 92–93; Lewis Meriam et al., *The Problem of Indian Administration* (Baltimore: Brookings Institution for Government Research, 1928), 7, 447–48.

22. New York State Assembly, "Report of the Indian Commission to Investigate the Status of the American Indian Residing in the State of New York, Transmitted to the Legislature, Mar. 17, 1922 (Albany: New York State, 1922), 2, 303–4, 324. A copy of this "buried" paper, known as the Everett Report, was found in the Akwesasne Cultural Center, St. Regis Mohawk Reservation.

23. *United States v. Boylan,* 265 F. 165 (1920); *Deere et al. v. State of New York et al.,* 22 F. 2d 851 (1927). For Kellogg, see chap. 9 of this book.

24. For Deskaheh, see chap. 8 of this book.

25. See George P. Decker's legal argument: "Trace of Title of Seneca Indians," in House of Representatives, Committee on Foreign Affairs, *Hearings on H.R. 2498, 11756, 16542, and 16587: Diversion of Water from the Niagara River,* 63rd Cong., 2nd sess., July 15, 1914

(Washington, D.C.: USGPO, 1914). For the Niagara River claim, see Laurence M. Haupt-man, "Who Owns Grand Island (Erie County, N.Y.)?" *Oklahoma City University Law Review* 23 (Spring/Summer 1998): 151–74. Recently the federal district court and federal court of appeals rejected the Senecas' claim to Grand Island.

26. 44 *Stat.*, 932 (Jan. 5, 1927).

27. Hauptman, *Iroquois and the New Deal,* 39–41.

28. Ray Jimerson to Congressman Mead, Jan. 28, 1933, with attached resolution of Seneca Nation Tribal Council and résumé of Alice Lee Jemison; Jimerson to Collier, Mar. 26, 1934, with attached resolutions of Seneca Nation Tribal Council dated Jan. 28, 1933, and Dec. 30, 1933, BIA CCF, 1907–39, #19086-1934-162 New York, RG75, NA.

29. Hauptman, " American Indian Federation," 378–402.

30. 48 *Stat.*, 984 (June 18, 1934). For a full analysis of the act, see Laurence M. Haupt-man, "The Indian Reorganization Act," in *The Aggressions of Civilization: Federal Indian Policy Since the 1880s,* ed. Sandra L. Cadwalader and Vine Deloria, Jr. (Philadelphia: Temple Univ. Press, 1984), 131–48.

31. Senate Subcommittee on Indian Affairs, *Hearings on S. Res. 79: Survey of Conditions of the Indians of the U.S.,* 71st Cong., 1st sess. (Washington, D.C.: USGPO, 1928–43), pt. 37, 20630–31, 20645, 21489–90, 21502; interview of Rupert Costo, Apr. 20–21, 1979, Geneva, N.Y. The late Rupert Costo, a Cahuilla Indian and the founder of the *Indian Historian,* testified against the IRA and the Indian New Deal.

32. George F. Newton to John Collier, Oct. 28, 1934, #4894-1934-066, pt. 12A, Records Concerning the Wheeler-Howard Act, box 9, RG75, NA.

33. House of Representatives, Committee on Indian Affairs, *Hearings on H.R. 7902,* 73rd Cong., 2nd sess. (Washington, D.C.: USGPO, 1934), 9:389.

34. Senate, Committee on Indian Affairs, *Hearings on S. 5302: Fish and Game Within the Allegany, Cattaraugus, and Oil Spring Reservations,* 72nd Cong., 2nd sess. (Washington, D.C.: USGPO, 1933), 7; William Zimmerman, Jr., to Alice Lee Jemison, Dec. 17, 1936, BIA CCF, New System (1936), #84524, RG75, NA; Ray Jimerson to John Collier, Jan. 27, 1934, #4894-1934-066, Records Concerning the Wheeler-Howard Act, box 4, RG75, NA.

35. Harold Ickes to John Collier, Aug. 31, 1933, John Collier MSS., box 8, folder 153, Sterling Library, Yale Univ.

36. Alice Lee Jemison to President Franklin D. Roosevelt, June 20, 1935, President Franklin D. Roosevelt MSS., OF 296, FDR Library, Hyde Park, N.Y.

37. Ibid.

38. Ibid.

39. House of Representatives, Committee on Indian Affairs, *Hearings on H.R. 7781 and Other Matters: Indian Conditions and Affairs,* 74th Cong., 1st sess. (Washington, D.C., 1935), 35–36.

40. Ibid., 48.

41. Alice Lee Jemison FBI file.

42. William Zimmerman, Jr., to Clarence A. Dykstra (director of Selective Service), Nov. 27, 1940, Office File of Commissioner John Collier, box 6, File: "Alice Lee Jemison," RG75, NA.

43. See Bilharz, *Allegany Senecas and the Kinzua Dam*.

44. Senate, Subcommittee of the Committee on Interior and Insular Affairs, *Hearings on S. 1683, S. 1686, S. 1687: New York Indians,* 80th Cong., 2nd sess. (Washington, D.C.: USGPO, 1948), 24. For Iroquois history in this era, see Hauptman, *Iroquois Struggle for Survival*.

45. *The First American* 2 (Feb. 3, 1954): 3.

PART THREE—INTRODUCTION

1. William C. Sturtevant, "Oklahoma Seneca-Cayuga," in Trigger, *Handbook of North American Indians,* 15:537–43; Erminie Wheeler Voegelin, "The 19th and 20th Century Ethnohistory of Various Groups of Cayuga Indians," MSS., NAA; Grant Foreman, *The Last Trek of the Indians* (1946; reprint, New York: Russell and Russell, 1972), 332–36; Hauptman, *Iroquois and the New Deal,* 88–92.

2. Wheeler Voegelin, "Ethnohistory," 92–126; James Howard, "Cultural Persistence," *Plains Anthropologist* 6 (1961): 21–30; and his "Environment and Culture: The Case of the Oklahoma Seneca-Cayuga," *Oklahoma Anthropological Society Newsletter* 18 (Sept. 1970): 5–13.

3. Interviews of Chief James Allen, Aug. 17, 1979, and Chief Vernon Crow, June 29, 1983, Miami, Oklahoma; Hauptman, Seneca-Cayuga Field Notes, 1979–83.

4. I was the expert witness providing oral and written testimony for both the Cayuga Nation of New York and the Seneca-Cayuga Tribe of Oklahoma in their litigation in 2000. For my written testimony, see "Expert Witness Report on Cayuga Indian Land Claims to Cayuga Lake lands," *Cayuga Nation of New York and Seneca-Cayuga Tribe of Oklahoma and United States of American v. George Pataki, et al.*," 80-CV-930; 80-CV-960, U.S. District Court, Northern District of New York, June 14, 2000. These two Cayuga communities were awarded $247.8 million by the federal district court, a decision overturned on appeal.

5. Hauptman, "Ditches, Defenses and Dispossession," 325–58.

6. Jack Campisi, "The Oneida Treaty Period, 1783–1838," in *The Oneida Indian Experience: Two Perspectives,* ed. Jack Campisi and Laurence M. Hauptman (Syracuse, N.Y.: Syracuse Univ. Press, 1988), 48–64; Graymont, "New York State Indian Policy," 438–74. For a full analysis of this dispossession, see Hauptman, *Conspiracy of Interests,* 1–97.

7. Jack Campisi, "Ethnic Identity and Boundary Maintenance in Three Oneida Communities" (Ph.D. diss., State Univ. of New York, 1974), 103–41.

8. For a full biography of Bread, see Laurence M. Hauptman and L. Gordon McLester III, *Chief Daniel Bread and the Oneida Nation of Indians of Wisconsin* (Norman: Univ. of Oklahoma Press, 2002).

9. I have been a consultant for and speaker at every Oneida History Conference since 1987. See the published proceedings: Campisi and Hauptman, *The Oneida Indian Experience*; Laurence M. Hauptman and L. Gordon McLester III, eds., *The Oneida Indian Journey: From New York to Wisconsin, 1784–1860* (Madison: Univ. of Wisconsin Press, 1999); Laurence M. Hauptman and L. Gordon McLester III, eds., *The Oneidas in the Age of Allotment, 1860–1920* (Norman: Univ. of Oklahoma Press, 2006).

10. Herbert Lewis (with the assistance of L. Gordon McLester III), ed., *Oneida Lives: Long Lost Voices of the Wisconsin Oneidas* (Lincoln: Univ. of Nebraska Press, 2005), ix–xli.

11. See chap. 9 of this book for the origins of the modern Oneida land claims movement (Laura Minnie Cornelius Kellogg).

12. Laurence M. Hauptman, Wisconsin Oneida Field Notes, 1977–2007.

6. THE GARDENER

1. A Friend, "Daniel Bread," *Green Bay Advocate,* Aug. 7, 1873 (obituary). For the fullest treatment of Bread's life, see Hauptman and McLester, *Chief Daniel Bread.* The meaning of Bread's Indian name, "Tekayá-tilu," is unknown. Clifford Abbott to Laurence M. Hauptman, Dec. 16, 1999. Dr. Abbott is the leading scholar of the Oneida language.

2. Reginald Horsman, "The Origins of Oneida Removal to Wisconsin, 1815–1822," in *An Anthology of Western Great Lakes Indian History,* ed. Donald Fixico (Milwaukee: American Indian Studies Program of the Univ. of Wisconsin, Milwaukee, 1987), 203–32; Campisi, "Ethnic Identity and Boundary Maintenance," 74–107. For a full description of the pressures on the Oneidas in New York that resulted in their "migration" to Wisconsin, see Hauptman, *Conspiracy of Interests,* chaps. 2–5.

3. Receipts (with Daniel Bread's name and mark) of Annuities Received by First Christian Party, Jan. 26, 1821, June 1, 1822, June 1, 1825, June 1, 1826, etc., Records of the Indian Commissioners, A0832B4F8, NYSA.

4. See, for example, Thurlow Weed, *Memoir of Thurlow Weed,* ed. Thurlow Weed Barnes (Boston: Houghton, Mifflin, 1884), 1:6.

5. Hauptman and McLester, *Chief Daniel Bread,* 9–12, 31–40, 71–74, 89–90; Horsman, 203–32; Karim Tiro, "The People of the Standing Stone: The Oneida Indian Nation from Revolution through Removal, 1768–1840" (Ph.D. diss., Univ. of Pennsylvania, 1998), 219–30. There is a dire need to write a corrective biography of Eleazer Williams because myth has replaced the facts of life and his influence. Examples of these poor entries include an article in the *American National Biography* written by Kenny A. Franks (20:452) and a fuller but poor treatment by Geoffrey Buerger, "Eleazer Williams: Elitism and Multiple Identity on Two Frontiers," in *Being and Becoming Indian: Biographical Studies of North American Frontiers,* ed. James A. Clifton (Chicago: Dorsey Press, 1989), 112–36. The older accounts are even more inadequate: Albert G. Ellis, "Advent of the New York Indians into

Wisconsin," *WHC* 2 (1856): 415–45; Albert G. Ellis, "Recollections of Eleazer Williams," *WHC* 8 (1879): 325–52; and Albert G. Ellis, "Fifty-four Years Recollections of Men and Events in Wisconsin," *WHC* 7 (1876): 207; William Wight, "Eleazer Williams," in *Papers* (Milwaukee, Wis.: Parkman Club, 1896), 1:133–203; Lyman C. Draper, "Additional Notes on Eleazer Williams," *WHC* 8 (1879): 353–69 (Madison, Wis.: SHSW); John N. Davidson, "The Coming of the New York Indians to Wisconsin," in *Proceedings of the Wisconsin State Historical Society* (Madison, Wis.: SHSW, 1900), 176–77.

6. Kappler, *Laws and Treaties,* 2:281–83, 2:319–23.

7. George B. Porter, Report to Lewis Cass, Feb. 8, 1832, OIA, MC234, GBAR, MR315, RG75, NA; Petition of the New York Indians to the President of the United States [including Chief Bread as one of the signatories], Jan. 30, 1831, OIA, MC234, GBAR, MR315, RG75, NA; Daniel Bread et al., (Petition of "New York Tribes") to Enos Troop, Apr. 13, 1831, Thomas Dean MSS., WHS.

8. Calvin Colton, *Tour of the American Lakes and Among the Indians of the Northwest Territory in 1830* (1833; reprint, Port Washington, N.Y.: Kennikat Press, 1972), 2:163–212; Viola, *Diplomats in Buckskin,* 11; George Catlin, *Letters and Notes on the North American Indians* (1841; reprint, New York: Dover Publications, 1973), 1:103.

9. Porter Report, Feb. 8, 1832.

10. Ibid.

11. Boyd went so far as to refer to Chief Bread as "our friend" and Eleazer Williams "as anything but an honest man." George Boyd to Governor George Porter, Jan. 1, 1833, George Boyd MSS., WHS. For Bread's (and the Oneidas') support of Boyd, see Clarence E. Carter and John Porter Bloom, eds., *The Territorial Papers of the United States: Wisconsin Territory* (Washington, D.C.: USGPO, 1934–56; National Archives, 1958–75), 28:154–57; and Daniel Bread to L. Hartley Crawford [Commissioner of Indian Affairs], Feb. 24, 1840, OIA, MC234, MR318, GBAR, RG75, NA. For more on Boyd, see Hauptman and McLester, *Chief Daniel Bread,* 109–10, 177 n28.

12. Daniel Bread to Henry Dodge [territorial governor], Aug. 29, 1836, OIA, MC234, GBAR, MR316, RG75, NA. For Schermerhorn's nefarious activities, see Laurence M. Hauptman, *Tribes and Tribulations: Misconceptions About American Indians and Their History* (Albuquerque: Univ. of New Mexico Press, 1995), chap. 4; see also James W. Van Hoeven, "Salvation and Indian Removal: The Career Biography of Rev. John Freeman Schermerhorn, Indian Commissioner" (Ph.D. diss., Vanderbilt Univ., 1972).

13. Kappler, *Laws and Treaties,* 2:517–18.

14. For the Orchard Party settlement in Wisconsin, see Henry Colman, "Recollections of the Oneida Indians," in *Proceedings for 1911* (Madison: State Historical Society of Wisconsin, 1912), 40–45.

15. See, for example, memorial of sixty Oneidas designating Daniel Bread, Jacob Cornelius, Henry Powless, and Elijah Skenandore to operate for them in negotiations with John C. Schermerhorn, Oct. 6, 1837, OIA, MC234, GBAR, MR316, RG75, NA.

16. Memorial of First Christian Party (Neddy Archiquette, Elijah Skenandore, et al.), Aug. 31, 1836, OIA, M234, GBAR, MR316, RG75, NA.

17. Daniel Bread, Jacob Cornelius, et al. to Henry Dodge, Sept. 2, 1836, OIA, M234, GBAR, MR316, RG75, NA.

18. New York State Legislature, *Assembly Doc. No. 260,* Mar. 7, 1835.

19. For the best treatment of the Iroquois Condolence Council, see Fenton, *Great Law and the Longhouse,* 3–18, 135–242. For its importance in Iroquoian diplomacy, see William N. Fenton, "Structure, Continuity and Change in the Process of Iroquois Treaty-making," in *The History and Culture of Iroquois Diplomacy: An Interdisciplinary Guide to the Treaties of the Six Nations and Their League,* ed. Francis Jennings et al. (Syracuse, N.Y.: Syracuse Univ. Press, 1985), 3–36.

20. Graymont, "Oneidas and the American Revolution," 341–42; Tiro, 99–146.

21. Alfred Cope, "Mission to the Menominee: A Quaker's Green Bay Diary," *Wisconsin Magazine of History* 50 (Winter 1967): 135–44.

22. "Celebration of the Fourth at Oneida Settlement: Speech of Daniel Bread," *Green Bay Advocate,* July 4, 1854.

23. Ibid.

24. Lyman C. Draper, "Report on the Picture Gallery," *WHC* 3 (1856): 56–58.

25. Fenton, *Great Law and the Longhouse,* 6–8.

26. Ibid., 99, 209; Fenton, "Structure, Continuity and Change," 16–18.

27. Fenton, "Structure, Continuity and Change," 21–27.

28. Fenton, *Great Law and the Longhouse,* 6.

29. Ibid., 27. For more on lacrosse, see ibid., 130, 618. On July 4, 2001, the Wisconsin Oneidas reintroduced lacrosse at their annual pow-wow.

30. Hauptman and McLester, *Chief Daniel Bread,* 127–40, 144–60.

PART FOUR—INTRODUCTION

1. Daniel K. Richter, "War and Culture: The Iroquois Experience," *William and Mary Quarterly,* 3rd ser., 40 (Oct. 1983): 528–59.

2. Ibid.

3. See Armstrong, *Warrior in Two Camps*; Roy Wright, "Silverheels, Jay," *Canadian Encyclopedia,* 2nd ed. (Edmonton, Alberta: Hurtig, 1988).

4. 132nd New York Volunteer Infantry, Company D, Abstract of Muster Rolls, NYSA; 132nd New York Volunteer Infantry, Regimental Books, Muster Rolls, Records of the Adjutant General's Office, War Department, RG94, NA.

5. Isaac Newton Parker to Martha Hoyt Parker, Aug. 15, 1863, Ely S. Parker MSS., APS. Parker, the brother of Ely S. Parker, was a sergeant in the Tuscarora Company.

6. Isaac Newton Parker to Sarah Jemison Parker, Dec. 24, 25, 1862, Jan. 15, 1863, Isaac Newton Parker MSS., BECHS.

7. For more on the Tuscarora Company's involvement in the battle, see *OR*, ser. 1, 33:62–76.

8. Interview of Julius Cook, Aug. 1, 1983, Akwesasne (St. Regis Mohawk) Indian Reservation. The late Mr. Cook was the crew chief of the sixty or more Iroquois ironworkers, mostly Mohawks, who built the two massive World Trade Center towers.

9. Quoted in Smithsonian Institution Traveling Exhibition Service, News Release: "Booming Out: Mohawk Ironworkers Build New York," <http://www.sites.si.edu/exhibitions/exhibits/booming/main.htm> This national exhibit documents the history of Mohawk ironworkers from the 1880s to today. Please note that all Iroquois communities, not just the Mohawks, have been involved in high-steel construction.

10. For the role of the Iroquois in high steel, see Joseph Mitchell, "The Mohawks in High Steel," in Wilson, *Apologies to the Iroquois*, 3–38; Donald L. Fixico, *The Urban Indian Experience in America* (Albuquerque: Univ. of New Mexico Press, 2000), 47–48, 78–80.

11. I am not the first to make the connections between the warpath and construction. See the classic article on this subject: Morris Freilich, "Cultural Persistence Among the Modern Iroquois," *Anthropos* 53 (1958): 473–83.

7. "WAR EAGLE"

1. New York State Historian, appendix f of *2nd Annual Report,* ed. Hugh Hastings (Albany, 1896–97); Elias Johnson, *Legends, Traditions and Laws, of the Iroquois or Six Nations, and History of the Tuscarora Indians* (Lockport, N.Y.: Union Printing and Publishing, 1881), 171–72; E. Roy Johnson, *The Tuscaroras: History—Traditions—Culture* (Murfreesboro, N.C.: Johnson Publishing Co., 1968), 2:228–29. I thank Professor Barbara Graymont for sharing with me her knowledge about the Cusick-Rickard family and Tuscarora history.

2. Cornelius C. Cusick to Adjutant General, U.S. Army, Apr. 2, f883, ACP Branch Document File, 1888, box 1168, Records of the Adjutant General's Office, RG94, NA; Cornelius C. Cusick's death certificate, Jan. 2, 1904, in widow's [Lizzie B. Cusick] pension application 800,281, certificate 587,550, CWPR, NA; E. Roy Johnson, *The Tuscaroras,* 220; Graymont, *Iroquois in the American Revolution,* 197; Elias Johnson, *Legends, Traditions and Laws,* 165–66; David Cusick, *Sketches of Ancient History of the Six Nations,* 2nd ed. (Lockport, N.Y.: Cooley and Lothrop, 1828); Barbara Graymont, "The Tuscarora New Year Festival," *New York History* 50 (Apr. 1969): 149–52. In approximately 1825, Nicholas and James Cusick prepared a vocabulary of the Tuscarora language at the behest of the War Department (MSS. 3803, APS). Nicholas Cusick and his son James supported the Buffalo Creek Treaty. See Nicholas Cusick to Ransom H. Gillet, Jan. 1838, and Cusick et al. to the United States Senate and House of Representatives, Oct. 3, 1838, Special Case File 29, RG75, NA. James Cusick's activities concerning removal are documented in New York Agency Records, OIA, M234, MR586, RG75, NA. The Cusicks' stance in favor of removal tarnished the

family's reputation among the Tuscaroras well into the twentieth century (interview with Chief Edison Mt. Pleasant, Nov. 30, 1984, Tuscarora Indian Reservation).

3. Clinton Rickard, *Fighting Tuscarora: The Autobiography of Chief Clinton Rickard,* ed. Barbara Graymont (Syracuse, N.Y.: Syracuse Univ. Press, 1973); Hauptman, *Iroquois Struggle for Survival,* 151–76.

4. Rickard, *Fighting Tuscarora,* 14.

5. Peter J. Claassen to Whom It May Concern, Jan. 14, 1865, ACP Branch Document File 1888, box 1168, Records of the Adjutant General's Office, RG94, NA; E. Roy Johnson, *The Tuscaroras,* 2:228–29.

6. E. Roy Johnson, *The Tuscaroras,* 2:228–29. Cusick was frequently referred to as chief of the Tuscaroras. See, for example, Claassen to Whom It May Concern, Jan. 14, 1865.

7. Cornelius C. Cusick to Abraham Lincoln, Jan. 23, 1865, ACP Branch Document File 1888, box 1168, Records of the Office of the Adjutant General, RG94, NA.

8. Approximately thirty-five Tuscaroras served with the U.S. military in the War of 1812; twenty-three Tuscaroras volunteered to serve in the Union army during the Civil War. Five were assigned to the Tuscarora Company in 1862: Cusick, George Garlow, Hulett Jacobs, Jeremiah Peters, and John Peters (Elias Johnson, *Legends, Traditions and Laws,* 167–72). Seventeen Tuscaroras received pensions from the U.S. government for service in the War of 1812, New York State, Adjutant-General's Office, 573).

9. For Cusick's enlistment efforts, see chap. 2 of this book and also New York State Historian, app. f of *2nd Annual Report.*

10. Cornelius C. Cusick, Military Service Record, Descriptive Muster Rolls of D Company, 132d NYS Volunteer Infantry, Records of the Adjutant General's Office, RG94, NA. For the removal of the Tuscaroras from the Carolinas in the early eighteenth century, see Douglas W. Boyce, "Tuscarora Political Organization, Ethnic Identity and Sociohistorical Demography, 1711–1825" (Ph.D. diss., Univ. of North Carolina, 1973); David Landy, "Tuscarora Among the Iroquois," in Trigger, *Handbook of North American Indians,* 15:518–24; and David Landy, "Tuscarora Tribalism and National Identity," *Ethnohistory* 5 (1958): 250–84.

11. Quoted in John G. Barrett, *The Civil War in North Carolina* (Chapel Hill: Univ. of North Carolina Press, 1963), 202.

12. Ibid., 203–12.

13. Ibid.

14. Ibid. The battle can be traced in *OR,* ser. 1, 33:60–76.

15. *OR,* ser. 1, 33:76.

16. R. Emmett Fiske to Whom It May Concern, Jan. 13, 1865, ACP Branch Document, File 1888, box 1168, Records of the Adjutant General's Office, RG94, NA.

17. New York State Historian, app. f of *2nd Annual Report.*

18. Fiske to Whom It May Concern, Jan. 13, 1865; *OR,* ser. 1, vol. 40, pt. 1, 814.

19. New York State Historian, app. f of *2nd Annual Report.*

20. Cusick to Lincoln, Jan. 23, 1865.

21. Claassen to Whom It May Concern, Jan. 14, 1865.

22. E. L. Porter to E. D. Morgan, May 28, 1866, ACP Branch Document, File 1888, box 1168, Records of the Adjutant General's Office, RG94, NA.

23. Cornelius C. Cusick, Oath of Office in the Military Service of the United States, Aug. 24, 1866, Exhibit F: Statement of the Military Service of Cornelius C. Cusick of the United States Army, compiled from the records of this office, Dec. 24, 1891, Army Retirement Book Records, Columbus, Ohio, Jan. 14, 1892, ACP Branch Document File 1888, box 1168, Records of the Adjutant General's Office, RG94, NA.

24. Exhibit F: Statement of the Military Service of Cornelius C. Cusick; E. Roy Johnson, *The Tuscaroras,* 2:227–28; Armstrong, 126; interview with Chief Edison Mt. Pleasant.

25. Jerome A. Greene, *Yellowstone Command: Colonel Nelson A. Miles and the Great Sioux War, 1876–1877* (Lincoln: Univ. of Nebraska Press, 1991), 293n. 13; Exhibit F: Statement of the Military Service of Cornelius C. Cusick; Cornelius C. Cusick Death Certificate. Jan. 2, 1904; Lizzie B. Cusick widow's pension application, Feb. 15, 1904; Lizzie B. Cusick's affidavit, June 9, 1904, widow's (of Cornelius C. Cusick) pension application 800,281, certificate 587,550, CWPR, NA.

26. J. S. Conrad, Efficiency Report in Case of C. C. Cusick, Captain, 22nd Infantry, ACP Branch Document File 1888, box 1168, Records of the Adjutant General's Office. RG94, NA.

27. Alton B. Cusick to Commissioner of Pensions, June 20, 1921, Certificate of Marriage: Cornelius C. Cusick and Lizzie M. Barnes, June 19, 1879, Cleveland, Ohio, ACP Branch Document File 1888, box 1168, Records of the Adjutant General's Office, RG94, NA.

PART FIVE—INTRODUCTION

1. Interview of Julius Cook, Aug. 1, 1983.

2. Fenton, *Great Law and the Longhouse,* 99–100.

3. See Herman Kvasnicka and Herman Viola, eds., *The Commissioners of Indian Affairs, 1824–1977* (Lincoln: Univ. of Nebraska Press, 1979). Three Iroquois were among the founders or original members of the Society of American Indians: Arthur C. Parker, Dennison Wheelock, and Laura Minnie Cornelius Kellogg. Alice Lee Jemison was the "brains," chief lobbyist, and publicist for the American Indian Federation. Louis Bruce, Jr., was one of the founders (and later chairman) of the National Congress of American Indians. Karen Rickard was an early organizer of the National Indian Youth Council.

4. Sally M. Weaver, "The Six Nations of the Grand River, Ontario," in Trigger, *Handbook of North American Indians,* 15:525–36.

5. For Iroquois views on and protest of "land takes," see Six Nations Council, *Six Nations of the Grand River: Land Rights, Financial Justice, Creative Solutions* (Ohsweken, Ontario: Six Nations Council, 2006).

6. Weaver, "Six Nations of the Grand River," 525–32.

7. Ibid., 531.

8. Joseph Heath to author, July 13, 2006, with the attachment of the United Nations Draft Declaration on the Rights of Indigenous Peoples, dated June 23 2006. Mr. Heath is the attorney for the Iroquois Confederacy at Onondaga. As in Deskaheh's case, the Canadian government was the primary opponent of this resolution. Alexander Ewen, ed., *Voices of Indigenous Peoples* (Santa Fe, N.M.: Clear Light Publishers, 1994), 31–36, 119–26; John Mohawk, comp., *A Basic Call to Consciousness* (Rooseveltown, N.Y.: *Akwesasne Notes,* 1979); *Akwesasne Notes, Voices from Wounded Knee, The People Are Standing Up* (Rooseveltown, N.Y., 1974); Interview of John Mohawk, Sept. 29, 2006, Allegany Indian Reservation. In John Mohawk's book, *A Basic Call to Consciousness,* he reprints Deskaheh's last speech, a radio address, and includes an article: "Deskahe[h]: An Iroquois Patriot's Fight for International Recognition," drawn largely from Carl Carmer's *Dark Trees to the Wind: A Cycle of York State Years* (New York: William Sloane Associates, 1949). *A Basic Call to Consciousness* was inspired by a visit to Geneva, Switzerland, following the path of Deskaheh made by Iroquois activists in 1977.

9. For differing views of Kellogg, see Hauptman, *Iroquois and the New Deal,* 11–15, 74–77; Hauptman, *Iroquois Struggle for Survival,* 178–87; Thelma McLester, "Oneida Women Leaders," in *The Oneida Indian Experience: Two Perspectives,* ed. Campisi and Hauptman, 109–11; Patricia Stovey, "Opportunities at Home: Laura Cornelius Kellogg and Village Industrialization," in *The Oneida Indians in the Age of Allotment, 1860–1920,* ed. Laurence M. Hauptman and L. Gordon McLester III (Norman: Univ. of Oklahoma Press, 2006), 143–75.

10. Laura Cornelius Kellogg, *Our Democracy and the American Indian* (Kansas City, Mo.: Burton Publishing Co., 1920).

11. Despite the failed effort, the *Deere* case fostered the modern Iroquois land claims movement. *Deere et al. v. State of New York et al.* See Hauptman, *Iroquois Struggle for Survival,* chap. 10.

12. Hauptman, *Conspiracy of Interests,* 121–43.

13. For the importance of the Jay Treaty and border crossing rights, see Rickard, *Fighting Tuscarora,* 76–89. For Mohawk (Kahnawake) efforts to assert rights, see Gerald Reid, *Kahnawà:ke: Factionalism, Traditionalism and Nationalism in a Mohawk Community* (Lincoln: Univ. of Nebraska Press, 2004), 134–67.

14. See illustration 9, the photograph of Chief Benedict and Pope John Paul II, in chap. 10.

8. THE IDEALIST AND THE REALIST

1. According to Annemarie A. Shimony, the original Deskáhe⁷ received his Iroquoian name in the following manner: "He was a leader of a group which was set off by itself from

the other groups who trapped fish. But the next morning the traps would be empty, and the fish caught during the night would have been stolen. Finally, the several trapping groups decided to stand guard all night, and the group of warriors under the leadership of Deska'he⁷ were caught. They were brought to the chief and asked what they were doing and where the rest of the group was. Deska'he⁷ told where they were and when asked how many there were, he could only answer, 'More than eleven.' That is how he was subjugated and captured, for he had been caught doing wrong and had to submit." Annemarie Shimony, *Conservatism Among the Iroquois at the Six Nations Reserve,* (1961; expanded ed., Syracuse, N.Y.: Syracuse Univ. Press, 1994), 115.

2. Grace Li Xiu Woo, "Canada's Forgotten Founders: The Modern Significance of the Haudenosaunee (Iroquois) Application for Membership in the League of Nations," *Law, Social Justice and Global Development Journal,* 2003, <http://elj.warwick.ac.uk/global/03-1/woo.html>; Joëlle Rostkowski, "The Redman's Appeal for Justice: Deskaheh and the League of Nations," in *Indians and Europe: An Interdisciplinary Collection of Essays,* ed. Christian F. Feest (Vienna: Rader Verlag, 1989), 435–54; Richard Veatch, *Canada and the League of Nations* (Toronto: Univ. of Toronto Press, 1975), 91–100; Carmer, 105–117. Carmer's portrayal of Deskaheh has been reprinted several times by the Iroquois: See *Akwesasne Notes, Basic Call to Consciousness,* rev. ed. (Summertown, Tenn.: Native Voices/Book Publishing Co., 1991), 18–35; and by the Akwesasne Mohawk Counsellor Organization as Ray Fadden, ed. *The Study of Des-ka-heh: Iroquois Statesman and Patriot* (St. Regis Mohawk Reservation: Six Nations Museum, no date).

3. Annemarie Shimony, "Alexander General, 'Deskahe': Cayuga-Oneida, 1889–1965," in *American Indian Intellectuals of the Nineteenth and Twentieth Centuries,* ed. Margot Liberty (1978; reprint, Norman: Univ. of Oklahoma Press, Red River Books, 2002), 185, 187–89. Alexander was Levi's brother and succeeded him as Deskáhe⁷.

4. See note 2 in this chapter.

5. Woo, "Canada's Forgotten Founders"; Rostkowski, "Redman's Appeal for Justice," 435–54.

6. The two exceptions are Nelly Katchukian-Freudig, "The Decker Papers II: Decker and Chief Deskaheh in Geneva, 1923," *The Iroquoian* 12 (Spring 1986): 79–83; and her earlier "Chief Deskaheh, George Decker, and the Six Nations v. The Government of Canada," *The Iroquoian* 11 (Fall 1985): 12–18.

7. For a brief summary, see Weaver, "Six Nations of the Grand River," 525–36.

8. Woo, "Canada's Forgotten Founders," 4–5.

9. Quoted in ibid., 5.

10. Weaver, "Six Nations of the Grand River," 532. According to Weaver, most were assigned to the 114th Battalion of the Haldimand Rifles in trench warfare in France. Wright, "Silverheels, Jay."

11. Weaver, "Six Nations of the Grand River," 532.

12. Deskaheh, *The Redman's Appeal for Justice,* London, 1923, pamphlet found in Howard Berman Coll., SUNY Buffalo Law Library, Archives and Special Coll., Amherst, New York.

13. Weaver, "Six Nations of the Grand River," 533. For the dispossession of an Iroquois community under provisions of the Burke Act, see Hauptman and McLester, *Oneidas Indians in the Age of Allotment,* 179–249.

14. See Rickard, *Fighting Tuscarora,* 58–89.

15. Six Nations Confederacy Council Resolution of April 6, 1921, Re: George Decker, D-Dec 87, Decker MSS., SJFC.

16. Six Nations Confederacy Council Resolution of May ?, 1921, Re: George Decker, D-Dec 86, Decker MSS., SJFC.

17. See note 6 in this chapter.

18. "Death Takes G. P. Decker," *Rochester Times-Union,* Feb. 24, 1936; "G. P. Decker, 74, Lawyer, Friend of Indian," *Rochester Democrat & Chronicle,* Feb. 25, 1936, both found in Decker MSS., SJFC. For his involvement with the Senecas, see House of Representatives, *Hearings on H.R. 2498, 11756, 16542, 16547, & 16587: Diversion of Water from the Niagara River,* 63d Cong., 2nd sess., July 15, 1914 (Washington, D.C.: USGPO, 1914).

19. For this Oneida case, see *United States v. Boylan.* See also Keith Reitz, "George P. Decker and the Oneida Indians," *The Iroquoian* 13 (Fall 1987): 28–33.

20. Decker wrote extensively on Indian matters. See his "Treaty Making with the Indians," *Research and Transactions of the New York State Archaeological Association.* (Rochester, N.Y.: Lewis Henry Morgan Chapter, 1920), 5–23. Decker discusses Canadian policies and Deskaheh's response in "Must the Peaceful Iroquois Go?" *Research and Transactions of the New York State Archeological Association* (Rochester, N.Y.: Lewis Henry Morgan Chapter, 1923), 5–23. He dedicates his article by placing a picture of Deskaheh with a caption about his international efforts in "America Europeanized," *Research and Transactions of the New York State Archeological Association* (Rochester, N.Y.: Lewis Henry Morgan Chapter, 1925), 5–17.

21. See note 6 in this chapter. Chiefs David Hill and Chauncy Garlow frequently visited or wrote to Decker, bringing information about events transpiring at Grand River and discussing strategy with their attorney. See, for example, Decker to Deskaheh, Jan. 14, Mar. 22, Aug. 18, 1924, Decker MSS., SJFC.

22. Woo, "Canada's Forgotten Founders," 5.

23. Winston Churchill to Lord Bing of Vimy [Governor General of Canada], Sept. 23, 1921, Decker MSS., SJFC.

24. Woo, "Canada's Forgotten Founders," 6; Veatch, *Canada and the League of Nations,* 92–93.

25. The Aborigines Protection Society had been founded in the 1830s in London and had branches throughout the British Commonwealth of Nations, including Canada, by the

early 1920s. The work of BIDI (the Archives of the Claparède Foundation are housed with the Archives of the League of Nations in Geneva) is nicely discussed in Rostkowski, "Redman's Appeal for Justice," 435–54.

26. Woo, "Canada's Forgotten Founders," 5–6.

27. A photocopy of this bond can be found in the Decker MSS., SJFC. See also Decker to Deskaheh, Oct. 19, 1923, SJFC. For Decker's concerns about the Thompson "commission," see Decker to Deskaheh, Apr. 30, June 15, Oct. 6, 1923, Mar. 22, Sept. 17, 1924, SJFC.

28. Shimony, "Alexander General," 185, 187–89; Weaver, "Six Nations of the Grand River," 531–32.

29. Deskaheh to Charles Stewart, Jan. 23, 1923, Decker MSS., SJFC.

30. Decker's underlined and marked copy of the Covenant of the League of Nations, Decker MSS., SJFC.

31. Covenant of the League of Nations, Article 17, Avalon Project, Yale University School of Law, <http://www.yale.edu/lawweb/avalon/leagueof.htm>.

32. Decker frequently focused Deskaheh's attention to this backdoor strategy. See, for example, Decker to Deskaheh, Oct. 6, Dec. 27, 1923, Jan. 14, 25, 1924, Feb. 12, 1924, Decker MSS., SJFC.

33. Decker to Deskaheh, Jan. 2, 17, 1923, Decker MSS., SJFC.

34. Decker to Deskaheh, Apr. 23, Decker MSS., SJFC.

35. Decker to Deskaheh, Apr. 30, 1923, Decker MSS., SJFC.

36. Decker to Robert P. Skinner, Jan. 5, 16, 1923, Decker MSS., SJFC.

37. Quoted in Veatch, *Canada and the League of Nations*, 93.

38. Ibid., 94.

39. Joseph Pope, "Statement Respecting the Six Nations Appeal to the League of Nations," to secretary-general of the League of Nations, Dec. 27, 1923, with letter of transmittal of Feb. 7, 1924, found in communiqué entitled "Tribe of the Six Nations: Note by the Secretary-General," D-Dec-44, Decker MSS., SJFC.

40. See, for example, Deskaheh to King Victor Emanuel III of Italy, Dec. 12, 1923, Decker MSS., SJFC.

41. Deskaheh to Decker, Sept. 24, Oct. 3, 4, 12, 29, Nov. 3, 15, 1923, D-Dec 104, Decker MSS., SJFC.

42. Deskaheh to Decker, Oct. 4, 1923, Decker MSS., SJFC.

43. Deskaheh to Decker, Nov. 3, 1923, Decker MSS., SJFC.

44. Deskaheh to Decker, Oct. 3, 1923, Decker MSS., SJFC; Veatch, *Canada and the League of Nations*, 95. Later, Deskaheh personally thanked the foreign ministers of these countries and the prince of Persia for their support in a series of letters dated Jan. 10, 1924, Decker MSS., SJFC.

45. Deskaheh to Decker, Oct. 3, Nov. 15, 1923; Deskaheh to Hjalmar Branting, Jan. 10, 1924; Decker to Deskaheh, Jan. 14, 1924, Decker MSS., SJFC.

46. Decker to Deskaheh, Jan. 14, 1924, Decker MSS., SJFC.

47. Ibid.

48. Decker to King Victor Emanuel III, Dec. 12, 1924, Decker MSS., SJFC.

49. Decker to Deskaheh, Dec. 3, 24, 1923, Decker MSS., SJFC.

50. Decker to Deskaheh, Dec. 24, 1923, Decker MSS., SJFC.

51. See note 45 in this chapter.

52. Deskaheh to Branting, Jan. 10, 1924, Decker MSS., SJFC.

53. Quoted in Veatch, *Canada and the League of Nations,* 95–99.

54. Mrs. S. Robertson Matheson to Deskaheh, May 26, 1923, Decker MSS., SJFC.

55. Decker to Deskaheh, Nov. 5, 1923; W. H. Stoker to Deskaheh, Sept. 21, 24, 1924, Decker MSS., SJFC.

56. Deskaheh to Decker, Sept. 24, 1924, Decker MSS., SJFC.

57. The BIDI published the *Circulars* of the International Office for the Protection of Native Races (Colored Races), which can be found in Decker MSS., D-Dec 104, SJFC. The statement about countering the Bolsheviks' influence is in fourth circular (p. 1), dated May 1928. Rostkowski suggests that BIDI's and the Anti-Slavery Society's legacy at the League heralded "the rule that the Non-Governmental Organizations (NGOs) currently play within the United Nations system." Rostkowski, "Redman's Appeal for Justice," 446–50. For their aid to Deskaheh, see the chief's letters to Decker: Oct. 16, 1923, Jan. 10, 18, 23, 1924, Aug. 13, 1924, Decker MSS., SJFC.

58. Professor Gilbert Murray, "Mandates," *Headway,* fragment of article, Decker MSS., D-Dec-12; Decker to Deskaheh, Nov. 15, 1923; Decker to S. Robertson Matheson, Nov. 15, 1923, Decker MSS., SJFC.

59. Deskaheh to Decker, Jan. 16, 1924; Decker to Deskaheh, Dec. 24, 27, 1923, Jan. 16, 1924, Decker MSS., SJFC.

60. Decker to Deskaheh, Jan. 14, 1924, Decker MSS., SJFC.

61. Ibid.

62. Ibid.; Deskaheh to Decker, Jan. 31, 1924, Decker MSS., SJFC.

63. Decker to Deskaheh, Feb. 7, 12, 1924, Mar. 22, 1924; Deskaheh to Decker, Jan. 23, Feb. 15, 1924, Apr. 8, 10, 1924, Decker MSS., SJFC; Deskaheh, *Chief Deskaheh Tells Why He Is Here Again* (London, 1923), found in Howard Berman Collection, State Univ. New York–Buffalo School of Law.

64. Decker to Deskaheh, July 7, 1924, Decker MSS., SJFC.

65. Decker to Deskaheh, Aug. 18, 1924, Decker MSS., SJFC.

66. Woo, "Canada's Forgotten Founders," 5–6.

67. Deskaheh to Decker, Sept. 17, 24, 1924, Decker MSS., SJFC.

68. Deskaheh to King George V, Oct. 22, 1924, Decker MSS., SJFC.

69. Deskaheh's Six Nations Proclamation, Nov. 4, 1924, Decker MSS., SJFC.

70. Decker to Robert Skinner, Dec. 18, 1924, Decker MSS., SJFC.

71. Deskaheh and the Iroquois were urged to arm themselves and resist; they rejected that course. See J. D. Burnham to Deskaheh, Oct. 12, 1924, Decker MSS., SJFC.

72. Interview of Keitz Reitz, July 21, 1984, Rochester, New York. Mr. Reitz is a descendant of one of the Oneidas who brought the case and settled, with the help of Decker, in Rochester. Reitz, "Urban Native Americans of Western New York," paper delivered at the Conference on New York History, June 9, 1984, Buffalo.

73. Rickard, *Fighting Tuscarora*, 63.

74. Quoted in *Akwesasne Notes, Basic Call to Consciousness,* 27.

75. Rickard, *Fighting Tuscarora*, 63–64.

76. Chief Clinton Rickard to Decker, July 2, 1925, Decker MSS., SJFC. See also Chief David Hill to Decker, July 1, 1925, Decker MSS., SJFC.

9. DESIGNING WOMAN

1. *Who Was Who in America with World Notables,* vol. 5 (Chicago: Marquis Who's Who, 1973), 387. Kellogg was the author of several books, booklets, and plays that are no longer available today; these include *The Last Empire; The Trail of the Morning Star; Eagle Eye; Indians Reveries*; and *Gehdos of the Lost Empire.* My views have been revised over the years as a result of conversations with her relative, Thelma McLester, of De Pere, Wisconsin, who has written about Minnie Kellogg; and by the recent writings by Patricia Stovey. See Thelma McLester, "Oneida Women Leaders," 109–11; and her "Kellogg [née Cornelius], Minnie (Laura Miriam)," in *Encyclopedia of New York State,* ed. Eisenstadt and Moss, 833. For Stovey, see her "Opportunities at Home," 143–75.

2. Fenton, "Iroquois in History," 131. Some of Kellogg's message of "redemption" parallels the ideas of the so-called Thunderwater movement that was active on Iroquois reservations in Canada from 1914 to 1927, although the connection between the two movements is nebulous. Interview with Ernest Benedict, Akwesasne (St. Regis Mohawk) Indian Reservation, Cornwall Island, Sept. 10–11, 1982.

3. Interviews of Norbert Hill, Sr., Oct. 18, 1978; Frank Danforth, Oct. 20, 1978, Oneida, Wis.; Jim Schuyler, Oct. 20, 1978; Anderson Cornelius, Oct. 21, 1978; and Melissa Cornelius, Oct. 21, 1978, Oneida, Wis. Interview of Ruth Baird, Oct. 20, 1978, Green Bay, Wis. All of the people interviewed are respected elders of the Oneida Tribe of Wisconsin. Melissa Cornelius was Minnie Kellogg's first cousin. Interview of Oscar Archiquette by Dr. Robert W. Venables (transcribed by Venables and Christopher Vecsey), Oct. 20, 1970, Shell Lake, Wis.

4. Kellogg is frequently accused of being responsible for the land sale in which the Oneida Indian School property at the core of the Oneida territory was sold to the Catholic Diocese of Green Bay. She in fact attempted to save the school property. Jack Campisi, Field Notes, 1972 (in possession of Campisi, State Univ. of New York–Albany). The property today is the Sacred Heart Seminary, Oneida, Wis. Stovey, 149–54.

5. *The Episcopal Church's Mission to the Oneidas* (Oneida, Wis.: n.p., 1899), 37–38.

6. The best ethnohistory of the Oneidas of Wisconsin is Campisi, "Ethnic Identity and Boundary Maintenance."

7. Ibid.; and Hauptman, *Iroquois and the New Deal,* 70–74.

8. Senate Subcommittee on Indian Affairs, *Hearings on S. Res. 79,* 5:1930; Graham D. Taylor, *The New Deal and American Indian Tribalism: The Administration of the Indian Reorganization Act, 1934–1945* (Lincoln: Univ. of Nebraska Press, 1980), 6.

9. See chaps. 3 and 4 of this book.

10. *The Episcopal Church's Mission,* 38. Professor Floyd Lounsbury of Yale University, who was in charge of the WPA Oneida Language and Folklore Project, was told by the Oneidas in 1939 that Kellogg suffered and faced white prejudice as a result of being "the only Indian at Grafton Hall." Personal communication, Floyd Lounsbury, Oct. 8, 1982, Rensselaerville, N.Y.

11. Kellogg, *Our Democracy,* 38–39.

12. *The Episcopal Church's Mission,* 38.

13. Interview of Ernest Benedict, Sept. 10, 1982, Lounsbury personal communication; Venables interview with Archiquette.

14. Hauptman, *Iroquois and the New Deal,* 80.

15. *The Episcopal Church's Mission,* 38–39; Kellogg, *Our Democracy,* 17–24.

16. Patricia K. Ballow to Laurence M. Hauptman, Oct. 22, 1982, in possession of the author. Ms. Ballow is the archivist of Barnard College. "Special Student" Bursar's Receipt No. 2725, Feb. 6, 1906, for Laura M. Cornelius, Barnard College Archives. Laura M. Cornelius, "Overalls and a Tenderfoot: A Story," *The Barnard Bear* 2 (Mar. 1907), 5–18. The author thanks Ms. Ballow for her help in this research.

17. Barnard College, *The Mortarboard: The Yearbook of Barnard College, Columbia University* (New York: Barnard College Class of 1908, 1907), 142.

18. Campisi, Field Notes, 1972. Kellogg, the Progressive Era reformer, worked to expose poor conditions in Milwaukee's tenements; was a muckraking investigator of Osage leases and the Indian school at Pawhuska, Oklahoma; objected to some of the conditions caused by the nonregulation of certain American industries; and favored the work of the key Progressive Era think-tank, the New York Bureau of Municipal Research. Kellogg, *Our Democracy,* 44–45, 84–88; Laura M. Cornelius, "Industrial Organization for the Indian," *Report of the Executive Council on the Proceedings of the First Annual Conference, Oct. 12–17, 1911* (Washington, D.C.: Society of American Indians, 1912), 46–49.

19. Kellogg, *Our Democracy,* 17 to end. *Akwesasne Notes, Basic Call to Consciousness.* Also, see any issue of *Akwesasne Notes,* 1968–82; Janey B. Hendrix, "Redbird Smith and the Nighthawk Keetowahs," *Journal of Cherokee Studies* 7 (Fall 1983): 83–85.

20. For example, Clinton Rickard (Indian Defense League of the Americas); Alice Lee Jemison (American Indian Federation); Louis R. Bruce, Jr. (National Congress of American

Indians); Ernest Benedict (Assembly of First Nations); Norbert Hill Sr. (Great Lakes Inter-tribal Council); Alcatraz (Richard Oakes); Wounded Knee, 1973, and the Longest Walk, 1978 (Oren Lyons).

21. *Report of the Executive Council on the Proceedings of the First Annual Conference,* Society of American Indians, 8, 10–15.

22. Ibid., 14–15.

23. Laura Cornelius Kellogg, "Some Facts and Figures on Indian Education," *Quarterly Journal* 1 (Apr. 15, 1913), 37.

24. *Ibid.,* 36–46.

25. William A. DuPuy, "Looking for an Indian Booker T. Washington to Lead their People," *New York Tribune,* Aug. 27, 1911.

26. Cornelius, "Industrial Organization," 50.

27. Ibid., 43–55.

28. Ibid., 44.

29. Ibid., 48.

30. Ibid., 50.

31. DuPuy, "Looking for an Indian Booker T. Washington."

32. Although listed as the vice president on education of the Society of American Indians in 1913, her name is missing from the membership lists provided in the proceedings of the society's annual meetings in 1914 and thereafter, nor is she represented as an author in the *Quarterly Journal (American Indian Magazine)* after that time.

33. Hazel W. Hertzberg, *The Search for an American Indian Identity: Modern Pan-Indian Movements* (Syracuse, N.Y.: Syracuse Univ. Press, 1971), 61.

34. "What Has Become of Investigators," *Tulsa Daily World,* Oct. 5, 1913; "Alleged Swindlers of Indians Caught," *Tulsa Daily World,* Oct. 12, 1913. The *Tulsa Daily World,* on Oct. 5, 1913, claimed that Mrs. Kellogg was for years involved in questionable collection schemes allegedly for the benefit of poor Oneidas and other Indians. For the Osage in this period, see John Joseph Mathews, *The Osages: Children of the Middle Waters* (Norman: Univ. of Oklahoma Press, 1961), 774–84; Bill Burchardt, "Osage Oil," *Chronicles of Oklahoma* 41 (Autumn 1963): 253–69.

35. Her differences with other Indians can be seen in Kellogg, *Our Democracy,* 60–61. For Montezuma, see Peter Iverson, "Carlos Montezuma," in *American Indian Leaders,* ed. Edmunds, 206–11. Arthur C. Parker was another member of the society who had little to do with his Iroquois colleague Laura Cornelius Kellogg. M. Friedman to Arthur C. Parker, June 12, 1913, Arthur C. Parker Manuscripts, Rush Rhees Library, Univ. of Rochester. For differences with Parker, see Joy Porter, *To Be Indian: The Life of Iroquois Seneca Arthur Caswell Parker* (Norman: Univ. of Oklahoma Press, 2001), 91–142.

36. Kellogg, *Our Democracy,* 40–41, 60–63, 92–97.

37. Ibid., 52–53.

38. Ibid., 28–29.

39. Ibid., 93.

40. Ibid., 96–99.

41. Ramona Herdman, "A New Six Nations: Laura Cornelius Kellogg Sees the Old Iroquois Confederacy Re-established on a Modern Business Basis," *Syracuse Herald,* Nov. 6, 1927, 11.

42. Ibid.; "Six Iroquois Nations File Suit for Ownership to 6,000,000 Acres in State," June 12, 1925, Warren H. Norton Scrapbooks, "Indians, 1916–1927," OHA; "Expects Decision Soon on Huge Indian Claim: Ottinger Says St. Regis Suit Is Test Case Involving Lands Worth $3,000,000,000," *New York Times,* Feb. 27, 1926.

43. J. N. B. Hewitt to Laura Cornelius Kellogg, May 19 and June 4, 1920, Apr. 17, 1926, July 9, 1932; Kellogg to Hewitt, Feb. 16, 1925, May 31, 1927, May 17, 1932; Hewitt to Chief David Russell Hill, Mar. 26, 1928, Apr. 21, 1929, J. N. B. Hewitt MSS., No. 4271, box 2, NAA.

44. Kellogg to Hewitt, May 17, 1932, ibid.

45. Hewitt to Kellogg, July 9, 1932, ibid.

46. Campisi, "Ethnic Identity and Boundary Maintenance," 152–53.

47. Senate Subcommittee on Indian Affairs, *Hearings on S. Res. 79,* 12:4858.

48. *United States v. Boylan.*

49. New York State Assembly, "Report of the Indian Commission to Investigate the Status of the American Indian Residing in the State of New York [Everett Report], Transmitted to the Legislature, March 17, 1922" (unpublished manuscript version), 303–24 (copy at Akwesasne Mohawk Library, Akwesasne Reservation.)

50. See notes 3 and 4 in this chapter. Kellogg tax receipt in author's possession. "Final Notice: to all Oneidas who may participate in the New York Claim," Dec. 31, 1925, Bureau of Indian Affairs, BIA CCF, 1907–1939, #9788–1923–260, 1, New York, RG75, NA. Freeman Johnson (Tonawanda Seneca) to Commissioner of Indian Affairs (hereafter cited as USCIA), Apr. 7 and 20, 1927; William Skenandore (Oneida) to USCIA, July 9, 1926, BIA CCF, 1907–1939, #9788–1923–260, NYAR, RG75, NA. Interview with Chief Irving Powless, Sr., May 15, 1979, Onondaga Indian Reservation.

51. Venables interview with Archiquette. Hewitt claimed that at the Six Nations Reserve in Ontario, the Kelloggs solicited eighty thousand dollars for the claim. Hewitt to M. W. Stirling, June 25, 1932, Bureau of American Ethnology MSS., Letters Received, 1909–1950, box 45, "J. N. B. Hewitt, 1929–1937," NAA.

52. New York State joined the case later as one of the defendants. 32 F. 2d 851 (1927).

53. Quoted in Helen M. Upton, *The Everett Report in Historical Perspective: The Indians of New York* (Albany: New York State Bicentennial Commission, 1980), 77–104.

54. Ibid., 114–15.

55. Ibid., 124–29.

56. Cf. ibid. A strong critic of Kellogg, Stillman was a major adviser to the Iroquois Confederacy until her death in 1969. Her extensive papers are available at NYSL.

57. "Three Go on Trial in Six Nations Case," *New York Times,* Oct. 4, 1927; "National Status of Iroquois Is Again Discussed," *Montreal Gazette,* Oct. 6, 1927, and "Verdict in Indian Case This Afternoon," *Montreal Gazette,* Oct. 13, 1927, both found in Hewitt MSS., No. 4271, box 2, NAA.

58. F. G. Tranberger to Commissioner Burke, with attached memorandum, Nov. 2, 1927 (date received), BIA CCF, 1907–1939, #9788–1923–260, NY, 2, RG75, NA. The attached BIA memorandum reads "As Kelloggs have been very troublesome to the Six Nations Confederacy Indians in the United States and to the United States Department of the Interior and Department of Justice, also the Post Office Department, it is probable that all trouble can be eliminated *by obtaining the conviction of these persons in the Canadian courts* [emphasis mine]."

59. "$2,000,000,000 Suit of Indians Rejected," *New York Times,* Oct. 25, 1927.

60. Senate Subcommittee on Indian Affairs, *Hearings on S. Res. 79,* 12:4879.

61. Campisi, "Ethnic Identity and Boundary Maintenance," 442. "'Fighting Squaw' Defends Rights of Oneida Tribe as Members of Six Nations," Mar. 14, 1924, 106; "Principles in Row Over Six Nations Leadership," Oct. 12, 1924, 47; "Indian Affairs Bureau Warns Six Nations as to Rights on State Claim," Nov. 21, 1924, 32; all found in Warren H. Norton Scrapbooks, "Indians, 1916–1927," OHA.

62. Quoted in Campisi, "Ethnic Identity and Boundary Maintenance," 442–43.

63. Hauptman, *Iroquois and the New Deal,* 1–18, 30, 70–87, 177–83.

64. "She [Kellogg] is entirely dissatisfied with anything that John Collier may do, and does not want to discuss tribal affairs with him saying that they are not under his jurisdiction." Henry Kannee Memorandum for Miss Barrows, Sept. 14, 1937, President Franklin D. Roosevelt MSS., OF 6–C, FDR Presidential Library, Hyde Park, N.Y. Kellogg had written to Senator Royal Copeland on Aug. 5, 1937, and Copeland forwarded his letter to M. H. McIntyre on Aug. 14, 1937. McIntyre refused to allow Kellogg to see Roosevelt. McIntyre to Kellogg, Aug. 25, 1937, President Franklin D. Roosevelt MSS., OF 296. Collier warned people of Kellogg's "collection schemes." Circular letter on "Activities of O. J. and L. C. Kellogg," undated (1933?), J. N. B. Hewitt MSS., No. 4271, box 2, NAA; John Collier to Mrs. Charles E. Reynolds, Oct. 7, 1935, BIA CCF, 1907–1939, #40728–1933–051 New York, RG75, NA.

65. Campisi, Field Notes, 1972; interview with Archiquette by Venables; interview of Ernest Benedict.

66. Kellogg appears to have been suffering from manic depressive behavior. Joseph Mendels, *Concepts of Depression* (New York: John Wiley and Sons, 1970), 19–33. After the death of her mother, Kellogg entered a sanitarium: "Our sorrow bothered my sister and myself completely, and I have even had to go to a sanitarium of late to be able to go on with our terrific job of re-habilitating our wonderful Six Nations into their former mode of government." L. C. Kellogg to J. N. B. Hewitt, Feb. 16, 1925, J. N. B. Hewitt MSS., No. 4271, box 2, File: Kellogg News clippings, et al., NAA. Interview of Ernest Benedict.

67. Minnie Kellogg was both a transactional and a transformational leader in the terminology of James MacGregor Burns. See Burns, *Leadership*, 4–5.

68. Campisi, "Ethnic Identity and Boundary Maintenance," 443.

10. WHERE THE PARTRIDGE DRUMS

1. For the formal setting of the boundary line, see Joseph Delafield, *The Unfortified Boundary: A Diary of the First Survey of the Canadian Boundary Line from St. Regis to the Lake of the Woods*, ed. Robert McElroy and Thomas Riggs (New York: privately printed, 1943), 137–62. See also William A. Bird, "Reminiscences of the Boundary Survey Between the United States and the British Provinces," in *Publications of the Buffalo Historical Society No. 4* (Buffalo, N.Y.: Buffalo Historical Society, 1896), 1–14. For an analysis of the boundary commission's work, see Hauptman, *Conspiracy of Interests*, 138–42.

2. *Minister of National Revenue [of Canada] v. Grand Chief Michael Mitchell also known as Kanentakeron; Mitchell v. MNR*, 2001, SCC33.

3. Interview of Salli Benedict (Ernest Benedict's oldest daughter), Aug. 1, 2006, Akwesasne (St. Regis Mohawk) Indian Reservation. For the past thirty-six years, I have personally witnessed this intrusion on Mohawk existence as a field researcher in Iroquoia.

4. Interview of Ernest Benedict, Aug. 1, 2006, Akwesasne (St. Regis Mohawk) Indian Reservation, Cornwall Island.

5. Ernest Benedict interview, Aug. 1, 2006. For the devastation of the Mohawk economy as a result of environmental contamination, see the testimony in New York State Legislature, Subcommittee on Indian Affairs on the Committee on Government Operations, *Public Hearings*, Massena, New York, Sept. 19, 1970, copy on file at the New York State Library, Albany. Ward Stone, *ENCON Progress Report RAGTW Project No.: W–4*, Apr. 1, 1985–Mar. 31, 1986, copy provided by Mohawk Nation to the author; Lennart Krook and G. A. Maylin, "Industrial Fluoride Pollution: Chronic Fluoride Poisoning in Cornwall Island Cattle," *Cornell Veterinarian* 69, suppl. 8 (1979): 1–70; Irving Selikoff, E. Cuyler Hammond, and Stephen Levin, *Environmental Contaminants and the Health of the People of the St. Regis Reserve: Report submitted to the Canadian Minister of Health and Welfare*, 2 vols. (New York: Mount Sinai School of Medicine, 1984–85).

6. New York State Legislature, Assembly [Everett], "Report of the Indian Commission to Investigate the Status of the American Indians Residing in the State of New York . . . ," Mar. 17, 1922. For more on the Everett Report, see Hauptman, *Iroquois Struggle for Survival*, 179–203.

7. Lulu Stillman to Chief Angus Diabo [Kahnawake], June 28, 1948, box 1, folder 6; Stillman to Chief George Thomas, Jr. [Tadodaho], Aug. 4, 1952, box 6, folder 1, Lulu Stillman MSS., NYSL. For Stillman's own views on Iroquois rights under the Jay Treaty, see Stillman to Secretary of State Cordell Hull, Mar. 30, 1940, box 1, folder 5, Stillman MSS.

8. Interviews of Ernest Benedict, Sept. 10–11, 1982, July 30, 1983, Aug. 1, 2006.

9. Rickard, *Fighting Tuscarora*, 53; "Chiefs of Six Nations Reject Citizenship," *Syracuse Post-Standard*, May 9, 1920.

10. See chap. 8 of this book. Ray Fadden and the Akwesasne Mohawk Counsellor Organization, a great influence on Benedict's life, inculcated the view among youngsters that Levi General was a modern Iroquois patriot and reprinted articles about him and his work.

11. *McCandless, Commissioner of Immigration v. United States ex. rel. Diabo*, 18 F. 2d 862, 25 F. 2d 71 (1927). For a first-rate treatment of this case and its impact on the rise of Iroquoian nationalism, see Reid, *Kahnawà:ke:*, 149–56.

12. Benedict interview, Aug. 1, 2006.

13. *United States v. Mrs. P. L. Garrow*, 88 F. 2d 318 (1937).

14. Ernest Benedict interviews, Sept. 10–11, 1982, July 30, 1983. Interview of Louis R. Bruce, Jr., June 30, 1982, Washington, D.C. Interviews of Ray Fadden, July 15, 1980, Sept. 11, 1982, Onchiota, N.Y. "Indian Youth Train for Camp Service," *New York Times*, Apr. 24, 1938. Louis R. Bruce, Jr., foreword to *Indian Counselor's Handbook of Legends and Information on the Iroquois* (Washington, D.C.: n.p., 1940), found in NYA Records, Publications File, series 330, New York, RG119, NA.

15. Ernest Benedict interview, Aug. 1, 2006.

16. Interviews of William N. Fenton, June 28, 1978, and May 18, 1983, Slingerlands, New York.

17. Extant issues of *War Whoop* are found in the office of the Akwesasne Mohawk Council of Akwesasne, Cornwall Island. The author would like to acknowledge the help of Salli Benedict in securing access to copies of this newspaper.

18. Ibid.

19. Rickard, *Fighting Tuscarora*, 127. See the following news articles: "Indians Register as Aliens Under Protest," *Niagara Falls Gazette*, Dec. 27, 1940; "Indians on the 'Warpath' Over Selective Service Act," *New York Herald Tribune*, Oct. 21, 1941, 25. See also the following articles in the *New York Times*: "Indians Seek Draft Test," Oct. 10, 1940, 4; "Mohawks Reject Draft," Oct. 12, 1940, 14; "Say Treaty Exempts Indians," Feb. 22, 1941, 8; "Indian Loses Draft Plea," May 15, 1941, 14; "Indian Drops Selectee Fight," Aug. 15, 1941, 22.

20. *Ex Parte Green*, 123 F. 2d 862 (1941); *United States v. Claus*, 63 F. Supp. 433 (1944); *Albany v. United States*, 152 F. 2d 267 (1945).

21. Resolution Date June 12, 1942, BIA CCF, 1940–52, Acc. #53A-367, box 1056, File #26556-1942-054 NY, RG75, NA; FDR to Chiefs Louis David, Peter Oake, Ulysses G. Pierce, Hilton Nickless, W. H. Rockwell, Jesse Lyons (separate letters), June 15, 1942, FDR MSS., PPF 2530, FDR Presidential Library, Hyde Park, N.Y.

22. Ernest Benedict to the American Civil Liberties Union, Mar. 27, 1941, ACLU MSS., Princeton Univ.

23. Ibid.

24. Ibid.

25. Interview of Louis R. Bruce, Jr., June 30, 1982.

26. Salli Benedict to Laurence M. Hauptman, personal communication, Sept. 21, 2006.

27. Ernest Benedict interview, Aug. 1, 2006.

28. See a full treatment in Hauptman, *Iroquois Struggle for Survival,* 45–64. For an excellent analysis of this period focusing on Utah, see R. Warren Metcalf, *Termination's Legacy: The Discarded Indians of Utah* (Lincoln: Univ. of Nebraska Press, 2002).

29. The best collection of *Kahwehras* is at the Akwesasne Library on the Akwesasne Reservation. The author would like to acknowledge the valuable help of Sue Herne and Brenda La France in locating back issues of this publication as well as *Akwesasne News.*

30. See *Kahwehras,* Feb. 21, 28, Mar. 13, Apr. 10, 17, May 15, 1948, found at Akwesasne Library, Akwesasne Mohawk Library.

31. *Kahwehras,* Mar. 6, 1948.

32. *Kahwehras,* Mar. 13, 1948.

33. Subcommittee of the Committee on Interior and Insular Affairs, *Hearings on S. 1683, S. 1686 and S. 1687: New York Indians,* 169–71.

34. The two acts passed were USC 232 (1948) and USC 233 (1950).

35. For a fuller treatment of the impact of the St. Lawrence Seaway on Mohawk life at Akwesasne and Kahnawake, see Hauptman, *Iroquois Struggle for Survival,* 123–50.

36. See note 5 in this chapter. See also Laurence M. Hauptman, "Circle the Wagons," *Capital Region* 2 (Feb. 1987).

37. Ernest Benedict interview, Aug. 1, 2006; Salli Benedict, personal communication, Feb. 12, 2007.

38. Salli Benedict to Laurence M. Hauptman, Aug. 10, 2006. Salli Benedict is Ernest Benedict's daughter.

39. Ernest Benedict interview, Aug. 1, 2006; Salli Benedict interview, Aug. 1, 2006.

40. *Francis v. The Queen,* 1956 SCR 618.

41. See chap. 8 of this book. For the Oneidas of the Thames, see Jack Campisi, "Ethnic Identity and Boundary Maintenance," 312–16.

42. Ernest Benedict interview, Aug. 1, 2006.

43. *St. Regis Tribe v. State of New York,* 4 Misc. 2d 110 (1956); 168 NYS 2d 894 (1957); 177 NYS 2d 289 (1958).

44. Ernest Benedict interview, Sept. 10–11, 1982, July 30, 1983.

45. Benedict's words are quoted in *Landmark: A Publication of the [Canadian] Indian Claims Commission* 7 (1999–2000): 1.

46. Wilson, *Apologies to the Iroquois,* 39–57.

47. See the following in the *Rochester Democrat and Chronicle*: "Mohawks Invade Upstate Area; Assert Treaty Gives Them Land," Aug. 17, 1957; "Mohawks Insist on Claim to Land," Aug. 26, 1957; "Indians Defy Eviction," Jan. 18, 1958; "Mohawks Defy Order to Break Camp Upstate," Feb. 16, 1958; "Mohawks Ordered Out," Feb. 21, 1958; "Mohawks

Are Adamant," Mar. 2, 1958; "Indians Get Land Grant," Mar. 6, 1958; "Eviction Hearing Set for Mohawks," Mar. 9, 1958; "Mohawks Quit Camp," Mar. 22, 1958; "Indian Population Doubles at New Site Near Thruway," June 26, 1957; "Legal Tomahawk Over City: Mohawks May Set Up Little White Teepee," Aug. 18, 1957; "Thruway Indians Defying Eviction," Feb. 16, 1958; "Standing Arrow Skedaddles, Too: Indian Squatters Quit Settlement," Apr. 1, 1958. See also "Seaway Indians Urged to Settle in State," *Niagara Falls Gazette,* Aug. 23, 1957.

48. Ernest Benedict interview, Aug. 1, 2006.

49. Edmund Wilson, *Letters on Literature and Politics, 1912–1973,* ed. Elena Wilson (New York: Farrar, Straus, and Giroux, 1977), 553.

50. Wilson, *Apologies to the Iroquois,* 153–54.

51. Wilson's notebooks contain further information about the meeting with Benedict. Edmund Wilson, *The Fifties* (New York: Farrar, Straus, and Giroux, 1986), 575. For an excellent biography of Wilson discussing his "Iroquois phase," see Lewis M. Dabney, *Edmund Wilson: A Life in Literature* (New York: Farrar, Straus, and Giroux, 2005), 420–25.

52. Ernest Benedict interviews, Sept. 10–11, 1982, July 30, 1983. Interview of Jerry Gambill, Aug. 22, 1984, Ottawa, Ontario. The translation of *Ronathahon:ni* is "They who paved the path."

53. Gambill interview, Aug. 22, 1984. Richard Oakes, "Alcatraz Is Not an Island," *Ramparts,* Dec. 1972, 35. See also Hauptman, *Iroquois Struggle for Survival,* 222–27; interviews of Adam Fortunate Eagle Nordwall, New Paltz, N.Y., May 4 and Oct. 20, 1983. Nordwall was *the* planner of the Alcatraz takeover.

54. "Benedict Wants Indian Justice," *Tekawennake,* Feb. 19, 1969.

55. The Mohawks recorded this incident in a film, *You Are On Indian Land,* which is obtainable from the National Film Board of Canada. "Indians Define Problems," *Massena Observer,* Dec. 17, 1968; "Indians to Seek MP, Threaten Blockade," *Cornwall Standard-Freeholder,* Dec. 16, 1968; "Red Faces for Palefaces," *Ottawa Citizen,* Dec. 20, 1968; "Chiefs from Six Nations Meet; Discuss Duty Problems with Canadian Customs," *Watertown Daily Times,* Dec. 20, 1968. See also the following articles in the *New York Times*: "41 Mohawks Seized in Protest at Border Bridge," Dec. 19, 1968; "Indians and Canada Report According in Customs Dispute," Dec. 21, 1968; "Canada Is Seeking a Mohawk Accord," Dec. 29, 1968. Interviews of Ernest Benedict, Sept. 10–11, 1982; Salli Benedict, Sept. 11, 1982, Brasher Center, N.Y. "They're Winning Some Battles: Vocal, Demonstrating Indian [Kahn-Tineta Horn] Emerging," *Rochester Democrat and Chronicle,* Dec. 23, 1968. [Kahn-Tineta Horn] "Speaks with Sharp Tongue," *New Yorker,* May 27, 1972, 28–31.

56. Both *Akwesasne News* and *Akwesasne Notes* were inspired by the sitdown at the International Bridge in 1968. Issues of *Akwesasne News* (January–June 1969) are found at the Akwesasne Library, Akwesasne Mohawk Reservation. Gambill interview, Aug. 22, 1984.

57. Gambill interview, Aug. 22, 1984; interview of Chief Burton Jacobs, New Paltz, N.Y., May 2–4, 1984; interview of Dean Jacobs, New Paltz, N.Y., May 2–4, 1984; interview

of Chief William Tooshkenig, New Paltz, N.Y., May 2–4, 1984. Chiefs Jacobs and Toosh-kenig as well as Dean Jacobs are from Walpole Island Reserve. Chiefs Jacobs and Tooshkenig were active in the Union of Ontario Indians. For more on Canadian efforts to "terminate" Indians in the White Paper, see Sally Weaver, *Making Canadian Indian Policy: The Hidden Agenda* (Toronto: Univ. of Toronto Press, 1981).

58. Salli Benedict interview, Sept. 11, 1982.

59. Ernest Benedict interview, Aug. 1, 2006. For Harold Cardinal's remarkable writ-ings, see *The Unjust Society: The Tragedy of Canada's Indians* (Edmonton, Alberta: M. G. Hurtig, 1969).

60. Canada Parliament, House of Commons, *Minutes of Proceedings of the Special Committee on Indian Self-Government* (Ottawa, Ontario: House of Commons, 1983). The chairman of the commission was Keith Penner. Roberta Jamieson was the ex officio mem-ber representing the AFN. Interview of Roberta Jamieson, May 28–29, 1984, Six Nations Reserve; Gambill interview, Aug. 22, 1984.

61. Doug George-Kanentiio, "Pope John Paul II Stands Tall Among the Mohawks," *Indian Time,* Apr. 7, 2005, 2 (guest editorial). Ernest Benedict interview, Aug. 1, 2006.

62. Salli Benedict to Laurence M. Hauptman, personal communication, Aug. 10, 2006.

63. Laurence M. Hauptman, Field Notes at Akwesasne, 1979 to 1991. Salli Benedict, personal communication, Aug. 10, 2006.

64. Hauptman Mohawk Field Notes, 1979–91.

65. Quoted in Bruce E. Johansen, *Life and Death in Mohawk Country* (Golden, Colo.: North American Press, 1993), 12.

66. *Mitchell v. MNR* (Minister of National Revenues), 2001 SCCC 33.

67. Canada, Ministry of Justice, "Akwesasne Residents Remission Order, June 13, 1991," <http://laws.justice.gc.ca/en/ showFullDoc/cr/SOR-91-412///en>

68. For Canada's Federal Court of Appeals ruling, see *Mitchell v. MNR,* 1 F.C. 375 (1999).

69. *Mitchell v. MNR,* 2001 SCC 33.

70. Salli Benedict, personal communication, Aug. 10, 2006.

71. Masthead of *Landmark* (Canadian Indian Claims Commission) 11 (July 2005): 1.

72. Dr. Alicia P. Magos, "Report on Lecture Tour of Dr. Alicia P. Magos, 1997 SEAMO-Jasper Fellowship Awardee," <http://www.seameo.org/vl/library/d/welcome/proj-ects/jasper/jasper9 . . . >.

73. Salli Benedict, personal communication, Aug. 10, 2006.

PART SIX—INTRODUCTION

1. Interview of Genevieve Plummer, July 28, 1977, Allegany Indian Reservation; inter-view of Carol Moses, Sept. 28, 1984, Allegany Indian Reservation; George Abrams, personal

communication, July 31, 2001. Carol Moses was Martha Bucktooth's granddaughter. Reva Barse was George Abrams's aunt.

2. Interviews of Pauline Seneca, July 15–17, 1982, Cattaraugus Indian Reservation; interview of Wini Kettle, July 27, 1977, Cattaraugus Indian Reservation; Hauptman, Seneca Field Notes, 1974–84.

3. Interview of Marlene Johnson, Aug. 15, 2001, Allegany Indian Reservation.

11. WOMEN'S LEADERSHIP AND THE SENECA NATION

1. The Seneca Nation Settlement Act, PL 101-503, on Nov. 3, 1990. For a brief history of the controversy and its resolution, see Laurence M. Hauptman, "Compensatory Justice: The Seneca Nation Settlement Act of 1990," *National Forum* 71 (Spring 1991): 31–33.

2. Bilharz, *Allegany Senecas and Kinzua Dam.*

3. PL 88-533; 78 *Stat.,* 738 (Aug. 31, 1964). I participated with the Seneca Nation in its twenty-year memorial, "Remembering the Removal, 1964–1984," held on Sept. 29, 1984 (as well as one on Sept. 29, 2006). The first memorial included a six-and-a-half-mile walk tracing the path of the Kinzua removal, addresses by Senecas and Quakers involved in fighting the dam, and a panel discussion on the history of the project. I saw adult Senecas choked up with emotion, unable to continue to speak about these events. I also had the opportunity and privilege to speak with the following Senecas: Rovena Abrams, Cornelius Abrams, Jr., George Abrams, DuWayne (Duce) Bowen, George Heron, Kelly John, and Carol Moses, as well as Walter Taylor, a member of the Society of Friends who had come to the Senecas' aid.

4. Martha Bucktooth was the first woman to be elected to the Seneca Nation Tribal Council, a landmark event that happened in the mid-1960s. Genevieve Plummer was an outstanding Seneca leader during the Kinzua crisis of the 1950s and 1960s. Interview of Genevieve Plummer, July 28, 1977; interview of Marlene Johnson, Aug. 15, 2001.

5. Interview of Lana Redeye, Aug. 15, 2001, Allegany Indian Reservation; George Abrams, personal communication, July 31, 2001.

6. For the state's historic failure to provide quality education to American Indians, see Hauptman, *Formulating American Indian Policy,* 75–88.

7. The annual reports of these Iroquois conferences, not to be confused with the annual convocation of scholars (the Iroquois Research Conference at Rensselaerville, New York), can be found in the Office of Library Development, New York State Library, Albany. One of these sessions was formally published: Roy H. Sandstrom, ed., *Educating the Educators: A Report of the Institute on "The American Indian Student in Higher Education"* (Canton, N.Y.: St. Lawrence Univ., 1971). I have also learned much about these conferences from two attendees: Gloria Tarbell Fogden (Mohawk) and Dr. Lloyd Elm (Onondaga). Interview of Gloria Fogden, June 21, 1984, New Paltz, N.Y.; interview of Lloyd Elm, July 31, 2005, Canton, N.Y.

8. Interview of Marlene Johnson, Aug. 15, 2001.

9. These women, along with Chief John Cook and Lincoln White of the State Education Department, pushed for the creation of a Mohawk Nation library in 1973 and were instrumental in lobbying for the American Indian Tribal Libraries Act of 1977 that secured 100 percent of the funding for tribal library operations. Philip Tarbell, Iroquois cultural affairs specialist in the New York State Museum of the State Education Department, lobbied continually from 1974 to 1977 to push for tribal library legislation. New York State, Interdepartmental Committee on Indian Affairs, *Annual Report, 1973–1974* (Albany, 1974), 23; Charles Townley to Dorothy Smith, Philip Tarbell, and Lincoln White, June 6, 1974, Native American Indian Education Unit Correspondence, 1954–1985, box 2, folder: Legislation, Records of the New York State Dept. of Education, NYSA; John McAvin Field Reports, 1/14/71–1/15/71, 3/24/71–3/25/71, 3/9/72–3/10/72, 3/15/72; Townley to Jean Connor, May 15, 1971; McAvin memo of meeting—American Indian Task Force, June 20, 1971, in Dallas, Records of the OLD, folder: Indian Library Advisory Board, NYSL OLD, Albany.

10. Interviews of Marlene Johnson and Ethel Bray, Aug. 15, 2001, Cattaraugus Indian Reservation; interview of Lana Redeye, Aug. 15, 2001, Allegany Indian Reservation; Bernard Finney, personal communication, June 5, 2001; Seneca Nation Tribal Council Minutes, Nov. 12, 1977–July 14, 1979.

11. Bernard Finney, personal communication, June 5, 2001; Ramona Charles, personal communication, June 5, 2001; interviews of Marlene Johnson, Ethel Bray, and Lana Redeye.

12. Bonnie Biggs, "Bright Child of Oklahoma: Lotsee Patterson and the Development of America's Tribal Libraries," *American Indian Culture and Research Journal* 24 (2000): 55–67.

13. Regents of the University of the State of New York, *Position Paper No. 22: Native American Education* (Albany, 1975).

14. McKinney's 1977 Session Laws, chap. 476, Aug. 1, 1977, 681–85.

15. Bernard Finney, personal communication.

16. Dadie Perlov to Governor Hugh Carey, July 13, 1977; Legislative Bill Jacket, New York State Statutes, chap. 476 (1977), NYSA.

17. Legislative Bill Jacket; interview of State Senator James Donovan, Apr. 17, 1986, Albany.

18. Interview of Ethel Bray, Aug. 15, 2001.

19. Joseph Shubert, "Native American Libraries and Their Library Systems in New York State," statement to U.S. National Commission on Libraries and Information Science, Hartford, Conn., Oct. 24, 1990, Records of the OLD, folder: Indian Libraries, NYSL, OLD; Joseph Shubert to Midge Dean Stock, Sept. 28, 1994, Records of the OLD, folder: Indian Library Correspondence, NYSL, OLD.

20. *Annual Reports of the Seneca Nation Libraries,* Records of the OLD, NYSL; interview of Marilyn Douglas (director, OLD, NYSL), Aug. 1, 2001, Albany; Ethel Bray, "The Seneca Nation Library," *The Bookmark,* Summer 1988, 246–47. The New York State Indian Library Act of 1977 has been hailed as a "landmark statute." See U.S. National

Commission on Libraries and Information Science, *Pathways to Excellence: A Report on Improving Library and Information Services for Native American Peoples* (Washington, D.C.: U.S. National Commission on Libraries and Information Science, 1992); Elizabeth Rockefeller-MacArthur, *American Indian Library Services in Perspective* (Jefferson, N.C.: McFarland and Co., 1998), 79–82.

21. See Hauptman, *Formulating American Indian Policy*, 49–53.

22. New York State Legislature, Assembly Subcommittee on Indian Affairs, *Report* (Albany, 1971), 41–43.

23. Henry P. Staub et al., "Health Supervision of Infants on the Cattaraugus Indian Reservation in New York: The Record Is No Better than in the Big City Slum Areas," *Clinical Pediatrics* 15 (Jan. 1976): 44–52.

24. D. W. Kaplan in cooperation with the Seneca Nation of Indians, *Indian Health Proposal* (Boston, Mar. 1, 1975).

25. Interviews of Wini Kettle, July 27, 1977, Cattaraugus Indian Reservation; Marilyn Anderson, Norma Kennedy, and Henry Staub, May 4, 1977, New Paltz, N.Y.; William Millar (former IHS official at Nashville and long-time friend and adviser to Lionel John), Oct. 24, 1987, Mashantucket Pequot Reservation, Ledyard, Conn. See also "Seneca Nation Health Department Celebrates Tenth Anniversary," *O-HI-YOH-NOH: Allegany Indian Reservation Newsletter* (Apr. 23, 1986), 1, 4–5.

26. Hauptman, *Formulating Indian Policy*, 49–53.

27. List of Seneca and Cayuga women who rebuilt the Seneca Nation of Indians, 1966–91: Marge Abrams, Rovena Abrams, Marilyn Anderson, Alberta Austin, Arliss Barrs, Reva Barss, Eleanor Bowen, Ethel Bray, Martha Bucktooth, Mae Chambers, Ramona Charles, Dorothy Cox, Loretta Crane, Marjorie Curry, Marge Farmer, Judy Greene, Alice Lee Jemison, Jeanne Marie Jemison, Grace John, Hazel V. Dean-John, Marlene Johnson, Norma Kennedy, Wini Kettle, Ann Lewis, Jean Lorette, Carol Moses, Betty Owl Nephew, Myrtle Peterson, Harriet Pierce, Genevieve Plummer, Maribel Printup, Cheryl Ray, Lana Redeye, Pauline Seneca, Tessie Snow, Virginia Snow, Rae Snyder, Midge Dean Stock, Alice Waterman, Nettie Watt.

CONCLUSION

1. Interview of William N. Fenton, Sept. 28, 1977, Albany, N.Y.

2. Robert Porter, personal communication, Sept. 29, 2006, Allegany Indian Reservation.

3. For more on this crisis, see Hauptman, *Iroquois Struggle for Survival*, 105–78.

4. Ibid., 45–84.

5. Ibid., 31–64.

6. See Weaver, *Making Canadian Indian Policy*.

7. Interviews of George Abrams, Aug. 26, 1983, Allegany Indian Reservation; Cornelius Abrams, Jr., Sept. 29, 1984, Allegany Indian Reservation; Jeanne Marie Jemison, July

14–17, 1982, and Sept. 8, 1984, Cattaraugus Indian Reservation; and Pauline Seneca, July 15–17, 1982, Cattaraugus Indian Reservation. George Abrams, Cornelius Abrams, Jr., and Jeanne Marie Jemison, all Senecas, worked for the Seneca Nation of Indians in the 1980s. Pauline Seneca, a Cayuga, was the wife of Cornelius Seneca, who held the presidency of the Seneca Nation of Indians several times in the 1940s and 1950s.

8. For the Indian Self-Determination and Education Assistance Act, see 88 *Stat.,* 2203–14.

9. Doug George-Kanentiio, *Iroquois on Fire: A Voice from the Mohawk Nation* (Westport, Conn.: Praeger, 2006), 133.

10. For the Indian Gaming Regulatory Act, see 102 *Stat.,* 2467–76.

11. The Oneida Nation of Indians of New York, *Annual Report for 2004.*

12. The Seneca Nation of Indians, *Annual Report for 2006*; David Staba and Ken Belson, "Temporary Seneca Casino Opens in Downtown Buffalo," *New York Times,* July 4, 2007, B5; "City Casino Gets 49,004 Visitors in First Month," *Buffalo News,* Aug. 4, 2007, D1. See also "Seneca Impact on WNY Economy Positive, Study Shows," *Buffalo News,* Feb. 23, 2007, D1; "Seneca Buffalo Creek Casino Opens for Business," Seneca Nation of Indians, *Official Newsletter,* July 13, 2007, 3.

13. Charles Bagli, "Spitzer Backs Indian Casinos in the Catskills," *New York Times,* Feb. 20, 2007, A1.

14. For the National Indian Gaming Association, see its report, *An Analysis of the Economic Impact of Indian Gaming in 2005* (Washington, D.C.: National Indian Gaming Association, 2005).

15. This section on the Oneidas is based on thirty years of fieldwork at Oneida, Wisconsin, and on my work as a historical consultant for this nation. Wisconsin Oneida Field Notes, 1977–2007.

16. George-Kanentiio, *Iroquois on Fire,* 95–137.

17. [*Smithsonian*] *Annual Report for 2002* (Washington, D.C.: Smithsonian Institution, 2002), 11; "Tribal Philanthropy: Oneida Nation's Giving Grows," *Indian Country Today,* Mar. 18, 2003. The Oneida Nation of Indians owns *Indian Country Today,* the Native American newspaper in the United States with the most subscriptions. Mark Libbon, "Oneida Giving to Indian Museum," *Syracuse Post-Standard,* Apr. 12, 2002, A5; Glenn Coin, "Leader [Halbritter] Shaped Oneidas' Success," *Syracuse Post-Standard,* Mar. 5, 2007, B1. For less favorable opinions, see George-Kanentiio, *Iroquois on Fire,* 90–94; Erik Kriss, "Halbritter Protest Held in Albany," *Syracuse Post-Standard,* Sept. 21, 2002, B3; "Albany Protesters Criticize Halbritter," *Syracuse Post-Standard,* Sept. 26, 2002, 6; and Glenn Coin, "Oneida Evict Four Families," *Syracuse Post-Standard,* July 30, 2003, A1.

18. George-Kanentiio, *Iroquois on Fire,* 76–77.

19. Arlinda Locklear, "Tribal Land Claims: Before and After Cayuga," New York State Bar Association *Government, Law and Policy Journal* 8 (Spring 2006): 40–43. Locklear is the attorney for the Oneida Nation of Indians of Wisconsin and also has represented the

Seneca Nation of Indians in the past. A Lumbee, she is recognized as a leading attorney and legal scholar on Native American issues relating to land and water rights.

20. *Oneida Indian Nation of New York v. County of Oneida, New York,* 414 U.S. 661 (1974).

21. *County of Oneida v. Oneida Indian Nation of New York,* 470 U.S. 226 (1985). For the federal Trade and Intercourse Act of 1790, see *USC,* 177.

22. *City of Sherrill v. Oneida Indian Nation,* 125 S.Ct. 1478 (2005).

23. Ibid., 1483.

24. *Cayuga Nation and Seneca-Cayuga Tribe of Oklahoma v. George Pataki,* 165 F. Supp. 266 (N.D.N.Y., 2001); Diane Carter, "U.S. Court Supports Cayuga Land Claim," *Rochester Democrat and Chronicle,* Nov. 2, 2001. For the reversal of this decision, see 413 F. 3d 266. I was the expert witness at the district court level for both the Cayuga Nation of Indians of New York and the Seneca-Cayuga Tribe of Oklahoma in this case. For the repercussions, see my "'Going Off the Reservation': A Memoir," *Public Historian* 25 (Fall 2003): 81–94.

25. 413 F. 3d 266, at 268.

26. *Seneca Nation of Indians and Tonawanda Band of Seneca Indians v. The State of New York, the New York State Thruway, et al.,* 206 F. Supp. 2d 448 (W.D.N.Y., 2002). The case was affirmed by the U.S. Court of Appeals in 2004. I was one of the expert witnesses for both Seneca communities at the federal district court level.

27. Vine Deloria, Jr., foreword to George-Kanentiio, *Iroquois on Fire.*

28. See Hauptman, *Iroquois Struggle for Survival,* 205–44.

29. Mad Bear was immortalized by Edmund Wilson. See Wilson, *Apologies to the Iroquois,* 160–68. He was always accessible to journalists and gave them a "good story," whether real or not.

30. Snow, *The Iroquois,* 221.

31. Hauptman, *Formulating American Indian Policy,* 27–32; cf. Gail Landsman, *Sovereignty and Symbol: Indian-White Conflict at Ganienkeh* (Albuquerque: Univ. of New Mexico Press, 1988).

32. There are no accurate, hard-and-fast statistics about the number of Iroquois speakers today in the seventeen communities, because ability varies from knowing phrases commonly used in greetings or in social gatherings to those few who know lengthy ritual addresses spoken in Longhouse ceremonies. My estimate is based on my fieldwork and my conversations with prominent linguists and with Iroquois and non-Indian scholars.

33. Snow, *The Iroquois,* 205.

34. Hauptman, Iroquois Field Notes, 1980–91.

35. George-Kanentiio, *Iroquois on Fire,* 95–136; Darren Bonaparte, "The History of Akwesasne from Pre-Contact to Modern Times," *The Wampum Chronicles,* <http://www.wampumchronicles.com/history.html>.

36. Snow, *The Iroquois,* 212–13; George-Kanentiio, *Iroquois on Fire,* 123–26.

37. For the Mohawk assertion of their claims, see "Fact Sheet: The Tsikaristisere/ Dundee Claim," *Akwesasne: A Special People in a Special Place* (Akwesasne: Mohawk Council of Akwesasne, 2006), 15–20.

38. Weaver, "Six Nations of the Grand River," 525.

39. CBC News in Depth: Caledonia Land Claim, Aug. 20, 2007, <http://www.cbc.ca/ news/background/caledonia-landclaim/>; "MNCC Sends Letter to Prime Minister Regarding Caledonia," *Indian Time,* Apr. 20, 2006, 3; Ian Austin, "Canada Issues Arrest Warrants for 7 in Land Dispute," *New York Times,* June 12, 2006, A11.

40. Six Nations Confederacy Council Statement, Six Nations Reclamation Haudenosaunee Confederacy Land Rights . . . , posted on July 21, 2007, <http://reclamationinfo. com/?=60/>. See also Six Nations Council, *Six Nations of the Grand River.*

41. "Letter to Canada Border Services Agency from MCA," *Indian Time,* May 12, 2005, 4, 6; "MCA Set to Meet with Canada Border Services Agency in Canadian Human Rights Commission Mediation," *Indian Time,* Apr. 27, 2006, 21; Organization of American States, Inter-American Commission on Human Rights, Report No. 74/03, Petition 790/01 Admissibility Grand Chief Michael Mitchell, Canada, Oct. 22, 2003; "Homeland Insecurity," in *Akwesasne: A Special People in a Special Place,* 10–12; "U.S. Ambassador [to Canada] David Wilkins Visits Akwesasne," in *Akwesasne: A Special People in a Special Place,* 24–25.

42. I was teaching at St. Bonaventure University, only fourteen miles from the Allegany Indian Reservation, in 1992 and witnessed the "tax war" firsthand.

43. "Tribe Seeks $2.1 Million for Road Use: Seneca Nation Gives Thruway Bill in Fight Against State Tax Effort," *Albany Times Union,* June 13, 2007, A3; "Seneca Start Billing State for Thruway Use of Land," *Buffalo News,* May 18, 2007, D1; "Tribe Rescinds 1954 Thruway Pact," *Albany Times Union,* Apr. 20, 2007, A3; "Senecas Blast Spitzer Plan for Taxes on Cigarettes," *Buffalo News,* Mar. 14, 2007, B1; "Senecas Target Thruway," *Buffalo News,* Apr. 19, 2007, A1.

44. Snow, *The Iroquois,* 216–18.

45. I was the expert witness called by Senator Inouye and Congressman Houghton to give oral and written testimony before committees of both houses of Congress. For a brief summary, see my "Compensatory Justice," 31–33.

46. Loretta Webster, "The Railroad and Wisconsin Oneida Lands: A Legal Memoir," in *Oneida Indians in the Age of Allotment,* ed. Hauptman and McLester, 232–39; Hauptman, Wisconsin Oneida Field Notes, 1993–2006. The New York Oneidas "bought back 17,370 acres from landowners." See Shadi Ramini, "A Tribe Turns to 3-D Animation for Modern Storytelling," *New York Times,* Feb. 10, 2007, B2; "Seneca Get Cuba Lake Acreage in Historic Settlement with the State," *Buffalo News,* June 23, 2005.

Bibliography

ARCHIVES AND MANUSCRIPTS

Akwesasne Mohawk Library. New York State Assembly. "Report of the Indian Commission to Investigate the Status of the American Indian Residing in the State of New York, Transmitted to the Legislature, Mar. 17, 1922." Albany: New York State, 1922. [Known as Everett Report.]

Allegany County Courthouse, Belmont, N.Y. Oil Spring Reservation. Land records and map.

Antioch College, Yellow Springs, Ohio. Arthur E. Morgan MSS.

Barnard College. Laura Cornelius [Kellogg] Academic Record.

Buffalo and Erie County Historical Society, Buffalo, N.Y.

    1. Howard Gansworth Collection.

    2. Arthur C. Parker MSS.

    3. Ely S. Parker MSS.

    4. Isaac Newton Parker MSS.

    5. Maris B. Pierce MSS.

    6. Peter B. Porter MSS.

    7. Wilkeson Family MSS. (letters concerning Indian volunteers in Civil War)

Canada. Department of Indian and Northern Affairs Records, Hull, Quebec. St. Lawrence Seaway Expropriation—Caughnawaga and St. Regis Files: 373/34-1-1 and 481/34-1-1.

Canada. National Archives of Canada [Public Archives of Canada], Ottawa.

    1. RG10 Indian Affairs.

    2. RG22 Deputy Minister Files

    3. RG52 St. Lawrence Seaway Authority

    4. RG89 Water Resources Files

Cattaraugus County Courthouse, Little Valley, N.Y.

    1. F. A. Gaylord, "Report on State Land in the Vicinity of Cuba Lake (1913)"

2. Map Book: Indian Reservations

Columbia University, New York, N.Y.

1. John Jay MSS.

2. Herbert Lehman MSS.

3. Charles Poletti MSS.

Cornell University

1. Earl Bates MSS.

2. Irving Ives MSS.

3. Daniel Reed MSS.

Eisenhower Library, Abilene, Kan.

1. Eisenhower Records as President. (a) White House Central Files, 1953–61. (b) Ann Whitman Files

2. John S. Bragdon MSS.

3. Bryce Harlow MSS.

4. James Lambie MSS.

Federal Bureau of Investigation. Alice Lee Jemison FBI File #60,431, released Aug. 17, 1978

Georgetown University, Washington, D.C. Robert F. Wagner Sr. MSS.

Hartwick College, Oneonta, N.Y. James Hanley MSS.

Haverford College

1. Smiley Family MSS.

2. Society of Friends MSS. Records of the Baltimore Yearly Meeting: Special Committee on Indian Concerns; Records of the Philadelphia Yearly Meeting: Indian Committee

Historical Society of Pennsylvania, Philadelphia. Indian Rights Association MSS.

Lyndon Baines Johnson Library, Austin, Tex.

1. U.S. Senate Files

2. White House Central Files, Johnson Records

3. Robert L. Bennett Oral History

John F. Kennedy Library, Boston, Kennedy Records

1. U.S. Senate

2. President's Office Files

3. White House Central Files

Library of Congress

1. Ulysses S. Grant MSS.

2. LaFollette Family MSS.

3. Wadsworth Family MSS.

Milwaukee Public Museum

    1. Photograph Collection

    2. Robert Ritzenthaler MSS.

National Anthropological Archives (Smithsonian Institution)

    1. American Indian Chicago Conference MSS.

    2. J. N. B. Hewitt MSS.

    3. National Congress of American Indians MSS.

    4. Erminie Wheeler-Voegelin MSS: "19th and 20th Century Ethnohistory of Various Groups of Cayuga Indians."

National Archives, Washington, D.C., and College Park, Md.

    1. Cartographic Records

    2. RG24 U.S. Navy Records

    3. RG48 Office Files of the Secretary of the Interior

    4. RG75 (a) Correspondence of the Office of Indian Affairs. Letters Received: Green Bay Agency; Keshena Agency; Neosho Agency; New York Agency and New York Emigration; Seneca Agency; Six Nations Agency; and Southern Superintendency. (b) Carlisle Indian School Records. © Indian Census Records. (d) Special Case File 29 (Treaty of Buffalo Creek)

    5. RG77 U.S. Army Corps of Engineers. Records of the Chief Engineer.

    6. RG94 War Department Records—War of 1812 and Civil War Records of the Adjutant General's Office: (a) Compiled Military Service Records. (b) Pension Records. (c) Regimental Books

    7. RG279 Indian Claims Commission

Newberry Library, Chicago. Jennings, Francis, et al., eds. *Iroquois Indians: A Documentary History of the Six Nations and Their League.* 50 microfilm reels. Woodbridge, Conn.: Research Publications, 1985.

New-York Historical Society, New York

    1. Rufus King MSS.

    2. Thomas Morris (Account of Treaty of Big Tree) MSS.

    3. Alfred Ogden MSS.

    4. Henry O'Reilly (Western Mementos) MSS.

    5. Rokeby Collection

    6. Robert Troup MSS.

New York Public Library. Special Collections Division, New York

    1. Jedidiah Morse MSS.

    2. Philip Schuyler MSS.

    3. Robert Troup MSS.

New York State Archives, Albany, N.Y.

1. Records of the Division of Military and Naval Affairs. (a) Abstract of Muster Rolls, War of 1812. (b) Abstract of Muster Rolls, Civil War.
2. Office of the New York State Surveyor-General, Land Office Records, ser. 1 and 2.
3. Records of Indian Deeds and Treaties, 1748–1847.
4. Records of New York State Canals. (a) Account books for the Genesee Valley Canal, 1843, 1863. (b) Canal damage awards by canal appraisers. © Canal System Survey Maps (Holmes Hutchinson Maps), 1832–1843. (d) Description of lands appropriated for the Genesee Valley Canal, 1839–1882. (e) Estimates for the Genesee Valley Canal, 1851–1855. (f) Minutes of the Board of Canal Commissioners. (g) Miscellaneous payments made for work done on the western division of the Erie Canal and the Genesee Valley Canal. (h) Original maps and surveys for the Erie Canal (Geddes Map), 1817. (i) Petitions and appeals to the Canal Board. (j) Records of land appropriations and damage records relating to the Genesee Valley Canals, 1843–1847. (k) Western Inland Navigation Company damage assessments and reimbursements, 1820. (l) Records of the New York State Court of Appeals *(Seneca Nation v. Christy; Seneca Nation v. Philonus Pattison)*. (m) Records of the New York State Governors, 1860–2006. (n) Records of the New York State Legislature. Assembly Papers. Indian Affairs. (o) Records of the State Comptroller's Indian Annuity Claims, Receipts and Related Documents, 1796–1925. (p) Records of the State Treasurer (Comptroller's Office), 1864–1866. (q) Records of the War of 1812, Certificates of Claims by War of 1812 Veterans. (r) Schoolcraft Indian Census (1845).

New York State Bureau of Land Management, Albany, N.Y. Minutes of the New York Board of Land Commissioners.

New York State Library. Manuscript Division, Albany, N.Y.

1. Banyar, Goldsbrow MSS.
2. Beauchamp, William M. MSS.
3. Bliss Family MSS.
4. Cayuga County, N.Y., Survey Map . . . formerly the Cayuga Reservation MSS.
5. Clinton, De Witt MSS.
6. Deardorff, Merle MSS.
7. Fish Family MSS.
8. Genesee Land Company Papers

9. Gillet, Ransom MSS.

10. Great Western Turnpike MSS.

11. Holland Land Company MSS.

12. Hough, Franklin Benjamin MSS.

13. Hutchinson, Holmes MSS.

14. Livingston Family MSS.

15. Ogden Land Company Record Book, 1811–1882

16. Parker, Arthur C. MSS.

17. Phelps-Gorham MSS.

18. Schuyler Family MSS.

19. Scriba, George MSS.

20. Seymour, Horatio MSS.

21. Stillman, Lulu MSS.

22. Tayler, John MSS.

23. Troup, Robert MSS.

24. Van Buren, Martin MSS.

25. Van Rensselaer Family MSS.

26. Wadsworth Family MSS.

27. Watson, Elkanah MSS.

28. Wright, Benjamin MSS.

New York State Library. Office of Library Development, Albany, N.Y. American Indian Library Files

Oklahoma Historical Society, Oklahoma City. WPA Indian-Pioneer History MSS.

Oneida Nation of Indians of Wisconsin. Cultural Heritage Department, Oneida, Wis.

1. WPA Oneida Language and Folklore Project Records

2. Genealogical Records

Onondaga Historical Association, Syracuse, N.Y.

1. William Beauchamp MSS.

2. New York State Comptroller Records (Albany Papers)

3. Vertical Files. (a) Aunt Dinah John. (b) Chief Samuel George. (c) Sanford Thayer

Pennsylvania Historical and Museum Commission, Harrisburg, Pa.

1. Merle Deardorff MSS.

2. David Lawrence MSS.

3. Paul A. W. Wallace MSS.

Princeton University, Princeton, N.J. American Civil Liberties Union MSS.

Franklin D. Roosevelt Library, Hyde Park, N.Y.
1. Eleanor Roosevelt MSS.
2. Franklin D. Roosevelt MSS. (a) Papers as Governor of New York, 1929–1932. (b) President's Alphabetical File MSS. (c) President's Personal File MSS. (d) President's Secretary File MSS. (e) President's Official File MSS.
Scholarly Resources, Wilmington, Delaware
1. Larner, John W., ed. *The Papers of Carlos Montezuma, M.D.* Wilmington, Del.: Scholarly Resources, 1983. 9 microfilm reels.
2. ———. *The Papers of the Society of American Indians.* Wilmington, Del.: Scholarly Resources, 1987. 10 microfilm reels.
St. John Fisher College, East Rochester, N.Y. George Decker MSS.
State University of New York, College at Buffalo. Paul Reilly MSS. (Indian Claims Commission)
State University of New York, Buffalo School of Law. Howard Berman MSS.—Pamphlets.
1. *Chief Deskaheh Tells Why He Is Here Again* (1923)
2. *The Red Man's Appeal for Justice* (1923)
Syracuse University, Syracuse, N.Y.
1. De Witt Family MSS.
2. Averill Harriman MSS. (recently transferred to New York State Archives)
3. Robert Moses MSS.
4. Peter Smith MSS.
Swarthmore College. Friends Historical Library, Swarthmore, Pa.
1. Elkinton Family MSS.
2. Society of Friends MSS. (a) Records of the Baltimore Yearly Meeting. Standing Committee on the Indian Concern. (b) Records of the Philadelphia Yearly Meeting. Indian Committee. (c) Records of the Joint Committee on Indian Affairs.
Harry S. Truman Library, Independence, Mo.
1. Truman Papers as President. (a) Bill File. (b) President's Secretary File. (c) White House Central Files
2. William A. Brophy MSS.
3. Clark Clifford MSS.
4. Indian Claims Commission MSS.
5. Dillon S. Myer MSS.
6. Philleo Nash MSS.
United States Military Academy, West Point, N.Y. John S. Bragdon Cullum File

University of Oklahoma. Western Historical Collection
   1. Doris Duke American Indian Oral History Project
   2. Elmer Thomas MSS.
University of Rochester. Rush Rhees Library
   1. Thomas E. Dewey MSS.
   2. Lewis Henry Morgan MSS.
   3. Arthur C. Parker MSS.
   4. Ely S. Parker MSS.
   5. William H. Seward MSS.
   6. George J. Skivington Collection.
University of Texas, Austin, Tex. Oliver LaFarge MSS.
University of Wisconsin, Green Bay, Wis. Area Research Center
   1. John Archiquette Diary
   2. Holy Apostles Episcopal Church (Oneida) Records
   3. Joseph Powless Diary
   4. Morgan Martin MSS.
   5. Eleazer Williams MSS.
Vassar College, Poughkeepsie, N.Y. Jasper Parrish MSS.
Wisconsin Historical Society, Madison, Wis.
   1. George Boyd MSS.
   2. Henry R. Colman MSS.
   3. Thomas Dean MSS.
   4. Lyman Draper MSS.
   5. Jackson Kemper MSS.
   6. James McLaughlin MSS.
   7. Morgan Martin MSS.
   8. Carlos Montezuma MSS.
   9. John F. Seymour MSS.
   10. Eleazer Williams MSS.
Yale University, New Haven, Conn.
   1. Beinecke Library. Richard Henry Pratt MSS.
   2. Sterling Library. John Collier MSS.

INTERVIEWS (CONDUCTED BY LAURENCE M. HAUPTMAN)

Abrams, Cornelius, Jr. Sept. 29, 1984, Mar. 21, 1986, Allegany Indian Reservation.
Abrams, George. Aug. 26, 1983, Allegany Indian Reservation.

Allen, Chief James. Aug. 17, 1979, Miami, Okla.; May 4–5, 1980, New Paltz, N.Y.

Anderson, Marilyn. May 4–5, 1977, New Paltz, N.Y.

Baird, Ruth. Oct. 20, 1978, Green Bay, Wis.

Benedict, Ernest. Sept. 10–11, 1982, July 30, 1983, Aug. 1, 2006, Akwesasne (St. Regis Mohawk) Indian Reservation.

Benedict, Salli. Sept. 11, 1982, Aug. 1, 2006, Brasher Center, N.Y., and Akwesasne (St. Regis Mohawk) Indian Reservation.

Black, Roy. Oct. 30–Nov. 1, 1983, May 2–5, 1984, Apr. 7, 1986, New Paltz, N.Y.

Bray, Ethel. Aug. 15, 2001, Allegany Indian Reservation.

Bruce, Louis R., Jr. Dec. 11, 1980, June 30, 1982, Washington, D.C.

Charles, Ramona. July 21, 1982, May 14, 1986, Sept. 18, 2007, Tonawanda Indian Reservation.

Cook, John Adrian. Feb. 24, 1986, Albany, N.Y.

Cook, Julius. May 27–June 1, 1982, New Paltz, N.Y.; Aug. 1, 1983, Akwesasne (St. Regis Mohawk) Indian Reservation.

Cornelius, Anderson. Oct. 21, 1978, Oneida, Wis.

Cornelius, Melissa. Oct. 21, 1978, Oneida, Wis.

Danforth, Frank. Oct. 20, 1978, Oneida, Wis.

Danforth, Jerry. May 17, Nov. 27, 2007, Oneida, Wis.

Dean-John, Hazel V. July 16, 1984, Apr. 18, 1986, Jan. 30, 1987, Albany, N.Y.

Deloria, Vine, Jr. May 4, 1982, New Paltz, N.Y.

Doxtator, Marlene. Nov. 21, 2003, Albany, N.Y.

Elijah, Howard. Nov. 21, 2003, Albany, N.Y.

Elm, Lloyd. July 31, 2005, Canton, N.Y.

Elm, Ray. Oct. 20, 1984, Rome, N.Y.; Apr. 21, 1985, Syracuse, N.Y.; May 6, 1990, June 13, 1991, Onondaga Indian Reservation.

Fadden, John. Sept. 11, 1982, Onchiota, N.Y.; Jan. 8, 1987, Albany.

Fadden, Ray. July 15, 1980, Sept. 11, 1982, July 14, 1985, Onchiota, N.Y.; Jan. 8, 1987, Albany, N.Y.

Fenton, William N. Sept. 28, 1977, June 28, 1978, May 18, 1983, Albany, N.Y.

Fogden, Gloria Tarbell. June 21, 1984, New Paltz, N.Y.

Gambill, Jerry (Rarihokwats). Aug. 22, 1984, Ottawa, Ont.

Gonyea, Ray. Jan. 22, 1988, Albany, N.Y.

Green, Elwood. Apr. 11, 1985, Niagara Falls, N.Y.

Halbritter, Gloria. Apr. 21, 1985, Syracuse, N.Y.

Halbritter, Ray. Oct. 20, 1984, Rome, N.Y.

Hill, Gerald. Aug. 14–16, 2003, Nov. 27, 2007, Oneida, Wis.

Hill, Norbert, Sr. Oct. 17 and 18, 1978, July 28, 1982, Oneida, Wis.

Hill, Rick. Sept. 8, 1982, Syracuse, N.Y.; May 28, 1984, Six Nations Reserve.

Horn, Kahn-Tineta. Nov. 3, 2007, Syracuse, N.Y.

Jamieson, Roberta. May 28–29, 1984, Six Nations Reserve.

Jemison, G. Pete. May 15, 1986, Ganondagan State Park.

Jemison, Jeanne Marie. Aug. 26, 1977, Herndon, Va.; Aug. 23, 1978, Tyson's Corners, Va.; May 2–4, 1978, New Paltz, N.Y.; July 14–17, 1982, Sept. 8, 1984, Mar. 21, Sept. 13, 1986, Cattaraugus Indian Reservation.

John, Calvin "Kelly". May 4, 1997, Allegany Indian Reservation.

Johnson, Marlene. Aug. 15, 2001, Allegany Indian Reservation.

Johnson, Nancy. May 27, 1986, Buffalo, N.Y.

Kennedy, Norma. May 4–5, 1977, New Paltz, N.Y.

Kettle, Wini. July 27, 1977, Cattaraugus Indian Reservation.

La France, Ron. Oct. 30–Nov. 1, 1983, New Paltz, N.Y.

Lewis, Anna. June 10, 1983, Albany, N.Y.

Lickers, F. Henry. June 10–13, 1986, Oneonta, N.Y.

Lyons, Chief Oren. Sept. 8, 1984, Syracuse, N.Y.; May 6, 1985, Queens, N.Y.; Nov. 3, 2007, Syracuse, N.Y.

McLester, L. Gordon III. Oct. 17–22, 1978, June 24, 1983, July 22–24, 1986, Oct. 24, 1998, Apr. 4, 2001, May 16, Aug. 14–16, 2003, May 18, Nov. 26–28, 2007, Oneida, Wis.

Martin, Kallen. Feb. 20, 1987, Albany, N.Y.

Moses, Carol. Sept. 28, 1984, Allegany Indian Reservation.

Mt. Pleasant, Chief Edison. Oct. 20–21, 1984, Rome, N.Y.; Nov. 30, 1984, Tuscarora Indian Reservation.

Mt. Pleasant, Ruth. Nov. 30, 1984, Tuscarora Indian Reservation.

Patterson, Elma. Nov. 30, 1984, Lewiston, N.Y.; Apr. 15, 1972, New Paltz, N.Y.

Plummer, Genevieve. July 28, 1977, Allegany Indian Reservation.

Porter, Tom. May 5–6, 1982, New Paltz, N.Y.

Powless, Chief Irving, Jr. Oct. 21, 1984, Rome, N.Y.

Powless, Chief Irving, Sr. May 15, 1979, Onondaga Indian Reservation.

Redeye, Lana. Aug. 15, 2001, Allegany Indian Reservation.

Reitz, Keith. May 2–4, 1982, New Paltz, N.Y.; July 21, 1982, June 8, 1984, Rochester, N.Y.

Richmond, Dave. Mar. 22, 1985, Washington, Conn.

Schuyler, Jim. Oct. 20, 1978, Oneida, Wis.

Seneca, Pauline. June 4, 1978, July 15–17, 1982, Sept. 13, 1986, Cattaraugus Indian Reservation.

Shenandoah, Chief Leon (Tadodaho). May 15, 1979, Onondaga Indian Reservation.

Staub, Henry. May 4, 1977, New Paltz, N.Y.

Sundown, Chief Corbett. May 22, 1980, Tonawanda Indian Reservation.

Swamp, Chief Jake. Apr. 25, 1985, New Paltz, N.Y.; May 6, 1985, Old Westbury, N.Y.

Tarbell, Michael. Sept. 2, 2005, Howes Caves, N.Y.

Tarbell, Philip. Dec. 7, 1981, New Paltz, N.Y.

Thompson, Jacob. Apr. 15, 1972, May 6, 1976, New Paltz, N.Y.

White, Lincoln. July 1, 1982, Washington, D.C.

Wilson, Duffy. Apr. 11, 1985, Niagara Falls, N.Y.

GOVERNMENT PUBLICATIONS

American Indian Policy Review Commission. *Final Report*. 2 vols. Washington, D.C.: USGPO, 1977.

American State Papers: Documents, Legislative and Executive of the Congress of the United States. 38 vols. Class 2: *Indian Affairs*. 2 vols., 1832–34. Washington, D.C.: Gales and Seaton, 1832–61.

The Balloting Book and Other Documents Relating to Military Bounty Lands in the State of New York. Albany: Packard and Van Benthuysen, 1825.

Canada. Parliament. House of Commons. *Minutes of Proceedings of the Special Committee on Indian Self-Government* (Penner Commission). Ottawa, Ontario, 1983.

Carter, Clarence E., and John Porter Bloom, eds. *The Territorial Papers of the United States*. 28 vols. Washington, D.C.: USGPO, 1934–56; National Archives, 1958–75.

Cohen, Felix. *Handbook of Federal Indian Law*. Washington, D.C.: USGPO, 1942.

Donaldson, Thomas, comp. *The Six Nations of New York*. Extra Census Bulletin of the 11th Census (1890) of the United States. Washington, D.C.: U.S. Census Printing Office, 1892.

Kappler, Charles J., comp. *Indian Affairs: Laws and Treaties*. 5 vols. Washington, D.C.: USGPO, 1904–41. (Vol. 2 reprinted as *Indian Treaties, 1778–1883*. New York: Interland, 1982.)

New York State. Adjutant-General's Office. *Index of Awards: Soldiers of the War of 1812*. Baltimore: Genealogical Society, 1969.

New York State Board of Canal Appraisers. *Digest of Claims . . . from 1866 to 1870, Inclusive*. Albany, N.Y.: Argus Co., 1870.

New York State Board of Canal Commissioners. *Annual Report* [1811–78].

New York State Historian. *2nd Annual Report*. Ed. Hugh Hastings. Albany, 1896–97.

New York State Land Office. *Proceedings of the Commissioners of the Land Office for the Year 1924*. Albany: J. B. Lyon Co., 1924.

New York State Legislature. Assembly. *Document No. 51: Report of the Special Committee to Investigate the Indian Problem of the State of New York. Appointed by the Assembly of 1888*. 2 vols. Albany: Troy Press, 1889 [Whipple Report].

New York State Legislature. Joint Legislative Committee on Indian Affairs. *Minutes of Public Hearings . . . November 9, 1963*. Albany, 1963.

New York State Legislature. Joint Legislative Committee on Indian Affairs. *Reports, 1944–1959*. Albany, 1944–59.

New York State Legislature. Subcommittee on Indian Affairs on the Committee on Government Operations [Lisa-Reilly Subcommittee]. *Public Hearings, 1970–1971*. Albany, 1970–71.

New York State. Regents of the University of the State of New York. *Position Paper No. 22: Native American Education*. Albany, 1975.

New York State. Superintendent of Common Schools. *Annual Reports, 1845–1854*. Albany, 1845–54.

New York State. Superintendent of Public Instruction. *Annual Reports, 1855–1900*. Albany, 1855–1900.

Richardson, James D., comp. *A Compilation of the Messages and Papers of the Presidents, 1789–1897*. 10 vols. Washington, D.C.: USGPO, 1896–99.

Royce, C. C., comp. *Indian Land Cessions in the United States. 18th Annual Report of the Bureau of American Ethnology, 1896–1897*. Washington, D.C.: USGPO, 1899.

Sims, J. N., comp. *Report to the Legislature of the State of New York Concerning the Onondaga Indians . . . , March 1883*. Albany, 1883.

U.S. Bureau of the Census. 1st (1790)–14th (1920) Censuses.

U.S. Congress. *Annals of Congress, 1789–1824*.

U.S. Congress. *Congressional Globe, 1833–1851*.

U.S. Congress. *Congressional Record*.

U.S. Congress. House of Representatives, Committee on Foreign Affairs. *Hearings on H.R. 2498, 11756, 16542, 16547 and 16587: Diversion of Water from the Niagara River.* 63rd Cong., 2nd sess., July 15, 1914. Washington, D.C.: USGPO, 1914.

U.S. Congress. House Committee on Indian Affairs. *Hearings on H.R. n: Indians of New York.* 71st Cong., 2d sess. Washington, D.C.: USGPO, 1930.

U.S. Congress. House Subcommittee on Indian Affairs. *Hearings: Seizure of Bureau of Indian Affairs.* 92nd Cong., 2nd sess. Washington, D.C.: USGPO, 1973.

U.S. Congress. House Committee on Interior and Insular Affairs. *Hearings on H.R. 6631: Settlement of the Cayuga Indian Nation Land Claims in the State of New York, March 3, 1980.* 96th Cong., 2nd sess. Washington, D.C.: USGPO, 1980.

U.S. Congress. Senate. Subcommittee of the Committee on Interior and Insular Affairs. *Hearings on S. 1683, S. 1686, and S. 1687: New York Indians.* 80th Cong., 2nd sess. Washington, D.C.: USGPO, 1948.

U.S. Congress. Senate. Committee on Interior and Insular Affairs. *Report No. 1489: Conferring Jurisdiction on Courts of New York over Offenses Committed by Indians.* Washington, D.C.: USGPO, 1948.

U.S. Congress. Senate. Committee on Indian Affairs. *Hearings on S. 5302: Fish and Game Within the Allegany, Cattaraugus, and Oil Spring Reservations.* 72nd Cong., 2nd sess. Washington, D.C.: USGPO, 1933.

U.S. Congress. Senate Select Committee on Indian Affairs. *Hearings on S. 2895: Renegotiation of Seneca Nation Leases.* 101st Cong., 2nd sess. Washington, D.C.: USGPO, 1991.

U.S. Congress. Senate. Subcommittee on Indian Affairs. *Hearings on S. Res. 79: Survey of Conditions of the Indians of the U.S.* 43 parts. 70th–76th Cong. Washington, D.C.: USGPO, 1928–43.

U.S. Congress. Senate Subcommittee on Indian Affairs of the Committee on Interior and Insular Affairs. *Hearings: Occupation of Wounded Knee.* 93rd Cong., 1st sess. Washington, D.C.: USGPO, 1974.

U.S. Congress. Senate Subcommittee to Investigate the Administration of the Internal Security Act and Other Internal Security Laws of the Committee on the Judiciary. *Hearings: Revolutionary Activities Within the United States: The American Indian Movement.* 94th Cong., 2nd sess. Washington, D.C.: USGPO, 1976.

U.S. Congress. Senate Select Committee on Indian Affairs. *Hearings on S. 2084: Ancient Indian Land Claims.* 97th Cong., 2nd sess. Washington, D.C.: USGPO, 1982.

U.S. Congress. House of Representatives and Senate. *Joint Hearings Before Subcommittee of the Committees on Interior and Insular Affairs: Termination of Federal Supervision over Certain Tribes of Indians.* 83rd Cong., 2nd sess. Parts 1–12. Washington, D.C.: USGPO, 1954.

U.S. Congress. Senate. *Report 101–511. Calendar No. 948: Providing for the Renegotiation of Certain Leases of the Seneca Nation, and for Other Purposes.* 101st Cong., 2nd sess. Washington, D.C.: USGPO, 1990.

U.S. Indian Claims Commission. *Decisions of the Indian Claims Commission.* Microfiche edition. New York: Clearwater Publishing Co., 1973–78.

U.S. Indian Claims Commission. *Final Report.* Washington, D.C.: USGPO, 1979.

U.S. Interior Department. *Annual Report of the Commissioner of Indian Affairs, 1849–1950.* Washington, D.C., 1849–1950.

U.S. Congress. House of Representatives. Committee on Indian Affairs. *Hearings on S. 2103: Wheeler-Howard Act—Exempt Certain Indians.* 76th Cong., 3rd sess. Washington, D.C.: USGPO, 1940.

U.S. National Commission on Libraries and Information Science. *Pathways to Excellence: A Report on Improving Library and Informational Services for Native American Peoples.* Washington, D.C.: U.S. National Commission on Libraries and Informational Science, 1992.

U.S. National Resources Board. Land Planning Committee. *Indian Land Tenure, Economic Status, and Population Trends.* Washington, D.C., 1935.

U.S. War Department. *The War of the Rebellion: A Compilation of the Official Records of the Union and Confederate Armies.* 128 vols. Washington, D.C.: USGPO, 1880–1901.

Whitford, Noble E. *History of the Canal System of the State of New York.* 2 vols. Albany: Office of the Chief Engineer and Brandon Printing, 1906.

COURT CASES

Albany v. United States. 152 F. 2d 267 (1945).

Cayuga Nation and Seneca-Cayuga Tribe of Oklahoma v. George Pataki. 165 F. Supp. 266 (N.D.N.Y., 2001); and 413 F. 3d 266.

City of Sherrill v. Oneida Indian Nation. 125 S.Ct. 1478 (2005).

County of Oneida v. Oneida Indian Nation of New York. 470 U.S. 226 (1985).

Deere et al. v. State of New York et al. 22 F. 2d 851 (1927).

Ex Parte Green. 123 F. 2d 862 (1941).

Federal Power Commission v. Tuscarora Indian Nation; Power Authority of (the State of) New York v. Tuscarora Nation. 80 S.Ct. 543 (1960).

Francis v. The Queen. 1956 SCR 618.

McCandless, Commissioner of Immigration v. United States ex. rel. Diabo. 18 F. 2d 862, 25 F. 2d 71 (1920).

Mitchell v. MNR. 2001 SCC 33.

New York Indians v. United States. U.S. Court of Claims. Doc. No. 17861 (1905).

Oneida Indian Nation of New York v. County of Oneida, New York. 414 U.S. 661 (1974).

People v. Redeye. 358 N.Y.S. 2d 632 (1974).

St. Regis Tribe v. State of New York. 4 Misc. 2d 110 (1956).

Seneca Nation v. Philonus Pattison. N.Y.S. Court of Appeals, vol. 487, case no. 1, 1860–61, New York State Library, Albany.

Seneca Nation of Indians and Tonawanda Band of Seneca Indians v. The State of New York, the New York State Thruway, et al. 206 F. Supp. 2d 448 (W.D.N.Y., 2002).

Seneca Nation of Indians v. Wilbur M. Brucker, et al. 360 U.S. 909 (1959); 262 F. 2d 27 (1958); 162 F. Supp. 580 (1958).

United States v. Boylan. 265 F. 165 (1920).

United States v. Claus. 63 F. Supp. 433 (1944).

United States v. Cook. 86 U.S. 591 (1873).

United States v. Elm. 25 Fed. Cas. 1006 (1877).

United States v. Mrs. P. L. Garrow. 88 F. 2d 318 (1937).

BOOKS/BOOKLETS/PAMPHLETS

Abernethy, Byron R., ed. *Private Elisha Stockwell, Jr. Sees the Civil War.* Norman: Univ. of Oklahoma Press, 1958.

Abler, Thomas S. *Cornplanter: Chief Warrior of the Allegany Senecas.* Syracuse, N.Y.: Syracuse Univ. Press, 2007.

———, ed. *Chainbreaker: The Revolutionary War Memoirs of Governor Blacksnake as Told to Benjamin Williams.* Lincoln: Univ. of Nebraska Press, 1989.

Abrams, George H. J. *The Seneca People.* Phoenix, Ariz.: Indian Tribal Series, 1976.

Alfred, Gerald R. *Heeding the Voices of Our Ancestors: Kahnawake Mohawk Politics and the Rise of Native Nationalism.* New York: Oxford Univ. Press, 1995.

Armstrong, William H. *Warrior in Two Camps: Ely S. Parker, Union General and Seneca Chief.* Syracuse, N.Y.: Syracuse Univ. Press, 1978.

Austin, Alberta, comp. *Né Ho Níyó De: No—That's What It Was Like.* 2 vols. New York: Rebco Enterprises, 1986–89.

Barnard College. *The Mortarboard: The Yearbook of Barnard College, Columbia University.* New York: Barnard College Class of 1908, 1907.

Barrett, John G. *The Civil War in North Carolina.* Chapel Hill: Univ. of North Carolina Press, 1963.

Beauchamp, William M. *A History of the New York Iroquois.* Bulletin No. 78. Albany: New York State Museum, 1906.

Belknap, Jeremy. *Journal of a Tour from Boston to Oneida, June 1796.* Edited by George Dexter. Cambridge, Mass.: John Wilson, 1882.

Benn, Carl. *The Iroquois in the War of 1812.* Toronto: Univ. of Toronto Press, 1998.

Bieder, Robert E. *Native American Communities in Wisconsin, 1600–1960: A Study of Tradition and Change.* Madison: Univ. of Wisconsin Press, 1995.

Bilharz, Joy. *The Allegany Senecas and Kinzua Dam: Forced Relocation Through Two Generations.* Lincoln: Univ. of Nebraska Press, 1998.

Bloomfield, Julia. *The Oneidas.* 2nd ed. New York: Alden Press, 1907.

Bonvillain, Nancy, ed. *Studies on Iroquoian Culture.* Occasional Publications in Northeastern Anthropology No. 6: *Man in the Northeast.* Rindge, N.H.: Dept. of Anthropology, Franklin Pierce College, 1980.

Britten, Thomas A. *American Indians in World War I: At War and at Home.* Albuquerque: Univ. of New Mexico Press, 1997.

Brown, Robert H. *The Republic in Peril: 1812.* New York: Columbia Univ. Press, 1964.

Bruce, Dwight H. *Onondaga's Centennial.* 2 vols. Syracuse, N.Y.: Boston History Co., 1896.

Burns, James McGregor. *Leadership.* New York: Harper and Row, 1978.

———. *Running Alone: Presidential Leadership—JFK to Bush II: Why It Has Failed and How We Can Fix It.* New York: Basic Books, 2006.

Burton, Lois. *A Quaker Promise Kept: Philadelphia Friends' Work with the Allegany Senecas, 1795–1960.* Eugene, Ore.: Spencer Butte Press, 1990.

Campbell, William W., ed. *The Life and Writings of DeWitt Clinton.* New York: Baker and Scribner, 1849.

Campisi, Jack, and Laurence M. Hauptman, eds. *The Oneida Indian Experience: Two Perspectives*. Syracuse, N.Y.: Syracuse Univ. Press, 1988.

Cardinal, Harold. *The Unjust Society: The Tragedy of Canada's Indians*. Edmonton, Alberta: M. G. Hurtig, 1969.

Carmer, Carl. *Dark Trees to the Wind: A Cycle of York State Years*. New York: William Sloane Associates, 1949.

Castile, George Pierre. *Taking Charge: Native American Self-Determination and Federal Indian Policy, 1975–1993*. Tucson: Univ. of Arizona Press, 2006.

———. *To Show Heart: Native American Self-Determination and Federal Indian Policy, 1960–1975*. Tucson: Univ. of Arizona Press, 1998.

Castile, George Pierre, and Robert L. Bee., eds. *State and Reservation: New Perspectives on Federal Indian Policy*. Tucson: Univ. of Arizona Press, 1992.

Caswell, Harriet S. *Our Life Among the Iroquois Indians*. 1892. Reprint. Lincoln: Univ. of Nebraska Press, 2007.

Catlin, George. *Letters and Notes on the Manners, Customs, and Condition of the North American Indians*. 1841. Reprint. New York: Dover Books, 1973.

Chazanoff, William. *Joseph Ellicott and the Holland Land Company: The Opening of Western New York*. Syracuse, N.Y.: Syracuse Univ. Press, 1970.

Clark, Joshua V. H. *Onondaga: or, Reminiscences of Early and Later Times*. 2 vols. Syracuse, N.Y.: Stoddard and Babcock, 1849.

Clarkin, Thomas. *Federal Indian Policy in the Kennedy and Johnson Administrations, 1961–1969*. Albuquerque: Univ. of New Mexico Press, 2001.

Colton, Calvin. *Tour of the American Lakes and Among the Indians of the Northwest Territory in 1830*. 1933. Reprint. Port Washington, N.Y.: Kennikat Press, 1973.

Congdon, Charles C. *Allegany Oxbow*. Little Valley, N.Y.: privately printed, 1967.

Cornplanter, Jesse. *Legends of the Longhouse*. New York: Lippincott, 1938.

Cusick, David. *Sketches of Ancient History of the Six Nations*. 2nd ed. Lockport, N.Y.: Cooley and Lothrop, 1828.

Dabney, Lewis M. *Edmund Wilson: A Life in Literature*. New York: Farrar, Straus, and Giroux, 2005.

Dearborn, Henry A. S. *Journals of Henry A. S. Dearborn*. Edited by Frank Severance. Buffalo Historical Society Publications No. 7. Buffalo, N.Y.: Buffalo Historical Society, 1904.

Delafield, Joseph. *The Unfortified Boundary: A Diary of the First Survey of the Canadian Boundary Line from St. Regis to the Lake of the Woods*. Edited by Robert McElroy and Thomas Riggs. New York: privately printed, 1943.

Deloria, Vine, ed. *The Indian Reorganization Act: Congresses and Bills*. Norman: Univ. of Oklahoma Press, 2002.

Densmore, Christopher. *Red Jacket: Iroquois Diplomat and Orator*. Syracuse, N.Y.: Syracuse Univ. Press, 1999.

Dowd, Gregory E. *A Spirited Resistance: The North American Indian Struggle for Unity, 1745–1815*. Baltimore: Johns Hopkins Univ. Press, 1992.

Edmunds, R. David. *The New Warriors: Native American Leaders Since 1900*. Lincoln: Univ. of Nebraska Press, 2001.

———, ed. *American Indian Leaders: Studies in Diversity*. Lincoln: Univ. of Nebraska Press, 1980.

Eisenstadt, Peter, and Laura-Eve Moss, eds. *The Encyclopedia of New York State*. Syracuse, N.Y.: Syracuse Univ. Press, 2005.

Engelbrecht, William. *Iroquoia: The Development of a Native World*. Syracuse, N.Y.: Syracuse Univ. Press, 2003.

Episcopal Church's Mission to the Oneidas, The. Oneida, Wis.: n.p., 1899.

Evans, Paul D. *The Holland Land Company*. Buffalo, N.Y.: Buffalo Historical Society, 1924.

Ewen, Alexander, ed. *Voices of Indigenous Peoples*. Santa Fe, N.M.: Clear Light Publishers, 1994.

Fenton, William N. *The Great Law and the Longhouse: A Political History of the Iroquois Confederacy*. Norman: Univ. of Oklahoma Press, 1998.

———, ed. *Symposium on Local Diversity*. Bureau of American Ethnology Bulletin No. 149. Washington, D.C.: Smithsonian Institution, 1951.

Fischer, David Hackett. *Growing Old in America*. New York: Oxford Univ. Press, 1977.

Fixico, Donald L. *Termination and Relocation: Federal Indian Policy, 1945–1960*. Albuquerque: Univ. of New Mexico Press, 1986.

———. *The Urban Indian Experience in America*. Albuquerque: Univ. of New Mexico Press, 2000.

———, ed. *An Anthology of Western Great Lakes Indian History*. Milwaukee: Univ. of Wisconsin, Milwaukee Indian Studies Program, 1987.

———, ed. *Rethinking American Indian History*. Albuquerque: Univ. of New Mexico Press, 1997.

Foreman, Grant. *The Last Trek of the Indians*. 1946. Reprint. New York: Russell and Russell, 1972.

Fortunate Eagle (Nordwall), Adam. *Heart of the Rock*. Norman: Univ. of Oklahoma Press, 2002.

Foster, Michael, et al., eds. *Extending the Rafters: Interdisciplinary Approaches to Iroquoian Studies*. Albany: State Univ. of New York Press, 1984.

Franco, Jeré. *Crossing the Pond: The Native American Effort in World War II*. Denton: Univ. of North Texas Press, 1999.

French, J. H., comp. *Gazetteer of the State of New York*. Syracuse, N.Y.: R. Pearsall Smith, 1860.

Ganter, Granville, ed. *The Collected Speeches of Sagoyewatha or Red Jacket*. Syracuse, N.Y.: Syracuse Univ. Press, 2006.

George-Kanentiio, Douglas. *Iroquois on Fire: A Voice from the Mohawk Nation*. Westport, Conn.: Praeger, 2006.

Gibson, Arrell, ed. *America's Exiles: Indian Colonization in Oklahoma*. Oklahoma City: Oklahoma Historical Society, 1976.

Glasson, William H. *Federal Military Pensions in the United States*. Edited by David Kinley. New York: Carnegie Endowment for International Peace and Oxford Univ. Press, 1918.

Glatthaar, Joseph, and James Kirby Martin. *Forgotten Allies: The Oneida Indians and the American Revolution*. New York: Hill and Wang, 2006.

Graymont, Barbara. *The Iroquois in the American Revolution*. Syracuse, N.Y.: Syracuse Univ. Press, 1972.

Greene, Jerome A. *Yellowstone Command: Colonel Nelson A. Miles and the Great Sioux War, 1876–1877*. Lincoln: Univ. of Nebraska Press, 1991.

Haber, Carole, and Brian Gratton. *Old Age and the Search for Security: An American Social History*. Bloomington: Indiana Univ. Press, 1994.

Hale, Horatio E. *The Iroquois Book of Rites*. 2 vols. Philadelphia: D. G. Brinton, 1883.

Hauptman, Laurence M. *Between Two Fires: American Indians in the Civil War*. New York: Simon and Schuster, 1995.

———. *Conspiracy of Interests: Iroquois Dispossession and the Rise of New York State*. Syracuse, N.Y.: Syracuse Univ. Press, 1999.

———. *Formulating American Indian Policy in New York State, 1970–1986*. Albany: State Univ. of New York Press, 1988.

———. *The Iroquois and the New Deal*. Syracuse, N.Y.: Syracuse Univ. Press, 1981.

———. *The Iroquois in the Civil War: From Battlefield to Reservation*. Syracuse, N.Y.: Syracuse Univ. Press, 1993.

———. *The Iroquois Struggle for Survival: World War II to Red Power*. Syracuse, N.Y.: Syracuse Univ. Press, 1986.

————. *Tribes and Tribulations: Misconceptions About American Indians and Their History.* Albuquerque: Univ. of New Mexico Press, 1995.

————, ed. *A Seneca Indian in the Union Army: The Civil War Letters of Sergeant Isaac Newton Parker, 1861–1865.* Shippensburg, Pa.: Burd Street/White Mane Publishing, 1995.

Hauptman, Laurence M., and L. Gordon McLester III. *Chief Daniel Bread and the Oneida Nation of Indians of Wisconsin.* Norman: Univ. of Oklahoma Press, 2001.

————, eds. *The Oneida Indian Journey: From New York to Wisconsin, 1784–1860.* Madison: Univ. of Wisconsin Press, 1999.

————, eds. *The Oneidas in the Age of Allotment, 1860–1920.* Norman: Univ. of Oklahoma Press, 2006.

Hertzberg, Hazel W. *The Search for an American Indian Identity: Modern Pan-Indian Movements.* Syracuse, N.Y.: Syracuse Univ. Press, 1971.

Hewitt, J. N. B. *Iroquoian Cosmology.* Part One: *Annual Report of the Bureau of American Ethnology for the Years 1899–1900.* Washington, D.C.: Smithsonian Institution, 1903.

————. *Iroquoian Cosmology.* Part Two: *Annual Report of the Bureau of American Ethnology for the Years 1925–1926.* Washington, D.C.: Smithsonian Institution, 1928.

Hitsman, J. Mackay. *The Incredible War of 1812.* Toronto: Univ. of Toronto Press, 1965.

Holm, Tom. *Strong Hearts, Wounded Souls: Native American Veterans of the Vietnam War.* Austin: Univ. of Texas Press, 1996.

Horsman, Reginald. *Expansion and American Indian Policy, 1783–1812.* East Lansing: Michigan State Univ. Press, 1967.

Houghton, Frederick. *The History of the Buffalo Creek Reservation.* Publication No. 24. Buffalo, N.Y.: Buffalo Historical Society, 1920.

Howland, Henry R. *The Old Caneadea Council House and Its Last Council Fire.* Perry, N.Y.: Comfort Craftsmen, 1932

Hoxie, Frederick E. *A Final Promise: The Campaign to Assimilate the Indians, 1890–1920.* Lincoln: Univ. of Nebraska Press, 1984.

Ickes, Harold L. *The Secret Diary of Harold L. Ickes.* 3 vols. New York: Dutton, 1954.

Jennings, Francis. *The Ambiguous Iroquois Empire.* New York: W. W. Norton, 1984.

Jennings, Francis, et al., eds. *The History and Culture of Iroquois Diplomacy: An Interdisciplinary Guide to the Treaties of the Six Nations and Their League.* Syracuse, N.Y.: Syracuse Univ. Press, 1985.

Johansen, Bruce E. *Life and Death in Mohawk Country.* Golden, Colo.: North American Press, 1993.

Johnson, E. Roy. *The Tuscaroras: History—Traditions—Culture.* Murfreesboro, N.C.: Johnson Publishing Co., 1968.

Johnson, Elias. *Legends, Traditions and Laws of the Iroquois or Six Nations, and History of the Tuscarora Indians.* Lockport, N.Y.: Union Printing and Publishing, 1881.

Johnston, Charles M., ed. *The Valley of the Six Nations: A Collection of Documents on the Indian Lands of the Grand River.* Toronto: Champlain Society, 1964.

Josephy, Alvin M., Jr. *The Patriot Chiefs: A Chronicle of American Indian Resistance.* New York: Viking, 1961.

Kellogg, Laura M. Cornelius. *Our Democracy and the American Indian.* Kansas City, Mo.: Burton Publishing Co., 1920.

Ketchum, William. *An Authentic and Comprehensive History of Buffalo.* 2 vols. Buffalo: Rockwell, Baker and Hill, 1864–65.

Krouse, Susan Applegate. *North American Indians in the Great War.* Lincoln: Univ. of Nebraska Press, 2007.

Kvasnicka, Richard, and Herman Viola, eds. *The Commissioners of Indian Affairs, 1824–1977.* Lincoln: Univ. of Nebraska Press, 1979.

Lafitau, Joseph-François. *Customs of the American Indians Compared with the Customs of Primitive Times.* 2 vols. 1724. Edited and translated by William N. Fenton and Elizabeth L. Moore. Toronto: Champlain Society, 1977.

Landsman, Gail. *Sovereignty and Symbol: Indian-White Conflict at Ganienkeh.* Albuquerque: Univ. of New Mexico Press, 1988.

Lewis, Herbert (with the assistance of L. Gordon McLester III), ed. *Oneida Lives: Long Lost Voices of the Wisconsin Oneidas.* Lincoln: Univ. of Nebraska Press, 2005.

Littlefield, Daniel F., Jr., and James W. Parins, eds. *American Indian and Alaska Native Newspapers and Periodicals, 1925–1970.* Westport, Conn.: Greenwood Press, 1961.

Loew, Patty. *Indian Nations of Wisconsin: Histories of Endurance and Renewal.* Madison: Wisconsin Historical Society Press, 2001.

Lurie, Nancy Oestreich. *Wisconsin Indians.* Rev. ed. Madison: Wisconsin Historical Society Press, 2002.

McKelvey, Blake. *Rochester on the Genesee*. Syracuse, N.Y.: Syracuse Univ. Press, 1973.

——. *Rochester: The Water-Power City, 1812–1854*. Cambridge, Mass.: Harvard Univ. Press, 1945.

McNall, Neil Adams. *An Agricultural History of the Genesee Valley, 1790–1860*. Philadelphia: Univ. of Pennsylvania Press, 1952.

Martin, Deborah B. *History of Brown County, Wisconsin: Past and Present*. 2 vols. Chicago: S. J. Clarke, 1913.

Mau, Clayton, ed. *The Development of Central and Western New York*. New York: Du Bois Press, 1944.

Meinig, D. W. *The Shaping of America: A Geographical Perspective on 500 Years of History*. 2 vols. New Haven, Conn.: Yale Univ. Press, 1986 and 1993.

Metcalf, R. Warren. *Termination's Legacy: The Discarded Indians of Utah*. Lincoln: Univ. of Nebraska Press, 2002.

Miller, Nathan. *The Enterprise of a Free People: Aspects of Economic Development in New York State During the Canal Era, 1792–1838*. Ithaca, N.Y.: Cornell Univ. Press, 1962.

Minard, John S. *History of Allegany County*. New York: W. A. Ferguson, 1876.

——. *The Indian Oil Spring*. Gowanda, N.Y.: privately printed, 1901.

Mohawk Council of Akwesasne. *Akwesasne: A Special People in a Special Place*. Akwesasne: Mohawk Council of Akwesasne, 2006.

Mohawk, John, comp. *A Basic Call to Consciousness*. Rooseveltown, N.Y.: *Akwesasne Notes*, 1979.

Morgan, Lewis Henry. *League of the Ho-de-no-sau-nee, or Iroquois*. 1851. Reprint, with new introduction by William N. Fenton. New York: Corinth, 1962.

Moses, L. George, and Raymond Wilson, eds. *Indian Lives: Essays on Nineteenth- and Twentieth-Century Native American Leaders*. Albuquerque: Univ. of New Mexico Press, 1985.

Murdock, Eugene C. *Patriotism Limited, 1862–1865: The Civil War Draft and the Bounty System*. Kent, Ohio: Kent State Univ. Press, 1967.

Myers, Merlin G. *Households and Families of the Longhouse Iroquois at Six Nations Reserve*. Lincoln: Univ. of Nebraska Press, 2006.

National Indian Gaming Association. *An Analysis of the Economic Impact of Indian Gaming in 2005*. Washington, D.C.: National Indian Gaming Association, 2005.

Newton, James K. *A Wisconsin Boy in Dixie: The Selected Letters of James K. Newton*. Edited by Stephen E. Ambrose. Madison: Univ. of Wisconsin Press, 1961.

Norton, John. *The Journal of Major John Norton, 1816.* Edited by Carl F. Klinck and James J. Talman. Toronto: Champlain Society, 1970.

Oneida Nation of Indians of New York. *Annual Report for 2004.* 2005.

O'Reilly, Henry. *Sketches of Rochester.* Rochester, N.Y.: William Alling, 1838.

Otis, D. S. *The Dawes Act and the Allotment of Indian Lands.* Edited by Francis Paul Prucha. Norman: Univ. of Oklahoma Press, 1973.

Parker, Arthur C. *Parker on the Iroquois.* Edited by William N. Fenton. Syracuse, N.Y.: Syracuse Univ. Press, 1968.

———. *Seneca Myths and Folk Tales.* 1923. Reprint, with an introduction by William N. Fenton. Lincoln: Univ. of Nebraska Press, 1989.

———. *The Life of General Ely S. Parker, Last Grand Sachem of the Iroquois and General Grant's Military Secretary.* Buffalo Historical Society Publication No. 23. Buffalo, N.Y.: Buffalo Historical Society, 1919.

Perdue, Theda, ed. *Sifters: Native American Women's Lives.* New York: Oxford Univ. Press, 2001.

Pevar, Stephen L. *The Rights of Indians and Tribes.* 3rd ed. Carbondale: Southern Illinois Univ. Press, 2002.

Philp, Kenneth R. *John Collier's Crusade for Indian Reform, 1920–1954.* Tucson: Univ. of Arizona Press, 1977.

———. *Termination Revisited: American Indians on the Trail to Self-Determination, 1933–1953.* Lincoln: Univ. of Nebraska Press, 1999.

———, ed. *Indian Self-Rule: First Hand Accounts of Indian-White Relations from Roosevelt to Reagan.* Salt Lake City, Utah: Howe Brothers, 1986.

Pilkington, Walter, ed. *The Journals of Samuel Kirkland.* Clinton, N.Y.: Hamilton College, 1980.

Porter, Joy. *To Be Indian: The Life of Iroquois Seneca Arthur Caswell Parker.* Norman: Univ. of Oklahoma Press, 2001.

Porter, Robert Odawi, ed. *Sovereignty, Colonialism and the Indigenous Nations.* Durham, N.C.: Carolina Academic, 2005.

Reid, Gerald F. *Kahnawà:ke: Factionalism, Traditionalism, and Nationalism in a Mohawk Community.* Lincoln: Univ. of Nebraska Press, 2004.

Richter, Daniel K. *The Ordeal of the Longhouse: The Peoples of the Iroquois League in the Era of European Colonization.* Chapel Hill: Univ. of North Carolina Press, 1992.

Richter, Daniel K., and James H. Merrell, eds. *Beyond the Covenant Chain: The Iroquois and Their Neighbors in Indian North America, 1600–1800.* Syracuse, N.Y.: Syracuse Univ. Press, 1987.

Rickard, Clinton. *Fighting Tuscarora: The Autobiography of Chief Clinton Rickard*. Edited by Barbara Graymont. Syracuse, N.Y.: Syracuse Univ. Press, 1973.

Ritzenthaler, Robert E. *The Oneida Indians of Wisconsin*. Bulletin No. 19. Milwaukee, Wis.: Public Museum of the City of Milwaukee, 1950.

Rockefeller-MacArthur, Elizabeth. *American Indian Library Services in Perspective*. Jefferson, N.C.: McFarland and Co., 1998.

Rosen, Deborah. *American Indians and State Law: Sovereignty, Race, and Citizenship, 1790–1880*. Lincoln: Univ. of Nebraska Press, 2007.

Sandstrom, Roy H., ed. *Educating the Educators: A Report of the Institute on "The American Indian Student in Higher Education."* Canton, N.Y.: St. Lawrence Univ., 1971.

Satz, Ronald. *American Indian Policy in the Jacksonian Era*. Lincoln: Univ. of Nebraska Press, 1975.

Schoolcraft, Henry Rowe. *Notes on the Iroquois, or Contributions to American History, Antiquities and General Ethnology*. Albany, N.Y.: Erastus H. Pease, 1847.

Seaver, James E., comp. *A Narrative of the Life of Mrs. Mary Jemison*. 1824. Reprint, with a foreword by George H. J. Abrams. Syracuse, N.Y.: Syracuse Univ. Press, 1990.

Selikoff, Irving, E. Cuyler Hammond, and Stephen Levin. *Environmental Contaminants and the Health of the People of the St. Regis Reserve: Report Submitted to the Canadian Minister of Health and Welfare*. 2 vols. New York: Mount Sinai School of Medicine, 1984–85.

Seneca Nation of Indians. *Annual Report for 2006*.

Shattuck, George C. *The Oneida Indian Land Claims: A Legal History*. Syracuse, N.Y.: Syracuse Univ. Press, 1991.

Shaw, Diane. *City Building on the Eastern Frontier: Sorting the New Nineteenth-Century City*. Baltimore: Johns Hopkins Univ. Press, 2004.

Shaw, Ronald E. *Erie Water West*. Lexington: Univ. of Kentucky Press, 1965.

Sheriff, Carol. *The Artificial River: The Erie Canal and the Paradox of Progress, 1817–1862*. New York: Hill and Wang, 1996.

Shimony, Annemarie A. *Conservatism Among the Iroquois at the Six Nations Reserve*. 1961. Expanded ed. Syracuse, N.Y.: Syracuse Univ. Press, 1994.

Six Nations Council. *Six Nations of the Grand River: Land Rights, Financial Justice, Creative Solutions*. Ohsweken, Ontario: Six Nations Council, 2006.

Snow, Dean R. *The Iroquois*. Oxford, U.K.: Blackwell, 1994.

Snyder, Charles M., ed. *Red and White on the New York Frontier: A Struggle for Survival—Insights from the Papers of Erastus Granger, Indian Agent, 1807–1819*. Harrison, N.Y.: Harbor Hill, 1978.

Society of American Indians. *Report of the Executive Council on the Proceedings of the First Annual Conference, October 12–17, 1911*. Washington, D.C., 1912.

Tanner, Helen Hornbeck, et al., eds. *Atlas of Great Lakes Indian History*. Norman: Univ. of Oklahoma Press, 1987.

Taylor, Alan. *The Divided Ground: Indians, Settlers and the Northern Borderland of the American Revolution*. New York: Alfred A. Knopf, 2006.

Taylor, Graham D. *The New Deal and American Indian Tribalism: The Administration of the Indian Reorganization Act, 1934–1945*. Lincoln: Univ. of Nebraska Press, 1980.

Tooker, Elisabeth. *The Iroquois Ceremonial of Midwinter*. Syracuse, N.Y.: Syracuse Univ. Press, 1970.

———, ed. *Lewis Henry Morgan on Iroquois Material Culture*. Tucson: Univ. of Arizona Press, 1994.

———, ed. *Proceedings of the 1965 Conference on Iroquois Research*. Albany: New York State Museum and Science Center, 1967.

Townsend, Kenneth William. *World War II and the American Indian*. Albuquerque: Univ. of New Mexico Press, 2000.

Trigger, Bruce G., ed. *Handbook of North American Indians*. Vol. 15: *The Northeast*. Washington, D.C.: Smithsonian Institution, 1978.

Turner, Orsamus. *History of Phelps' and Gorham's Purchase*. Rochester, N.Y.: William Alling, 1851.

———. *Pioneer History of the Holland Purchase of Western New York*. 1850. Reprint. Geneseo, N.Y.: James Brunner, 1974.

Upton, Helen M. *The Everett Report in Historical Perspective: The Indians of New York*. Albany: New York State Bicentennial Commission, 1980.

Veatch, Richard. *Canada and the League of Nations*. Toronto: Univ. of Toronto Press, 1975.

Vecsey, Christopher, and William A. Starna, eds. *Iroquois Land Claims*. Syracuse, N.Y.: Syracuse Univ. Press, 1988.

Viola, Herman J. *Diplomats in Buckskin: A History of Indian Delegations in Washington City*. Washington, D.C.: Smithsonian Institution Press, 1981.

Wallace, Anthony F. C. *The Death and Rebirth of the Seneca*. New York: Alfred A. Knopf, 1970.

Weaver, Sally. *Making Canadian Indian Policy: The Hidden Agenda.* Toronto: Univ. of Toronto Press, 1981.

Weed, Thurlow. *Memoir of Thurlow Weed.* Edited by Thurlow Weed Barnes. Boston: Houghton Mifflin, 1884.

White, Richard. *The Middle Ground: Indians, Empire and Republic in the Great Lakes Region, 1650–1815.* New York: Cambridge Univ. Press, 1991.

Wilson, Edmund. *Apologies to the Iroquois.* 1960. Reprint, with new introduction by William N. Fenton. Syracuse, N.Y.: Syracuse Univ. Press, 1991.

——. *The Fifties.* New York: Farrar, Straus, and Giroux, 1986.

——. *Letters on Literature and Politics, 1912–1973.* Edited by Elena Wilson. New York: Farrar, Straus, and Giroux, 1977.

Wonderley, Anthony. *Oneida Iroquois Folklore, Myth and History.* Syracuse, N.Y.: Syracuse Univ. Press, 2004.

ARTICLES

Abler, Thomas S. "Friends, Factions and the Seneca Nation Revolution of 1848." *Niagara Frontier* 21 (Winter 1974): 74–79.

——. "Protestant Missionaries and Native Cultures: Parallel Careers of Asher Wright and Silas T. Rand." *American Indian Quarterly* 26 (Winter 1992): 25–37.

Allen, Orlando. "Personal Recollections of Captain Jones and Parrish, and the Payment of Indian Annuities in Buffalo." In *Buffalo Historical Society Publications No. 6.* Edited by Frank Severance, 539–46. Buffalo, N.Y.: Buffalo Historical Society, 1903.

Berkhofer, Robert F., Jr. "Faith and Factionalism Among the Senecas: Theory and Ethnohistory." *Ethnohistory* 12 (1965): 99–112.

Biggs, Bonnie. "Bright Child of Oklahoma: Lotsee Patterson and the Development of America's Tribal Libraries." *American Indian Culture and Research Journal* 24 (2000): 55–67.

Bilharz, Joy. "First Among Equals? The Changing Status of Seneca Women." In *Women and Power in Native North America,* edited by Laura F. Klein and Lillian A. Ackerman, 101–12. Norman: Univ. of Oklahoma Press, 1995.

Bird, William A. "Reminiscences of the Boundary Survey Between the United States and the British Provinces." *Publications of the Buffalo Historical Society No. 4* Buffalo, N.Y.: Buffalo Historical Society, 1896, 1–14.

Bray, Ethel. "The Seneca Nation Library." *The Bookmark,* Summer 1988, 246–47.

Brown, Judith K. "Economic Organization and the Position of Women Among the Iroquois." *Ethnohistory* 17 (Summer–Fall 1970): 151–67.

Cohn, Benjamin S. "History and Anthropology: The State of Play." *Comparative Studies in Society and History* 22 (Apr. 1980): 198–221.

Colman, Henry. "Recollections of Oneida Indians, 1840–1845." *Proceedings of the State Historical Society at Its Fifty-ninth Annual Meeting*, 152–59. Madison, Wis.: State Historical Society, 1912.

Cope, Alfred. "Mission to the Menominee: A Quaker's Green Bay Diary." *Wisconsin Magazine of History* 49 (1966): 302–23; 50 (Winter 1967): 18–42, 120–44, 211–41.

Cornelius [Kellogg], Laura M. "Overalls and a Tenderfoot: A Story." *The Barnard Bear* 2 (Mar. 1907): 5–18.

Decker, George. "America Europeanized." *Research and Transactions of the New York State Archaeological Association, Lewis Henry Morgan Chapter*, 1925, 5–17.

———. "Must the Peaceful Iroquois Go?" *Research and Transactions of the New York State Archaeological Association, Lewis Henry Morgan Chapter*, 1923, 5–23.

———. "Treaty Making with the Indians." *Research and Transactions of the New York State Archaeological Association, Lewis Henry Morgan Chapter*, 1920, 5–23.

Fenton, William N. "Iroquoian Culture History: A General Evaluation." *Bureau of American Ethnology Bulletin* 180 (1961): 253–77.

———. "The Iroquois Confederacy in the Twentieth Century: A Case Study of the Theory of Lewis Henry Morgan in 'Ancient Society.'" *Ethnology* 4 (July 1965): 251–65.

———. "The Lore of the Longhouse: Myth, Ritual and Red Power." *Anthropological Quarterly* 48 (1975): 131–47.

———. "The Roll Call of the Iroquois Chiefs: A Study of a Mnemonic Cane from the Six Nations Reserve." *Smithsonian Miscellaneous Collections* 111 (1950): 1–73.

———. "This Island, the World on the Turtle's Back." *Journal of American Folklore* 75 (Oct.–Dec. 1962): 283–300.

———. "Toward the Gradual Civilization of the Indian Natives: The Missionary and Linguistic Work of Asher Wright [1803–75] Among the Senecas of Western New York." *Proceedings of the American Philosophical Society* 100 (1956): 567–81.

————, ed. "Seneca Indians by Asher Wright 9(1859)." *Ethnohistory* 4 (1957): 302–21.

Freilich, Morris. "Cultural Persistence Among the Modern Iroquois." *Anthropos* 53 (1958): 473–83.

Geary, James W. "Civil War Conscription in the North: An Historiographical Review." *Civil War History* 32 (Sept. 1986): 208–28.

Graymont, Barbara. "New York State Indian Policy After the American Revolution." *New York History* 58 (Oct. 1976): 438–74.

————. "The Tuscarora New Year Festival." *New York History* 50 (Apr. 1969): 149–52.

Gunther, Gerald. "Governmental Power and New York Indian Lands—A Reassessment of a Persistent Problem of Federal-State Relations." *Buffalo Law Review* 7 (Fall 1958): 1–14.

Hauptman, Laurence M. "Alice Lee Jemison: Seneca Political Activist, 1901–1964." *Indian Historian* 12 (June 1979): 15–22.

————. "Circle the Wagons." *Capital Region* 2 (Feb. 1987): 29–31, 52–53.

————. "Compensatory Justice: The Seneca Nation Settlement Act of 1990." *National Forum* 71 (Spring 1991): 31–33.

————. "Four Eastern New Yorkers and Seneca Lands: A Study in Treaty-Making." *Hudson Valley Regional Review* 13 (Mar. 1996): 1–19.

————. "'Going Off the Reservation': A Memoir." *Public Historian* 25 (Fall 2003): 81–94.

————. "State's Men, Salvation Seekers and the Senecas: The Supplemental Treaty of Buffalo Creek, 1842." *New York History* 78 (Jan. 1997): 51–82

————. "Senecas and Subdividers: Resistance to Allotment of Indian Lands in New York, 1875–1906." *Prologue* 9 (Summer 1977): 105–16.

————. "The American Indian Federation and the Indian New Deal: A Reinterpretation." *Pacific Historical Review* 52 (Nov. 1983): 378–402.

————. "The Indian Reorganization Act." In *The Aggressions of Civilization: Federal Indian Policy Since the 1880s,* edited by Sandra L. Cadwalader and Vine Deloria, Jr., 131–48. Philadelphia: Temple Univ. Press, 1984.

————. "The Iroquois Indians and the Rise of the Empire State: Ditches, Defense and Dispossession." *New York History* 79 (Oct. 1998): 325–58.

————. "Who Owns Grand Island (Erie County, N.Y.)?" *Oklahoma City University Law Review* 23 (Spring/Summer 1998): 151–74.

Katchukian-Freudig, Nelly. "Chief Deskaheh, George Decker and the Six Nations v. The Government of Canada." *The Iroquoian* 11 (Fall 1985): 12–18.

———. "The Decker Papers II: Decker and Chief Deskaheh in Geneva, 1923." *The Iroquoian* 12 (Spring 1986): 79–83.

Kellogg, Laura Cornelius. "Some Facts and Figures on Indian Education." *The Quarterly Journal* [of the Society of American Indians] 1 (Apr. 15, 1913): 36–46.

Krook, Lennart, and G. A. Maylin. "Industrial Fluoride Pollution: Chronic Fluoride Poisoning in Cornwall Island Cattle." *Cornell Veterinarian* 69, suppl. 8 (1979): 1–70.

Landy, David. "Tuscarora Tribalism and National Identity." *Ethnohistory* 5 (1958): 250–84.

Locklear, Arlinda. "Tribal Land Claim: Before and After Cayuga." New York State Bar Association *Government, Law and Policy Journal* 8 (Spring 2006): 40–43.

Manley, Henry S. "Buying Buffalo from the Indians." *New York History* 28 (July 1947): 313–29.

———. "Red Jacket's Last Campaign." *New York History* 31 (Apr. 1950): 149–68.

Miller, Nathan. "Private Enterprise in Inland Navigation: The Mohawk Route Prior to the Erie Canal." *New York History* 11 (Oct. 1950): 398–413.

Parker, Arthur C. "The Senecas in the War of 1812." *Proceedings of the New York State Historical Association* 15 (1916): 78–90.

Pound, Cuthbert W. "Nationals Without a Nation: The New York State Tribal Indians." *Columbia Law Review* 22 (Feb. 1922): 97–102.

Reitz, Keith. "George P. Decker and the Oneida Indians." *The Iroquoian* 13 (Fall 1987): 28–33.

Richter, Daniel K. "War and Culture: The Iroquois Experience." *William and Mary Quarterly*, 3rd ser., 40 (Oct. 1983): 528–59.

Rostkowski, Joëlle. "The Redman's Appeal for Justice: Deskaheh and the League of Nations." In *Indians and Europe: An Interdisciplinary Collection of Essays*, edited by Christian F. Feest. Vienna: Rader Verlag, 1989.

Shimony, Annemarie A. "Alexander General, 'Deskahe': Cayuga-Oneida, 1889–1965." In *American Indian Intellectuals of the Nineteenth and Twentieth Centuries*, edited by Margot Liberty. 1978. Reprint. Norman: Univ. of Oklahoma Press, Red River Books, 2002.

Shoemaker, Nancy. "The Rise and Fall of Iroquois Women." *Journal of Women's History* 2 (Winter 1991): 39–57.

Snyderman, George S. "Behind the Tree of Peace: A Sociological Analysis of Iroquois Warfare." *Pennsylvania Archaeologist* 38 (Fall 1948): 3–93.

———, ed. "Halliday Jackson's Journal of a Visit Paid to the Indians of New York (1806)." *Proceedings of the American Philosophical Society* 101 (Dec. 1957): 565–88.

Staub, Henry P., et al. "Health Supervision of Infants on the Cattaraugus Indian Reservation in New York: The Record Is No Better than in the Big City Slum Areas." *Clinical Pediatrics* 15 (Jan. 1976): 44–52.

Tooker, Elisabeth. "On the Development of the Handsome Lake Religion." *Proceedings of the American Philosophical Society* 133 (1989): 35–50.

———. "On the New Religion of Handsome Lake." *Anthropological Quarterly* 41 (1968): 187–200.

Wallace, Anthony F. C., ed. "Halliday Jackson's Journal to the Seneca Indians, 1798–1800." *Pennsylvania History* 19 (1952): 117–46, 325–49.

DISSERTATIONS

Abler, Thomas S. "Factional Dispute and Party Conflict in the Political System of the Seneca Nation (1845–1895): An Ethnohistorical Analysis." PhD dissertation, Univ. of Toronto, 1969.

Basehart, Harry S. "Historical Changes in the Kinship System of the Oneida Indians." PhD dissertation, Harvard Univ., 1952.

Boyce, Douglas W. "Tuscarora Political Organization, Ethnic Identity and Sociohistorical Demography, 1711–1825." PhD dissertation, Univ. of North Carolina, 1973.

Campisi, Jack. "Ethnic Identity and Boundary Maintenance in Three Oneida Communities." PhD dissertation, State Univ. of New York–Albany, 1974.

Conable, Mary. "A Steady Enemy: The Ogden Land Company and the Seneca Indians." PhD dissertation, Univ. of Rochester, 1995.

Flad, Harvey. "City and the Longhouse: A Social Geography of American Indians in Syracuse, N.Y." PhD dissertation, Syracuse Univ., 1973.

Geier, Philip Otto. "A Peculiar Status: A History of the Oneida Indian Treaties and Claims: Jurisdictional Conflict Within the American Government, 1775–1920." PhD dissertation, Syracuse Univ., 1980.

Patrick, Christine. "Samuel Kirkland: Missionary to the Oneida Indians." PhD dissertation, State Univ. of New York–Buffalo, 1992.

Rothenberg, Diane B. "Friends Like These: An Ethnohistorical Analysis of the Interaction Between Allegany Senecas and Quakers, 1798–1823." PhD dissertation, City Univ. of New York, 1976.

Tiro, Karim. "The People of the Standing Stone: The Oneida Indian Nation from Revolution through Removal, 1765–1840." PhD dissertation, Univ. of Pennsylvania, 1998.

Van Hoeven, James W. "Salvation and Indian Removal: The Career of Rev. John Freeman Schermerhorn, Indian Commissioner." PhD dissertation, Vanderbilt Univ., 1972.

NEWSPAPERS AND PERIODICALS

Akwesasne News
Akwesasne Notes
Albany Knickerbocker News
Albany Times-Union
American Indian
American Indian Journal
Appleton Crescent
Asheville Citizen
Atlantic Monthly
Baltimore Sun
Batavia News
Brooklyn Daily Eagle
Brown County Democrat
Buffalo Courier-Express
Buffalo Evening News
Christian Century
Commentary
Commonweal
Conservationist
Cornwall Standard-Freeholder (Cornwall, Ont.)
Daily Oklahoman (Oklahoma City)
De Pere Journal Democrat (De Pere, Wis.)
Empire State Report (Albany, N.Y.)
The First American (Washington, D.C.)
Green Bay Advocate
Green Bay Intelligencier
Green Bay Press Gazette
Harlow's Weekly (Tulsa, Okla.)

Indian Country Today

Indian Helper (Carlisle Indian School)

Indian Historian (San Francisco)

Indian Time (Mohawk Nation, via Rooseveltown, N.Y.)

Indian Truth (Philadelphia, Pa.)

Indians at Work (Washington, D.C.)

KA-WEH-RAS (Akwesasne Reservation)

Kingston Freeman

Kinzua Planning Newsletter (Salamanca, N.Y.)

Life

Massena Observer

Miami Daily News-Record

Milwaukee Indian News

Milwaukee Journal

Milwaukee Sentinel

Montreal Gazette

Nation

Native American Rights Fund Announcements (Washington, D.C.)

Native Peoples

New Republic

New York Herald Tribune

New York Times

Newark Evening News

Newburgh News

News from Indian Country

Newsweek

Niagara Falls Gazette

Ogdensburg Journal

Olean Times Herald

Ottawa Citizen

Pine Tree Chief (Six Nations Reserve, Ohsweken, Ont.)

Progressive

Raleigh News and Observer

Red Man (Carlisle Indian School)

Rochester Democrat and Chronicle

Rochester Times-Union

Salamanca Republican-Press

San Francisco Chronicle
Saturday Review
Si Wong Geh (Cattaraugus Reservation, Irving, N.Y.)
Syracuse Courier
Syracuse Herald American
Syracuse Herald-Journal
Syracuse Post-Standard
Talking Leaf (Brooklyn, N.Y.)
Tekawennake (Six Nations Reserve, Ohsweken, Ontario)
Time
Tulsa Daily World
Tulsa Tribune
Warren Observer
War Whoop (Akwesasne Reservation)
Washington Post
Wassaia (San Francisco, Calif.)
Watertown Daily Times
Wisconsin State Journal (Madison, Wis.)

Index

Italic page number denotes photograph or map.

208–9; criticism of over casino gambling, 207; cultural crisis and, 211; drawing on past to deal with the present, 6–7, 14, 89, 93–97, 213–14, 216; extension of power of, xix–xx, 120, 148–49, 246n. 3, 253n. 18, 253n. 20; pitting of nation against nation, xx, 136; pursuit of land claims in courts, 208–10; selection of chiefs, xix, 45, 46, 65, 85; since World War II, 204; successes of, 215–16; use of metaphors, xxi, 96; variation of opinion among, 203; Warriors' Movement and, xxvii, 211–12

Iroquois Loyalists, 1, 4, 16–17, 30, 83, 118, 125–26. *See also* Six Nations Confederacy Council of Chiefs; Six Nations of Ohsweken; Six Nations Reserve

Iroquois nationalism, xx, 70–71, 117–18, 148–49, 178, 187. *See also* Iroquois sovereignty and treaty rights; nationhood

Iroquois sovereignty and treaty rights: asserted in Canada, 126–28; assertion of in 1920s, 71; Ernest Benedict's appeal to, 174–75; Ernest Benedict's teaching of, 122; Daniel Bread's promotion of, 88; Canadian/U.S. denial of, 76, 187; casino gambling and, 207; civil/criminal jurisdiction and, xxvi, 127, 174–75, 208–9; Civil War conscription and, 38–40; Deskaheh's advocacy of, 71, 119–20, 129–41; education in New York State and, 197, 199–200; established in Haldimand Treaty, 214; Samuel George's advocacy of, 31, 40; Indian Citizenship Act and, xxv, 168, 171, 172; Alice Lee Jemison's advocacy

of, 48, 68–69, 70, 73–76, 77, 79; Dinah John's belief in, 63–64; Minnie Kellogg's belief in, 156, 163; lobbyists championing, 197; location of Seneca Nation Libraries as symbol of, 196–97; loyalty oaths and, 57, 59, 74, 112, 235n. 38; nationhood and, 117; Selective Service Act and, xxvi, 47, 77, 171–72; Society of American Indians and, 149; tax on Indians and, 12, 54, 68, 146, 184, 208–9, 214; Two Row Wampum symbolizing, 49, 214, 232n. 1. *See also* border crossing rights; conscription; Iroquois nationalism; land claims movement; nationhood; *specific treaty by name*

Iroquois Warriors' Movement, xxvii, 211–12

Irvine, Lowry, and Macomber lease, 24–25

Jackson, Andrew, 83, 91
Jackson Mills, Battle of, 103, 111
Jacob, Susan, 53, 233–34n. 16
Jacobs, Burton, 181
Jacobs, Hubert, 245n. 8
Jacobs, Margaret, 198, 201
Jamieson, Roberta, 182, 261n. 60
Jandrew, Andrew, 166
Jandrew, Julia, 166
Jay Treaty (1794): Ernest Benedict's appeal to, xxi, 172; denial of rights guaranteed by, xxiii, 1, 122, 123, 127, 169–70, 184–85; Diblo's appeal to, 169; Louis Francis's challenge to Canada based on, 176; Anna Garrow's appeal to, 169–70; International Bridge protest and, 179–80; Mitchell case and, 184–85; provisions of, xxiii, 165

land speculators: on Buffalo Creek Reservation, 35; failure of Indians to stop, 42; in Genesee Valley, 26; in New York in 1700s, 2, 3, 17; Oneida Carrying Place and, 84–85, 90; Senecas and, 66; in Wisconsin, 146
language. *See* Iroquois languages
Lavell-Corbier, Jeannette, 182
leadership, xvii, xvii–xix. *See also* Iroquois leadership
League of Nations: Canadian membership in, 125; Deskaheh's/Decker's appeal for recognition as nation, xxv, 71, 124, 125, 131, 132–33; Deskaheh's proclamation to, 141
League of the Ho-de-no-sau-nee, or Iroquois, The (Morgan), xviii, 34
Lee, Daniel A., 69
Lee, Robert E., 108–9
Letchworth, William Pryor, 28
Lewis, Ann, 197, 264n. 27
Lincoln, Abraham, 38–39, 42, 59, 111
Little Beard's Town, 22
Little Water Society, 85
Locklear, Arlinda, 208, 265n. 19
Lolomi plan, 153–54
Longare, Bonin, 136
Lorette, Jean, 264n. 27
Lounsbury, Floyd, 86, 253n. 10
Lyons, Jesse, 173, 232n. 12

Magos, Alicia P., 186
Marchand murder case, 71–72
Matheson, Mrs. S. Robertson, 131, 137–38
McIntyre, M. H., 256n. 64
McLester, L. Gordon, III, 86
McLester, Thelma, 252n. 1
media representation, 210–11

men: arena of influence of, 45, 66; role in horticulture, 6, 32, 67
Menominee Indians of Wisconsin, 78–79, 91
Mercier Bridge protest, 212
metaphors: extending the rafters, xx, 118; Minnie Kellogg's use of, 144; purpose of use of, xxi; of seven generations to come, xxi, 14, 66, 216; of Silver Covenant Chain, 96, 214; Two Row Wampum as, 49, 95, 131, 214, 232n. 1; used in Condolence Council Ceremony, 96
Métis rights, 182
Michigan Territory, 88, 89, 91
Miles, Nelson A., 112
Miskito Indians, 120
missionaries: on Allegany Reservation, 19, 29; Americanization of Indians by, 37; division among Onondagas by, 32; John's view of, 55; Onondagas' resistance to, 35–36, 42; work among Iroquois, 4, 11, 13, 30
Mitchell, Mike, xxviii, 168, 179, 181, 184–85, 214
Mitchell case, xxviii, 184–85, 214
Mohawk, John, 120, 168
Mohawk Council of Akwesasne, 176, 214
Mohawk lands and dispossession: customs officials on, xxvi, 122, 165, 175; Darnhart Island, 175, 177; Dundee claim, 213; Eagle Bay takeover, xxvii, 200, 211; environmental degradation of, xxvi, 167–68, 175, 183, 204, 210; Ganienkeh, 200-211; New York State Power Authority and, xxvi, 175, 210; occupation of Racquette Point, xxvii, 177; protest of Oka golf course construction, xxvii, 184, 212; St. Lawrence Seaway project and, xxvi, 123, 172, 175, 177, 204, 212

Mohawk Nation Library, 198, 263n. 9

Mohawk radio station, 183

Mohawks: aid in rescue at World Trade Center, xxviii; in American Revolution, 1; attempt to recover land, 208; battles with New York State, 198; border crossing rights and, 164, 175, 179–80, 210, 214; casinos established, xxvii, 206, 212; civil war among, xxvii; creation of Mohawk Nation Library, 198; Eagle Bay takeover, xxvii, 200, 211; health care, 202; as high-steel workers, xx, xxviii, 101, 103–4, 117, 207, 244n. 8, 244n. 8-9; interference from outside sources, 122; International Bridge protest, 175, 179–78, 210, 260n. 55-56; Mohawk Nation Library, 198; New York State taxes on, 184; protest of Oka golf course construction, xxvii, 184, 212; radio station, 183; school boycotts, xxvi, 210; Treaty of Fort Stanwix, 2; Treaty with the Seven Nations of Canada and, 2; tribal economy of, 167–68. See also Benedict, Ernest

Montezuma, Carlos, 47, 70, 72, 78, 153

Morgan, Lewis Henry, xviii, 34, 41

Mormon economic model, 121, 150–51, 154

Morris, Robert, xxiii, 3, 20

Morris, Thomas, 3, 20

Morse, Jedidiah, 90

Moses, Carol, 237n. 13, 261–62n. 1, 264n. 27

Moses, Robert, 106, 175

mothers of the nation, xx, 45–46, 66–68, 70. See also clan mothers; women; specific woman by name

Mountpleasant, Caroline Parker, 50

mourning-wars, 101

Mulroney, Brian, 212

Mundt, Karl, 78

Munro, Robert, 21

Murray, Gilbert, 138

Mussolini, Benito, 136

Nash, George, 127–28

National Congress of American Indians, xxvi, 118, 246n. 3

National Indian Brotherhood (NIB), 177, 181

National Indian Education Association, 199

National Indian Gaming Association, 206

National Indian Youth Council, 118, 246n. 3

nationalism. See Iroquois nationalism; Iroquois sovereignty and treaty rights; nationhood

National Youth Administration's Indian programs, 170

nationhood, 117–18, 120, 203–4, 214, 215. See also Iroquois nationalism

National Museum of the American Indian (Smithsonian), 207

Native American Indian Education Unit (SED), 197

Native American religious revitalization, 4–5, 12–13. See also Gaiwiio; Hall, Louis; Handsome Lake

Nephew, Betty Owl, 201–2, 264n. 27

Netherlands, 131, 134

New Deal: clash of Iroquois/non-Indian belief systems during, 75–76; effect on Kellogg's plans, 161–62; Alice Lee Jemison's attacks on, 47, 48; Minnie Kellogg's view of, 122; political problems of, 76. See also Indian reorganization

and, 157–60; migration into Wisconsin, 84–85; move to the West, 35; Oneida Business Committee formed, *xxv;* pursuit of tribal land restoration, 128; removal to Wisconsin, 83; social disintegration following American Revolution, 90; transition to Wisconsin life, 90; *United States v. Boylan,* 128–29, 142, 156, 252n. 72. *See also* Bread, Daniel; Kellogg, Laura Minnie Cornelius; Wisconsin Oneidas

Onondaga Council of Chiefs, 36, 37–38

Onondaga lands and dispossession: in 1820s, 32; in American Revolution, 1; Buffalo Creek Treaty and, 53–54; loss of lands after American Revolution, 2, 3; survey of Onondaga Reservation, 37–38; treaties/lease with New York State in 1788/1795, 52–53

Onondaga Nation Arena, 49

Onondaga Reservation: Confederacy Council at, 36; effects of Kellogg's efforts, 155, 161; missionaries at, 42; population in 1806, 52; school on, 12, 42, 54; timber stripping on, 40; Whipple Report and, 63. *See also* George, Samuel; John, Dinah A.

Onondagas: acceptance of Handsome Lake's teachings, 32–33; American Revolution and, 1, 51–52; on Buffalo Creek Reservation, 31–32; education of, 31; government of, 63; missionaries among, 13; opposition to Seneca political revolution, 35; protest over Interstate 81 expansion, xxvi, 210; rejection of assimilation policies, 37; relocation of some to Kansas, 54; resistance to missionaries, 35–36; return of wampum belts to, 215; school boycott, xxvi, 210; significance

of Two Row Wampum, 49; sitdown on Interstate 81, xxvi, 210; treaty annuities, 52–53, 61; Treaty of Fort Stanwix (1784), 2; in War of 1812, 33, 35; Whipple Report and, 63. *See also* George, Samuel; John, Dinah A.

Ontario Provincial Police, 180

Oras, Henry, 58

Orchard Party (Oneidas), 92–93, 145

Our Democracy and the American Indian (Kellogg), 121, 152–53

Panama, 135, 137

Paris, Treaty of, 1

Parker, Arthur C., xviii, 149, 192, 246n. 3, 254n. 35

Parker, Ely S.: as commissioner of Indian Affairs, xxiv, 118; drafting of surrender at Appomattox, xxiv, 102; historical sources for life of, 30; service in Civil War, 102, 105, 113

Parker, Isaac Newton, 102

Parker, John S., 60

Pataki, George, 215

Patriot Chiefs, The (Josephy), xvii

Patterson, Lotsee, 199

Pattison, Philonus, 26–27

peach stone game, 84

Peck, John, 102

Penner, Keith, 261n. 60

Penner Commission, 182, 261n. 60

Perdue, Theda, 46

Perlov, Dadie, 200

Permanent Court of International Justice, 125, 128, 130–31, 133, 136, 140

Persia, 135, 137

Peters, John, 245n. 8

Peters, Susannah, 60

Peterson, Myrtle, 264n. 27

Wisconsin Oneidas (*cont.*)
    links to New York Iroquois, 86;
    migration into Wisconsin, 84–85,
    90–91; reacquisition of lost lands,
    xxv, 22, 215; reaffirmation of past,
    86; social structure of, 85, 144–46;
    Strambaugh Treaty, 91; taxes on, 146;
    timber stripping on lands of, 146; *See
    also* Bread, Daniel; Kellogg, Laura
    Minnie Cornelius
witchcraft, 5, 6, 7, 18, 32
women: accommodation to change,
    54–55; activism of, 65, 67–68; arena
    of influence of, 45–46, 66, 194–95;
    Handsome Lake's revision of role of,
    6, 32, 67; as protector of the land, xx,
    70; recovery from Kinzua Dam trag-
    edy by, 67, 191–92, 196–203; response
    to changing world, 52; role in creation
    of Seneca Nation Libraries and
    Museum, 196–201; role in creation of
    Seneca Nation Health Clinics, 196,
    201–2; role in Indian-white economic
    exchange, 46, 54–56, 64; role in Iro-
    quoia, xxi, 146; role in Seneca Nation
    of Indians, 65–67, 191, 238n. 17; role
    in Tonawanda Band of Indians, 65;
    selection of chiefs, xix, 45, 46, 65,
    85; as victims of war in American
    Revolution, 52; voting rights, 46, 47,
    66, 67–68, 191; in War of 1812, 53,
    233n. 16. *See also* Jemison, Alice Lee;
    John, Dinah A.; Kellogg, Laura Min-
    nie Cornelius; Seneca, Pauline Lay
Women's, Infant's and Children's Center
    (WIC), 194
Works Progress Administration, xxv, 86,
    253n. 10
World Trade Center, xxviii, 104, 117,
    244n. 8
World War I, xxv, 71, 102, 126
World War II, xxvi, 77, 173, 204,
    232n. 12
Wounded Knee occupation, xxvii, 120